976.944 Wright, George C.
WR I
      Life behind a veil

DATE			

LIFE BEHIND A VEIL

LIFE BEHIND A VEIL

Blacks in Louisville, Kentucky
1865–1930

GEORGE C. WRIGHT

Louisiana State University Press
Baton Rouge and London

Designer: Rod Parker
Typeface: Sabon
Typesetter: Moran Colorgraphic
Printer and Binder: Edwards Brothers

Grateful acknowledgment is hereby offered to The Littlefield Fund for Southern History, University of Texas at Austin, for a grant that has assisted in the publication of this volume.

For permission to reprint portions previously published, acknowledgment is made to the *Journal of Negro History*, the Kentucky Historical Society, and *Southern Studies: An Interdisciplinary Journal of the South*.

Library of Congress Cataloging in Publication Data
Wright, George C.
    Life behind a veil.

    Bibliography: p.
    Includes index.
    1. Afro-Americans—Kentucky—Louisville—History. 2. Louisville (Ky.)—History.
3. Louisville (Ky.)—Race relations. I. Title.
F459.L89N49 1985   976.9′44   84-28838
ISBN 0-8071-1224-0

To Valerie

CONTENTS

MAPS AND TABLES

ACKNOWLEDGMENTS

My research and writing benefited greatly from the generous support and encouragement I received from colleagues and friends. I would like to thank the library personnel at all of the libraries where I conducted my research. Especially helpful were Dwayne Cox and Thomas Owen of the Department of Archives and Records at the University of Louisville. They answered numerous letters, provided me with an ideal place to work, and gave me access to a copying machine. Terry Birdwhistell of the Department of Special Collections at the University of Kentucky greatly assisted my project. While I was a member of the history department at UK, Terry worked with me on several oral history projects, provided me with a tape recorder and cassettes, and offered constructive criticism on interviewing techniques. In addition, he often provided me with food, shelter, and conversation during my return trips to Kentucky.

The final draft of the manuscript was completed at Harvard University where I held an Andrew W. Mellon Faculty Fellowship for the school year 1983–1984. I would like to thank Professor Nathan I. Huggins, W. E. B. DuBois Professor of History and director of Afro-American Studies, for my office and encouragement in my work.

I owe a great intellectual debt to Professor August Meier of Kent State University, whose scholarship in the field of Afro-American history has set a standard of excellence for all scholars to emulate. Professor Meier read the entire manuscript and made numerous insightful comments. An earlier draft of the manuscript was read by Professors Humbert S. Nelli and Daniel Blake Smith of the University of Kentucky, Dr. James Klotter of the Kentucky Historical Society, Dr. Benjamin S. Baker, pastor of the Main Street Baptist Church in Lexington, Professor David Katzman of the University of Kansas, and Professor Paul Finkelman of the University of Texas. My good friend from graduate school, Professor Albert S. Broussard of Southern Methodist University, took time from his own research on San Francisco blacks to read all of the manuscript drafts.

While pursuing the B.A. and M.A. degrees at the University of Kentucky, I took courses taught by Steven A. Channing and Richard Lowitt.

Both men helped shape my understanding of American history and challenged my views on race relations and the role of white liberals. At Duke University I had the good fortune to work with Raymond Gavins, William Chafe, and Lawrence Goodwyn. These scholars gave me the confidence to complete the doctorate degree and have remained sources of advice and encouragement.

I would like to acknowledge the financial support I received from the University of Texas. Robert D. King, Dean of the College of Liberal Arts, and William S. Livingston, Vice President and Dean of the Graduate School, were instrumental in my being awarded several grants from the University of Texas Research Institute. The African and Afro-American Studies Department, under the directorship of John L. Warfield, and the History Department's Dora Bonham Fund financed several research trips to Washington, D. C., and Kentucky. My chairman, Lewis L. Gould, and Professor Robert A. Divine wrote letters in support of my financial requests and were helpful in my securing a grant from the George W. Littlefield Fund in Southern History. Lew also took time from his many administrative chores to read and comment on my manuscript.

In direct and indirect ways, my family has aided this project. My mother, Amanda Wright Knox, and in-laws, William and Ida Ellison, have always applauded my efforts and expressed their pride in whatever I accomplished. My three sisters and two brothers expressed a genuine concern about my research; one of them was always there to ask, "When will the book be done?" My daughter Rebecca, by being a normal (active) child, helped me keep my perspective on all things, intellectual and otherwise. Finally, this study could not have been attempted, much less completed, without the emotional support and constant encouragement of Valerie Ellison Wright. Valerie read and made extensive comments on every draft; this was in addition to being a full-time mother and wife, and while pursuing her own career. My dedicating this book to her is a small repayment for all she has done for me.

LIFE BEHIND A VEIL

INTRODUCTION

Although this study of blacks in Louisville, Kentucky, covers the years 1865–1930, the motivation for this history lies in events of more recent decades. In May 1968 a riot tore through Louisville's black community, resulting in two deaths, numerous injuries, the arrest of over 400 persons, and widespread destruction of property. Louisville's white and black leaders expressed amazement over the riot's occurrence, explaining that Louisville had always enjoyed good race relations and had been blessed with city officials sensitive to racial matters. They pointed to the peaceful school desegregation of 1956 (the first successful school integration plan in the country) as proof of Louisville's progressive spirit.

Beneath this tranquil appearance, however, lay a more somber record. Adequate housing has been a continuing problem for blacks, who are excluded from many of Louisville's neighborhoods. In 1967 the Rev. Martin Luther King, Jr., spent several weeks in Louisville leading open housing demonstrations. These efforts were without significant effect. Moreover, King and his followers were taunted and stoned in nearly all of the white areas they entered. King said that he encountered more white hatred in Louisville, a border city, than in any city in the Deep South.[1] Racial tension increased in the city in the early 1970s as the likelihood of school busing became a reality. When busing finally began, only Boston outdid Louisville's resistance and violence. With these events in mind— school desegregation in 1956, open housing demonstrations in 1967, the riot of 1968, and school busing conflicts in the 1970s—I began my study of Louisville, looking at its life from the Civil War to the Great Depression, with emphasis on race relations, black response to white discrimination, and black activities behind the walls of segregation.

1. Throughout this book the term "border city" will apply to any city located in the former slave states that border on the North. These states—Missouri, Kentucky, Virginia, Maryland, and Delaware (and the District of Columbia)—were often prosouthern in sentiment, but only Virginia joined the Confederacy. Economic considerations played a key role in the decision of the other border states to remain loyal to the Union. Yet a considerable number of men from these states, especially Kentucky and Missouri, joined the Confederate Army.

During the years under study, the black experience in Louisville differed from what Afro-Americans often experienced in southern cities. As one observer of Louisville explained, "since North and South meet in Louisville, the more intense forms of race conflict are missing."[2] No lynchings or race riots occurred in Louisville between 1865 and 1930. Although there were times when local Democratic politicians denounced blacks as part of their campaign strategy, the city was usually spared the virulent political campaigns that became all too common in the South. Moreover, blacks in Louisville, unlike their counterparts in the urban South, were given the right to vote from the 1870s on. Maintaining their franchise was extremely crucial to the black quest for equality in Louisville, for, at the very least, it assured them of the right to protest, and it gave them the leverage necessary to sustain that protest.

An essential aspect of Louisville life that kept racial friction to a minimum (and often gave the appearance of idyllic race relations when compared to the South) was the attitude of Louisville's upper-class whites and their desire to maintain racial order in the city. From antebellum days, when most of the slaves had worked in close contact with their masters and mistresses, a form of paternalism had developed akin to what Kenneth Stampp describes in his classic, *The Peculiar Institution*.[3] Louisville's leading white citizens often seemed genuinely concerned about Afro-Americans and generously supported a number of black causes. But these whites were very selective in choosing what to support, and in return they demanded that blacks be passive and remain in the place assigned them in Louisville society. The paternalism exhibited by Louisville whites, just like that of slave owners, was a form of control. In the years after the Civil War, when Louisville was firmly controlled by ex-Confederates, it was important for blacks to remain on friendly terms with their former masters. These ex-Confederates opposed all federal civil rights legislation and the constitutional amendments granting citizenship and the franchise to their former slaves, but they reluctantly concluded that the Negro, now free, needed to be uplifted and guided in the right direction. Local newspaper editor Henry W. Watterson, literary critic and businessman Basil Duke, and others viewed blacks as inferiors, and they feared that without their guidance the Negroes would retrogress back to their barbaric African ways of life. Furthermore, these whites had fond memories of the "faithful darkies" produced by slavery. Well into the twentieth century, these whites, who re-

2. George R. Leighton, *Five Cities: The Stories of Their Youth and Old Age* (New York, 1939), 54.

3. Kenneth M. Stampp, *The Peculiar Institution* (New York, 1956), 322–31.

ferred to themselves as the "friends of the Negro," repeatedly proclaimed that they had the solution to the never-ending "Negro problem." These paternalistic racists could not conceive that blacks were human and that their "solution" was merely a new form of slavery, one assuring the continuation of white supremacy.

Fortunately, the city always had a small, yet influential, group of liberal whites who championed black concerns and who were relatively free of the racist views of the ex-Confederates. For a decade or more after the Civil War, Louisville was home to a number of prominent Republicans. Led by future Supreme Court Justice John Marshall Harlan, these Republicans demanded fair treatment for blacks and were responsible for the softening of the Democratic party's initial resentment to blacks as freedmen and voters. Outside the political arena, several leaders of the Jewish community were consistent supporters of black civil rights. The Brandeis family, of which Supreme Court Justice Louis Brandeis was a member, worked in volunteer organizations that made improvements in black neighborhoods. Many Jews served on the boards of black institutions and donated funds to keep these institutions open. Equally important were the actions of several well-known attorneys who worked consistently to end housing discrimination and who tried, though in vain, to prevent the playing of outrageous racist plays in local theaters. One of these lawyers, Huston Quin, was elected mayor in the 1920s and was then in a position to be of even more help to Afro-Americans. Finally, Louisville also had Robert W. Bingham, a former mayor and judge and the owner of the highly influential *Courier-Journal* in the 1920s, who served on local branches of the Urban League and the Commission on Interracial Cooperation, two organizations that worked to improve living conditions for blacks and to promote good race relations.

Given these developments in Louisville—the absence of race riots and lynchings, blacks maintaining their franchise, and whites calling for the uplifting of Afro-Americans—it is not surprising that white Kentucky historians, novelists such as James Lane Allen, politicians, newspaper reporters, city boosters, and even travelers to the city have concluded that blacks were treated far better in Louisville than in the Deep South and in many places in the North. These whites obviously concluded that the absence of the most violent and virulent forms of racism meant the presence of amicable race relations. They took it for granted that blacks were denied equal access to public accommodations, housing, and employment. Indeed, when looking at black-white problems in Louisville from a historical perspective, the *Courier-Journal* concluded in 1942: "The relations between the races in Louisville have been good. By comparison with some other communities they have been almost Utopian. The progress of the Negro toward justice here economically and politically has been slow, but it has been steady and it is continuing."[4]

Significantly, the recollections of Afro-Americans about race relations in Louisville often mirror the white assessment. Bishop Alexander Walters, a black active in the formation of the National Association for the Advancement of Colored People, fondly recalled his teenage years in Louisville. He thought that Louisville was one of the most beautiful and progressive cities in the South. To illustrate the fairness of the "broad-minded" white citizens, Walters pointed out that "the school buildings for colored pupils are among the largest, handsomest and best equipped in the country; well heated and lighted and every facility for the intellectual and physical development of the students."[5] In his memoirs of his youth in Louisville in the early 1900s, Blyden Jackson, the holder of a doctorate in English from the University of Michigan and a professor at Southern University and most recently (the 1970s) at the University of North Carolina, explains that "in my Louisville, while it was understood that Negroes had a place and should be kept therein, it was also understood that Louisville was a better than average town where ugly, brutal, open, racial friction was not the accepted thing."[6] Another black, Robert White, who came to Louisville in the 1920s to work as a printer for a black newspaper, agreed that race relations in Louisville were superior to those in the Alabama city he left behind. "Here whites did recognize that you could grow from a boy to a man and from a girl to a woman."[7] These glowing testimonies were substantiated by most of the interviews conducted for this study, and these positive assessments cannot be totally dismissed. Nevertheless, a most revealing statement about the nature of race relations in Louisville was made by a black news reporter in 1891, when he astutely observed that the "races get along nicely—like oil and water—the whites at the top and the Negroes at the bottom."[8] What existed in Louisville was racism in a polite form; it would remain polite as long as Afro-Americans willingly accepted "their place," which, of course, was at the bottom.

4. Louisville *Courier-Journal*, May 22, 1942.
5. Alexander Walters, *My Life and Work* (New York, 1917), 38–39.
6. Blyden Jackson, *The Waiting Years: Essays on American Negro Literature* (Baton Rouge, 1976), 3.
7. Robert White, interview with author, Louisville, July 17, 1979.
8. Indianapolis *Freeman*, February 21, 1891. More than a dozen Afro-American newspapers were published in Louisville at various times from 1870 to 1930. But, except for the *Leader*, which started in 1917, and a handful of copies from three others, these newspapers

This polite racism often deluded both blacks and well-meaning whites into believing that real progress was being made in their city. This politeness allowed local whites to say that they were different from other whites—fairer in dealing with blacks—and yet it served to warn blacks that they should be appreciative of the treatment they received. This attitude led black leaders, though by no means all of them, to accept racial indignities for fear that upsetting the status quo might result in a much harsher racial order. After the passage of the Civil Rights Act of 1875, local black leaders advised their community to avoid entering white establishments where they were not welcomed lest they offend whites. Almost four decades later the black leadership counseled the city's blacks to willingly accept the start of segregation in public parks and to be grateful that the city had constructed a swimming pool for blacks. It might be argued that these moderate black leaders were being realistic in dealing with intransigent whites. But their statements reveal that the city's polite racism had lulled them into believing that Louisville's racial situation was eminently better than elsewhere and that such polite racism was the best that could be hoped for. Continued agitation on the part of black people for their full rights would offend white allies, so blacks in Louisville often accommodated themselves to a second-class status for fear of increasing racial tension.

Local whites were content with making minimal changes in black life, and they were quick to oppose anything that would drastically improve overall conditions for blacks or put them on equal footing with whites. The historian Howard N. Rabinowitz notes that in many instances the start of segregated schools and other facilities during Reconstruction was an improvement because previously there were no institutions available for Afro-Americans. That is true, but segregation also maintained the system of inequality and insured that blacks would remain firmly cemented at the bottom of society. Blacks and whites alike applauded the opening of public schools for Louisville blacks in the 1870s. Most of the schools—though

---

have not been preserved. One newspaper, the *Ohio Falls Express*, which was published for two decades in the late nineteenth century, is lost. Fortunately, however, several out-of-state black newspapers had correspondents in Louisville. For example, in the 1860s and 1870s, the AME *Christian Recorder* carried news on Louisville's black churches and schools; in the mid-1880s, the New York *Freeman* had articles on black employment and race relations in the city; and in the 1890s the Indianapolis *World* occasionally discussed local black leaders and the public schools. The best newspaper source on black Louisville is the Indianapolis *Freeman*. From the early 1880s to 1916, this newspaper, which was edited by George L. Knox, had several reporters in the city, and Louisville events—ranging from race relations to community affairs—were discussed in great detail.

far superior to other black schools in Kentucky and most of the South—
were vastly inferior to the white public schools. Over the years the gap in
quality between white and black schools grew wider. Yet Louisville whites
could correctly say that blacks had good schools in their city. With their
temperate form of racism, Louisville whites never seriously considered
disfranchising blacks, but they were largely insensitive to the black electorate and gave them few political plums and no real voice in government.
In the 1870s and 1880s, when blacks held elective and appointive positions elsewhere and were hired as policemen and firemen in many southern and border cities (and even in a few northern cities), Louisville blacks
were completely shut out of these positions. Instead, local whites, even the
supposed friends of blacks, said repeatedly that the time was not right for
such innovations because putting blacks in responsible positions in city
government would inflame racial hatred. Furthermore, despite the assertions of white leaders that they aided black institutions for humanitarian
reasons, it can be argued that their prevailing motives were to maintain
control over black activities and, with a clear conscience, to exclude Afro-
Americans from white institutions. All of the black institutions that whites
gave financial support to, including several Negro churches, were shack-
led in the area of racial protest. In summary, despite the absence of physical violence and derogatory racial epithets, Louisville whites maintained
a system that allowed few breakthroughs for blacks. Professor Blyden
Jackson, though saying that Negroes were better off in Louisville than in
the South, describes life there as living behind a veil.

Through a veil I could perceive the forbidden city, the Louisville where white folks
lived. It was the Louisville of the downtown hotels, the lower floors of the big movie
houses, the high schools I read about in the daily newspapers, the restricted haunts
I sometimes passed, like white restaurants and country clubs, the other side of windows in the banks, and of course, the inner sanctums of offices where I could go
only as a humble client or a menial custodian. On my side of the veil everything
was black: the homes, the people, the churches, the schools, the Negro park with
the Negro park police. . . . I knew that there were two Louisvilles and in America,
two Americas. I knew, also, which of the Americas was mine.[9]

It is impossible to do a study about the period 1865–1930 without
addressing the thesis put forward by Professor C. Vann Woodward on the
origins of Jim Crow. After carefully examining the rash of segregation ordinances enacted in the 1890s, Woodward concludes that the law was the
crucial factor in the dramatic increase in segregation during the decade. A

9. Jackson, *The Waiting Years*, 3-4.

number of scholars, however, have shown that segregation practices were well entrenched decades earlier; furthermore, social customs, not the law, largely determined race relations. Howard N. Rabinowitz, building on the work of the critics of the Woodward thesis, goes a step further and explains that segregation in most institutions not only started immediately after slavery but was often initiated by the Radical Republicans with the full backing of Afro-Americans. These two groups, Rabinowitz informs us, viewed segregation in education and health facilities as an improvement since it replaced exclusion. Most scholars do agree with Woodward that for the period 1865–1890 race relations in public accommodations were "relatively fluid." [10]

This study shows that black Louisvillians found racial exclusion far from uniform and often very baffling. For instance, blacks protested and won, so they thought, the right to ride and sit where they desired on the streetcars in 1871. Yet the "victory" was challenged within a short period of time, and over the years a vocal minority of whites attempted to have legislation enacted to segregate the races on the streetcars. From the late 1860s, blacks were excluded from white-run theaters, hotels, and restaurants. Yet there were a few exceptions: some of the theaters would allow Afro-Americans to purchase balcony tickets for special occasions, and in 1909, during the convention of the National Negro Business League, blacks were granted equal access to downtown facilities. Kentucky's leading railroad, the Louisville and Nashville, whose executives generously supported black education, often allowed blacks to ride first class in the 1870s and 1880s. Yet on several occasions the company executives succumbed to protest from its white customers and relegated blacks to the coach class. By the mid-1890s the state had formally segregated the races on railroads, even though most railroad companies found the law unneccessary and extremely costly to enforce.

In addition to discussing the growth of segregation, some of the most important works on urban blacks have emphasized the pathological effects of racism on blacks. By the standards of the 1980s, to speak of blacks as "pathological," as constantly "reacting" to white society, is negative and can be viewed as a subtle form of racism. But a number of early schol-

10. C. Vann Woodward, *The Strange Career of Jim Crow* (2nd rev. ed.; New York, 1966); Howard N. Rabinowitz, *Race Relations in the Urban South, 1865–1890* (New York, 1978); Charles E. Wynes, *Race Relations in Virginia 1870–1902* (Charlottesville, 1961); Joel Williamson, *After Slavery: The Negro in South Carolina During Reconstruction 1861–1877* (Chapel Hill, 1965); August Meier and Elliott Rudwick, "A Strange Chapter in the Career of 'Jim Crow'," in A. Meier and E. Rudwick (eds.), *The Making of Black America* (2 vols.; New York, 1974), II, 14–19.

ars who were sympathetic to blacks and who attempted to inform and arouse the white public about the horrible conditions under which urban blacks attempted to eke out a living, largely discussed the negative aspects of Afro-American life. These scholars, primarily trained as sociologists, spoke of broken families, crime, poverty, and, above all, despair as the logical results of racism in America. This negative view of black life predominates in the work of the brilliant black scholar E. Franklin Frazier, who not surprisingly is widely criticized on a number of fronts today. His work, especially *The Negro Family in the United States* with its controversial section on "The City of Destruction," catalogs the ills besetting blacks in an urban environment.

The most recent debate on black pathology was begun by the late Gilbert Osofsky in his essay "The Enduring Ghetto." Writing in a tone that expressed his deep concern for the plight of black Americans, Osofsky noted that "there is an unending and tragic sameness about black life in the metropolis over the two centuries." He wrote that each succeeding generation of blacks in the cities has been subjected to overcrowded and unsanitary housing, inferior schools, white racism, and the denial of equal access to public facilities. Blacks also have been denied the opportunity to advance through employment: "Over the decades one finds an essentially similar pattern: a relatively small, though presently growing urban Negro middle class, and an overwhelming working-class or semi-skilled Negro majority employed in marginal occupations. In unending repetition the largest number of city Negroes work as domestics, janitors, porters, servants, cooks, waiters, . . . general factory help of some kind and lower class clerks." Osofsky concluded that "despite occasional periods of racial reform, little has ever been done that permanently improved the fundamental conditions of life of most Negroes. . . . What has in our time been called the social pathology of the ghetto is evident throughout history; the wounds of centuries have not healed because they've rarely been treated. By all standard measurements of human troubles in the city, the ghetto has always been with us—it has tragically endured." [11]

Several students of the Afro-American urban experience have commented on Osofsky's thesis. David Katzman and Allan Spear agree with Osofsky about the tragic sameness of black life in the cities. "In spite of all the changes in American society," Katzman writes, "so much of the quality of black life dependent upon the rest of society remains disturb-

11. Gilbert Osofsky, *Harlem: The Making of a Negro Ghetto* (2nd ed.; New York, 1971), 189–201.

ingly inferior to that of white people." Spear notes that nothing, not even the civil rights movement, changed the basic structure of the black ghetto. Blacks faced the same restrictions in the 1960s that hindered an improvement in their status in the 1920s. Kenneth Kusmer, on the other hand, concludes that "if we are to understand the black urban experience in its totality, we need to revise and move beyond ahistorical concepts like the 'enduring ghetto' by exploring the variations that have existed in the history of black communities." Indeed, Douglas H. Daniels has produced a study on San Francisco blacks that discusses the social and cultural activities of Afro-Americans. His study shows that despite the presence of racism, black life is diverse, enjoyable, and even "shady." In other words, it has the same dimensions as white life.[12]

Many of the problems Louisville blacks faced were the same over the entire sixty-five year period examined in this study. Yet it is important to point out that changes did occur; to compare and contrast them with the experiences of blacks in cities in both the North and South; and to show that what happened to blacks in one particular city did not take place in a vacuum, that blacks as well as whites were often influenced by events occurring elsewhere. Especially enlightening in this regard are the experiences of blacks in border cities. A significant number of blacks, even during the Great Migration of 1915–1918, remained in border cities instead of moving farther north. The black population in the five largest border cities—Baltimore, Washington, D.C., St. Louis, Richmond, and Louisville—increased from 135,167 in 1870 to 468,069 by 1930.[13] For a full understanding of how white America dealt with its "Negro problem" it is extremely important to discuss the circumstances of blacks in border cities. Except for Washington, all of these cities enacted residential segregation ordinances to prevent blacks from moving into white neighborhoods. Were these ordinances enacted because of white insecurities? Since blacks in all of these cities, except for Richmond, had the right to vote, did whites worry that blacks might get out of their place? In each of these cities, blacks established NAACP and Urban League affiliates to combat racial discrimination and to improve their quality of life. By not concen-

12. David M. Katzman, *Before the Ghetto: Black Detroit in the Nineteenth Century* (Urbana, 1973), 208; Allan H. Spear, *Black Chicago: The Making of a Negro Ghetto* (Chicago, 1967), 224; Kenneth L. Kusmer, *A Ghetto Takes Shape: Black Cleveland, 1870–1930* (Urbana, 1976), xii; Douglas Henry Daniels, *Pioneer Urbanites: A Social and Cultural History of Black San Francisco* (Philadelphia, 1980).

13. Hollis Lynch (ed.), *The Black Urban Condition* (New York, 1973), appendix A, 421–28.

trating on the tragic sameness of black life, this study of Louisville blacks will, first, illuminate some of the problems faced by border-city blacks; second, describe the actions they took in the name of racial justice; and third, show the diversity and richness of life in Afro-American communities.

PART I

*The Struggle for Freedom and
Civil Rights: 1865–1870*

## 1

The Civil War and Reconstruction
Years of Change, Years of Hope

The passage of the Fifteenth Amendment to the U.S. Constitution on March 30, 1870, inaugurated a period of celebration by Afro-Americans to commemorate their struggle for emancipation and civil rights. According to one source, all of Detroit's blacks turned out for the parade and speeches held on April 7, 1870. In Paris, Kentucky, over 6,000 Negroes participated in the ceremonies held in remembrance of the black past.

In Louisville, however, the black leaders were more deliberate in planning their celebration of black franchisement. A formal program was planned; on June 30, 1870, black Louisvillians heard speeches from several ministers and prominent citizens, held a contest to select the "Goddess of Liberty," feasted at picnics, played games, and swayed to the rhythm of music. Symbolically, the Court Square, where many slaves had been sold and separated from their families, was the place chosen to conduct the final service. After paying due respect to the dark days of their past, the 10,000 blacks concluded the service by singing a song composed for the celebration.

Come all ye Republicans, faithful and true, here is a work for you.
The Fifteenth Amendment has fought its way through true as the boys in blue.
The Democrat party its race has run, to give away for an era that freedom has won.
Bring out your gun! Bring out your gun! Bring them, ye brave and true.
. . . .
Our country's flag we do revere, for we love the Constitution;
The Declaration doth declare, All men are free and equal.
The Fifteenth Amendment hath abolished caste, servitude, color, are
Buried at last, Never to rise! Never to rise! Under the Constitution.

Black Louisvillians drew so much inspiration from their celebration that they made it an annual event for several years.[1]

---

1. A detailed discussion of the black celebration in Louisville can be found in William

The holding of festivities in honor of the ratification of the Fifteenth Amendment and the Emancipation Day celebrations were important events for blacks throughout the nation.[2] These commemorative occasions gave Afro-Americans an opportunity to look back at the road they had traveled. But, even more important, the celebrations also reinforced their determination to improve themselves and to continue agitating for all of their rights as citizens. They stressed above all political rights and the right to an education, goals that a number of sympathetic whites also viewed as essential for the well-being of all. Wisely, Afro-Americans scrupulously avoided mentioning issues that touched on "social equality," the great bugbear of southern whites. These celebrations clearly show that blacks did not merely observe the unfolding events during Reconstruction but that they tried to exert whatever pressure they could. Blacks were optimistic that better days lay ahead.

Looking back on the events of the 1860s, black Louisvillians could find a number of incidents that reinforced their optimism. At the same time, several things had happened that made them guardedly worried about the future direction of black-white relations. First of all, they had endured— and indeed did their part in—the Civil War, a conflict that led to the end of slavery. Yet the war years witnessed a brutal suppression of the few rights they enjoyed, such as the closing of their churches and schools. Several groups of sympathetic whites had come to Louisville at the close of the war to assist the freedmen in receiving medical care, in obtaining adequate housing, and in reopening their churches and schools. Despite some initial setbacks—caused by white resentment—the Freedmen's Bureau had been especially helpful. Employment was an immediate concern for the newly freed, and many were successful in their job searches. These freedmen helped put to rest the white assertion that blacks would work only when compelled. Perhaps one of the early symbols of the optimism and perse-

---

H. Gibson, *Historical Sketch of the Progress of the Colored Race in Louisville, Ky.* (Louisville, 1897), 62–63. Gibson, an accomplished musician, probably composed the song for the program. For celebrations elsewhere, see Ross A. Webb, "Kentucky: Pariah Among the Elect," in Richard O. Curry (ed.), *Radicalism, Racism, and Party Realignment* (Baltimore, 1969), 128; Katzman, *Before the Ghetto*, 3–5.

2. For the significance of Emancipation Day celebrations in black communities, see William H. Higgens, Jr., "January 1: The Afro-American's 'Day of Days'," in Jack Salzman (ed.), *An Annual of American Cultural Studies* (New York, 1979), 331–55; see Emma Lou Thornbrough, *The Negro In Indiana* (Indianapolis, 1957), 231–32, 255, for similar celebrations in the Hoosier State.

verance of blacks at this time was their desire to deposit whatever money they could afford in the Freedmen's Savings and Trust Company. Branches of the bank opened in 1865 in cities with large black populations. The Louisville branch, with its very capable black leadership, quickly became one of the most successful branches of the bank.

Nevertheless, a number of ominous events occurred during the early days after the Civil War that made Afro-Americans realize that obtaining their political and educational rights would require difficult struggles. Most white Kentuckians had supported the Union during the war because of the federal government's promise to protect their right to own slaves. Therefore, emancipation, the recruitment of black soldiers, and the continued presence of blacks in the military after the war left these whites extremely bitter. Unlike the whites of the defeated Confederacy, Kentucky whites were in a position to vent their frustrations on blacks; since their state had remained "loyal" they were free from the federal government's restrictions that hampered the old Confederacy, be it ever so briefly, from doing solely as it pleased with Afro-Americans.

This state of affairs played a significant role in the development of race relations in Louisville. Revisionist historians have shown that the South was "redeemed" within a matter of years after the Civil War, placing blacks once again firmly under the control of their former masters. But at least the federal government had been active in the South, thus giving the illusion that attempts were made to protect blacks and to upgrade their status. But from the start of Reconstruction, whites and blacks in the Bluegrass State knew that except for extending the Freedmen's Bureau to Kentucky virtually nothing was being done by the government to aid or protect the freedmen. An ex-Confederate officer, Basil Duke, who agreed fully with the view that the white South was made to suffer during "Radical Reconstruction," freely admitted that his home state of Kentucky, and most especially Louisville, escaped radical control. Not surprisingly, then, for several years after the war whites handled the "Negro problem" in Louisville by adhering to a system that was reminiscent of the old regime: blacks could not vote or testify in court against whites; violence against blacks was widespread, in fact tens of thousands of blacks—far more than in the other border states—quit Kentucky for the North between 1865–1870; and no public education was provided for blacks. Whites were determined that even under the new system blacks would remain at the bottom. Howard N. Rabinowitz explains that whites in the cities were especially concerned with keeping blacks in their place. "Social control far outweighed any desire to ease the transition of the blacks from slavery to freedom in the Urban South."[3]

I.

White Kentuckians watched the outbreak of the Civil War with great apprehension. As a border state, Kentucky had important kinship and commercial ties with both North and South. Louisville had always been an important supplier of goods to the South, but with the advent of the Louisville and Nashville Railroad in the 1850s, the city also began a brisk trade with the North and the developing western states. For several months Kentucky proclaimed her neutrality, but this proved impossible because both sides desperately needed to control her rivers to win the war. Ultimately, Kentucky chose the Union. Except for the southwestern section, the Bluegrass region around Lexington, and Louisville, most of the state had no slaves. Though antiblack feelings were widespread, the average white citizen had little sympathy for slavery. The purse strings also convinced some Kentuckians to remain loyal. This was most definitely the case among a number of Louisville businessmen who initially spoke favorably of the southern nation until learning that their city would serve as a military headquarters for the Union Army (which would mean that they would be called upon to supply the army with accommodations, food, liquor, and entertainment). Kentucky's decision to remain loyal did result in about 25,000 of its sons leaving to fight for the southern cause. But 75,000 joined the Union forces.

Both free blacks and slaves suffered hard times in Louisville during the Civil War. Though comprising only 10 percent of the city's population (4,903 slaves and 1,917 free blacks in 1860), they were viewed with much suspicion by whites at the start of the war. City officials enacted an ordinance prohibiting them from being on the streets after dark without a pass. Black men were arrested for the slightest offense or indeed at the whim of the police. "The darkies . . . were picked up by the hundreds on the streets, and all of the lazy idle characters set to work," the *Daily Journal* informed its readers in 1864 when the city feared attack.[4] On several occasions, city officials forced blacks to build entrenchments around the city. B. L. Brooks, correspondent for the AME *Christian Recorder*, described how city officials treated blacks when Louisville feared an invasion from the Confederate Army in September 1862.

3. Basil Duke, *Reminiscences of General Basil W. Duke* (New York, 1911), 407; Rabinowitz, *Race Relations in the Urban South*, 26.

4. Louisville *Daily Journal*, August 18, 1864.

Our city is in a state of great excitement and they fear an attack from the enemy and are preparing for it. They are throwing up entrenchments all around the city. They called for one thousand negroes to work on the entrenchments. They are taking men everywhere they can get them—on the streets or at their houses. They came to my house this morning, between one and two o'clock. They found no male . . . but myself—and seeing that I was very lame, they let me be for the present, and said perhaps they would call for me today.[5]

This suppression of blacks was common throughout the nation during the war. In Indiana, a northern state with strong southern ties, practically all of the black institutions were closed. Once the decision was made to recruit blacks into the army, Indiana officials did so vigorously, often "forcing" blacks to join. A race riot occurred in New Albany, a city across the Ohio River from Louisville. Some blacks attempted to come to Louisville to escape the racial violence in New Albany.[6]

From the very beginning the Civil War threatened the continued existence of slavery in Kentucky. Louisville and other Kentucky cities on the Ohio River witnessed an alarming increase in slave escapes. Numerous citizens in Indiana complained to Kentucky officials about the number of blacks coming illegally into their state. President Abraham Lincoln's Emancipation Proclamation and his decision to recruit black troops further undermined slavery. The Emancipation Proclamation, freeing the slaves in the rebellious states as of January 1, 1863, did not apply in the loyal state of Kentucky. Nevertheless, the proclamation transformed the war of secession into a war of emancipation, and this was not lost on Kentucky blacks. Though Kentucky was exempt from the proclamation, black men could legally gain their freedom by joining the Union Army. Furthermore, an act of Congress on March 3, 1865, extended this freedom to their wives and children. Not surprisingly, many black Kentuckians seized this opportunity to become free while helping to defeat the Confederacy. All told, over 28,000 Kentucky blacks, both slave and free, enlisted in the Union Army. Only Louisiana supplied more black soldiers.[7]

After realizing that their slaves could gain their freedom by enlisting in the army, many white Kentuckians, though professing their allegiance

5. Charles K. Messmer, "City in Conflict: A History of Louisville, 1860–65" (M.A. thesis, University of Kentucky, 1953), 76; AME *Christian Recorder*, September 27, 1862.
6. Messmer, "City in Conflict," 155–62; *Daily Journal*, August 18, 1864. Slaves were impressed to do work for the Union Army. See, for example, a letter from the Union Army Headquarters of Kentucky to Issaac Clark, November 13, 1863, in Issaac Clark Papers, Filson Club, Louisville; see also Herbert G. Gutman, *The Black Family in Slavery and Freedom, 1750–1925* (New York, 1976), 368; Thornbrough, *The Negro in Indiana*, 187–96.
7. Lowell Harrison, *The Civil War in Kentucky* (Lexington, 1975).

to the Union, adamantly opposed the use of black soldiers. U. S. Senator John J. Crittenden said that no self-respecting white Kentuckian should fight next to a black. "I would rather see our young men brought home corpses than see them saved by such unsoldierlike means," he angrily concluded. George Prentice, the influential editor of the Louisville *Journal*, ridiculed the idea of "General Cuffee" and "Rear Admiral Sambo." The recruitment of black soldiers started in Maryland and Missouri in late 1863 but was delayed until March 1864 in Kentucky because of the strong opposition in the state. Numerous clashes occurred throughout Kentucky when slaves attempted to leave their masters to join the Union Army. Indeed, many blacks were beaten, maimed, murdered, and their children and wives threatened over the enlistment of the slaves in the army. In addition, at least seven white recruiting officers were fatally wounded for enticing slaves to join the army.[8]

Once sworn into the army, the black soldiers were stationed in Louisville, a city very hostile to their presence. Southern sympathizers made life unbearable for blacks by denying them the services extended to other soldiers, by shouting obscenities at them, and by making it dangerous for them to be on the streets alone or at night. The blacks also encountered problems with many of the Union soldiers who resented the recruitment of Afro-Americans into a "white man's army." While southern sympathizers were doing all in their power to keep blacks from joining the army, Union recruiting officers, with the backing of city officials, tried to force local blacks into the military to fill the city's quota. Indeed, on August 16, 1864, the police raided a black fair and carried all of the men to a military prison. The next day the men were forced to "enlist" in the army or remain in jail.[9]

A noticeable improvement in the treatment of blacks occurred in early 1865 after General John M. Palmer took over as commander of the Union Army in Kentucky. Palmer, an abolitionist and strong supporter of the Republican party, viewed his appointment as an opportunity to undermine the final vestiges of slavery in the state. Many years later he recalled how he felt upon arriving in Louisville: "I made up my mind that all that was left of slavery was its mischiefs, and that I would encourage a system of gradual emancipation, a thing that had been desired so long, and which

8. Crittenden was quoted in John David Smith, "The Recruitment of Negro Soldiers in Kentucky, 1863–65," *Register of the Kentucky Historical Society*, LXXII (October, 1974), 366; John W. Blassingame, "The Recruitment of Colored Troops in Kentucky, Maryland, and Missouri, 1863–65," *Historian*, XXIX (August, 1967), 533–45; Louisville *Daily Democrat*, June 21, 1864.

9. *Daily Journal*, August 18, 1864; Elijah P. Marrs, *Life of Reverend Elijah P. Marrs* (Louisville, 1885).

the colored people had pretty well established for themselves." Outraged at how city officials and military recruiters had conspired against blacks, Palmer named a black man, Rev. Thomas James, to tour the prisons to see if any black men were being held for refusing to join the army. James discovered five slave pens where, so he said, hundreds of blacks—"some had iron bars on their legs, reaching from the hip to the ankle and fastened on with iron straps"—were being held. James's actions led to their freedom and to numerous threats on his life. Palmer responded by giving him military escorts and warning the mayor and councilmen that "if James is killed, I will hold responsible for the act every man who fills an office under your city government. I will hang them higher than Haman was hung, and I have 15,000 troops behind me to carry out the order. Your only salvation lies in protecting this colored man's life." [10]

Palmer's actions in Louisville indicate that the ending of slavery was his primary task. He organized a series of meetings to inform black soldiers and their families of their freedom and to reassure them that the Union Army would intervene on their behalf if necessary. Even though Palmer's statement applied only to soldiers, fugitive slaves throughout Kentucky converged on Louisville. They believed—and Palmer did nothing to disprove their belief—that the Union Army under his command would protect them. By April 1865, an average of two hundred blacks a week were entering the city. In early May, Palmer used his power to further undermine slavery by issuing Order No. 32, which annulled the slave code that limited the movement of slaves and free blacks. He gave passes to any blacks desiring to cross the Ohio River to freedom in the North. [11]

Word spread that Palmer had unlimited power and that he would free all slaves who came to Louisville on July 4, 1865. Palmer staunchly denied the rumor. Yet on July 4 a black crowd, estimated between 20,000 and 50,000, gathered in Louisville and waited for Palmer to declare an end to slavery. In his autobiography, Palmer said that before addressing the crowd he became "determined to 'drive the last nail in the coffin' of the 'institution' even if it cost me the command of the department." Palmer told the black crowd, "my countrymen, you are free, and while I command . . .

---

10. John M. Palmer, *Personal Recollections of John M. Palmer* (Cincinnati, 1901), 233–34; AME *Christian Recorder*, March 25, April 1, June 3, 1865; Gutman, *The Black Family in Slavery and Freedom*, 375–76; James L. Smith, *Autobiography of James L. Smith* (Norwich, Conn., 1881), 128.

11. AME *Christian Recorder*, April 1, June 3, 1865; Gutman, *The Black Family in Slavery and Freedom*, 375–78; E. Merton Coulter, *The Civil War and Readjustment in Kentucky* (Chapel Hill, 1926), 263.

this department, the military forces of the United States will defend your right to freedom." Pandemonium broke out! [12]

Palmer's declaration of emancipation was purely a symbolic act. He lacked the power to free the slaves. Practically, however, slavery ceased in Louisville with the start of the Civil War and especially with the coming of the Union Army. Slavery officially ended in Kentucky only with the ratification of the Thirteenth Amendment on December 18, 1865. This important date has special significance for Kentucky blacks. Lincoln's Emancipation Proclamation gave slaves in the rebelling states their freedom. The proclamation was enforced by the conquering Union Army, though some blacks in Texas were unaware of the Emancipation Proclamation and did not gain their freedom until June 19, 1865. The Thirteenth Amendment was directed at blacks in the loyal border states. During the war, Maryland and Missouri voluntarily abolished slavery, while Kentucky and Delaware refused to do so. But by the end of the war, slavery was virtually dead in Delaware, with most of the slaves having escaped and no more than 900 blacks still in bondage. It was a different matter entirely in Kentucky, for scattered throughout the state were some 100,000 blacks still enslaved. As Herbert G. Gutman notes in his study *The Black Family in Slavery and Freedom*, the final battle over slavery occurred in Kentucky as violence erupted between black soldiers, returning to get their families, and slave owners. Ironically, Kentucky, a state that claimed that slavery played only a minor role in its economy and that the institution was more of a bother to the ruling class than a hardship to the slaves, can make a legitimate claim to being the last state to free its slaves. [13]

II.

As Louisville blacks soon realized, the ending of slavery did not lead to their acceptance into the body politic but rather to increased white resentment of all their attempts for political and educational rights. In most respects the situation faced by Kentucky blacks was worse than that experienced farther South because at least in most of the old Confederate states blacks could participate in running the local governments, thus as-

12. Palmer, *Personal Recollections*, 242. There are several other versions of what occurred in Louisville on July 4, 1865. See Gutman, *The Black Family in Slavery and Freedom*, 380; Smith, *Autobiography*, 129; AME *Christian Recorder*, July 22, 29, 1865; and John M. Langston, *From the Virginia Plantation to the National Capital* (Hartford, 1894), 237–39.

13. Gutman, *The Black Family in Slavery and Freedom*, 375–85.

suring that the concerns of blacks were raised and often enacted into law. In Kentucky the Democratic party remained firmly in control. After sensing the people's desire to end the bitterness with their friends who had joined the "lost cause," the party moved quickly to repeal the Civil War liabilities against the Confederates. In fact, as Kentucky scholars Hambleton Tapp and James Klotter explain, "the pendulum swung so far pro-southern that ex-Union soldiers were in danger of being persecuted for legitimate wartime acts." With all the liabilities removed, it was but a short step for the ex-Confederates, many of whom were leaders in the Democratic party before the war, to reclaim their political positions.[14]

Historians have accurately labeled Reconstruction in Kentucky "Confederacy Supremacy." A recent scholar of Louisville has called the influx of ex-Confederates into the city "remarkable." It seems that a part of the "rite of passage" into the business world of the city was to have been an officer in the Confederacy. Nearly all of Louisville's journalists, lawyers, realtors, and merchants were former rebels. By 1871 ex-Confederates dominated the Louisville School Board. Louisville's ex-Confederates were determined to keep the memory of the Confederacy alive. They, like others throughout the South, established a dozen or more Confederate organizations—ranging from the Confederate Monument Association, which was responsible for placing statues in the parks honoring their fallen comrades, to the Confederate Association, an organization that worked "to see that no worthy Confederates shall ever become an object of public charity."[15]

Just as Afro-Americans held Emancipation Day celebrations, the ex-Confederates held special events to keep alive the spirit of the rebellion and to honor their heroes. The Orphan Brigade of the Confederacy had annual reunions in the 1870s and 1880s. In 1889 the Confederate Monument Association sponsored a dance for 600 veterans in the Louisville Armory. The hall was appropriately draped in Confederate colors and the walls adorned with Confederate flags. An even larger gathering occurred in 1908 when the United Confederate Veterans of the Kentucky Division met "to keep alive the memory of 1861." Louisville's most prominent lawyer, Bennett

14. Hambleton Tapp and James C. Klotter, *Kentucky, Decades of Discord 1865–1900* (Frankfort, 1977), 12–29; Coulter, *The Civil War and Readjustment in Kentucky*, 287–312. In Maryland the ex-Confederates also gained control of the Democratic party. See Margaret Law Callcott, *The Negro in Maryland Politics 1870–1912* (Baltimore, 1969), 14–18.

15. George H. Yater, *Two Hundred Years at the Falls of the Ohio: A History of Louisville and Jefferson County* (Louisville, 1979), 95; *Courier-Journal*, October 3, 1908; James P. Sullivan, "Louisville and Her Southern Alliance 1865–1890" (Ph.D. dissertation, University of Kentucky, 1965), 319–24.

H. Young, was honored during the ceremonies by being named a life-long major-general of the Kentucky Division. But perhaps Louisville's greatest outpouring of admiration for the "lost cause" and its leaders occurred in the 1870s: first, at the death of Robert E. Lee, when more than 250 businesses closed and a large procession marched silently through the town; second, in May 1, 1877, when federal troops left South Carolina and Louisiana, the last two states to be "redeemed" from Republican control. In anticipation of the troop removal, newspaper editor Henry Watterson suggested holding a grand celebration to mark the occasion. City officials responded by decorating all of the businesses in the downtown area, the mayor's home, and the homes of prominent ex-Confederates. Several clubs held dances that evening. A crowd estimated between 25,000 and 30,000 gathered at City Hall to enjoy a concert of popular southern songs. The *Courier-Journal* proudly concluded that the celebration "proved most clearly how much in sympathy with the sorely distressed southern people Louisville is." [16]

Reminiscing on their formative years in Louisville in the late 1800s, Abraham Flexner and Arthur Krock recalled that the city had a Confederate flair and that without question the ex-Confederates were the "movers and shakers" in Louisville. Flexner, a leading authority on education and for many years an employee of the General Education Board, and Krock, a well-known journalist, said that Louisville's ex-Confederates had all of the trademarks of the Old South—long legs, lean build, mustache, and goatee—and talked on and on about '61. It is clear from reading their colorful anecdotes about "Marse Henry" Watterson and the others that both Flexner and Krock, though the offspring of immigrants who arrived in Louisville after the war, greatly admired the manner and dignity in which the ex-Confederates carried themselves. The ex-Confederates were, so Flexner believed, Louisville's best citizens. [17]

The role of the Negro in the New South was a major concern of Louisville's ex-Confederates. Should Negroes be given the franchise and the other rights of citizenship? Should they remain in the South? In fact, could anything be done to aid the newly freed Negroes, or would they merely retrogress back to their African ways? These men, of course, were not of one mind on all questions relating to Afro-Americans. Some believed that ed-

16. Tapp and Klotter, *Kentucky, Decades of Discord*, 109–10; *Courier-Journal*, May 2, 1887, September 20, 1889, October 3, 1908.

17. Arthur Krock, *Myself When Young* (Boston, 1973), 196–98; Abraham Flexner, *I Remember: The Autobiography of Abraham Flexner* (New York, 1940), 19–36. See also Arthur Krock (ed.), *The Editorials of Henry Watterson* (New York, 1923).

ucation was an important means of teaching the former slaves the judicious use of the ballot box and the value of working for a living. Many more, however, opposed extending the right of franchise to blacks and spoke of a guardianship stage for the race. They all firmly agreed on the necessity of the separation of races in social activities. Yet they realized that the progress and productivity of blacks in the work force would depend on their contact with whites, that total exclusion would have a negative effect on the city's economy. These white leaders did not fear blacks because they remembered blacks as being loyal and passive slaves. They were convinced that once they made the rules of their new order known the blacks would do as commanded. Without a doubt the ex-Confederate leaders believed that since they were the "better element of whites" the intelligent Negroes would naturally look to them for direction.[18]

Of all the ex-Confederate leaders in Louisville, journalists Basil Duke and Henry Watterson speculated most on how best to solve the "Negro problem." Duke, a general in the Confederacy and a close associate of the dashing rebel soldier John Hunt Morgan, made Louisville his home after the war and lived there for sixty years. He edited *The Southern Magazine*, contributed short pieces to another local magazine, *The Southern Bivouac*, and gave numerous speeches on the Negro question. Like many of his contemporaries, Duke had fond memories of life on a plantation surrounded by slaves. Slavery, so he repeatedly explained, produced the superior Negro, one with insights and a great sense of humor.[19] The Civil War and the recruitment of blacks as soldiers, however, did a great injustice to blacks, more so than to whites. "If previously he had been ignorant and half savage, he had at any rate been a 'gentle savage.' Given the bayonet and turned loose on those he had formerly served, it would have been a marvel if all the insolence, ferocity, and evil passion that might have been latent in his nature had not been aroused."[20]

Fully three decades after the end of slavery, Duke was still informing his readers that "the average negro is yet a savage."[21] He did acknowledge that a few blacks had progressed (this he called "extraordinary") but quickly added that the vast majority had retrogressed in morality and in-

18. See Woodward, *The Strange Career of Jim Crow*, 28–51, for a good discussion of southern conservatives.

19. Duke's writings are sprinkled with stories about loyal plantation darkies. See, for example, Basil Duke, "Charcoal Sketch," *Southern Magazine*, III (August, 1893–January, 1894), 669–70; Duke, *Reminiscences*, 232.

20. Duke, *Reminiscences*, 241.

21. Quoted in Leighton, *Five Cities*, 76.

tegrity. And to make a bad situation even worse, blacks (at least in Kentucky) had the right to vote: "The political rights granted the negro have done him little benefit. Suffrage was given him suddenly and before he was . . . prepared to judiciously or safely exercise it. With no previous training, hereditary or individual, he was entrusted with powers on the proper use of which good government depends, and was expected to use them wisely—something the Anglo Saxon has 800 years of racial experience, and has scarcely yet learned to do." He chided naive northerners and Englishmen for believing that "the negro is merely a white man with black skin," and that given the same opportunities enjoyed by whites the Negro would develop in a similar manner. Instead, those who knew the Negro best were well aware of his limited potential and inherent weaknesses.

It will not surprise those who know the negro best, if in another generation it produces orators, poets, and artists who shall rival their contemporaries of white blood. But in the art of government; in the knowledge of and capacity for the conduct of political and social affairs; and in self-control; in an acute perception of what ought to be done and what should be attempted; in the organizing instinct which detects how best to adapt the means to an end, and the ability to subordinate passion to judgment; in those qualities, in short, which it has been asserted make the Aryan race capable of self-government and the Anglo-Saxon preeminent in that great faculty—the negro is vastly and unmistakably beneath the level of the white man. His distinguishing characteristics are a worship of power, an adoration of might, and a ductile susceptibility to the influence of any one stronger than himself who is immediately in contact with him.[22]

Duke was confident that racial problems would end as soon as blacks accepted their lot in the South and returned to the care of their former masters—"the real and intelligent friends among the colored people of the South." Like the Louisville businessmen who needed the manual labor of blacks, he scoffed at the idea of blacks leaving the South, for it "is the true habitat of the negro on this continent." White southerners, unlike northerners, appreciated the labor performed by blacks. "In the South, among the descendants of his former masters, the old relations between the whites and blacks . . . may be restored; and there, I hope and believe, he will receive the best incentives and the best help to attain the highest plane to which he may be destined."[23]

Duke's influence, though considerable, could in no way match that of Henry Watterson. Indeed, in Watterson, Louisville had a newspaper editor whose views on race, politics, and American society were read not only

22. Duke, *Reminiscences*, 224, 413.
23. *Ibid.*, 242.

in Kentucky and the South, but throughout the nation. Next to Henry W. Grady, he is the best known of the spokesmen for the "New South," one built on progress and industrialism and peaceful race relations. As Paul Gaston explains in his study, *The New South Creed*, the region's spokesmen agreed on the inherent inferiority of blacks and the need for white supremacy. Yet, Watterson realized that unless the "retarded" blacks were uplifted and given a basic education and employment skills they would "inevitably retard white progress"; therefore cooperation between the races was essential. But at all times these New South spokesmen assured white southerners that nothing would change southern mores, that the races would be separate and white supremacy preserved.[24]

A native of Tennessee who reluctantly joined the Confederacy, Watterson arrived in Louisville in the late 1860s to edit the *Courier-Journal*. As described by Arthur Krock, he was a man of middle height, with one blazing blue eye (having lost the other in his youth), a high voice, and the usual "badges of the old Confederacy"—white mustache and goatee. As editor of a prosouthern paper, Watterson was quickly admitted to the prominent circles in Louisville. And undoubtedly he fit right in with the other ex-Confederates, for he adhered to and ultimately helped to shape their view of what should be done with the Negro. Like fellow journalist Duke and other ex-rebels, Watterson never took blacks seriously and constantly poked fun at them; even worse, in his paper he often referred to them in uncomplimentary terms such as "niggers," "darkies," and "Sambos." Watterson often made disparaging remarks about their habits, their attempts to improve themselves, and their culture. Speaking of black religion, he quipped "with the old darky at the camp meeting, who, whenever he got happy, went shouting: 'Bless the Lord! I'm getting fatter an' fatter!'"[25]

Throughout his long career Watterson consistently opposed black involvement in politics, and he often wrote of the bad will they brought on themselves by blindly following the Republican party. As a spokesman for the Democratic party in 1870, he wrote an editorial entitled "A Short

24. Paul M. Gaston, *The New South Creed: A Study in Southern Mythmaking* (New York, 1970), 125.

25. Krock, *Myself When Young*, 110–13; Henry Watterson, *The Compromises of Life* (New York, 1903), 290; Krock, *Editorials of Watterson*, 315. Krock, obviously a great admirer of Watterson, said the following: "So far as the writer of these notes was ever able to discover during an intimacy of many years, Mr. Watterson had no social or racial prejudices. In smiling speech he would now and then consign to Hades 'A Cockney Jew' or an 'Ourishman,' or a 'naygur' especially if these nationals were writing articles attacking him." See the *Courier-Journal*, February 21, 1875, for two articles with derogatory references to blacks.

Epistle to Sambo." He explained that the Democracy "does not need the Negro vote. It can get along well, or better, without it." Watterson advised blacks to stay out of politics and to improve their condition by laboring and building their culture, "which [you] will not get out of the Fifteenth Amendment nor be able to filch from the wrangles of party warfare." He concluded that his "opposition to their enfranchisement has been steady, intense, and resolute, founded upon a conviction that their habits of life and general condition disqualify them for the judicious exercise of suffrage." [26] He rarely deviated from this view, and he often urged the Democrats to take whatever steps necessary to eliminate black influence in local elections. In October 1908, Watterson wrote an editorial, "The Negro and His Vote," which largely restated his positon of thirty-eight years earlier. In terms that were strikingly similar, Watterson informed his readers that the Democratic party did not want or need the black vote. By voting, blacks offended the very whites they relied on for employment. Moreover, black voting was offensive to lower-class whites. "Everytime, therefore, that a black man votes a Republican ticket he puts a cudgel in the hands of a mean white man to lay upon the entire negro race." His suggestion: blacks should not vote at all, and if they refrained, conditions would improve for them. [27]

Despite his opposition to black involvement in politics and "race mixing," Watterson proclaimed himself a friend of the Negro and said the Negro deserved "a white man's chance" to succeed in life. He proudly told black audiences that after the Civil War he had denounced the Negro codes in Kentucky, the formation of the Ku Klux Klan, and all forms of racial violence. In reality Watterson called for an end to lawlessness in Kentucky and the granting of new rights to Afro-Americans, not out of genuine concern for them but out of fear that the federal government would intervene if Kentucky failed to accept fully the end of slavery and the new status of blacks. Moreover, he said that lawlessness would have a detrimental effect on the state's attempt at economic recovery, for few industries would move into the state until law and order returned. Also, the Freedmen's Bureau, which he viewed as totally worthless, would remain until the violence ceased. In other words, the best way for Kentucky whites to be left alone to handle "their Negroes" was to acknowledge that the war was over and to willingly make a few changes. Significantly, white Democratic leaders in another border state, Maryland, arrived at a similar conclusion. As Margaret Law Callcott explains in her study, *The Negro in Maryland Pol-*

26. *Courier-Journal*, February 17, 19, 1870; Louisville *Commercial*, May 4, 1870.
27. *Courier-Journal*, October 27, 1908.

itics: "Moderation . . . was a calculated strategy for heading off federal interference in the state's election processes. At the time the Fifteenth Amendment was ratified the Radical-dominated Congress was considering the first of the Federal Enforcement Acts, laws that would give federal officials power to enforce the amendment by, among other things, creation of a federal administrative and police force to oversee the conduct of elections. By seeming to accept and comply with the amendment Maryland Democrats hoped to discourage passage of such acts and to retain undisputed control over the state's elections."[28]

Watterson repeatedly told black and white audiences that "the Negro must labor." Like so many conservative whites of that day, Watterson would begin his speech by deploring Reconstruction, a time when blacks had attempted to take a shortcut on the long road of progress. Now, however, intelligent Negroes realized that there was dignity in laboring; as laborers, instead of politicians, blacks were assured the goodwill of whites. After Booker T. Washington's rise to prominence in the 1890s, Watterson included in his address to blacks his whole-hearted endorsement of the realistic approach of the Tuskegeean. Watterson and most whites heard only what they wanted to hear from Washington: that he was for mutual economic growth, for blacks remaining and working in the South, and for racial separation in social activities. The only time Watterson criticized Washington was after his dinner at the White House, an act that most white Americans found offensive for it smacked of social equality.[29]

In addition to the ex-Confederates, a number of Unionists came to Louisville after the war. These Unionists—Benjamin H. Bristow, John Marshall Harlan, and others—were the backbone of the Republican party in the state. They gave the minority party a strong voice, and though seldom victorious on the local or state level, they occasionally made the political races lively and often pushed the Democrats into supporting more liberal legislation. With their political party getting virtually no hearing in Louisville's Democratic-controlled newspapers, they launched a paper of their own, the Louisville *Commercial* in 1868. This paper was in existence for over thirty years. Blacks found this Republican-dominated paper far more concerned about their situation and more willing to denounce the injustices they suffered. Ultimately, however, Louisville proved to be such

28. Krock (ed.), *Editorials of Watterson*, 15; *Courier-Journal*, November 9, 1868, October 27, 1908; Henry Watterson, *"Marse Henry": An Autobiography* (New York, 1919); Callcott, *The Negro in Maryland Politics*, 22.

29. New York *Freeman*, December 13, 1886; *Courier-Journal*, October 21, November 5, 1901, June 21, 1902; Indianapolis *Freeman*, August 10, 1907.

an unfriendly city for strong Republican supporters that many of them left the state. Bristow accepted a cabinet post in the Grant Administration, and Harlan, of course, became a justice on the Supreme Court. A number of other prominent Republicans simply left for the new western states.[30]

With the Republican party unable to prevent their actions, Kentucky's Democratic legislators, led by the ex-Confederates, overwhelmingly rejected all legislation calling for political, social, and educational rights for blacks. The General Assembly moved very quickly in the weeks after the war to restore all rights to the ex-Confederates; yet at the same time they kept in place a number of discriminatory laws regarding blacks, even refusing to abolish the slave codes. The same legislature, in a very defiant mood, voted against the Thirteenth Amendment in December 1865 (and would do likewise to the Fourteenth and Fifteenth) and strongly protested the adoption of the Civil Rights Act of 1866. Louisville's city officials followed suit. They refused to change ordinances that restricted the activities of free blacks and slaves, and they refused to open hospitals or schools to the freedmen. Furthermore, Louisville officials disrupted as much as possible the humane efforts to assist the blacks that were being undertaken by several missionary groups. In fact, by the end of 1865 several of the northern missionary societies stopped sending their workers to Louisville and elsewhere in Kentucky because of the numerous threats on their lives and the state's refusal to protect them. With local and state officials refusing to aid blacks or to prevent outbreaks of violence, the U.S. Government extended the Freedmen's Bureau to Kentucky in January 1866, selecting Louisville as its headquarters. Kentucky was the only loyal state to have the bureau, and this action only further aroused the hostilities of many embittered whites toward Afro-Americans.[31]

In Louisville the Freedmen's Bureau devoted most of its time to establishing schools and providing health care, programs that the officials thought would meet only minimal opposition. But, as the Freedmen's Bureau Monthly Reports repeatedly emphasized, white resentment was the major obstacle the Bureau faced in Louisville. Thomas K. Noble, head of the bureau's education program in Kentucky, explained that Louisville blacks strived to better themselves in an atmosphere of bitter hostility to-

30. Yater, *A History of Louisville*, 96; Thomas Owen, "The Pre-Court Career of John Marshall Harlan" (M.A. thesis, University of Louisville, 1970).
31. Mary S. Donovan, "Kentucky Law Regarding the Negro, 1865–77" (M.A. thesis, University of Louisville, 1967), 28–31; Lewis Collins and Richard H. Collins, *History of Kentucky* (2 vols.; Covington, Ky., 1874), I, 332; Ross Webb, *Kentucky in the Reconstruction Era* (Lexington, 1979).

ward "nigger schools." "Everywhere the colored man hears these schools spoken of with contempt," Noble sadly pointed out. "The very idea of 'educating the nigger' is held up before him as the climax of the absurd." [32]

In one instance bureau officials made a difficult search before finally securing a building for a school. Shortly thereafter, a contingent of prominent businessmen ordered the owner of the building to void the lease, warning that if he refused they would cease doing business with him. He refused and violence followed. A white mob stormed the building, breaking all of the windows and smashing the door. Guards were placed at the school for several weeks to prevent bodily harm to the students and teachers (who were jeered as they went to school) and the further destruction of property. In March 1867, the American Missionary Society and the Western Freedmen Aid Society, in conjunction with the bureau, purchased a lot as a site for a new school building. Irate whites tried to halt construction. When that failed, they circulated a petition urging city authorities to declare the school a public nuisance. Then they tried to burn it down. Again, the use of guards was necessary to prevent the school from being destroyed. In his report of January 1868, Noble told his superiors in Washington that "almost every school in Louisville has been interfered with in one way or the other. . . . In many portions of Louisville . . . it would be positively unsafe for an officer or an agent of the Bureau to undertake to organize a school without protection." [33]

Whites directed much of their anger at the white northern teachers who came to Louisville to teach black children. Their presence, so local whites said, would lead to social equality and then the blacks would become uppity. The teachers were treated with contempt; they were verbally assaulted on the streets, refused admission to white social circles, and denied services in stores and restaurants. On one occasion a young woman applied for membership at the Walnut Street Baptist Church. After being thoroughly examined about her religious experiences by the pastor and deacons, the young woman was accepted into the congregation and arrangements were made for the baptismal service. But several days before the ceremony, church officials were informed that the woman taught at a Negro school and boarded with a black family. The church met and unan-

---

32. For information on the activities of the Freedmen's Bureau in Kentucky, see Educational Division of the Bureau of Refugees, Freedmen, and Abandoned Lands, Records, 1865–1871, "Monthly Reports from Kentucky," National Archives, Washington, D.C. See, for example, "Bureau Monthly Reports," October 1, 1866, February 11, March 11, December 1, 1867, May 1, 1868, July 20, 1869.

33. "Bureau Monthly Reports," February 11, December 1, 1867, January 1, May 1, 1868.

imously rejected her application for membership. Local whites denied white teachers housing accommodations and then complained about the impropriety of the teachers, especially the women, living in black households. Indeed, as Thomas Noble pointed out, "the old hue and cry of miscegenation would then be raised and mobs would doubtless break up the school. This is not fantasy but actual fact." [34]

In addition to its educational efforts in Louisville, the bureau maintained a hospital, an orphanage, and a home for the destitute. Indeed, providing for the sick and homeless became the primary concern of bureau agents in 1868 as they made plans to end their activities in the state. That July, bureau officials sent a proposal to Louisville officials urging the city to assume control of the bureau's hospital. The mayor and city council rejected the offer. Fortunately, General O. O. Howard received word of the situation in Louisville and sent sufficient food and medical supplies to last until the spring of 1869. In March 1869, bureau agent Ben Runkle again approached the mayor about the city taking over the hospital. This time, Runkle's request had the backing of several prominent local whites. The mayor endorsed the request and sent his recommendation to the city council. Again, however, the councilmen refused to assume responsibility for the freedmen's hospital. Shortly thereafter, the national office directed Runkle to send all of the patients remaining under the bureau's care to the Freedmen's Hospital in Washington. On April 30, forty-one blacks, most of whom were fifty and over, boarded a train for Washington. Runkle noted their departure by saying, "Thus it is the black paupers, the decrepit and worn out freedmen, worn out in the service of their masters, made helpless toiling to make Kentucky what it is, are driven from their homes by the very men for whom they wasted the strength of their lives." [35]

III.

White resentment only compounded the many problems that thousands of freed slaves faced in Louisville during the weeks and months after the Civil War. Their arrival in the city severely strained available housing and often resulted in families living in very congested quarters. Their presence caused alarm among city officials, and the council urged the military authorities to continue giving passes to blacks allowing them to move to Indiana and Ohio. As in other cities throughout the South, Louisville's of-

34. *Ibid.*, July 8, 1867, January 1, July 1, October 13, 1868.
35. *Ibid.*, July 20, 1869.

ficials tried to discourage blacks from remaining in their city by arresting many of them on vagrancy charges, but this simply overtaxed the jail and workhouse. In response to the potential health menace caused by the overcrowded conditions, the city council created a Board of Health in September 1865 and instructed the superintendent to begin working in earnest to bring the large number of freedmen in the city under control, "for unless prevented, they will crowd in numbers of from 10 to 20 in one room, and when warm weather begins, it cannot help but breed disease." [36]

Unfortunately, this dire prediction proved prophetic. By January 1866 infectious diseases were moving unchecked among the freedmen. A local newspaper noted the "alarming prevalence of smallpox among the negro residents in Louisville." The new Board of Health immediately went to work, hoping to stop the spread of the disease. "I have supplied the Dispensaries of the city with vaccine matter," explained the superintendent, "and had notice given to the colored population . . . that they would be vaccinated." This vaccinating of the new migrants—which was often done against their will—helped control smallpox, but, as the *Daily Courier* reported, because so many blacks were living in dingy rooms, cellars, and even outhouses, other infectious diseases also spread, complicating health care. Though no official figures exist, the death rate among the freedmen was undoubtedly high, especially among the old and very young. The hardships experienced in Louisville during the winter of 1865–1866 were also experienced by freedmen in several other southern cities. In southeast Georgia thousands of freedmen quit the countryside and flocked into Savannah. Many of them died, while others barely survived. Meanwhile, city officials refused to admit blacks to white welfare institutions. [37]

A major problem hampering the attempts of city officials to end the spread of infectious diseases was their own unwillingness to quarantine blacks in the city's welfare institutions. For several years after the war, city officials continued the antebellum practice of restricting blacks to the basement of the city hospital, an area with only a few cots and with inadequate light and ventilation. Even hospital officials admitted that the basement was inadequate and urged the construction of a separate hospital building for black patients. The Freedmen's Bureau had opened a

---

36. George F. Lawson, "A Brief Outline of Louisville Health Prior to 1880 with Special Consideration of the Yellow Fever Epidemic of 1878" (June, 1937), Filson Club, Louisville.

37. Louisville *Daily Courier*, January 4, 1866; *Louisville Municipal Reports for the Year Ending December 31, 1868* (Louisville, 1869), 5; Robert E. Perdue, *The Negro in Savannah* (New York, 1973), chap. 1.

hospital. The hospital was constantly overcrowded and often had to turn patients away. At the closing of the bureau's hospital in 1868, pressure was put on city officials to admit blacks to the city's Almshouse. In his report to city fathers, Almshouse director Dr. John J. O'Reilly complained that he was obliged to receive a black woman simply because there was nowhere else for her to go. He concluded with a warning that unless something was done soon the unfortunate people of both races would be mixed together: "As it now is, if the keeper of the Almshouse is compelled to receive them, there is no alternative but to place them with the whites. This is objectionable, and should be attended to in time." In 1870 a building was erected for the housing and treatment of poor blacks.[38]

The inadequate and congested housing for Louisville's newcomers led to many health problems. During the Civil War the city simply could not house all of the people, black and white, flowing in from the state's rural areas. Indeed, Louisville's population soared during the decade, reaching 14,956 blacks in 1870, an increase of 120 percent; the total population increased by 48.1 percent, to more than 100,000 people.[39] These figures do not include the number of people who migrated to Louisville but stayed only a few years. The housing situation eased somewhat during the summer of 1866 when new construction started all over the city, opening up some of the older tenement houses in the downtown area to blacks. Afro-Americans fortunate enough to find employment and to afford better housing began moving into a few of the neighborhoods west of the downtown area, primarily on Congress and Magazine Alleys and into the California District, which was located on Fifteenth Street. But perhaps the most significant breakthrough for blacks was the construction of small houses and tenements in an area east of downtown, which came to be called "Smoketown." As Henry Clay Weeden, a black chronicler of Louisville explained, "In 1866 the colored people began to lease lots and build homes on Breckinridge Street, from Preston to Jackson and Jackson to Caldwell." He quickly added that "the houses were not the finest but furnished a neat appearance."[40] The Afro-Americans who bought or leased these

38. In Municipal Reports for 1868, see "Report of the Hospital," 8–9; "Report of Almshouse," 24–62; also see *Municipal Reports for 1869*, "Report of Almshouse," 3; *Municipal Reports for 1870*, "Report of Almshouse," 325–33.

39. Bureau of the Census, *Ninth Census of the United States*, "1870: Population" (Washington, D.C., 1872), I, 150.

40. Henry Clay Weeden, *Weeden's History of the Colored People of Louisville* (Louisville, 1897), 28. Weeden, a long-time black resident of Louisville, published at his own expense this small book, an excellent source of information on black leaders, institutions, and cultural life. For many years Weeden was active in the Republican party, working to keep

small houses or moved into the new tenements were the lucky ones. Because of poverty, a segment of the black population would always live in cellars and basements, as they did in the early days of freedom.

Finding work in postbellum Louisville did not prove unduly difficult for most Afro-Americans. To be sure, some blacks from rural areas, who lacked skills and familiarity with the city, experienced difficult times. For the most part, however, local whites readily hired blacks but relegated them to jobs identical to the ones they had performed during slavery. Black women labored as laundresses, washerwomen, and domestic servants. Many black men also found employment as domestic and personal servants, working as gardeners, barn cleaners, carriage drivers, and as waiters and cooks in hotels. Blacks, both male and female, worked in tobacco factories and manufacturing concerns as common laborers, positions that paid very poorly and offered little chance for advancement to better jobs. William and W. F. Robertson, English travelers to Louisville, noted that "all of the porters and servants in the tobacco warehouses we visited were black. . . . When any work is required they perform it cheerfully, but do not get any extra pay. The wage they are paid is 25 shillings a week all year round, whether there is work for them or not. We were informed that on the whole, the blacks here are working pretty well."[41]

Two occupations held almost exclusively by blacks in antebellum Louisville, barbering and cartage, offered the possibility of economic success. Though a service occupation, barbering allowed blacks to work for wealthy whites as well as giving them the free time to venture into other vocations. As the *Commercial* correctly pointed out, it was an "occupation that embraces some of the most influential, intelligent, and prosperous of our colored citizens." One barber owned a small candy store and several others accumulated enough money to speculate in real estate. Meanwhile, several black draymen, led by James Brown who was reputedly worth $10,000, accumulated small fortunes. By 1870, an estimated 150 draymen owned teams, and ten boss draymen owned several teams. Moreover, freedmen with skills made inroads as blacksmiths, wagonmakers, carpenters, builders, painters, and bricklayers. Having a skill was crucial, for it ensured many blacks of a decent livelihood. John W. Blassingame, in his study of black New Orleans, explains that having skills

---

blacks loyal to the "party of Lincoln." Paul J. Lammermeier, "The Urban Black Family of the Nineteenth Century: A Study of Black Family Structure in the Ohio Valley, 1850–1880," *Journal of the Marriage and Family*, XXXV (August, 1973), 446.

41. William Robertson and W. F. Robertson, *Our American Tour* (Edinburgh, 1871), 100; Edward King, *The Great South: A Record of Journey* (2 vols.; New York, 1875), I, 696.

protected blacks from a complete strangulation during Reconstruction by white unions, city officials, and antiblack employers. In Savannah, for example, the skilled freedmen had the easiest transition to freedom and were most likely to be successful. As prestigious as the barbers, draymen, and skilled occupations were, black workers could aspire to yet another job level. A handful of blacks found jobs as messengers for banks, railroad companies, and other businesses. Free blacks had an exclusive hold on these jobs, because the positions required persons with a basic education. Moreover, only blacks who personally knew whites in the company were hired. These jobs, the closest thing to "white collar" jobs available to blacks, carried status in the Afro-American community.[42]

A few black business enterprises also developed. Practically all of them were small grocery stores, requiring modest capital investments and operating out of the owners' homes. But there were several notable exceptions, such as George and Dan's Restaurant which opened in the 1860s and had a number of employees. Also, by the early 1870s there were several furniture dealers with locations in the center of Louisville's business district, three undertaking establishments, a newspaper (*The Weekly Planet*), and two monthly religious newspapers.[43]

Once they acquired the essentials to sustain life, black Louisvillians began agitating for admission to public schools.[44] At every turn, however, they met opposition from local and state officials, many of whom expressed their resentment at the very idea of educating blacks. For instance, H. A. M. Henderson, state superintendent of public instruction in the early 1870s and a former Confederate soldier, viewed blacks as a "non-conformable element," who at best could acquire only the very basics of an education. He insisted that under no circumstances should blacks and whites attend the same schools, because blacks, being naturally inferior, could not compete with whites and their very presence in the classroom would be harmful to whites. The General Assembly readily agreed, decreeing that schools would be segregated. A letter to the *Daily Courier* ex-

---

42. *Commercial*, July 3, 1874; *Courier-Journal*, June 28, 1874; Weeden, *History of the Colored People*, 8; John W. Blassingame, *Black New Orleans 1860–1880* (Chicago, 1973), 60; Perdue, *The Negro in Savannah*, 105.

43. *Commercial*, July 3, 1874; C. K. Caron's *Directory of Louisville 1872* (Louisville, 1872).

44. Louisville blacks played a prominent part in several educational conventions held by black Kentuckians. See, for example, *Proceedings of the State Convention of Colored Men, held at Lexington, Kentucky, in the AME Church, November 26, 27, 28, 1867; Kentucky State Colored Education Convention Held at Benson's Theatre, Louisville, Kentucky, July 14, 1869; Courier-Journal*, July 15, 16, 1869.

pressed the white sentiment well: "It is proper that all necessary legislation should be made for his assistance and benefit, . . . but it would be unjust and odious to oppress white taxpayers for his benefit. Let Sambo be made to educate his own children. . . ." This became the law. The legislature ruled that only revenue raised from black taxpayers would be used to finance black schools and that Negro tax rolls would be kept separate. But, as Thomas Noble of the Freedmen's Bureau explained, even this very mild measure went unenforced: "This law is a dead letter, and until the public sentiment changes, will never be enforced. More than a year has passed since its enactment and not a single school has been established. The law was passed to ensure Washington that something was being done." [45]

From the end of the Civil War until October 1870, the only schools available to blacks were directed by the churches, the Freedmen's Bureau, and the missionary societies. With the arrival of General Palmer to Louisville, several Negro churches, led by Rev. Henry Adams of First African, reopened schools that the authorities had closed in 1861. A generous grant from a white Episcopal church allowed a recently formed black church, St. Mark's Colored Episcopal, to start a school in 1866 and to hire two northern-trained blacks to direct the program. The school existed for three years, offering day classes for young children and evening classes to more than one hundred adults. Local blacks benefited greatly from schools run by the bureau and missionary societies. But even these schools could not have existed without the invaluable assistance of the black churches: the churches allowed their facilities to be used for most of the schools, and the ministers often provided housing for white teachers. [46]

The Afro-American response to the opening of the schools was overwhelming. Hundreds of former slaves rushed to enroll their children. So many potential students came that all of the schools had to limit enrollment because of a shortage of teachers. For weeks after classes had started, parents continued to bring their children to the schools, hoping for a va-

45. *Daily Courier*, February 7, March 9, 1867; *Annual Reports of the State Superintendent of Public Instruction for the Year Ending June 30, 1871* (Frankfort, 1871), 99–100; *State Superintendent of Public Instruction Report of November 22, 1871* (Frankfort, 1871), 22–23; "Bureau Monthly Reports," February 11, 1867.

46. "Bureau Monthly Reports," November 1, 1867; *Freedmen's Record*, I (May, 1865), 72–73; Charles Wynes, "Bishop Thomas U. Dudley and the Uplift of the Negro," *Register of the Kentucky Historical Society*, LXV (July, 1967), 230–38.

Two of the best sources on black Louisville are the Minutes of Fifth Street Baptist Church (formerly First African), 1829–1930, which are located at the church, and the Minutes of Green Street Baptist Church (formerly Second African), 1844–1930, Archives Department, University of Louisville. See minutes of Green Street, April 7, 1865.

cancy so they could enroll. Officials of the bureau were astonished at the number of blacks who were not only willing to pay tuition so their children could attend school but were also willing to sacrifice any income the children might earn by working instead of attending school. By 1870 there were at least fifteen schools in Louisville providing education for about 1,500 black students.[47] Considering the white violence they faced and the fact that their schools existed on prayer as much as money, blacks had a right to be proud of their schools. In his travels throughout the South, John W. Alvord found no better schools being operated by and for the freedmen than those in Louisville.

> The colored people themselves have a species of public school system. Aided by the bureau, and in connection with the several colored churches, some 15 schools, under the care of the colored assistant of Genr. Runkle, are in operation. They are in good condition . . . though the places in which they are kept are inconvenient. I took great interest in visiting these schools. They show what people *can do themselves*. What is here accomplished, may become universal as soon as the Freedmen have, from their own color, a sufficient number of competent teachers.[48]

Despite their burning desire for an education, black Louisvillians had to wait until October 1870, fully five years after the Civil War, for their first public schools.

The years immediately following 1865 witnessed the rapid growth of black churches in Louisville. With the aid of the white Walnut Street Baptist Church, a group of free blacks had formed First African Baptist in November 1829. The church grew steadily throughout the remainder of the antebellum period. Indeed, on the eve of the Civil War, First African had over 800 members and a building worth $15,000. The church's growth was even more impressive in the late 1860s as it added 400 more members and renovated its structure. By 1870 First African had changed its name to Fifth Street Baptist and was reigning as the leading black church in Kentucky. Two other churches formed in the antebellum period also grew rapidly after the war. Green Street Baptist, formerly Second African, boasted of having 1,000 members, and Quinn Chapel Episcopal, though not rivaling the Baptist churches in membership, doubled its congregation in less than ten years. Afro-Americans formed three churches in 1866, and in 1867 white Episcopalians aided them in organizing St. Mark's. Within

47. "Bureau Monthly Reports," February 11, 1867, December 1, 1868, January 13, 1869; Philip C. Kimball, "Freedom's Harvest: Freedmen's Schools in Kentucky After the Civil War," *Filson Cub*, LIV (July, 1980).

48. John W. Alvord, *Letters from the South Relating to the Condition of the Freedmen* (Washington, D.C., 1870), 33.

a few more years, blacks founded a Catholic church, Broadway Temple African Methodist Episcopal Zion, a Christian church called Church of Our Merciful Savior, and additional Baptist churches. Louisville had at least twenty-four black churches by 1880.[49]

From the beginning the church assumed very broad areas of responsibilities in the black community—far wider than those accepted in white denominations. The church served as a center of worship, but equally important, as a school for literacy, a center for recreation, and an agent for social control. During Reconstruction in Louisville the church, more than any other institution or organization, provided stability in black life. Fifth Street held services three nights a week in addition to all-day Sunday services. Other churches started programs to instruct their members in the duties of citizenship. Without a doubt, the churches accepted the responsibility of helping their people become model citizens. The ministers talked constantly about vice and laziness and how any misdeeds reflected poorly on the entire race. For many former slaves the church (and especially the minister) seemed to assume the paternalistic role of the former master. Often the leadership of the churches was conservative. Rev. Henry Adams of Fifth Street, whose congregation was comprised primarily of free blacks and people with stable roots in the community, lectured on the value of working hard and saving for the future, and on the dangers of becoming overly concerned with civil rights. Yet several of the churches would lead the first black assault on Jim Crow. Throughout its past, to the present, the Afro-American church has performed dual roles.[50]

Most local blacks were self-motivated and did not need the prodding of ministers to realize the importance of planning for their future. Their attitude toward the start of the Freedmen's Savings and Trust Company clearly showed their desire and determination to postpone immediate pleasures and to save for an education, a house, or the capital for a small

49. *AME Christian Recorder*, May 27, 1865; *Courier-Journal*, June 28, 1874; *Church of Our Merciful Savior* (Louisville, 1979); Charles H. Parrish (ed.), *Golden Jubilee, of the General Association of Colored Baptists in Kentucky* (Louisville, 1915), 257, 281; *Souvenir Program of Lampton Baptist Church, 1966* (Louisville, 1966); *100th Anniversary 1878–1978, Zion Baptist Church* (Louisville, 1978); *Portland Memorial Baptist 1866–1977* (Louisville, 1977); *Souvenir Brochure, Green Street Baptist Church, November 17–21, 1965* (Louisville, 1965); *Centennial Celebration, Broadway Temple AME Zion Church 1876–1976* (Louisville, 1976).

50. See Minutes of Green Street, January 10, 1868, October 5, 1870, February 19, 1875; Minutes of Fifth Street, December 18, 1872, November 26, 1873; Clarence E. Walker, *A Rock in a Weary Land: The African Methodist Episcopal Church During the Civil War and Reconstruction* (Baton Rouge, 1982).

business. A group of New York businessmen and philanthropists organized the bank toward the close of the war to encourage and facilitate black
savings. The bank's founders established branches in a number of cities,
including Louisville and Lexington, Kentucky. Louisville's branch opened
in September 1865 in a building owned by the U. S. Army. Several highly
respected white citizens were connected with the bank: Dr. William H.
Goddard served as cashier, and Judge Bland Ballard directed the advisory
board. Horace Morris, Washington Spradling, and Rev. Henry Adams
represented the black community on the board. As Carl R. Osthaus, the
historian of the bank, notes "one of the best and most influential advisory
boards was at Louisville." [51]

The Louisville branch quickly became one of the most successful of
the Freedmen's Banks. Three months after its inception, the bank had deposits totaling more than $300,000. Each month saw black artisans,
teachers, laborers, servants, and even whites (11 percent of the bank's depositors were white) open accounts. The bank's assets multiplied in 1868
after the advisory board selected Horace Morris as cashier. Under his
leadership the number of depositors grew from 709 in 1868, to 1,074 in
1869, to 3,000 by 1874, and the amount of deposits reached $3 million.
Morris was an excellent administrator with "his books and entire prem-
ises in perfect order." This was no small accomplishment, for the collapse
of the bank nationally in 1874 resulted from fraud and inept bookkeeping. Louisville, however, shared no blame in the bank's failure. Indeed, for
some time after the close of the national bank, the Louisville branch thought
that it could still make a go of it. This ultimately proved impossible, and
the people in Louisville like those elsewhere lost their savings, even though
their branch had remained solvent. [52]

Black involvement with the ill-fated bank was in several respects symbolic of the Civil War and Reconstruction years for Louisville's Afro-
Americans. Many events had occurred (including the opening of the bank)
that made blacks optimistic and encouraged them to plan for the future.
Yet their many setbacks made them fully aware of the difficulties involved
in acquiring all of their rights. White hostility was always present, often
working effectively to negate black gains. The events of the late 1860s and

51. Carl R. Osthaus, *Freedmen, Philanthropy, and Fraud: A History of the Freedman's Savings Bank* (Urbana, 1976), 1, 5, 18, 23, 108; Louisville *Daily Union Press*, September 18, 1865; *Daily Democrat*, September 29, 1865.

52. *Daily Union Press*, December 23, 1865; *Commercial*, April 2, 1870; Alvord, *Letters from the South*, 34; "Registers of Signatures of Depositors in Branches of the Freedman's Savings and Trust Company 1865–1875," National Archives Microfilm Publications,
M816, roll 11, National Archives, Washington, D.C.

early 1870s led some local blacks to be extremely cautious, unwilling to challenge the racial status quo. But others—though always a minority—were compelled to consistently campaign for racial justice on a number of different fronts.

During the Reconstruction years several free blacks logically emerged as the leaders of Afro-American Louisville. In a study of free blacks, Ira Berlin notes that "blacks who had enjoyed freedom before the war generally remained at the top of the new black society." [53] After 1865, these blacks controlled the wealth that existed in the black community, comprised the social elite, and received political patronage. These black leaders, led by Rev. Henry Adams, Horace Morris, and William H. Steward (a native of Brandenburg, Kentucky, who came to Louisville around 1860), made few demands on whites. Instead they urged the race to uplift itself. These men had lived as free men during the antebellum period, a time when their mere survival depended on the goodwill of whites. Immediately after slavery ended, Rev. Adams disappointed many newly freed blacks by counseling them to return to their old jobs and to cultivate relationships with their former masters. Steward, who would have enormous influence in Louisville throughout the entire period from 1865 to 1930, always reminded blacks of the importance of maintaining alliances with whites because those alliances were essential to black progress.

At the close of the war, local blacks began agitating for admission to the public schools. For several years their request was denied. In 1870 they were finally admitted to segregated schools that were housed in old buildings. A new school built exclusively for blacks opened in 1873. Both Steward and Morris held prominent places on the dedication program for the new school (Rev. Adams had died), and the choir of Fifth Street Baptist Church provided the music. For this significant occasion, the choir appropriately chose as its first song "I Waited Patiently." [54] To wait patiently, a strategy often appropriate during the antebellum period, was what the black leadership often advised their followers to do during Reconstruction and throughout the remainder of the nineteenth century.

After examining the Afro-American experience in Louisville during the Civil War and Reconstruction, this significant fact is clear: despite all the obstacles they faced, these former slaves and free blacks believed fully in

53. Ira Berlin, *Slaves Without Masters: The Free Negro in the Antebellum South* (New York, 1974), 384.

54. Minutes of Fifth Street, October 7, 1873; *Daily Commercial*, October 8, 1873; See Berlin, *Slaves Without Masters*, 393–95, for an excellent discussion of the cautious strategy of race relations advocated by free black leaders.

the American sense of fairness; in the idea that hard work and sacrifice would lead to success and, most assuredly, to the respect of others. They believed the whites who said that no one would help them but they would have to help themselves, so blacks strived to care for their own poor and to educate their own children. Their positive attitude and strong determination were all the more remarkable given their recent experience of slavery and given the degree of white hostility existing in Louisville at practically every turn.

Most whites, especially the ex-Confederate leaders, were equally determined that blacks would remain at the bottom of society. And they controlled most of the political machinery necessary to enforce their will.

PART II

A Time of Worsening Race Relations: 1870–1917

The trend of blacks migrating to Louisville from rural Kentucky that started during the Civil War would continue through the last three decades of the nineteenth century. Several factors drew Afro-Americans to the state's largest city. First, Louisville offered far more employment and entrepreneurial opportunities. Indeed, while the state's economy suffered as a whole during the war, Louisville enjoyed relatively prosperous times. A second reason cited by blacks for moving to Louisville was the opportunity for a public education. Louisville, though dragging its feet, did develop a public school system, including a high school, for blacks quicker than other Kentucky cities and counties. Unfortunately, in many places throughout the state, black public schools were not opened until ten to fifteen years after the war, and high schools for blacks would await the twentieth century. Other blacks simply were caught up in the adventure of moving to the city, following their relatives and friends to Louisville. Many soldiers who had been stationed in Louisville during the war returned to the city with their families.

The migration of rural blacks to Louisville was part of a sectional trend involving Afro-Americans in virtually every southern state moving from rural to urban areas. Though it would be the middle of the twentieth century before most of the nation's blacks lived in cities, the urbanization of blacks started after the Civil War. By 1870 the black population in the fourteen largest cities in the South had increased by 91 percent (as compared to only 17 percent for whites). This trend would remain high for decades and was well underway before the Great Migration of the World War I years. For example, in the decade 1900–1910 the black population in southern cities increased by 886,173. Whites were also migrating to the cities although at a lower rate. Hundreds of thousands of black and white Americans—tired of watching their crops being ruined by the weather and insects, angered at the abuse they received from planters and country storekeepers under the farm tenancy system, discontented with the extremely low wages in rural areas, frustrated with the lack of education opportunities for their children, and for blacks, upset with the pattern of race relations—came to view the city as a place for a fresh start and a chance to better themselves. By 1920 more than three and one-half million of the nation's 10,400,000 blacks lived in the cities, a significant increase from sixty years earlier.[1]

A large number of migrants stopped in the border cities. The black population in the five largest border cities—Baltimore, Washington, D.C., St. Louis, Richmond, and Louisville—more than tripled between 1870 and 1930 (see table 1). Though its increase was never as large as that of the other border cities, Louisville's black population increased substantially during this time. This was especially true from 1870 to 1900 when Louisville's black population increased by at least 35 percent each decade.

Table 1

Black Population in Border Cities, 1870–1930[a]

National Ranking in Number of Blacks	Percent Increase in 10 Years	Population
1870		
# 2 Baltimore	41.8%	39,558
# 3 Washington	222.8%	35,455
# 5 Richmond	61.9%	23,110
# 7 St. Louis	569.9%	22,088
#11 Louisville	119.6%	14,956
1880		
# 2 Baltimore	35.8%	53,716
# 3 Washington	36.4%	48,377
# 5 Richmond	20.4%	27,832
# 7 St. Louis	0.8%	22,256
# 8 Louisville	39.8%	20,905
1890		
# 2 Baltimore	24.9%	67,104
# 1 Washington	56.2%	75,572

1. Bureau of the Census, *Negro Population in the United States, 1790–1915* (Washington, D.C., 1918), 43–44; Bureau of the Census, *Negroes in the United States, 1920–1932* (Washington, D.C., 1935), 1–15. As scholars have repeatedly pointed out, the U.S. Census and city directories must be used with caution, realizing that blacks and poor people are vastly undercounted.

Table 1 (Continued)

National Ranking in Number of Blacks	Percent Increase in 10 Years	Population
# 6 Richmond	16.2%	32,330
#12 St. Louis	20.7%	26,865
#10 Louisville	37.1%	28,651
1900		
# 2 Baltimore	18.1%	79,258
# 1 Washington	14.7%	86,702
#10 Richmond	−0.3%	32,230
# 9 St. Louis	32.3%	35,516
# 7 Louisville	36.6%	39,139
1910		
# 4 Baltimore	6.9%	84,749
# 1 Washington	8.9%	94,446
# 9 Richmond	45.0%	46,733
#11 St. Louis	23.8%	43,960
#12 Louisville	3.5%	40,522
1920		
# 5 Baltimore	27.8%	108,322
# 3 Washington	16.4%	109,966
#11 Richmond	15.6%	54,041
# 8 St. Louis	58.9%	69,854
#15 Louisville	−1.1%	40,087
1930		
# 4 Baltimore	31.2%	142,106
# 5 Washington	20.0%	132,068
#15 Richmond	−1.9%	52,988
#10 St. Louis	34.0%	93,580
#18 Louisville	18.1%	47,354

[a]Hollis Lynch (ed.), *The Black Urban Condition* (New York, 1973), appendix A, 421–28.

The percentage increases for blacks and whites in Louisville were very similar. They differed, however, between 1910 and 1920 when the black population actually declined (see table 2). Additionally, unlike the remainder of the state, Louisville always attracted a number of foreign-born whites. Most of them were Irish or German, and their numbers increased substantially in the two decades following the Civil War. By 1910 Louisville had 17,436 foreign-born whites, comprising 7.8 percent of the population.

Table 2

Total Population of Louisville, 1870–1930[a]

Year	Total Population	Black Population	Percent Black
1870	100,753	14,956	14.8
1880	123,758	20,905	16.8
1890	161,129	28,651	17.7
1900	204,731	39,139	19.1
1910	223,928	40,522	18.0
1920	234,891	40,087	17.0
1930	307,745	47,354	15.3

[a] Bureau of the Census, *Fifteenth Census of the United States*, "1930: Population" (Washington, D.C., 1932), I, 432.

Blacks were migrating to Louisville and other cities during a time of increasing racial hatred. Most of the ex-Confederate states were controlled by the "Redeemers" within a matter of years after the beginning of Reconstruction in 1867. By 1877 it was obvious that the federal government had turned its back on Afro-Americans, allowing southern whites to handle the "Negro problem." The historian Rayford Logan has called this period the nadir for black Americans, and it would last for roughly four decades. Perhaps the worst and most consistent offender of black rights was the United States Supreme Court, which ruled in 1896 that the policy of separate but equal was constitutional, and which upheld the laws in the former Confederate states which deprived blacks of the right to vote. During these years an estimated 3,000 blacks were lynched in the United States. Race riots occurred in cities both North and South. Segregation intensified; blacks were excluded from places of amusement, public accommodations, welfare institutions, and hospitals. Black ghettos burgeoned as more and more Afro-Americans were forced to live in only a few, restricted neighborhoods, regardless of their economic means.

Discrimination in employment and access to public accommodations was a common experience for Louisville blacks, and they were often the victims of police brutality. Adequate housing was a continuing problem, with the poor being relegated to places not fit for animals and middle- and upper-class blacks meeting sharp opposition to their attempts to move into better housing in white neighborhoods. All Louisville blacks felt the sting of racial discrimination, but the group most affected was black women. They were confined to the worst jobs, often having to leave their children unattended while working. Helen Irvin, in her definitive study of women in Kentucky, points out that many women turned to prostitution as a means of survival. Despite the presence of churches and racial uplift organizations, virtually nothing was done to alleviate the special problems of women. In Louisville a YMCA opened twenty-five years before a YWCA. In a male-dominated society, where all women faced discrimination, Afro-American women carried a double burden.[2]

Despite the discrimination they faced on several fronts, the population growth of Afro-Americans in Louisville did have some positive results. By the 1890s blacks were receiving political recognition for the first time, though nowhere near what their numbers and importance to the Republican party warranted. But just keeping the right to vote was an accomplishment, considering the success of the disfranchisement movements in several states bordering Kentucky. As the number of blacks increased, city officials were compelled to build schools, libraries, and hospitals for them. The black churches continued to grow in both membership and programs, providing leadership training for the community. Black social clubs flourished. The rise in black population, creating a need

2. In Louisville, as was generally the case elsewhere, black women outnumbered men.

	1890	1900	1910
Males	13,330	18,842	19,602
Females	15,321	20,297	20,920

See Bureau of the Census, *Negro Population*, 202. Of course, this meant that not all women could get married; furthermore, many of the men were far from desirable as husbands, lacking both stable jobs and roots in the Afro-American community. Professor DuBois called the predominance of black women one of the most striking problems of the urban Negro population. W. E. B. DuBois (ed.), *The Negro American Family*, Atlanta University Publications, no. 13 (Atlanta, 1908), 36–37; Helen D. Irvin, *Women In Kentucky* (Lexington, 1979).

for black teachers, lawyers, physicians, and businessmen, contributed to the development of a black professional class.

Not surprisingly, many whites were troubled by the increase in the black population and even more so by the "quality" of blacks coming to Louisville. Always careful to avoid harsh racial indictments, white leaders repeatedly explained that young blacks lacked the manners and indeed the white guidance that helped shape the character of antebellum blacks. In reality, what troubled whites most was not black laziness or indifference but attempts by blacks to better themselves. "The average Louisville citizen would be surprised to see aged darkies, barely able to totter under their weight of age, trudging with books under their arms to night school," quipped the *Courier-Journal* in 1903. Educated blacks, especially lawyers and doctors, were subjected to ridicule. Jokes were told about the lack of morality among black ministers. The white newspapers spoke fondly of slave life in Louisville. The Louisville *Post* of May 22, 1893, carried a typical story about slavery, this one described "Aunt Mildy," an old ex-slave. In very sentimental terms, the paper told of Aunt Mildy's devotion to the Zachary Taylor family and then contrasted that with the lack of respect and devotion on the part of present-day Afro-Americans. Aunt Mildly was said to be very astute: "Her intelligence on commonplace subjects is far greater than that of the average Negro." Also, the reporter explained that Aunt Mildy, who readily accepted her lot in life, abhorred "high fluttin' niggers." This was Louisville's polite racism, not nearly as bitter in the denunciation of blacks. Another excellent example is a newspaper story about blacks entertaining whites at a Shriner's Convention. The paper enjoyed detailing the entire program, and depicting the blacks as buffoons:

> Pickaninnies, with their faces buried in huge cuts of watermelon; the sporty young negro dressed in his "ice cream suit" dancing a cake-walk with his dusky bell, dressed to kill; the old mammy and the old darkies singing their plantation melodies and every other interesting feature associated with the care-free life of the negro in years gone by . . . were told in song, story and dance to a crowd that was estimated at 7,000 persons at the First Regiment Armory last night when 150 negro men, women, and children took part in the "Grand Colored Jubilee and Festival," which had been arranged by Kosair Temple for the Imperial Council and other visiting Shriners and their women folk.

The blacks performed many exotic dances. They sang and acted out numerous songs, with the crowd thoroughly enjoying "Kinky," performed by a three-year old boy with unkempt hair, and "All Coons Look Alike to Me." According to the paper, the audience was amazed that the 150 blacks could devour 50 huge watermelons "in less time than it takes to tell about it." The entertainment closed with blacks singing "My Country 'Tis of Thee." [3] Such were the attitudes and conditions Louisville blacks faced during the nadir period.

3. Louisville *Post*, May 22, 1893; *Courier-Journal*, April 12, 1903, June 10, 1909.

## 2

The Color Line

Throughout the 1870s, racial discrimination in Louisville was very inconsistent; blacks were totally excluded from some areas of society while, for some unexplained reason, they faced little or no white resistance in others. This inconsistency was baffling, embarrassing, and frustrating to blacks and whites alike. During the 1880s and 1890s, whites took steps to eliminate the inconsistencies, to make racial exclusion more uniform and as complete as possible. Blacks found it impossible to challenge every exclusion, so they carefully selected a specific battleground and formed a united campaign of protest.

As Professor C. Vann Woodward notes, prior to the 1890s blacks did not face a uniform system of Jim Crow Laws. In Savannah, blacks could attend the theaters, and most white churches admitted Negroes, though in some they were confined to seats in the rear. Also before the 1890s blacks and whites in Savannah rode together on streetcars. In New Orleans, writes John Blassingame, race relations "swung like a crazy pendulum back and forth between integration and segregation." Blacks received equal treatment on streetcars but generally not in restaurants and hotels. At times blacks were totally uncertain of the treatment they would receive when pursuing equal access to white establishments. In Virginia, according to Charles E. Wynes, the "most distinguishing factor in the complexity of social relations between the races was that of inconsistency." Discrimination was common in public inns and hotels, but this could vary from city to city, or from hotel to hotel. Ohio is an excellent example of the absence of a uniform code of discrimination before the 1890s, for in some areas of the state blacks were accepted on an equal basis, while in others racial discrimination rivaled that found in the South. In Cleveland and the Western Reserve region, blacks were received at the best hotels, restaurants, and theaters. Cleveland even went a step further and adopted integrated public schools and employed black teachers. Meanwhile, in Cincinnati blacks faced total exclusion from public accommodations, and their children were taught by whites in segregated schools. After excluding blacks from the YMCA, Cincinnati whites were offended that blacks started their own branch. Pressure was exerted until blacks changed the name of theirs to YBCA—Young Boys Christian Association. Finally, Douglas Daniels, writing about San Francisco blacks, notes that racial discrimination in that city was mild by comparison with the South, but it was nevertheless disturbing "partly because it was not as iron-clad as elsewhere." As was the case in most cities, San Francisco blacks never knew what to expect when venturing into white restaurants, hotels, or saloons.[1]

I.

In the last decades of the nineteenth century, Louisville's elite whites found it desirable to segregate not only blacks but also poor whites and "foreigners." City officials created Male High School, designed for the professional class (although no white boys could be denied admission), who wanted their sons to receive preparatory training that would lead to their admission to prestigious colleges and to careers as lawyers, doctors, and bankers. Manual High School offered training for industry or small shops and catered almost entirely to young white men from middle- and lower-middle-class backgrounds. Female High School, for white females, had two tracts of study: college preparatory, and domestic science and business training.

The various private clubs in Louisville practiced an especially rigid system of exclusion. Leading the way was the Pendennis Club, whose only members were upper-class ex-Confederates and the city's wealthiest whites. The city also offered the Tavern Club to young enterprising white men on the make. Much later the Jewish community established the Standard Club. Scattered throughout the city were several country clubs that provided recreational facilities to its members; thus upper-class whites could avoid going to the public pools, tennis courts, and golf courses. A woman who lived in Louisville during these years proudly remembered:

When I was a girl there was a German caterer named Klein whose daughter went to the school attended by my sister and myself. We were always very polite to her but it was understood that we were from different worlds. True, her father no longer appeared at the parties for which he did the catering; he sent his waiters. He kept a carriage and had a handsome residence, but that made no difference.[2]

1. Woodward, *The Strange Career of Jim Crow*, 31–109; Perdue, *The Negro in Savannah*, 25–73; Blassingame, *Black New Orleans*, 173–210; Wynes, *Race Relations in Virginia*, 68–83; David A. Gerber, *Black Ohio and the Color Line 1860–1915* (Urbana, 1976), 52–59; Daniels, *Pioneer Urbanites*, 108.
2. For information on many of Louisville's exclusive clubs, see Robert W. Brown (ed.),

With that attitude prevalent among the upper class, the exclusion of blacks was natural, and seemed irreversible.

Immediately after the Civil War, blacks were allowed limited access to public transportation, health and welfare agencies, and white business establishments in Louisville. At the first Negro statewide educational convention in 1867, Louisville blacks called attention to the discrimination they faced on steamboats and railroads where "we are not allowed the privileges of travelers, but are put in second class and disagreeable places, where we are frequently abused and insulted by drunken and ill-behaved white persons." Yet in the early 1870s, Louisville's amusement places, restaurants, and hotels often extended their services to Afro-Americans. Prominent black visitors, such as Frederick Douglass and John M. Langston, had no trouble securing overnight hotel accommodations or service in restaurants. But the city's leading hotel, the internationally known Galt House, consistently denied all services to blacks.[3]

Of greatest concern to the majority of blacks was the treatment they received on the streetcars. Only a small number of blacks could afford to dine in restaurants or attend the theater, but using the streetcar was a necessity to blacks who lived in outlying districts but worked in the center of the city. Moreover, it was a personal affront to middle-class blacks who could easily afford the fare and found riding the streetcar preferable to walking throughout the city. All three streetcar companies serving Louisville discriminated against blacks. On the Main and Fourth Street line, rear seats were set aside for blacks, both male and female. The Walnut Company allowed black women to sit in the car, but black men had to ride on the platform. The Market Street line permitted black women to ride in the cars; black men were not allowed in the cars or on the platform. United States Senator Hiram Revels from Mississippi, while visiting in Louisville, was refused admission to the Market Street line. A white news reporter witnessed a second incident: "A very respectable looking, elderly colored man, two-thirds white, entered the car. He was innocently reaching forward to put his money in the fare box when the driver said 'Get out; you can't ride here. You can't even ride on the platform on this road. . . . We don't carry niggers.'"[4]

Book of Louisville (Louisville, 1915); see also Krock, *Myself When Young*, 187, and Flexner, *I Remember*, 19–20. Both vividly recall the stratified white society in Louisville. The quote comes from Leighton, *Five Cities*, 68.

    3. *Proceedings of the State Convention of Colored Men, held at Lexington, Kentucky, in the AME Church, November 26, 27, 28, 1867; Commercial*, July 20, 1870.

    4. *Daily Commercial*, April 2, July 20, 1870.

Discrimination on the streetcars led to the first organized protest movement by Louisville blacks. Robert Fox, a mortician, the "respectable looking, elderly colored man," would lead the movement. After church services on October 30, 1870, Fox, his brother Samuel, and Horace Pearce, who worked for the Fox brothers, boarded the Market Street line, paid their fare and sat down. This led to a disturbance on the streetcar and ultimately to their arrest. The black community quickly united behind the three men. The following evening a meeting was held at Quinn Chapel Church, and a subscription drive begun to defray the cost of fighting the case in court. A resolution was adopted: "That we hereby approve of the course pursued by Messrs. Fox and Pearce in their determination to make their expulsion recently from the streetcars a test case, and we pledge ourselves to sustain them in all prudent legal measures which they or others may take to secure redress." [5]

With the aid of two white attorneys, black leaders based their case on the grounds that the streetcar was a common carrier and that blacks had a right to ride and sit wherever they desired. In City Court, however, Judge J. Hop Price refused to hear any black testimony and fined each defendant five dollars for disorderly conduct. As a final point, Judge Price stated that common carriers could regulate their passengers. The black leaders refused to admit defeat and appealed to the U.S. District Court. They also decided that Robert Fox should sue the streetcar companies for damages. Since the court was recessed for several months, other methods had to be adopted to keep the movement going. Therefore, a few blacks, after being refused equal service on the streetcars, complained to railway officials about the treatment they received and petitioned them to change their discriminatory practices. Many other blacks boycotted the streetcars entirely as a way of convincing the companies to change their practices. Finally on May 11, 1871, the U.S. District Court ruled in favor of blacks in *Fox v. Central Passenger Company*. Fox won his case on the Federal Enforcement Acts of the Thirteenth and Fourteenth Amendments and the common law provisions relevant to common carriers. The court awarded Fox fifteen dollars in damages.[6]

The District Court's ruling did not immediately end the controversy. Several black men were attacked for exercising their right to ride all of the railway lines and to sit where they desired in the cars. The local white newspapers advocated segregated cars as the way of ending the violence

5. AME *Christian Recorder*, November 19, 1870.

6. Marjorie Norris, "An Early Instance of Non-Violence: The Louisville Demonstrations of 1870–71," *Journal of Southern History*, XXXII (November, 1966), 494–99.

and disruptions on the streetcars. This position was proposed by railway officials when attempting to reach a peaceful settlement with black leaders. Blacks quickly rejected the suggestion of segregated cars and threatened to continue their protest unless treated with equality on the lines. Railway officials then capitulated and opened all the streetcar lines to blacks because they feared that additional black denouncements would lead to a further disruption of their business.[7]

Several factors led to the successful demonstrations by Afro-Americans. Members of the U.S. District Court were Republicans, and their sympathy with the black protest movement effectively prevented local authorities from continuing to segregate blacks on the streetcars. Very important was the fact that blacks had a specific goal in mind—the ending of discrimination on the streetcars—and they remained well organized and united, and thus were able to persevere when it took several months to reach a conclusion. An example of the united effort during the boycott was the work of the city's black draymen who provided transportation for black people who lived in the city's outlying areas. Also, the churches gave financial and moral support to the cause and exhorted their people to remain committed to the boycott.[8]

But, as was so often the case in Louisville, the success of blacks was short-lived. In the future some whites would still protest the right of blacks to sit in "their section" of the streetcars. By the mid-1880s, in fact, blacks were often relegated to seats in the back and forcibly removed when sitting elsewhere. Arthur Krock recalled an incident on a streetcar: "I still remember the sense of shame I felt when, on a hot summer day, a Negro having boarded a crowded streetcar in Louisville and stood in the vestibule for a breath of fresh air, one of my uncles ordered him to the rear." However, even this pattern of Jim Crow streetcars was far from uniform. Blacks found discrimination when riding on certain routes but enjoyed the right to sit wherever they desired on others. Some whites, desiring a consistent Jim Crow policy, called for an ordinance to segregate streetcars on several different occasions in the early 1900s, but it failed every time.[9]

This failure to pass a streetcar ordinance made Louisville different from

7. *Courier-Journal*, May 15, 1871; AME *Christian Recorder*, May 19, 1871; Norris, "The Louisville Demonstrations," 500–502.

8. August Meier and Elliott Rudwick, "The Boycott Movement Against Jim Crow Streetcars in the South, 1900–1906," A. Meier and E. Rudwick, *Along the Color Line: Explorations in the Black Experience* (Urbana, 1976); Rabinowitz, *Race Relations in the Urban South*, 194.

9. Krock, *Myself When Young*, 79–80; Charles Dudley Warner, *Studies in the South and West* (New York, 1889), 387; New York *Freeman*, January 15, 1887.

many cities. A score of southern cities enacted Jim Crow streetcar ordinances between 1900 and 1905. Blacks protested and then boycotted the lines. In several cities they formed their own streetcar companies to compete against white-owned lines. But, except for Nashville where a black company operated for several months, the protest movements failed completely because Afro-Americans lacked the financial resources to sustain the companies. Also, white officials through legal and illegal means undermined the boycotts. Although in many of the cities the white streetcar companies opposed the ordinances because they were difficult to enforce and costly, the white citizens left no doubt about their desire for segregation on streetcars. Yet, when given the same opportunity, Louisville whites failed to enact such an ordinance. Maybe they rightly understood that the protest movement by blacks was a conservative movement and not a challenge to the established order. As historians August Meier and Elliott Rudwick explain, black leaders, by protesting the Jim Crow streetcars, were seeking to maintain the status quo. "The boycotts fitted the conservatism of Negro leaders in southern cities during a period of accommodation. . . . The boycotts were a natural and spontaneous response, for they sought to preserve dignity in the face of a humiliating social change." [10] Also, maybe Louisville's whites found satisfaction in not enacting yet another Jim Crow ordinance. Through informal means, the whites who thought it necessary to segregate the races on the streetcars did so, while other whites could correctly say that blacks in their city did not suffer the same legal discrimination that existed in most cities in the South.

Local whites may have been divided over the need for a Jim Crow streetcar ordinance, but on another controversial issue, the Federal Civil Rights Acts of 1875, they spoke as one voice in opposition to the law. The act, which Massachusetts Senator Charles Sumner had been trying to pass for years, forbade discrimination in hotels, restaurants, public conveyances, and public amusement places. It smacked too much of racial equality and was roundly condemned in white Louisville. New South spokesman Henry Watterson called the Civil Rights Act "an insult to the white people of the southern states." This law, he explained, was merely the latest in a long series of actions by the Republicans to create tension between blacks and whites. As usual, blacks were "blindly being led to believe that a measure would lead to a 'Revolution' in their condition and elevate them to affluence, social status, and political power," things, Watterson once again reminded his black readers, that could be obtained only through hard

10. Meier and Rudwick, "Jim Crow Streetcars," 279–83; Lester C. Lamon, *Black Tennesseans 1900–1930* (Knoxville, 1977), 24–34.

work. In the weeks that followed the passage of the bill, the *Courier-Journal* kept its white readers informed about attempts by blacks all over the nation to "try it on"—to see if they would be served in white establishments. This cataloging had its desired effect as local white businessmen resolved that their blacks had better refrain from entering places where they were not welcomed.[11]

When queried by the newspaper, all of the proprietors expressed their displeasure over the bill, stating emphatically that nothing would disturb "the even tenor of their businesses by the imposition of the Civil Rights Bill." One businessman noted that despite the new law, hotel owners still reserved the right to assign their guests to seats in the dining room and sleeping quarters, hinting that they would not allow the law to disrupt their practices of discrimination. Furthermore, local proprietors were convinced that, unlike blacks in some cities, Louisville blacks were decent people who would not want to force themselves on whites. "They [the Negroes] appear from their conversations, now that they have full liberty to put little value on it, so far as the social feature of the Civil Rights Bill is concerned, preferring to remain separated rather than to avail themselves of any privileges calculated to stir up strife between the races," so one hotel owner said to a *Courier-Journal* reporter.[12]

Local Republicans, who had been trying since the end of the war to broaden their base of support, found the Civil Rights Act a source of embarrassment. After assuring Afro-Americans of their continued commitment to black civil rights, party officials quickly added, "our objection to the bill has been based on our doubts of the Constitutional right of Congress to pass a bill relating to such subjects." Just like Henry Watterson and the ex-Confederates, the Republicans advised blacks to simply ignore the bill and continue improving themselves. Above all, they hoped that no blacks would foolishly hurry "to exercise their new privileges in an offensive way."[13]

Realizing that most whites found the law offensive, and fearful that they would be denied services, local blacks were reluctant to "try it on" in Louisville. Five days after the law had been in effect, however, several unknown black men (who the *Courier-Journal* pointed out were "all yellow") took it upon themselves to test the new law. They first went to McCauley's Theater where two of them asked for tickets to the dress circle. The cashier, unsure of what the owner wanted, sold them the tickets.

11. See the *Courier-Journal* for the two-week period of March 1–15, 1875.
12. *Ibid.*, March 9, 1875.
13. *Daily Commercial*, March 2, 12, 1875.

Their presence in the dress circle upset the entire audience. According to a reporter, most of the people ignored the play and stared at the men. A few people with cameras took pictures of the two men since, as the reporter explained, they were "the first of all Kentucky's colored population to transcend the bounds that the customs and traditions of the Commonwealth had prescribed for their race." Later that same evening, two blacks tried to purchase tickets to a play at the Public Library Hall. The owner, W. B. Hays, was present and he directed them to the balcony, saying that as usual the dress circle and parquet were reserved for whites only. The men passively accepted this arrangement. The very next evening, two Afro-Americans dined at the Rufer Hotel. According to the newspaper account, the men were treated properly, but upon leaving the hotel the men were attacked and beaten by a white mob—an incident that the *Courier-Journal* found deserving and humorous.[14]

Meanwhile, Louisville's black leadership was bitterly divided over what action to take. Some, mostly ministers and school teachers, were fearful that rushing to demand their civil rights would lead to racial friction. A group headed by Henry Fitzbutler, the state's first black physician, said that the Civil Rights Act was the culmination of their drive for all of their rights as citizens, and that though blacks should not throw themselves on whites they did have the right to public facilities. This group held a meeting at the saloon of William Spradling (son of a late free black leader) to decide how best to proceed. No definite plan resulted, so they held a second meeting at a church. This time they agreed, in honor of the men who had backed the bill, to pass a resolution: "That judicious, prudent, and continuous use of the Civil Rights law by colored people in all necessary cases, is indispensable in securing good by the enactment of the law." They called on the entire Afro-American community to participate in a celebration on March 25 in honor of the passing of the bill.[15]

Led by William H. Steward and Nathaniel R. Harper, the more conservative black leaders quickly responded to this announcement by the more activist blacks. Steward, a trusted employee of the president of the Louisville and Nashville Railroad, explained that instead of a celebration, which could lead to a riot, the black community should hold a quiet church service. Furthermore, he bitterly denounced the actions of the other blacks, labeling them as troublemakers. Harper, the first black admitted to the bar in Kentucky and a loyal Republican and office seeker, concurred with Steward. He took part in working out the details for the church service

14. *Courier-Journal*, March 6, 7, 8, 9, 1875.
15. *Ibid.*, March 12, 1875.

and announced that his popular singing group would provide the entertainment.

Surprisingly, by March 25 Fitzbutler's group canceled their celebration, leaving the church service as the only public black acknowledgment of the passing of the Civil Rights Act. After his group finished singing, Harper gave a long speech, urging his fellow black citizens to go slow and avoid making demands on whites. "We must," Harper said, "educate ourselves to a higher morality than exists at present within the race." Harper also noted that blacks needed to patronize black-owned businesses. "This will in time, make the Hotels, etc., of negroes as good as those of the whites, and do away with the necessity of troubling white people with their presence." [16]

With Harper's passive attitude dominating the actions and opinions of most black leaders, coupled with the united resistance of whites, the Civil Rights Act was a dead letter in Louisville. For one thing, too few blacks could afford such luxuries as dining at the Galt House or attending the theater. Blacks who could afford the luxuries were rightfully fearful that white resentment might cost them their jobs or white patronage. They also knew that two blacks had already been assaulted after dining at a local hotel. There are no records of Louisville blacks filing suit after being denied their rights under the new law. This indicates, first, that very few blacks challenged the white establishment by venturing into hotels and restaurants, and second, if they did and were denied services, they felt too powerless to seek legal redress. In many cities, especially in the North, blacks sued after being denied equal access to public accommodations. But more often than not their efforts were wasted, with the courts either dismissing their suits or awarding them only modest sums of money. The Louisville white press highlighted these unsuccessful attempts to make sure that local blacks understood that the Civil Rights Act had not changed the status quo.

Farther south, whites were even more hostile to the measure than their Louisville counterparts. To insure that the bill would be ineffective in their state, the Tennessee legislature abolished the common-law right of "any person excluded from any hotel or public means of transportation, or place of amusement" to sue. This was to prevent a rash of lawsuits. Other states simply ignored the Civil Rights Act. Emma Lou Thornbrough notes that the bill "attracted little attention in Indiana, where Negroes rarely attempted to invade the places designated by custom and economic circum-

16. *Ibid.*, March 21, 26, 1875; *Daily Commercial*, March 21, 1875.

stances for the use of white persons." In several cities in Ohio, black leaders counseled the race in the same tone as that of Louisville's conservative
leaders—go slow, uplift themselves, and forget about public accommodations.[17]

In 1883 the U.S. Supreme Court declared the Civil Rights Act unconstitutional, saying in essence that nothing could be done to prevent individual discrimination. Once again Louisville's black leaders met to decide
on an appropriate response. All agreed that for the race to succeed they
needed the goodwill of whites. They then urged whites to live up to the
American creed and to voluntarily admit respectable blacks to their establishments. The black leaders concluded with a familiar theme, that if blacks
could somehow work hard and acquire wealth they would be accepted by
whites. Louisville whites, other than praising the court, said very little about
the overturning of the Civil Rights Act. The noted southern historian C.
Vann Woodward explains why the repeal of the act caused little excitement in 1883, why the act never had much impact. "The Negro bred to
slavery was typically ignorant and poor and was not given to pressing his
rights to such luxuries as hotels, restaurants, and theaters even when he
could afford them or was aware of them. So far as his status was concerned, there was little need for Jim Crow laws to establish what the lin-
gering stigma of slavery—in bearing, speech, and manner—made so apparent.[18]

II.

Louisville blacks had already been experiencing a more consistent
pattern of discrimination by the time the Civil Rights Act was declared unconstitutional in 1883. Indeed, by the 1880s blacks were totally excluded
from several white establishments and welfare institutions where previously they had been admitted. Most of the theaters in the 1870s had allowed blacks to sit in a designated area, reserving the dress and parquet

17. Thornbrough, *The Negro in Indiana*, 258–63; Gerber, *Black Ohio*, 48, 189–90;
Rabinowitz, *Race Relations in the Urban South*, 186–87.

18. *Courier-Journal*, October 16, 17, 19, 20, 1883; *Daily Commercial*, October 20,
1883; Woodward, *The Strange Career of Jim Crow*, 32. See John Marshall Harlan Papers,
box 20, "Civil Rights Case Scrapbook," Archives Department, University of Louisville, for
the reaction of Louisville whites to Harlan's dissent in the Civil Rights case. A letter from a
Republican, A. E. Willson, a future governor of Kentucky, dated October 19,1883, praised
his action. A letter from another lawyer, Wallace S. Gudgell, dated November 5, 1883, said
that "many in Louisville are angry at Harlan."

circles for whites. But according to a correspondent for the New York *Freeman*, by 1885 the four theaters no longer admitted blacks at all. At one time, black women were allowed to sit in the ladies stands at baseball games and at the race track. However, this policy changed when Colonel M. Lewis Clark, president of the Louisville Jockey Club, informed his workers not to "admit colored patrons for love nor money in the ladies stand." Also, by the mid-1880s annual fairs and expositions were closed to blacks. They responded by holding their own fair, a tradition that continued into the twentieth century.[19]

In the early 1880s, Moses Fleetwood Walker, the only Negro on the Toledo, Ohio, professional baseball team, risked bodily harm while playing in Louisville. The Toledo management benched him after whites threatened to riot over Walker's presence on the baseball diamond. But on the team's return engagement to the city Walker was allowed to play. The fans responded by shouting racial slurs, booing his every move, and throwing objects on the playing field. To the delight of the all-white and highly partisan crowd, their rowdiness greatly affected Walker's performance. But as *Sporting Life* concluded, "Walker's poor playing in a City where the Color line was closely drawn as it is in Louisville should not be counted against him. . . . It is not creditable to the Louisville management that it should permit such outrageous behavior to occur on the grounds."[20]

During these years, blacks continued to be totally excluded from or, at best, segregated in Louisville's welfare institutions. The city established Industrial Schools of Reform for delinquent white youths in the 1870s. The schools were not only an alternative to sending youthful offenders to jail, they were also designed to prepare them for employment. White boys received instruction in carpentry and woodworking; white girls learned how to sew, cook, and perform other basic skills. Black juvenile delinquents were excluded from these institutions and sent to jail. After much pressure from the black community, city officials opened a reform school for black boys in 1885. They delayed another eleven years before starting one for black girls. A law enacted in 1884 called for segregation of the races at the Louisville School for the Blind. Blacks were denied the right to use most of the free public bathhouses scattered throughout the city.[21]

19. *Commercial*, April 2, July 20, 1870; New York *Freeman*, May 23, October 17, 1885, November 27, 1886; *Courier-Journal*, February 24, 1882, August 21, 1902; Indianapolis *Freeman*, July 20, 1901; Louisville *Evening Post*, September 21, 1910.

20. *Sporting Life* is quoted in Robert Peterson, *Only the Ball was White* (Englewood Cliffs, N.J., 1970), 23.

21. Gilbert T. Stephenson, *Race Distinction in American Law* (New York, 1910), 78–

Despite the increasing Afro-American population, the public hospitals refused to increase the beds and rooms available to blacks. Moreover, several Democratic city administrations in the 1880s and 1890s refused to hire a black physician, which meant that poor blacks did without the free medical services that the city provided poor whites. There were at least eight private hospitals in Louisville, ranging from Children's Hospital to a tuberculosis center; none of them extended services to blacks. The University of Louisville Medical School and the Hospital College of Medicine did not receive blacks and adamantly opposed admitting blacks to their medical programs. "The Hospital College of Medicine never matriculated a 'coon' in all of its history and never will so long as I am Dean," was the reply Professor W. E. B. DuBois received from Louisville. Even the private clinics, which were established to prevent the spread of contagious diseases, saw their purpose as serving whites only. In a letter to Rev. E. L. Powell of the First Christian Church, Dr. W. D. Berry expressed the following sentiment:

> Would suggest that only white women and children be treated at this clinic, because at our other clinics all classes are treated, men, women, and children, both whites and blacks, and there is no pretense made at separating them. Therefore I believe it would be a good thing to relieve our poor white women and children of this embarrassment. This clinic could gradually be advertised to a desirable class of poor white people, without cost, by giving each patient properly printed cards to distribute among their friends, and church-working bodies would send worthy women and children to the clinic.[22]

More than ever before, Louisville whites drew the color line in religion, refusing memberships to blacks and tolerating them as visitors only as long as they remained passively in the back of the church. Carter Helm Jones, pastor of the Broadway Baptist Church, told a *Courier-Journal* reporter that black seminary students from State University, a local Negro Baptist college, attended several white churches but were not allowed to participate in the services and were restricted to seats in the rear. On one occasion the interracial General Baptist Convention of America held a meeting in Louisville despite much difficulty in seating arrangements. Local white Baptists wanted to entertain the convention but were opposed to

---

101, 148; New York *Freeman*, September 26, November 6, 28, 1885; *Courier-Journal*, January 1, 1880, August 12, 1913; Warner, *Studies in the South and West*, 286–87.

22. W. E. B. DuBois (ed.), *The Health and Physique of the Negro American*, Atlanta University Publications, no. 11 (Atlanta, 1906), 98; Letter from Dr. W. D. Berry to Rev. E. L. Powell, June 27, 1911, Filson Club, Louisville.

blacks assembling with them. Despite Negro opposition, the General Baptists decided to hold the convention in Louisville with blacks restricted to the balcony. However, one Sunday shortly after Booker T. Washington's famous dinner with President Roosevelt, two black women entered a white church and occupied seats down front. The service continued even though the entire congregation was visibly upset. The paper speculated that Washington's dinner at the White House had encouraged the women to break yet another racial barrier.[23]

Yet even in the worsening racial climate of the 1880s and 1890s, racial segregation was far from complete. This most surely was the case in Louisville's public parks. On weekends and holidays it was not uncommon for both races to be seen picnicking and even playing baseball and other games side by side. Blacks also used the public swimming pools and tennis courts. Though there would be repeated attempts to oust blacks from the parks, all of these efforts would fail until the summer of 1924.[24]

Also, many Louisville whites did not see the necessity of passing a formal Jim Crow law for the railroads. Given the general racial beliefs prevailing, it is safe to assume that most white passengers would rather not sit next to a Negro. Yet the group using the railroads most—businessmen—did not take the time to complain about a lack of racial separation. Such ex-Confederates as Watterson and Duke, who never backed away from stating their opposition to social equality, failed to comment on this issue. Without a doubt, the railroad companies were opposed to laws segregating the races in travel, since they would bear the expenses of adding a Jim Crow car or building a partition and bear the responsibility of enforcing the law. Milton H. Smith, president of the L & N Railroad, explained that most of the railroads had too few black passengers to justify a separate car, nor were partitions necessary since so few blacks wanted or could afford first-class services. In all likelihood, the main supporters of Jim Crow railroads were rural Kentuckians, whose villages and farms the trains passed through. They were offended that blacks were even on the trains, and even more so at the thought that some of them might be traveling first class. Legislators representing the rural areas were the first to call for railway segregation in the state.[25]

23. *Courier-Journal*, October 21, 1901; Stephenson, *Race Distinction in American Law*, 142; Raleigh *News and Observer*, April 6, 1906.

24. Rabinowitz, *Race Relations in the Urban South*, 182–97; Ray Stannard Baker, *Following the Color Line: American Negro Citizenship in the Progressive Era* (New York, 1908); Wynes, *Race Relations in Virginia*, 68–84; Gunnar Myrdal, *An American Dilemma: The Negro Problem and Modern Democracy* (2 vols.; New York, 1944), I, 341–46.

25. Leighton, *Five Cities*, 72–74, has a discussion of Milton H. Smith and his attitude

Until the 1880s, the railroad companies apparently had no consistent policy and could be easily swayed by public protest to segregate or admit blacks to first class. From their protest in the late 1860s, we know that blacks were denied first-class services immediately after the war. Yet by the next decade Afro-American women were allowed into all cars, while all blacks could ride on the Chesapeake and Ohio and the Southern Railroads, two competitors of the L & N. The policy of the L & N during the 1870s is unclear. Unquestionably, by the early 1880s the L & N denied blacks first-class service. Also by that time the company had a separate waiting room for black passengers. In 1886 a group of black leaders met with President Smith of the L & N and presented him with a list of grievances, hinting that unless changes resulted they would boycott his railroad. Smith made a token gesture, lifting the ban on the selling of first-class tickets to black women. But this led to protests from whites, and within two months Smith reinstated segregation in first class. At this same time sufficient pressure was also placed on the Chesapeake and Ohio and the Southern Railroads, until they also joined the L & N in prohibiting first-class services to blacks.[26]

The enactment of a Jim Crow railroad law was inevitable since the state legislature had already passed laws segregating the races in every other conceivable area of society. Accordingly, in December 1891, State Senator Tipton Miller, a Democrat from Calloway County, introduced a bill calling for equal accommodations, but in separate coaches, for black and white passengers. "Each compartment of a coach [is to be] divided by a good and substantial wooden partition, with a door therein . . . and shall bear in some conspicuous place appropriate words in plain letters indicating the race it is set apart for." Fines would range from $500 to $1,500 for any railroad company failing to comply with the law. Legislators in both houses and the state's Democratic governor expressed some initial reservations about the proposed bill. But they ultimately succumbed lest their political careers be ruined by this "nigger issue." The measure passed overwhelmingly on May 24, 1892.[27]

Louisville blacks, in conjunction with Afro-Americans throughout the

---

toward Jim Crow railroad cars. Carl N. Degler, *The Other South: Southern Dissenters in the Nineteenth Century* (New York, 1974), 353–58, explains that poor whites were afraid that any social contact blacks might have with whites would lead to blacks being regarded as their equals. They wanted laws to clearly state the distinctions between the races.

26. *Courier-Journal*, October 14, November 29, 1881; New York *Freeman*, July 31, September 4, October 16, 1886, January 15, 1887.

27. *Acts of the General Assembly of the Commonwealth of Kentucky, 1891–93* (Frankfort, 1893), 63–64. See also S. E. Smith (ed.), *History of the Anti-Separate Coach*

state, formed the Anti-Separate Coach Movement and developed a test case to challenge the law in court. On October 30, 1893, Rev. W. H. Anderson, a leading black minister from Evansville, Indiana, boarded an L & N train for a trip to Madisonville, Kentucky. He was allowed to sit in first class while the train was in Indiana, but once the train reached Kentucky he was told to move. When he and his wife refused to do so, they were forced off the train. Anderson sued the L & N for $15,000. Ironically, the L & N had opposed the law but was now put in a position of defending it. Anderson won his case in U.S. District Court. The L & N appealed the decision. Meanwhile, another case had been developed by the Chesapeake and Ohio to test the constitutionality of the Kentucky law. The U.S. Supreme Court agreed to hear the case of *Chesapeake and Ohio Railroad Company* v. *Commonwealth of Kentucky*. On December 3, 1900, the court ruled that Kentucky's law was valid. Justice John M. Harlan, native of Kentucky and former leader of the state's Republican party, dissented. He said that the Kentucky Separate Coach Law interfered with interstate commerce and that the state legislature had no right to classify citizens by color in railway coaches.[28]

So by the force of law the railroad companies were compelled to maintain racial separation. This law, in addition to being a burden to the companies, was an insult to blacks. Separate but equal accommodations were never a reality. A Nashville black sued the L & N in 1905 for failure to provide equal services, noting that the car reserved for blacks lacked toilet facilities and a smoking section. Blacks such as Booker T. Washington used the L & N on long trips and were subjected to these inferior services and denied sleeping berths. In 1914, William Pickens of the National Association for the Advancement of Colored People was determined to have the use of a sleeping berth on the L & N from Louisville to Birmingham, Alabama. After calling in his reservation early in the morning, Pickens sent a messenger to get his ticket. The messenger returned empty handed, explaining that Pullman tickets had to be purchased directly by the user from the Pullman conductor. Pickens, well aware that the L & N would refuse him the Pullman berth once they saw him, tried a number of

---

Movement of Kentucky (Evansville, n.d.), for a detailed account of black resistance to the law.

28. Smith (ed.), *Anti-Separate Coach Movement*; Letter from the Headquarters of the Anti-Separate Coach Movement's State Central and Executive Committee, January 15, 1895, William H. Steward Scrapbook, in the possession of Carolyn Steward Blanton, Louisville; *W. H. Anderson* v. *Louisville and Nashville Railroad Company*, 6th Circuit Court of Owensboro, June 4, 1894; *Chesapeake and Ohio Railway Company* v. *Commonwealth of Kentucky*, 179 U.S. 388 (1900); *Courier-Journal*, December 4, 1900.

different methods to obtain the ticket, all of which failed. Finally, the only way Pickens succeeded in obtaining a sleeping berth was by boarding the train with a fellow NAACP worker, Joel Spingarn, and acting as his servant while Spingarn purchased the ticket. Pickens was thoroughly disgusted about his experience in Louisville: "The berth cost me: a messenger's fee, thirteen hours of work, worry, and strategy, my attendance at morning services, part of my dinner, part of my time for evening address, the assistance of at least six other persons, three trips to the station, and *the regular fare*. And yet they say that 'Jim Crowism' is no burden to the black man." After hearing about Pickens's experience, the L & N announced that it would upgrade the services offered blacks by giving them two toilets, a smoking room, and arrangements for meals. But with black business remaining small, nothing was done about providing sleeping cars for them.[29]

III.

Blacks hoped that their protests would lead to an end of Jim Crow railroads and to equal access to other public accommodations, but they well knew that it was futile to argue for integration in the public schools. Instead they hoped that local and state officials would provide equal funding for white and black schools. Although the first measures to finance black schools went largely unenforced, Kentucky's General Assembly continued to pass laws relating to black public education. In 1867 a poll tax for education was levied on black males eighteen and over. (But the very next year the legislature ordered that the poll tax first be used to care for black paupers.) There was a step forward in 1874, when legislators increased the money for black education by appropriating all taxes, fines, and forfeitures paid by Afro-Americans to the black education fund. But that was rendered moot in August 1882 by a decision of the electorate to equalize distribution of school funds for white and black schools. This remarkable act was motivated by political necessity rather than humanitarianism. On April 4, 1882, Judge John Baxter of the federal circuit court ruled in *Commonwealth of Kentucky* v. *Jesse Ellis* that "any fund created by the state for educational purposes must be equally and uniformly distributed among both classes, and neither in the raising of the fund by taxation, nor in the distribution of it, must there be any inequality or any discrimination on

---

29. Rabinowitz, *Race Relations in the Urban South*, 388; *Crisis*, VIII (September, 1914), 248–49, IX (December, 1914), 64; Lamon, *Black Tennesseans*, 7.

account of race or color." Judge Baxter then strongly implied that Kentucky schools had the same alternatives that he had recently presented to the state of Ohio in the case of *U.S.* v. *Buntin*: equalize funds for white and black schools, desegregate, or close. Kentucky's Democratic legislators, fearful of making any decision on the matter, submitted the alternatives to the electorate. Not surprisingly, the voters approved equal funding.[30]

Yet in total disregard for the law, the Louisville school board made no pretense of providing equal school facilities for blacks. In fact, the opening of the new $32,000 Central Colored School in 1873 proved to be the only occasion when a new school for blacks was on par with the new white schools. Thereafter, the schools constructed for blacks were inadequate from the start. After spending a day observing at a black school, a reporter for the New York *Freeman* explained that all of the classrooms were overcrowded, with "some of the classes having 100–120 scholars to a teacher. They have to be seated upon the platform," since there were not enough desks for everyone. "I saw one of the little ones standing with a watch waiting for [his] turn to get a seat." For a number of years the only second-grade class provided for blacks was at Central Elementary. Therefore, black children had to walk great distances to attend the second grade. None of the black schools had libraries until the early 1900s. In fact, by the early 1900s some of the "schools" for blacks were little more than old stores or run-down houses.[31]

Blacks complained unceasingly about the deplorable condition of Central High School. The school started in 1874 and was housed in the same building as Central Elementary. Central High moved to what the Board of Education called a "renovated" building at Ninth and Magazine in 1893 that had been vacated by a white elementary school. A fire occurred at Central High in January 1896, slightly damaging the building. The Indianapolis *Freeman* said blacks would have been better off if Central had burned to the ground because the building was one of the oldest

30. *Commercial*, April 11, 1882; *Courier-Journal*, April 12, 1882. J. Morgan Kousser and Victor B. Howard have thoroughly investigated the entire controversy surrounding the equalizing of the school funds. See Kousser, "Making Separate Equal: The Integration of Black and White School Funds in Kentucky, 1882," *Journal of Interdisciplinary History*, X (Winter, 1980), 399–428; Howard, *Black Liberation in Kentucky: Emancipation and Freedom, 1862–1884* (Lexington, 1983), 160–70.

31. New York *Freeman*, October 17, 1885, July 13, 1886; see "A Few of the Worst Units in Louisville's Free Public School System," *Courier-Journal*, January 27, 1909. Fortunately, the Jefferson County Board of Education has preserved the minutes of the old Louisville Board of Education and numerous pamphlets relating to the Negro schools. See Louisville Board of Education Papers, Durrett Education Center, Louisville.

and worst structures in Louisville. Thereafter, a number of black organizations called for the construction of a modern building for Central, pointing out that the city had three fine structures for white high school students. The school board ignored black demands for a new building, and Central High remained at Ninth and Magazine until 1916 when the school moved to yet another renovated structure at Ninth and Chestnut. In the 1950s Central High finally received a new building.[32]

Louisville, with its long history of educating white youths (since 1829) at the public expense, offered far more training to whites than was available to blacks. Louisville had separate high schools for white males and females and a normal school for whites desiring to be teachers. The white schools also had classes for the gifted, the mentally handicapped, and those interested in a trade. Meanwhile, Central High was little more than a junior high school, unable to offer a four-year course of study until 1893. Thereafter, Central offered few advanced courses in mathematics or the sciences. In fact, by the early twentieth century, the courses emphasized most were those in domestic science and manual training. Blacks agitated for a separate school for girls modeled after Female High and a normal school to train black teachers. School officials responded by opening a black normal school in 1897, but ignored all pleas for a Negro Female High School.[33]

Despite having equal credentials and far more students per class than their white counterparts, black teachers received lower salaries. In the 1870s, white teachers made an average salary of $702 a year, while blacks earned $439. This disparity in salaries would continue. By the 1890s, white high school teachers made salaries ranging from $1,000 to $1,800 a year, while the highest for a black teacher was $1,000. White elementary teachers earned at least $300 more than blacks. White high school principals

32. The reporter for the Indianapolis *Freeman* speculated that arson might have been the cause of the fire at Central High: "The Colored High School was partially damaged Thursday evening, January 23, by fire of incendiary origin at an extent of $5,000. The school had been threatened several times by white neighbors, because of the school being removed from Sixth and Kentucky to Ninth and Magazine." Indianapolis *Freeman*, February 1, 1896, February 29, 1908.

33. *Announcement of the Central Colored High School and Colored Normal School of Louisville, Kentucky, 1907–1908* (Louisville, 1908); Brenda F. Jackson, "The Policies and Purposes of Black Public Schooling in Louisville, Kentucky, 1890–1930" (Ph.D. dissertation, Indiana University, 1976); Henry A. Ford, *History of the Ohio Falls Counties* (Louisville, 1871), 410–14; Lacomis C. Curry, "The History of Industrial Education for Males at Central High School" (M.A. thesis, University of Louisville, 1957), 6, 22–27; George D. Wilson, "A Century of Negro Education in Louisville" (manuscript prepared by the project workers of the WPA, n.d.), 76, 93, 105; *Courier-Journal*, September 7, 1875.

earned $2,500 a year, compared to $1,750 for the principal of Central High.[34]

Another injustice heaped on black teachers was the school board's policy of writing morality clauses into their contracts. The Board of Education did not interfere in the private lives of white teachers, yet whatever black teachers did was open to public scrutiny. When opening the black schools, city officials organized the Committee on Colored Schools and later a Board of Visitors. As explained in Article VI of the Rules Governing Ward Schools, it was the duty of the Board of Visitors "to visit said schools and report to said committee the efficiency of the teachers and schools, and who shall exercise a general supervision over said schools, and through whom the moral character of all applicants for positions in said Colored Schools shall be made known to said committee." In conjunction with the Board of Visitors, the Committee on Colored Schools reported to the Board of Education on the morality of black teachers. Much apprehension and speculation surrounded the annual July school board meeting when blacks from the two committees would advise the school board on teacher appointments for the coming year. Large crowds attended and heard a series of charges and countercharges with each teacher's nomination.[35]

Several bitter controversies occurred in the 1880s and 1890s over the selection of school principals. W. T. Peyton, an elementary principal and an opportunistic politician, coveted the more prestigious (and higher paying) position of principal of Central High School, which was then held by John Maxwell. In 1893 Maxwell was ousted from his position by local politicians, but Peyton lacked the support he needed to be appointed in Maxwell's place. The principalship of Central eventually went to Albert E. Meyzeek. Peyton remained as head of an elementary school and Meyzeek directed Central High until 1896, when several changes were made at the July school board meeting. The board reinstated Maxwell as principal of Central, moved Meyzeek to Eastern Elementary, moved William H. Perry from Eastern to Western Elementary, and fired Peyton from the school system. Peyton's dismissal was a result of unsubstantiated charges of immorality. William H. Steward and several well-known ministers were

34. Jackson, "Black Public Schooling in Louisville," 197–98; W. E. B. DuBois (ed.), *The Negro Common School,* Atlanta University Publications, no. 6 (Atlanta, 1901), 57.

35. *Report of the Board of Trustees of the Public Schools of Louisville for the Year Ending June 30, 1873* (Louisville, 1873), 41; Jackson, "Black Public Schooling in Louisville," 208; Wilson, "A Century of Negro Education," 32–33; Weeden, *History of the Colored People,* 32.

given credit for the changes in the black schools: "The welding influence of Reverends J. H. McMillen, C. C. Bates, John Frank, and William H. Steward, who deserves special mention, will long be remembered and appreciated by the citizens," the Indianapolis *Freeman* said.[36]

From the mid-1890s to 1910, Steward and several ministers completely dominated the hiring and firing of black school employees. Reverends E. G. Harris and John Frank became notorious for soliciting church contributions from teachers and principals, explaining that their blessing would help the teachers keep their jobs. A black newspaper reporter summed up the situation in the black school system correctly when he wrote that Louisville's black schools had been corrupted by black leaders and that, as a result, obtaining a teaching job took "influence" rather than "ability." A campaign to rewrite the city's charter began in 1909, and one prominent feature proposed was the creation of a new Board of Education. It was hoped that a new board would end the unfair method used to select black teachers. However, the new Board of Education, which started in 1910, did not end favoritism in black school appointments. The board still relied, though to a lesser degree, on black ministers when selecting teachers. Worse, to the dismay of black leaders, the board began consulting a white social worker, John Little, before selecting black principals.[37]

Writing morality clauses into the contracts of black teachers proved to be an effective method of control. Black teachers, realizing that any questionable action on their part could lead to dismissal, remained aloof from controversial issues. It is highly possible that in some instances charges of "immorality" might actually have meant "militancy," that black teachers were disciplined after speaking out against white racism or criticizing established black leaders. Only Albert E. Meyzeek was bold enough to consistently denounce discrimination and to become involved in racial uplift movements. And in a way, he was disciplined as well: despite being the best qualified principal in the system, he spent his career, except for three years, as an elementary principal, not as principal of Central High.

Despite the existence of morality clauses and undue pressure from several ministers, a black could nevertheless teach in Louisville and maybe become the principal of a school, a fact that both white and black Louisvillians repeatedly pointed to with pride. In many cities, both North and

36. See the Minutes of the Louisville Board of Education from September 1, 1890, through July, 1896, Durret Education Center, Louisville; New York *Freeman*, November 6, 1886; *Courier-Journal*, September 8, 1891, July 4, 1893; Indianapolis *Freeman*, July 25, 1896.

37. *Ohio Falls Express*, September 29, 1884; Indianapolis *Freeman*, April 11, 1896, April 6, 1900, November 26, 1910, March 18, 1911.

South, blacks were not hired to teach in the Negro schools. Hiring whites to teach black students was a way of insuring that blacks would be educated in such a way that they would not be likely to challenge the white establishment. As Charles Wynes explains, "White teachers were not likely to indoctrinate their Negro charges with the philosophy of human equality, while assuredly many Negro teachers would. And white teachers in Negro schools were often accused of lacking sympathy for the Negro." Many school systems that eventually yielded to black demands and hired blacks as teachers continued to hire only white principals until well into the twentieth century.[38]

Most observers gave nothing but glowing accounts of the black schools in Louisville. It is obvious, however, that by the 1880s a great disparity in the pay and conditions of employment existed between white and black teachers and, if anything, the gulf widened over the years. Another important distinction existed between white and black education: a greater emphasis was placed on educating the hands rather than the mind in the black schools. In Louisville, blacks occupied the lowest rung on the social ladder. In school they were taught, to use a saying popular in that day, "to be drawers of water and hewers of wood." True, Louisville's polite racism provided blacks with an education, but it was designed to reinforce the idea that they rightfully belonged at the bottom of society.

However, not even the racism of the school board hindered the gallant efforts by blacks to acquire an education. By the early 1900s many blacks, after working all day, attended night school, paying ten cents a week for the privilege. When asked why, a seventy-one-year-old ex-slave said that he wanted to learn something; a forty-three-year-old woman wanted to learn how to write so she could correspond with friends; a middle-aged porter wanted to learn numbers. G. H. Richardson, an employee of the Louisville Hotel, eloquently expressed his reasons for going to school: "I go to help build up my race. I am educating my children and want to keep up with them and give them encouragement."[39]

IV.

After passing Jim Crow laws and adopting informal patterns of racial segregation, white Louisvillians took one additional step to insure that their

38. Wynes, *Race Relations in Virginia*, 127; Rabinowitz, *Race Relations in the Urban South*, 174; Gerber, *Black Ohio*, 334; Lilian Brandt, "The Negroes of St. Louis," *Publications of the American Statistical Association*, VIII (March, 1903), 240–41.

39. *Courier-Journal*, April 12, 1903.

blacks would remain in place. In many cities, violent mobs wreaked havoc with a vengeance on blacks with the tacit approval of the authorities. Louisville leaders, however, abhorred the thought of mob rule. Instead they used the police. A symbol of law and order, the police controlled blacks with the full approval of the city's legal apparatus. For a fifty-year period, starting in the 1880s, police abuse of blacks would be consistent, occurring whenever whites thought blacks were getting out of "their place." This remained a problem for so long because only on the rarest of occasions would the local courts prosecute police officers for assaulting blacks.

Louisville's police had always taken seriously its mandate to control the Negro. In the period from 1865 to 1880, blacks were far more likely to be arrested than whites, especially native-born whites. The police felt justified in arresting blacks, for as city officials constantly pointed out, blacks caused most of the petty crimes—stealing, fighting, vagrancy, and public drunkenness. According to the police reports, in 1873 blacks accounted for 22 percent of the total arrests in Louisville, and by 1881 this had jumped to 32 percent. During these years blacks comprised 15 percent of the city's population. The Irish comprised Louisville's largest immigrant group, and the percentage of Irish arrests fluctuated from a high of 17 percent in 1873 to a low of 7 percent in 1881. A social worker in St. Louis made the following observation on the declining number of foreign-born whites being arrested at the same time that the number of black arrests was increasing: "A large proportion of the policemen are Irish, a circumstance that would argue a charitable attitude of forbearance towards the offenses of a large part of the foreign-born population and an abnormal vigilance over the Negroes." [40]

Indeed, that the percentage of Irish being arrested dropped in the 1880s was no coincidence, for the police department had begun hiring Irish as officers and an Irishman, John Whallen, emerged as boss of Louisville's Democratic party. Previously the Democratic party, though occasionally condemning blacks and Republicans, usually ignored them since they offered only token opposition to the Democrats. But Whallen's rise to power became closely associated with increasing problems for blacks. Under his guidance, race became a political issue—sometimes the only issue—in several crucial campaigns. Also, the policemen would take an active role

---

40. *Ibid.*, June 28, 1874. Most of the Louisville Annual Reports failed to classify the people arrested by race or ethnicity. Therefore, the figures mentioned come from the *Louisville Annual Report of 1873* (Louisville, 1874), 41, and *Louisville Annual Report of 1881* (Louisville, 1882), 268; Stanley Ousley, "The Irish in Louisville," (M.A. thesis, University of Louisville, 1974), 27; Brandt, "The Negroes of St. Louis," 252–53.

in political campaigns, adopting any tactics necessary to undermine the black vote. Friction had existed for years between blacks and Irish. They competed for jobs as common laborers and house servants. To the dismay of the Irish, blacks often lived in or near their neighborhoods. Indeed, those blacks who could afford decent housing complained that Irish landlords often refused to rent to them or charged double or triple the normal price. That blacks and Irish backed different political parties further divided the two groups. With bitterness seething throughout their relationship, small outbreaks of violence occurred on several occasions.[41]

John Whallen arrived in Louisville in 1871 from Covington, Kentucky, and immediately opened a theater, the Buckingham. He then applied for a liquor license, but his request was denied until Councilman Barney McAtee intervened on his behalf. Whallen returned the favor by engineering McAtee's surprising victory in the mayoral election of 1880. Whallen continued in politics, and his efforts led to the election of Booker Reed as mayor in 1884. Reed rewarded Whallen by naming him police chief, the first of numerous city jobs he would hold. By the mid-1880s Whallen controlled practically all of the patronage jobs in city government, and he handpicked the candidates for most elective offices. The Buckingham became a popular gathering place for working-class men after Whallen introduced the five-cent beer in Louisville. He gained additional support by giving generously to labor unions and by holding benefits for striking Irish workers. Whallen even cultivated a friendship with Henry Watterson, editor of the *Courier-Journal*, a move Whallen viewed as necessary because of the enormous influence of Watterson's paper.[42]

With Whallen in control of city government, Louisville acquired a reputation as a "wide-open town." The number of gambling houses, saloons, and houses of prostitution multiplied, and they conducted a booming business, blatantly ignoring city ordinances and Sunday closing laws. For one large convention, an enterprising publisher sold a *Sporting Guide* to Louisville, listing all of the madames, the services they provided, and the type of girls available "to assist visitors in making life one continuous round of pleasure." Most of Louisville's houses of prostitution, including the "red light district" that developed under Whallen, were located in the

<hr/>

41. Ousley, "The Irish in Louisville," 27–28; New York *Freeman*, October 10, 1885, September 4, 1886.

42. Ousley, "The Irish in Louisville," 142–44; Yater, *A History of Louisville*, 131; Pier Luigi Gregory DePaola, "Management and Organized Labor Relations of the Louisville and Nashville Railroads During the Depression Year 1893," (M.A. thesis, University of Louisville, 1971), 93–96.

downtown area within close proximity to black neighborhoods. Indeed, in the Annual Police Report for 1885, Whallen stated that "the 'social evil' has been kept under good control. I have confined the known houses of ill repute to certain territorial limits wherein the neighbors seem to make no complaints, and have forced all prostitutes to leave respectable localities when made known to me." Moreover, as various newspaper accounts mentioned, the police department was directly involved in virtually all of the city's illegal activities.[43]

Whallen's police officers were often lenient toward white offenders while being intolerant toward blacks. "The police are busy watching and searching every colored man and boy they meet after dark," protested the Louisville correspondent for the New York *Freeman* in February 1886. "The white culprits are aware of the fact that the color line is drawn distinctively by the police and therefore it is no trouble for them to rob and plunder without detection." According to the *Freeman*, under Whallen's regime in the mid-1880s at least seven blacks were killed by policemen under highly questionable circumstances. In July 1885, a group representing the black community presented Mayor Booker Reed with a long list of complaints against the police. They urged the mayor to appoint blacks to the force. Mayor Reed expressed his disbelief at black complaints of the police department. He also replied that the city charter prohibited blacks from being policemen. In fact, a Louisville ordinance excluded blacks from the police and fire departments. But the real issue was not this ordinance, which could easily have been repealed if the Democratic machine had been interested in doing so. Rather, it was the attitude of whites toward blacks, as the mayor honestly observed, "The time is not yet ripe for such an innovation, and it would inflame race prejudice. . . . Gentlemen, it is too soon yet."[44]

Despite the complaints of black leaders, police officers continued to use excessive force on blacks. In December 1885 the police raided the black saloons and beat several men as retribution for the killing of a police officer by a drunken black. Not surprisingly, the black who shot the police officer was killed before he could surrender. As Whallen explained in his annual report of 1886, "The blood-thirsty fiend lived only a few minutes to gloat over his cowardly act, as Officer G. L. Ferguson . . . shot the scoundrel dead." Several years later a black resisted arrest and fired at sev-

43. *Wentworth's Souvenir Sporting Guide* (New York, 1895); *Courier-Journal* June 12, December 30, 1881; New York *Freeman*, July 25, 1885, January 30, 1886; *Louisville Annual Report of 1885* (Louisville, 1886), 202.

44. New York *Freeman*, July 25, December 19, 1885, February 13, 1886.

eral policemen, wounding one of them. The *Commercial*, the Republican newspaper, noted that the police killed "the black fiend" after he had emptied his gun. The paper concluded that the police were justified in shooting the black even though they could have easily overpowered him: "Jeff Arnett was one of the toughest negroes in the city. Eleven years ago he tried to cut a policeman, and only a few months ago he made an attempt to kill another one."[45]

In the 1890s blacks played an important role in local politics. In 1895 the Republican party won in Louisville for the first time. To regain control of the city in 1897, Whallen's police officers intimidated black voters and kept many from the polls. If they insisted on voting, numerous blacks, including well-known attorney Albert S. White, were assaulted. His assailant, Irish policeman John Murphy, reputedly said, "I have worn out four billies and I will wear this one out on you, as I want to get a new one."[46]

In the early 1900s a group of militant blacks formed the Negro Outlook Committee, declaring that they would protect blacks from police brutality. Unfortunately, except for mention of the organization in a black newspaper, virtually nothing exists detailing the Outlook Committee's activities and plans to end police mistreatment of blacks. It is known, however, that Dr. John A. C. Lattimore, who arrived in Louisville in 1902 from Meharry Medical College and quickly became involved in all of the protest movements, was the driving force behind the organization. On at least one occasion, city officials dismissed a police officer after the committee demonstrated that he had been "too free with the use of his billet" on blacks. But the tenure of the Outlook Committee was all too brief, lasting less than a decade. The organization suffered from a lack of an on-going program and the shortage of much-needed funds to fight cases of police brutality through the courts.[47]

Despite the presence of the Outlook Committee and the constant protests of prominent blacks, police abuse of Negroes remained pronounced in the early 1900s. Especially vulnerable were blacks who were not well known by police officers or blacks who were engaged in any activities that the police might label "suspicious." These "suspicious looking" Negroes were often taken to police headquarters, even when no crime had been

45. *Ibid.*, December 19, 1885; *Commercial*, November 4, 1897. See the *Courier-Journal*, March 20, 1894, for an account of an unarmed black burglar who was killed by the police. *Louisville Annual Report of 1886* (Louisville, 1887), 226.

46. *Commercial*, November 3, 4, 1897.

47. Indianapolis *Freeman*, April 13, 20, October 20, December 22, 1906, March 1, 1913.

committed. In his autobiography, journalist Arthur Krock mentions an episode he witnessed when working as the police reporter for the Louisville *Herald*.

> Lieutenant Kinnarney . . . [an Irishman] was a constant source of delight because of his informal methods of law enforcement. Witness: One morning, about three a.m., Captain Krakel and I were sitting outside Police Headquarters with Kinnarney. Suddenly he jumped from his chair, darted across Fifth Street and fired three shots at a vanishing, shadowy figure. Captain Krakel demanded furiously to know the reason. "Well," said the Lieutenant, "it was a Negro and he was acting suspicious." [48]

In September and October 1910, a white daily, the Louisville *Evening Post*, carried a series of stories detailing police abuse of blacks. A story in the paper on September 8 told about a police officer following a black woman for several blocks and firing several shots at her once she started running. Another article protested the arrest of innocent blacks, noting that on one occasion an officer arrested four men for no apparent reason. On October 10 the *Evening Post* explained that the cause of police mistreatment of blacks "was to establish in every home of a negro man or woman in this city a condition of terrorism, a living fear of the billy and the revolver." [49]

Throughout these years the Louisville police abused blacks at will, knowing that the courts would likely uphold their actions, even when the injustice to blacks was obvious. For example, in 1885 the city court fined a black woman $25 for disorderly conduct, even though several eyewitnesses testified that the officers had attacked her for no apparent reason. The woman brought charges against the police officers, but the judge, though acknowledging that the officers had used excessive force, dismissed the charges. In every decade from 1880 to 1910 several blacks were gunned down by the police. Yet there is no record of a police investigation into the shootings. As *The Crisis*, the journal of the NAACP, noted after conducting its own investigation of the Louisville police force, "The policemen [act] upon the assumption that the Negro [has] no rights, civil or political, that a police bully [is] bound to respect." [50]

In many cities throughout the country, blacks responded with violence of their own as a way of fighting police brutality. They made it extremely dangerous for one or two policemen to enter black bars and at-

---

48. Krock, *Myself When Young*, 138–39.
49. *Evening Post*, September 1, 2, 6, 8, 15, 23, 24, October 5, 8, 10, 12, 14, 1910.
50. New York *Freeman*, September 12, October 17, November 2, 14, 1885; *Crisis*, I (December, 1910), 15, IV (June, 1912), 66; Indianapolis *Freeman*, April 20, 1912.

tempt to arrest well-known figures in the Afro-American community.[51] Black Louisvillians, however, did not respond with violence, but with resentment, suspicion, and disrespect for law officials. None of the city's black leaders advocated retaliation against the police, nor did they publicly urge blacks to defend themselves when attacked. Usually they investigated all instances of police brutality and then protested to city officials. But their pleas to city officials to end police brutality fell on deaf ears.

In the final analysis, the racial oppression that blacks faced in Louisville differed only in degree from what their southern brothers and sisters experienced. Undoubtedly, it would be a mistake to conclude that the racial climate in Louisville was identical to that of the Deep South, for Louisville was spared the race riots, lynchings, and race baiting that occurred in southern cities and that caused blacks to live in a nearly perpetual state of fear. Moreover, during these years, Louisville whites failed to enact a Jim Crow streetcar ordinance or to segregate the races in the public parks. Also, as will be discussed, Louisville blacks maintained their right to vote. But, like their counterparts in the Deep South, Louisville whites had no qualms about resorting to violence to suppress black aspirations for changes. The difference was that Louisville whites always made sure that it was done legally—by the police. In Louisville the police force was an ever-present symbol of white authority, reminding Afro-Americans to remain in their place and that any attempts to change the racial status quo would be met with resistance.

51. See Elliott M. Rudwick and August Meier, "Negro Retaliatory Violence in the Twentieth Century," *New Politics*, V (Winter, 1966), 41–51; Howard N. Rabinowitz, "The Conflict Between Blacks and the Police in the Urban South, 1865–1900," *Historian*, XXXIX (November, 1976), 62–76.

## 3

The Color Line in Employment

Louisville's polite racism limited employment opportunities for Afro-Americans. For the most part they were relegated to unskilled jobs. Of course in late-nineteenth-century America the vast majority of whites worked at jobs that required little formal education or training. Blacks, however, were usually assigned the worst tasks, most often doing jobs that were stigmatized as "Negro work." Identifying these jobs was really a simple matter: either the wages were extremely low or the work was dirty, unpleasant, and often dangerous. Service jobs in Louisville were performed almost exclusively by blacks. Local whites boasted that the wages they paid their black employees were higher than the wages paid in the South, and that they compared favorably with wages in the North. Furthermore, they tried to give the impression that their black gardeners, chauffeurs, and maids were part of the family and that ideal accommodations were provided for the maids living in their homes.

Additionally, Louisville differed from most other cities by consistently refusing to hire blacks in local government as firemen, policemen, or clerical workers. Throughout Reconstruction and for decades thereafter, it was not uncommon to find black civil servants in a number of southern cities. Nashville had black firemen from the 1870s until the early 1900s. In Indianapolis, a city with a black population considerably smaller than Louisville's, there were at least a dozen Negro police officers in the late 1800s. One of them remained on the force for twenty-five years, rising to the rank of detective. Louisville's custom, however, was to bar blacks from city employment. To make it official, city officials passed an ordinance in 1877 stating that "all persons belonging to the pay department shall be white citizens of the United States and qualified voters of the city of Louisville." [1]

---

1. Rabinowitz, *Race Relations in the Urban South*, 41–42; Lamon, *Black Tennesseans*, 141; Thornbrough, *The Negro in Indiana*, 360; *Louisville Municipal Reports for the Year Ending December 31, 1877* (Louisville, 1878), 303.

I.

Louisville, a wholesale and retail trade center before the war, continued to grow after 1865 as local businessmen shipped the unfinished products of the South northward and the manufactured goods of the North southward. Extension of railroads after the war gave Louisville dominion over trade between the different sections of the country. An L & N line running from Louisville to Montgomery, Alabama, provided Louisville businessmen a virtual monopoly over north-south trade that lasted for years.[2]

Local businessmen prided themselves on the many products they manufactured and sold. The dominant market for Kentucky-grown tobacco, Louisville became one of the largest tobacco markets in the nation, selling cigarettes and cigars, and shipping unprocessed tobacco to out-of-state tobacco companies. In 1871, for example, 50,000 of the 66,000 hogsheads of tobacco from the Kentucky crop were sold in Louisville. By the 1870s the city had surpassed New Orleans as the world's largest tobacco market. The making of whisky, which had been important since early days, remained significant. In 1887 alone, bourbon shipments totaled 119,637 barrels, and there were at least twenty distilleries in the city. Louisville also had a thriving pork business. In proclaiming the importance of these three products to the city's economy, its leading booster, Henry Watterson, said, "a union of pork, tobacco, and whisky, will make us all wealthy, healthy, and frisky." A few of the many other articles manufactured in Louisville were plows, farm wagons, woolen and cotton goods, leather, hardware implements, and railroad supplies. The *Courier-Journal* boasted that the city led the world in publishing books for the blind, producing ice and refrigeration machinery, manufacturing enameled iron and brass, plumbing supplies, boxes, and the "Louisville Slugger" baseball bat, the most widely used bat in organized baseball.[3]

Unfortunately, most blacks did not share in the economic success of Louisville. Though there were a handful of black businessmen, the vast

2. Leighton, *Five Cities*, 54–65; Robert W. Brown (ed.), *Book of Louisville* (Louisville, 1915); *The Industrial News: A Semi-Monthly Journal Devoted to the Industries and to Science and Art* (August 21, 1883), 189.

3. Gary P. Kocolowski, "Louisville at Large: Industrial-Metropolitan Organization, Inter-City Migration, and Occupational Mobility in the Central U.S., 1865–1906" (Ph.D. dissertation, University of Cincinnati, 1978); Herbert Finch, "Organized Labor in Louisville, Kentucky 1880–1914" (Ph.D. dissertation, University of Kentucky, 1965), 105; *Courier-Journal*, June 17, 1924. Watterson was quoted in Tapp and Klotter, *Kentucky, Decades of Discord*, 307; Yater, *A History of Louisville*, 122–23.

majority of Afro-Americans found employment as servants and common laborers, marginal positions that paid very poor wages and were vulnerable to economic slowdowns. This was especially true for black females. As David Katzman notes in his important study, *Seven Days a Week: Women and Domestic Service in Industrializing America*, the occupation of domestic servant included a number of jobs: general servants, chambermaids, cooks, children's nurses, waitresses, laundresses, and day workers. Black women dominated these jobs (in 1890, of Louisville's 11,703 servants, 5,684 were black women; see table 3) because most white women found domestic work demeaning and unappealing and the wages too low. Indeed, in 1885 and again in 1886, the Louisville correspondent for the New York *Freeman* reported that black female servants worked sixty hours a week for $3.00. The servants performed all of the household chores and worked outdoors as well, even in inclement weather. One servant informed the *Freeman* that whites were hard to please, that they

Table 3

Males and Females over Ten Working as Servants, 1890–1920[a]

Year	Total	Native White	Foreign White	Black	Percent Black
			Females		
1890	8,745	2,152	969	5,684	64.9%
1910	12,239	2,021	368	8,848	72.2%
1920	8,376	1,354	168	6,849	81.7%
			Males		
1890	2,958	891	302	1,765	59.6%
1910	4,178	1,019	237	2,934	70.2%
1920	3,620	857	163	2,580	71.2%

[a] Bureau of the Census, *Eleventh Census of the United States*, "1890: Vital and Social Statistics" (Washington, D.C., 1896), XVI, 684; Bureau of the Census, *Thirteenth Census of the United States*, "1910: Population" (Washington, D.C., 1913), IV, 562–63; Bureau of the Census, *Fourteenth Census of the United States*, "1920: Population" (Washington, D.C., 1923), IV, 1132–35. The censuses for 1870, 1880, 1900, and 1930 do not list occupations in Louisville by race.

abused their servants, and that "the beds they give the servants are not meant for pigs to sleep in." Another servant, after describing the rigorous chores she performed during a normal day, concluded that "every colored woman that can get money enough ought to leave the city." White women, meanwhile, could often avoid domestic service by working in the woolen industry or as telephone operators, jobs that were totally closed to black women. Moreover, as Katzman notes, domestic service was usually a temporary occupation for whites, something they did between leaving home and getting married. This was far from the case for black women: in 1920, for example, fully one-half of the black women doing domestic service in Louisville were married.[4]

Black men also worked in and around the homes of whites as house servants, gardeners, and coachmen. As coachmen, they transported their employers to work, to the country club, and on pleasure drives. But like black female servants, they were poorly paid. One coachman informed a reporter in the 1880s that he received only $12 per month and worked extremely long hours. "I have worked in Chicago, Cleveland, and Buffalo, but this is by far the worst in all respects. A person can't find a decent place to work."[5]

Though poorly paid, some black men remained in service work for decades. In the 1930s, the *Courier-Journal* interviewed several prominent whites and used their interviews as the basis for an article "They've Grown To Be Part of the Families They Serve." The article cited George Hughes as a loyal servant who had worked for Mrs. Henning Chambers for thirty years. "George, as a little boy, used to pull weeds for Mrs. Chambers' parents, later became coachman and now chauffeur," the paper noted with obvious pride. Special mention was also made of Frank Leslie and Frank Hardin who had worked thirty-five and forty-six years, respectively, for the same white families. Uniformly, the whites considered these blacks to be "family" and gave them presents at Christmas and on their birthdays. To be sure, not all servants were poorly paid and overworked. But the primary reason black men and women continued to work these jobs was a lack of other opportunities. As long as they were denied better jobs, they

4. Bureau of the Census, *Eleventh Census of the United States,* "1890: Vital and Social Statistics" (Washington, D.C., 1896), XVI, 684. Many of my comments on employment are based on the U.S. Censuses from 1870 to 1930. I also used Bureau of the Census, *Negro Population*; David Katzman, *Seven Days a Week: Women and Domestic Service in Industrializing America* (New York, 1978), 24, 44, 72–82; New York *Freeman,* October 17, 1885; September 11, 1886.

5. New York *Freeman,* October 17, 1885; Indianapolis *Freeman,* July 17, 1911, January 4, 1913.

had little choice but to work as servants. In fact, most uneducated women (and many college graduates as well) who reached maturity before the 1960s probably did a stint as a servant. This practice ended for some blacks when industry, retail sales, and clerical jobs began opening up for blacks.[6]

Blacks continued to find employment as waiters and barbers to whites, even though whites coveted these jobs during hard economic times. Black men dominated the position of waiter. (The 1910 census, the first one to have a separate category for waiters, listed 421 blacks out of 545 waiters; and in 1920, 336 blacks out of 442.) All of the fancy hotels and private clubs used black men exclusively. Being a waiter must have been a part of the "rite of passage" for black males reaching maturity in Louisville. Alexander Walters, who became a leading bishop in the AME Church as well as one of the founders of the NAACP, worked as a waiter in Louisville for several years. "I had already during the summer of 1871, lived a while in Louisville and worked at the old St. Cloud Hotel and also at the Willard Hotel." Along with his brother, Walters left Louisville in 1876 because of a better opportunity as a waiter in Indianapolis. Roland Hayes, the famous singer, worked at the Pendennis Club as a youth. After making it big, Hayes was something of a celebrity in Louisville, and all of the men at this posh club patted themselves on the back for having given him encouragement and a job. A number of the city's future black leaders served terms as waiters while attending school. But there were also any number of men like Neal Walton, the leading waiter at the Pendennis Club for four decades, who spent their entire working careers as waiters in Louisville's hotels, restaurants, and private clubs.[7]

Like other servants, waiters received low pay for the long hours they worked. Furthermore, their salary was unsure since most of it was based on tips. Only the headwaiter received an adequate salary and the patrons' respect in hotels and restaurants. Unfortunately for most waiters, the men chosen as headwaiters were experienced captains or headwaiters from exclusive out-of-town hotels. W. R. Harris, the headwaiter at the Louisville Hotel in 1900, had served as the headwaiter at "three of the best hotels in Baltimore." In 1908 Harris left Louisville and was replaced by C. C. Lewis, who had served as the headwaiter at the Tremont Hotel in Chicago for

6. Newsclip, *Courier-Journal*, 1935; Dr. Charles H. Wesley, interview with author, December 21, 1981, Washington, D.C. Dr. Wesley's grandfather, Douglass Harris, was a chauffeur for a wealthy white family in Louisville for several decades. Over the years, Douglass Harris finally accumulated enough money to purchase a modest home.

7. Walters, *My Life and Work*, 30–32; *Courier-Journal*, December 22, 1936. For additional information on black waiters at the Pendennis Club, see Krock, *Myself When Young*, 203–205.

twelve years and had worked in hotels in Denver, Kansas City, and Cincinnati. In 1912 a new hotel named in honor of editor Watterson opened. William Mathias, who had once worked in Louisville at the Seelbach Hotel as the second waiter, returned to the city as the headwaiter. The three captains serving under Mathias had worked in "some of the best hotels in the United States."[8]

Barbering paid the best wages of all the service occupations. In the 1870s and 1880s, when newspaper stories highlighted Louisville's wealthiest blacks, barbers were prominently mentioned. As in antebellum days, the wealthiest barbers continued to rent space in white hotels and relied on the business of the rich and the many visitors to the city. Louisville would always have more white than black barbers, but some of the whites, especially the Irish, wanted complete control of this potentially lucrative occupation and resented competing with blacks. In 1885 an Irishman, well aware that black barbers would lose their white customers if they provided the same services to Negroes, said to a newspaper reporter, "Why don't they discontinue discriminating in their business? What would the Germans and Irish think of one of their countrymen doing that? He would be denounced. It is nothing more nor less than selling [their] birthright for a few dollars. If their barbers had race pride at heart they would step down and out of such business."[9] Despite such self-serving criticism, black barbers held their own in Louisville, at least until the 1930s (see table 4).

Table 4

Barbers in Louisville, 1890–1920[a]

	Total	Native White	Foreign White	Black	Percent Black
1890	427	219	88	120	28.1
1910	592	402	70	120	20.2
1920	579	415	45	119	20.5

[a] Bureau of the Census, *Eleventh Census of the United States* (Washington, D.C., 1896), XVI, 684; Bureau of the Census, *Thirteenth Census of the United States* (Washington, D.C., 1913), IV, 562–63; Bureau of the Census, *Fourteenth Census of the United States* (Washington, D.C., 1923), IV, 1132–35.

8. Indianapolis *Freeman*, July 7, 1900, October 3, December 12, 1903, May 4, July 6, 1912. According to an article in the *Freeman*, July 20, 1901, waiters were paid a straight salary of $2.00 per day for working at the various conventions held in Louisville.

9. New York *Freeman*, November 27, 1885.

It is significant that black barbers and waiters held their jobs in Louisville, given the trend in other cities. Black barbers in cities in Georgia, Tennessee, and elsewhere in the South were being squeezed out by the early 1900s. They came under attack from white supremacists who said that blacks were taking jobs that rightfully belonged to white men. In St. Louis, black waiters were installed in several hotels in 1913 after the employers failed to reach an agreement with the union representing the white waiters. Once they reached an agreement, however, all of the blacks lost their jobs. In the North in the late nineteenth and early twentieth centuries, a number of factors contributed to blacks losing their monopoly on service occupations. Scholars Lorenzo J. Greene and Carter G. Woodson explain that the unionization of waiters led to blacks losing their jobs since whites prohibited blacks from joining their unions. Many of the jobs were upgraded and so were more attractive to whites. In Cleveland, the declining importance of black waiters and barbers occurred when upper-class whites left the inner city and started living in the suburbs. By 1918 only two of the leading establishments in Cleveland still employed black waiters. In a number of cities (like Detroit) blacks lost their service occupations to foreign competitors. Several scholars have concluded, after considering a number of factors affecting the decline in the number of black waiters and barbers, that racism was the leading cause. In city after city the growing antipathy of whites toward blacks led directly to the decline in the number of blacks serving whites.[10]

However, in Louisville whites felt secure with blacks performing services for them, since they viewed this as part of the southern tradition. They were unaffected by the argument that black barbers and waiters were taking jobs from whites. In 1906, the owners of the Seelbach Hotel fired their white workers and replaced them with a full crew of black waiters. And this pattern persisted: before the opening of the Henry Watterson Hotel in 1912, the owners decided to use blacks in all of the service occupations in the hotel. A survey conducted a decade later by the Urban League found that blacks still dominated these occupations: "With the exception of white girls in one or two of the small tea rooms, colored waiters are used exclusively in all of the hotels in Louisville," the report concluded. Once stig-

10. Lamon, *Black Tennesseans*, 140–41; John Dittmer, *Black Georgia in the Progressive Era 1900–1920* (Urbana, 1977), 38; William A. Crossland, *Industrial Conditions Among Negroes in St. Louis* (St. Louis, 1914), 68; Lorenzo J. Greene and Carter G. Woodson, *The Negro Wage Earner* (Washington, D.C., 1930), 94–96; Spear, *Black Chicago*, Chaps. 6, 10; August Meier, *Negro Thought in America 1880–1915* (Ann Arbor, 1963), 139–42; Kusmer, *A Ghetto Takes Shape*, 77–78; Katzman, *Before the Ghetto*, 116.

matized as domestic work, service occupations had little appeal to whites. Employers also learned that whites were not nearly as dependable as blacks in these jobs because they could easily find jobs in the numerous industries that refused to hire blacks. As the *Courier-Journal* correctly pointed out, using blacks in hotels and restaurants was necessary because whites refused to work for the paltry tips waiters received. It is difficult to say exactly when black barbers quit providing tonsorial services to whites. One newspaper story, in June 1924, nostalgically lamented that "along with the old-time negro hotel porter, the negro barber that shaved 'white folks' has about passed . . . " Yet several interviewees contradicted that view.[11] It seems likely that in Louisville blacks maintained their positions as barbers for whites at least until the Great Depression. And, of course, to this very day black waiters can be found in the city's exclusive clubs.

Though dominating the service occupations, an even larger number of blacks found employment as common laborers. In Louisville in the late 1800s, "common laborer" described a wide range of occupations: digging ditches, hauling boxes, cleaning streets, sweeping floors, working in the sewers, and the like. Also, common laborers performed a wide range of functions in industry, at the race track, and at the warehouses on Main Street. Many of these jobs were seasonal, and all were poorly paid. Blacks, of course, were not the only ones confined to these jobs. For example, under the general heading of "Laborers" in the 1890 Census, out of a total of 7,442 males listed, native whites numbered 2,730, foreign whites, 1,590, and blacks, 3,123. It should also be remembered that because of discrimination, a black and a white could be doing the very same job but the white might be considered a skilled worker and receive a higher salary than the black, who would be classified as an unskilled worker.

Black women working as common laborers were hired almost exclusively in laundries, preserving companies, and tobacco factories. In 1890, of the city's 2,891 laundresses, 2,455 or 84 percent were black. They performed the back-breaking chore of washing and cleaning. An equally large number of black women worked in the tobacco industry, where they did the unpleasant task of rehandling the tobacco, turning it into snuff, cigars, and cigarettes. Black women dominated these jobs because rehandling tobacco was dusty and unhealthy and paid very poor wages, with some women receiving considerably less than a dollar per day in the 1880s. The

11. Indianapolis *Freeman*, January 27, 1906, May 4, 1912; *Courier-Journal*, June 8, 1924; *Opportunity*, IV (February, 1926), 72; *Courier-Journal*, January 1, 1918; Wesley interview; Dr. Charles H. Parrish, Jr., interview with author, May 19, 1976, Louisville; Mrs. Carolyn Steward Blanton, interview with author, May 18, 1976, Louisville.

women, paid by piece rate, would sit at their jobs all day, even while eating lunch. White women, meanwhile, worked the skilled jobs in the tobacco factories and received weekly salaries. Moreover, white women eventually quit working in tobacco factories altogether in order to work in cleaner factories or to take advantage of new opportunities as clerks, stenographers, and telephone operators. Indeed, by the early 1900s virtually all of the women tobacco workers in Louisville were black. A federal investigator, when looking at the horrible conditions these women worked under, had very little sympathy for them: "The working women in [Louisville] are as a class, honest, respectable, industrious, and polite, but from this statement must be excepted all of those who are employed in the tobacco factories. These, with few exceptions, are ignorant, coarse, and filthy." [12]

In her study of women in Kentucky, Helen Irvin points out that although white women in industry were poorly paid, they at least were able to avoid the most dangerous and dirty jobs. Many young white women worked in the city's numerous woolen mills. This industry, which refused to employ blacks in any capacity, manufactured jeans and work clothes. The young women, primarily from German and Irish families, earned more than $4.50 a week, an excellent salary for women in the 1880s and 1890s. Also, unlike black women, the young white women workers received union recognition and admission into the Knights of Labor. [13]

Black men were employed on the most strenuous and unpleasant jobs, the ones that whites often refused to work. Practically all of the city's sewer workers were black. These men worked long hours in unsanitary conditions and were paid $1.50 a day. In July 1877, the sewer workers went on strike, demanding improved working conditions, higher wages, and recognition as a union. They gathered at the mayor's home to voice their complaints. After the mayor proved unsympathetic to their cause, a few of the more volatile sewer workers began smashing the mayor's windows and those of his well-to-do neighbors. The next day the mayor formed a

12. *Fourth Annual Report of the Commissioner of Labor, 1888*, "Working Women in Large Cities" (Washington, D.C., 1889), 19; *Courier-Journal*, March 13, 1887; U.S. Department of Labor, Women's Bureau, *Negro Women in Industry in Fifteen States*, Bulletin no. 70 (Washington, D.C., 1929), 15. See also U.S. Department of Labor, Women's Bureau, *Women in Kentucky Industries*, Bulletin no. 29 (Washington, D.C., 1923); Greene and Woodson, *The Negro Wage Earner*, 116–19, 152, 283–85; *Monthly Labor Review*, XVII (October, 1923), 70–71.

13. Irvin, *Women In Kentucky*, 67–88; Nancy S. Dye, "Louisville Women and Knights of Labor: The 1887 Textile Strike," paper presented at the Centennial Symposium on the Knights of Labor, Newberry Library, Chicago, May 1979.

militia to walk the streets and enforce a curfew. The strike of the sewer workers was quickly crushed, and all of the instigators were fired. As long as horses and mules were important to transportation, blacks dominated another unpleasant job, that of livery stable keepers. Blacks were hired to feed and wash the animals and to keep the stables clean. Finally, the city government employed blacks to work on road and bridge construction crews and to demolish old buildings.[14]

Blacks also worked for the L & N Railroad Company, one of the largest employers in the state. Though precise data on occupations at the L & N are unavailable, from the end of the Civil War to the 1890s a number of blacks worked as skilled workers—conductors, engineers, firemen, switchmen, and brakemen. But as the various divisions within the railroad formed unions, blacks were excluded from most of the skilled jobs. For instance, the constitution adopted by the Brotherhood of Locomotive Firemen in 1892 said that "an applicant . . . must be white born, of good moral character, sober, and industrious."[15] This too was part of a national trend. Black men, who had previously worked on railroads, were finding their opportunities severely limited. In numerous places in the South, white railroad workers went out on strike until companies replaced skilled black workers with white union men. By the 1920s in Louisville and elsewhere, very few if any blacks worked the skilled occupations on the trains.[16]

At the railroad companies, therefore, the overwhelming majority of blacks were eventually relegated to backbreaking jobs or menial tasks. Many worked as track men—helping to lay and repair the railroad track. These men spent weeks away from home, living in camp cars on the railway. One southern historian has noted that these black men earned no more than a dollar a day and were "subject to attack from fearful white communities, and lived often in a state of peonage which rivaled that found in the Congo Free State." As a rule, all of the water boys and cooks traveling with the work crews were black. Blacks also cleaned the coaches, loaded and unloaded the train cars, with many of these gangs having black supervisors. Again, given the limited employment opportunities in Louisville for Afro-Americans, it was not uncommon for blacks to work as la-

14. New York *Times,* July 25, 26, 1877; *Courier-Journal,* July 25, 26, 1877.
15. See DePaola, "Management and Organized Labor Relations," for a discussion of the unions within the L & N and their exclusionary clauses.
16. Lamon, *Black Tennesseans,* 160–63; Gerber, *Black Ohio,* 74, 302; Sterling D. Spero and Abram L. Harris, *The Black Worker: The Negro and the Labor Movement* (New York, 1931), 284; Maury Klein, *History of the Louisville and Nashville Railroad Company* (New York, 1972).

borers at the L & N for twenty to thirty years (in at least one instance for fifty-four years). Unfortunately, however, because of discrimination these men rarely progressed through company ranks.[17]

A significant number of blacks found jobs at the L & N by providing services for whites. The *Louisville and Nashville Employee's Magazine*, which started in the mid-1920s but is an excellent source for the earlier period, shows that most blacks worked in the dining cars, on the Pullman sleeping cars, and as baggage handlers and waiters. By having blacks waiting on their customers' every need, the railroad company hoped to make white travelers feel right at home. The company magazine consistently published features on black porters, such as George Lightfoot, who had worked for the company for decades and who took extreme pride in serving prominent whites. The articles neglected to mention the long hours, the subsistence-level wages the porters received, and the fact that the men were required to buy their uniforms and supplies out of their salaries. Perhaps the best benefit received for working as a porter or waiter on a train was the opportunity to travel and visit many different cities.[18]

At no time in the history of Louisville were all black workers confined to unskilled jobs. Slave and free-black skilled workers performed vital jobs in the infancy of the city and were the primary reason that Afro-Americans found an important niche in the city. In the years immediately after slavery, the services of Negro blacksmiths, brickmakers, cabinetmakers, carpenters, and painters were important to the growth occurring in the city. All of the stories highlighting the progress of the race spoke with pride of the city's skilled black workers. Black leaders constantly told the race to learn skills, that this would uplift the race, gain the respect of whites, and insure a good livelihood. One of the city's black leaders, William J. Simmons, president of the black Baptist college, preached this philosophy, and, of course, school principal Booker T. Washington would become promi-

17. The quote is from Lamon, *Black Tennesseans*, 161. Greene and Woodson, in *The Negro Wage Earner*, 102–104, estimated that by 1910, 80 percent or more of all black railroad workers were unskilled. They also pointed out that in the South some blacks remained railroad firemen, but they were paid less than white firemen. See *Louisville and Nashville Employee's Magazine* that began publication in 1925. Especially see vol. I (March, 1925), 33; (February, 1926), 43. The February issue has an article on "Uncle Link" Turner who worked as a laborer for the L & N for fifty-four years, retiring on December 1, 1925. "The L & N has never had a more loyal or faithful employee than Uncle Link."

18. See *Louisville and Nashville Employee's Magazine* from vol. I (March, 1925) to vol. IX (March, 1932) for many stories on black porters; William H. Harris, *Keeping the Faith: A. Philip Randolph, Milton P. Webster, and the Brotherhood of Sleeping Car Porters, 1925–1937* (Urbana, 1977).

nent nationally as an advocate of industrial training for blacks. Indeed, in Louisville, in Kentucky, and in the South, learning a skill was an important part of black education. Local white businessmen were often very generous in giving grants to help start schools that taught skills to blacks.[19]

Despite the encouragement of black leaders and white business leaders, the percentage of blacks with skills declined. Having a skill was no guarantee for employment. Like Afro-Americans all over the nation in the late nineteenth century, Louisville's skilled blacks met staunch white resentment and resistance, especially in the building trades. According to a story in the Indianapolis *Freeman* in October 1890, the only black brickmaker in Louisville was being forced out of business by his white competitors. A suit was brought against him by one of his white neighbors who claimed that the smoke from the brickmaker's yard was causing injury to his family. For months the case was tied up in court. Meanwhile, the black brickmaker's business came to a halt, costing him $100 a day. Other newspaper stories pointed out that by the 1890s apprenticeships were virtually closed to blacks. In his study of skilled artisans, DuBois found only eight black apprentices in Louisville. Finally, the changing transportation system and improved technology made some skills—for example, blacksmiths and shoemakers—obsolete. So despite the proliferation of industrial schools and the emphasis on learning a trade at Central High, blacks often acquired skills that were essentially outdated or, because of racism, were of little use to them. According to DuBois, Louisville had only 1,272 skilled black workers in 1900.[20]

Important concerns of Louisville's skilled and unskilled black workers were their total exclusion from most labor unions and the discrimination they suffered in the few locals that did admit them as members. It should be kept in mind that, in general, Louisville was an anti-union town, leaving white unions often quite powerless. Large employers viewed unions as a nuisance. These large businesses did reluctantly agree to the formation of unions, primarily to bring stability and order to the work force. But even after recognizing unions, the employers were still very arbitrary and

19. William J. Simmons, "What the Colored People Are Doing in Kentucky," *American Baptist Home Mission Society*, jubilee volume (1883), 85–90; see also William J. Simmons, *Men of Mark: Eminent, Progressive, and Rising* (Cleveland, 1887).

20. Indianapolis *Freeman*, October 4, 1890, August 1, December 19, 1896, September 25, 1897, August 31, 1907; W. E. B. DuBois (ed.), *The Negro Artisan*, Atlanta University Publications, no. 7 (Atlanta, 1902), 90, 126–27; William H. Harris, *The Harder We Run: Black Workers Since the Civil War* (New York, 1982).

dictatorial when dealing with their workers. In 1893 the L & N cut the wages of its employees by 10 percent. A number of the railroad unions protested. The result: their leaders were fired. Most black workers—servants, seasonal workers, and common laborers—were in occupations that had very little bargaining power, and thus they were unable to organize. This was not the case, however, with the brickmakers, hod carriers, musicians, and others. Since they often competed successfully with whites for employment, they were admitted into unions; a move by whites to control blacks as much as anything else. For example, the white musicians' union, tired of seeing blacks get the better jobs, encouraged the formation of a black musicians' union in an attempt to regulate the number of black musicians in Louisville. Whites excluded the black musicians from their union, but they did allow a black to serve on the consolidated union board, which, of course, the white musicians dominated.[21]

In the 1880s most of Louisville's organized black workers were members of the Knights of Labor. The principles espoused by the Knights—unity in strikes, election of blacks to office in labor organizations, and interracial social functions—appealed to black workers. Interracial worker solidarity reached a high point in the city on May 1, 1886, when 6,000 black and white workers participated in the day-long Knights of Labor demonstration for an eight-hour working day. After marching together in a show of brotherhood, the men retired to a local park and socialized together. A New York news correspondent, viewing the actions of black and white Knights in Louisville, proclaimed: "thus have the Knights of Labor broken the walls of prejudice."[22]

Not all of the whites affiliated with the Knights of Labor were elated over blacks being a part of their union. As the president of the black hod carriers union learned, some whites within the union attempted to exclude blacks from their locals. After being snubbed repeatedly by white union men, the black president stated, "There [should be] an agreement of all colored unions in the city to stand aloof from white organizations that refuse to recognize us as brothers." The black hod carriers eventually struck when a dispute developed with an employer over wages and working conditions. As the black hod carriers feared, the white union workers did not support them. With the blacks on strike, the white contractor, with the consent of white union workers, hired white strikebreakers to replace the

21. Finch, "Organized Labor in Louisville," 75.
22. Quoted in Philip S. Foner, *Organized Labor and the Black Worker 1619–1973* (New York, 1974), 50; *Courier-Journal*, May 2, 1886.

black hod carriers. The whites did not hide their hopes that this action would destroy the black union.[23]

After the demise of the Knights of Labor, some blacks joined the American Federation of Labor (AFL). But once in the AFL they found discrimination to be far more prevalent than it had been under the Knights. Union meetings were completely segregated, and no blacks could hold positions in the union. To their dismay, blacks found that the entire philosophy of the AFL was different than the Knights: the union was opposed to the idea of an inclusive industrial brotherhood and was more concerned about individual crafts, having little sympathy for most laborers, black or white, who had been the chief concern of the Knights. As the scholars Harris and Spero so well explain, the AFL wanted to be a very exclusive union of highly skilled craftsmen. "The smaller it is kept the higher will be the value of the craftsman's service. It is therefore made as difficult as possible for new members to join. If whole classes, such as Negroes, can be automatically excluded, the problem of keeping the membership down is made that much easier." Samuel Gompers, president of the union, came to Louisville on May 1, 1890, for the May Day parade. Blacks marched in the grand parade but then adjourned to a separate park for picnicking and games. This act symbolized the spirit of the AFL in Louisville and elsewhere. Throughout the 1890s, though calling for worker solidarity in Louisville, the AFL maintained a strict policy of segregation.[24]

A few of Louisville's black workers rejected the hypocrisy of the AFL and formed unions of their own. By the late 1890s there were six all-black unions in the city: the Colored Waiters' and Cooks' Alliance #261, Waiters' Union #261, Coopers' Union, Hod Carriers' Union #10 (there was also a white Hod Carriers' Union), Hackmen's Union, and Teamster Union #261. The Waiters' and Cooks' Alliance was probably the most active of the black unions. The business manager of the organization, acting in many respects like an employment agent, found jobs for blacks at local hotels, clubs, and restaurants. Whites contacted the business manager to get help for banquets, balls, and receptions. The Waiters' and Cooks' Alliance rented a room on Fifth Street to use as a headquarters for union meetings and social activities. Indeed, recreational activities were some of the main functions of the unions. Local white unions also made social activities an important part of their unions. This factor, as much as anything, explains why whites strongly wanted segregated unions. For the most part their

23. Quoted in Foner, *Organized Labor*, 51; Fitch, "Organized Labor in Louisville," 37–38.
24. Spero and Harris, *The Black Worker*, 47–54, 461–62.

unions were fraternal orders and only rarely involved in economic issues.[25]

There was, however, at least one exception to racially segregated unions. Black men comprised at least one-fourth of the tobacco workers in Louisville, with some of them having semi-skilled jobs. These workers were welcomed into the local tobacco workers' union. In 1895 one of these black workers, Thomas N. Williams, became the first of his race to be initiated into the Rainbow Union No. 14, and he was immediately elected an officer. He quickly started recruiting other Negro tobacco workers into the union. As an officer, Williams represented the Rainbow Union at the Tobacco Workers' International Union in Detroit in 1900. At the meeting Williams was selected as the fifth vice-president of the international union.[26]

For a local black to be accepted into a white union and allowed to practice a skill happened on occasion; more rare, however, was for blacks to be hired as clerks or in positions of authority in local government or private businesses. It was one thing to hire blacks to help with the construction of a department store and quite another to hire a black to serve white customers once the store opened. Even though Louisville's black community could boast of many graduates from business and commercial schools, very few could find positions in white establishments. The very idea of a black clerk waiting on whites was offensive to the white public. Blacks, therefore, were excluded from clerical jobs in white businesses that required serving white customers. It would have been surprising, even shocking, if it had been otherwise. The 1910 Census listed 8 black men out of 1,307 clerks in stores and 4 black women out of 408 (see table 5). For women, the Census also had another category—saleswomen—and only two of Louisville's 1,307 saleswomen were black. In all likelihood the fourteen black clerks and saleswomen worked for black concerns, for no mention was made in the local press of blacks being hired by white department stores.[27] The Census material also reveals that very few foreign-born whites were hired as sales personnel. They probably found positions only in the businesses owned by people from their native country. About

25. C. K. Caron, *Directory of Louisville for 1908* (Louisville, 1908), 66; Indianapolis *Freeman*, November 25, 1908, March 5, 1910, January 7, 1911.

26. Finch, "Organized Labor in Louisville," 74.

27. Surprisingly, in Lexington, Kentucky, several white businesses employed blacks as clerks. The following quote appeared in the *Colored American Magazine*, I (October, 1900), 330: "The white business stores of Lexington are employing colored clerks. Graves, Cox and Co. set the example by employing Sam L. Tolley, who has held the post a number of years. The Kaufman Clothing Co. was next, who have in their charge Noah Woolridge. Also, Mr. Louis Adler, the shoe manager, has recently added to his force J. B. Caulder."

Table 5
Clerks, Saleswomen, and Deliverymen in Louisville, 1910[a]

	White	Foreign Born	Black
Women			
Clerks in Stores	387 (94.8%)	17 (4.1%)	4 (0.9%)
Saleswomen	1,246 (95.7%)	59 (4.1%)	2 (0.14%)
Men			
Clerks in Stores	1,221 (93.4%)	78 (5.9%)	8 (0.6%)
Deliverymen	777 (50.4%)	36 (2.3%)	728 (47.2%)

[a] Bureau of the Census, *Thirteenth Census of the United States* (Washington, D.C., 1913), IV, 562–63.

the best job a black man could hope for in a white store was to be a deliveryman, a position that required no direct contact with the public.

Black women found that even the clerical jobs that did not require dealing with the public were closed to them. They were excluded from the businesses that hired women for positions as bookkeepers and stenographers. Even during Republican administrations, black females were not hired for clerical jobs at City Hall. The job of telephone operator, which came to be dominated by females because of the long hours and short pay, was virtually closed to blacks. In 1910 only one black female worked as an operator out of a labor force of 346. Ten years later, despite an increase of 270 telephone operators, there was still only one black.[28]

For educated blacks, the United States Post Office offered the best employment opportunity in Louisville. A number of black college graduates got jobs at the Post Office by passing the civil service examination. These blacks viewed their positions as security, and a number of them, led by William H. Steward, kept their jobs at the Post Office while pursuing other business ventures or attending school. Steward published the *American Baptist*, a religious newspaper, for years before resigning his mail carrier job. Two young men, William Warley and Felix Fowler, worked at the Post

28. *Fourteenth Census*, IV, 1132–35; Irvin, *Women In Kentucky*, 74.

Office while attending college; both remained there for several years after graduating. By the early 1900s, about forty blacks had positions at the Post Office as clerks and letter carriers. Several whites resented the presence of blacks and called for a halt to hiring them, claiming that it was "disgraceful" for whites to work with blacks. They explained that the number of black letter carriers had increased because "the wages paid are so low, the work is so hard, especially in winter, and living is so high that white people are not taking the exam for such a position. You see we have to buy uniforms and all these things eat up our salaries. A negro don't care whether he makes anything or not, so long as he can wear a uniform." Louisville's postmaster heard the complaints of white workers. The number of blacks working at the Post Office barely increased during the 1910s, and in the early 1920s several local black groups were protesting loudly over discrimination at the Post Office.[29]

II.

One way that blacks could avoid the daily insults and discrimination in employment was by operating businesses of their own. Of all the ideas in the late-nineteenth-century Afro-American community, blacks put most faith in business ownership as a way to economic independence. After praising Henry Abel in his venture as owner of a shoe store, the Indianapolis *Freeman* then explained its importance to black Louisville: "The thousands of colored people should see to it that his business expands to such an extent that a number of young people could find employment with him."[30] Black-owned businesses were seen as a means of increasing the wealth of the community as well as a means of showing whites that the race was making substantial progress.

Repeatedly, black newspapers and journals praised the virtue of owning businesses. The New York *Freeman* in May 1885 highlighted black businesses in Louisville in an article entitled "Progress of the Race." Several furniture dealers—Jackson Burk and Son, James Tate, Moses Lawson, and Cain, Bazil, and Sons—had been in business since the late 1860s and were profiting from being ideally located in the city's business district. The newspaper mentioned with pride the large number of "fine" black-

29. Cary B. Lewis, "Louisville and Its Afro-American Citizens," *Colored American Magazine*, X (April, 1906), 265; Indianapolis *Freeman*, November 17, 1906, December 24, 1910. December 16, 1911.
30. Indianapolis *Freeman*, July 20, 1901.

owned barbershops that served white men exclusively. Louisville blacks owned eight grocery stores and several other businesses. The paper pointed out that the most lucrative enterprise was undertaking, and that, surprisingly, only two black men were engaged in the business. In 1896 the Indianapolis *Freeman* surveyed black Louisville and found that blacks owned two tailor shops, twenty restaurants, ten saloons, three newspapers, twenty barbershops, three carpenter shops, three blacksmith shops, and several funeral homes. This proved, so the *Freeman* explained, that the race was still progressing and advancing economically. Thirteen years later, yet another survey was done by the Indianapolis *Freeman*. The number of businesses was still increasing; blacks now owned too many grocery stores, restaurants, and barbershops to count, two drugstores, and a large office building completely occupied by black businessmen.[31]

The newspaper articles failed to mention that the successful black businesses depended primarily on white customers or that black-owned mortuaries and saloons were necessary because of discrimination. The successful black furniture dealers located on Main and Fourth Streets made expensive furniture that was purchased by wealthy whites. The most prominent black barbers had always owned shops in white neighborhoods or rented space in white establishments. For example, David Steward, whose father had probably been a barber in antebellum Louisville, ran a barbershop at a white hotel from 1876 to the early 1900s. Black barbers fully realized that their economic success depended on serving whites. During these years they came under attack not only by whites desiring to push them out of the business but also by blacks who viewed many black barbers as traitors to their race for refusing to serve blacks or doing so "only when the shop is closed and the shades drawn." As one disgruntled black explained, "It may be from a spirit of selfish indifference, or an uncalled for dependence upon the white men; yet the fact is that as a rule this class of people have no interest in the race's advancement." Louisville was, of course, far from being the only place where barbers were involved in such a practice. George L. Knox, the prominent editor of the Indianapolis *Freeman* and also a barber, refused services to Afro-Americans in his barbershop.[32]

31. New York *Freeman*, May 16, 1885; Indianapolis *Freeman*, August 1, 1896, September 4, 1909. For other estimates of the number of black-owned businesses in Louisville, see W. E. B. DuBois (ed.), *The Negro in Business*, Atlanta University Publications, no. 4 (Atlanta, 1899), 26; Carter G. Woodson, *The Negro Professional Man and the Community* (Washington, D.C., 1934), 338.

32. Indianapolis *Freeman*, July 20, 1901, August 10, 1907; New York *Freeman*, September 12, 1885; Thornbrough, *The Negro in Indiana*, 264.

The careers of two of the better-known black businessmen during this time further illustrates the close ties they had with whites. E. I. Masterson, the city's leading black tailor and a graduate of the tailoring department of Tuskegee Institute, specialized in stylish clothes. Previously, the city's black tailors had catered to blacks, making inexpensive clothing, but Masterson's fashionable and expensive gowns, suits, and other clothing appealed to whites. Located for ten years in downtown Louisville at the corner of West and Walnut Streets, Masterson's tailor shop made him economically secure; according to the Indianapolis *Freeman* he earned a minimum of $2,500 a year in profits. Likewise, David L. Knight, the first black in Kentucky to establish a transfer-line company, depended entirely on contracts from white businessmen to keep his business afloat. Knight learned his trade from a white employer. After gaining experience and saving the needed capital, he purchased a horse and wagon and started his own business, calling it "The Lightning Transfer Company." Knight's business grew rapidly; by the early 1900s he owned eleven wagons and employed "a great number of colored men." He performed a much needed service for local businessmen, moving their products from one place to another, and, as the name of his company implied, he prided himself on moving goods quickly. His business lasted for about fifteen years.[33]

Louisville had several profitable black enterprises that benefited from discrimination. Prior to the mid-1880s, most of the city's black funeral homes had failed, largely because of competition from white undertakers. But during the time of increasing segregation, local whites began complaining about white undertakers also providing services for blacks. The white funeral companies responded by declining black business or by charging blacks double the regular price.[34] A young black businessman, William Watson, soon realized the opportunity that was opening for him. He started an undertaking company in 1887 and it grew rapidly. Since he enjoyed a virtual monopoly on the black business, he was able to earn a profit in a very short time. He wisely put most of his profits back into his company and bought elegant horses and equipment. Reportedly, his equipment was so fancy that white undertakers rented it. By the time of his death in December 1905, he was perhaps the city's wealthiest black.

33. For information on both Masterson and Knight, see Lewis, "Louisville and Its Afro-American Citizens," 259–64; Indianapolis *Freeman*, April 5, 1902. For examples of other businessmen who relied on contracts with white businessmen, see the Indianapolis *Freeman*, December 19, 1896, April 5, 1902, September 11, 1909; George F. Richings, *Evidences of Progress Among Colored People* (Philadelphia, 1899), 302–303, 506–10.
34. New York *Freeman*, May 16, 1885.

His widow remarried, and, under the management of her new husband, John B. Cooper, the Watson Undertaking Company continued to do well, earning profits totaling $34,523.95 between 1907 and 1912. Not surprisingly, the number of black undertakers increased in the city (all of them were trained by Watson): in 1900 there were only two; by 1908, ten.[35]

Tom Cole, who rivaled Watson in wealth in the early 1900s, made several business ventures that succeeded primarily because blacks were excluded from white establishments. Cole erected an office building in 1908 that provided space for blacks to conduct medical and law practices and other businesses. He owned Cole's Cafe, which blacks viewed as a good alternative to white restaurants. Cole and several other black businessmen had prosperous saloons. Cole's saloon is remembered as being very "fancy and high class." Cole invested in several other entertainment businesses that appealed to blacks, the most successful being the Louisville Giants, a black baseball team that existed for years.[36]

The lucrative black businesses in Louisville—those conducted by furniture makers, Masterson's tailor shop, Knight's transfer-line company, undertaking establishments, Cole's enterprises, and several others—were far and away exceptions. In Louisville, and in cities throughout the nation, the vast majority of black enterprises struggled just to stay in business and could never seriously compete with white enterprises. Also, despite all of the boasting by the black press, most of the businesses that relied on white customers were declining by the early 1900s and gone by 1915. How much white racism contributed to the end of these businesses is open to speculation, because without white patronage the cabinetmakers, Knight's business, and Masterson's shop would never have succeeded in the first place. Moreover, black barbers were able to hold off white competitors and keep their customers. It is highly possible that the lack of both business experience and needed capital was a leading factor in the demise of some black-owned businesses. Banks were often criticized for refusing loans to black businessmen. Yet, in all fairness, most black businesses were small mom-and-pop operations with few assets, the very kind of enterprise that banks found too risky. So few blacks had acquired experience

35. Gibson, *Progress of the Colored Race in Louisville*, 29; Clement Richardson (ed.), *The National Cyclopedia of the Colored Race* (Montgomery, 1919), 161; Indianapolis *Freeman*, April 5, 1902, June 19, August 31, 1907, September 4, 1909, April 14, December 14, 1910, March 23, 1912. Alexander Walters was a close friend of William Watson; see Walters, *My Life and Work*, 41–42.

36. Lewis, "Louisville and Its Afro-American Citizens," 265; Indianapolis *Freeman*, April 5, 1902, February 9, August 31, 1907, February 29, 1908, March 5, April 23, 1910; Blanton interview.

in business that highly profitable enterprises, like those operated by the furniture makers, ended when the owners died. Indeed, despite some gallant attempts, most younger blacks found it impossible to sustain the businesses started by their fathers.[37]

Changes in technology also undermined black businesses. The automobile destroyed businesses like Knight's that relied literally on horsepower. Most black manufacturing businesses were small operations that could not compete with cheaper goods made by machines. What DuBois noticed happening in Philadelphia was undoubtedly occurring in Louisville as well: "Today, the application of large capital to the retail business, . . . the wonderful success of trained talent in catering to the whims and tastes of customers almost precludes the effective competition of small stores. Thus the economic conditions of the day militate against the negro; it requires more skill and experience to run a small store than formerly and the large store and factory are virtually closed to them on any terms." [38]

A lack of sufficient patronage from members of their own race also increased the likelihood of failure for most black businesses. Afro-Americans were the poorest group in Louisville, so any business that depended solely on them for success would experience some hard times. Black newspapers were started regularly, and they practically all failed within a matter of months. If the Negro press is correct, too often blacks lacked faith in members of their race to conduct businesses and chose to patronize white establishments even though a black-owned enterprise could perform the same service. The Indianapolis *Freeman*, hardly an unbiased observer, said that blacks could not expect whites to support black businesses when they themselves refused to spend their money in black stores and shops. In 1909 the paper complained that the two Negro-owned drugstores were failing, not because of poor business procedures, but because the black physicians did not encourage their patients to have prescriptions filled by the black pharmacists. The *Freeman* asked bluntly, "Do the physicians doubt the ability of the pharmacists?" Shortly thereafter, in an attempt to increase black awareness and support of black businesses, twenty-five businessmen formed the Young Men's Business Club. They agreed to "call the attention of the masses of our people to the fact that by giving their patronage to members of their own race . . . they will not only gain commercial prestige, but will make it possible for merchants and other businessmen to

37. Lewis, "Louisville and Its Afro-American Citizens," 259–65; Blanton interview; Parrish interview; see C. K. Caron's *Directory of Louisville* for the years 1900–1910.

38. W. E. B. DuBois, *The Philadelphia Negro* (Philadelphia, 1899), 123; Greene and Woodson, *The Negro Wage Earner*, 111.

employ our boys and girls who are coming out of schools and have no avenues open to them." This effort by the Young Men's Business Club failed. Two years later, in February 1911, The *Freeman* was still complaining that blacks failed to support black businessmen.

Here in this city we have several fine restaurants owned and conducted by our own people, but very poorly supported because there are a few white men running places for negroes. We have two very fine theaters controlled by colored men, yet a week ago our people deserted these playhouses to patronize a house that charges colored people double the price and inferior accommodations offered to whites.

One negro order, whose headquarters are in this city, and which boasts of a membership counted by the thousands—all of the money in its treasury being produced by the toil and sacrifice of black men—proposes to erect a large building at a cost of $35,000 and yet not one dollar goes to a negro contractor, mechanic or architect. The whole thing is being planned to enrich the members of labor unions that use every effort that can be effected to cut the negro off from employment of any kind but as a menial servant. . . .Our druggists and pharmacists are required to meet the standard of competency set forth by the state board, yet they stand idly behind their counters and watch the colored people flock into the white man's place down the street.[39]

Perhaps the best-known organization to promote black business in Louisville was the National Negro Business League (NNBL). Founded by Booker T. Washington in 1903, the NNBL tried to advise and encourage ventures by Afro-Americans. Forever showing optimism despite the worsening conditions during the nadir period, Washington informed black businessmen that "if you can make a better article than anybody else, and sell it cheaper than anybody else, you can command the markets of the world." The NNBL held annual meetings where successful black men, such as H. A. Tandy of Lexington, Kentucky, who constructed that city's new courthouse in 1899, told the large gatherings how they had "made it."[40]

Led by David L. Knight, a number of Louisvillians quickly formed a branch of the NNBL. They spread Washington's message and tried to use his name to increase black patronage of their businesses. Washington was so impressed with their enthusiasm and glowing accounts of their city that he selected Louisville as the site of the 1909 NNBL convention. At that convention, held August 18–20, Washington and the delegates heard speaker after speaker, including the city's white leaders, extol the local

39. Indianapolis *Freeman*, April 10, September 4, 18, November 13, 1909, February 4, 1911.
40. Booker T. Washington, "The National Business League," *World's Work* (October, 1902), 2671–74.

businesses owned by blacks and express their willingness to promote additional black enterprises. (They also boasted about the almost idyllic race relations enjoyed by the citizens of Louisville.) Washington, obviously not aware of the true nature of race relations or the poor state of most black businesses, exclaimed that Louisville served as a model of a successful black community. Immediately after the convention, however, the interest expressed in investing in and promoting black businesses evaporated. The local correspondent for the Indianapolis *Freeman* complained that it had all been just for show. Another black weekly, the Louisville *News*, was much harsher in its criticism. It asserted that the NNBL had no constructive effect in increasing black business over the years. "What does the Business League do but exaggerate and pretend? The tales of hardship overcome and wealth made 'in the sweat of their brows,' as told by some member of the Business League, would make Ananias blush for shame."[41]

Simply put, the NNBL refused to acknowledge the reality of the early twentieth century. Washington's group encouraged small black entrepreneurs during a time when large corporations were changing the face of America. These powerful companies were backed by millions of dollars. Black capitalism stood little chance against such power.

III.

Closely following the successful businessmen at the top of the economic scale were the city's black professionals. Black professionals obviously viewed Louisville as an ideal city for they migrated there from all over the country (even from the North) in sizeable numbers. By 1890, for example, the city had thirteen physicians, eight lawyers, fifty-nine clergymen, and well over a hundred teachers. Twenty years later the black professional class was still growing, especially the doctors, who then numbered over forty. The number of black professionals in the city compared favorably with that of any city its size; in fact, Louisville had more black lawyers during these years than the entire state of Georgia, and probably more black doctors than any city in Ohio.[42]

Despite their large number (in some ways, maybe because of it), blacks found it difficult to start and maintain medical and legal practices in

41. Indianapolis *Freeman*, April 17, August 14, 28, September 4, 11, 1909; The Louisville *News* was quoted in *Crisis*, IX (December, 1914), 71.

42. Indianapolis *Freeman*, August 1, 1896, September 4, 1909; Dittmer, *Black Georgia*, 37; Gerber, *Black Ohio*, 318–19.

Louisville. Relying totally on the substantially impoverished black community for a livelihood, black doctors found the going so rough that many
of them left the city or switched to other types of work. Henry Fitzbutler,
the first Negro to graduate from the medical school at the University of
Michigan, was Louisville's first black doctor, arriving in 1871. For years
his practice suffered; as one contemporary observer noted, "at first the
people did not take favorably to the colored man of this profession, but
with enlightenment doctors have fared better." Discrimination was part
of the problem—black doctors were not allowed in any of the hospitals in
the city. Black doctors became more successful with the opening of the Red
Cross Hospital and Nurse Training Department in 1899. Yet, for most of
them the first year or two in practice was still a test of survival. For example, Dr. Pendar Flack collected only $1.25 during his first month of
practice in 1902. Flack never collected more than $20 a month for his ser-
vices until his seventh month in Louisville, and not until his second year
did his practice begin to grow.[43]

Black lawyers received even poorer compensation than doctors. With
lawyers relying on their reputations to attract clients, black attorneys were
at a disadvantage because they were not part of the city's power structure.
Blacks who were in trouble with the law sought out the services of prominent white lawyers, like ex-Confederate Bennett H. Young. The black press
complained bitterly that the average black citizen had little faith in Negro
lawyers. "We have a number of well-educated lawyers who can present a
case with intelligence and command the respect of the bar, yet our people
. . . give all of their business to white shysters who never read a law book."
The city's first black attorney, Nathaniel R. Harper, arrived in 1871. He
barely eked out a living until he became an active campaigner for Republican candidates. The Republican party rewarded Harper by giving him a
succession of minor posts. Attorney Albert S. White's career paralleled
Harper's. A graduate of Howard University Law School, he stumped Kentucky for Republican candidates and in turn was appointed to office, with
the best position being U.S. Revenue Agent. White tried in vain over the
years to win the federal appointment to be Minister to Liberia.[44]

Many black professionals in Louisville taught school full-time and
practiced law or medicine or ran a newspaper part-time. Although black
leaders fought bitterly over the running of the schools, it is important to

43. Weeden, *History of the Colored People*, 44; Indianapolis *Freeman*, December 24,
1910. For information on the career of Dr. Flack, see Louisville *Leader*, October 29, 1930.
44. Indianapolis *Freeman*, December 12, 1896, August 31, 1907, December 26, 1908,
March 5, 1910, January 7, July 29, 1911.

remember that they did have a say in who taught at the schools. Like the U.S. Post Office, the school system offered more security (as long as the teacher remained free of controversial issues) and a higher wage than most jobs. A big problem, however, was always the competition for the jobs. Black leaders used their influence to win jobs in the school system for themselves, their friends, and, most especially, their children. In fact, a group of black teachers and principals developed a vested interest in running the black schools. So segregation in public education benefited blacks in one way by providing guaranteed jobs for well over a hundred black professionals each year. As long as most professional positions offered little chance for economic success, and as long as the skilled and white-collar clerical jobs were closed to blacks, the teaching field would remain very crowded in Louisville.

Overall, black Louisvillians made few gains in employment between 1870 and 1915. By limiting employment opportunities for blacks, whites assured themselves of a source of cheap, exploitable labor. Moreover, by maintaining control over the jobs available, whites could often intimidate blacks to support the white political power structure by threatening them with the loss of their jobs at election time. By 1915 blacks remained underrepresented in the skilled trades and overrepresented as common laborers and domestics. Black Louisville had an adequate number of professionals only because a segregated society created a need for black doctors, lawyers, and teachers. Black business enterprises did little to affect the limited employment opportunities available to the race. Moreover, though there were instances of successful black-owned businesses, most black businessmen—drugstore owners, storekeepers, and shoemakers— could not compete with the white businessmen who sought the black market. What hampered these businessmen most was that blacks themselves had little confidence in the ability of black entrepreneurs and would not support their enterprises. As DuBois once said, "Negro merchants are so rare that it is natural for customers, both white and colored, to take it for granted that their business is so poorly conducted without giving it a trial."[45]

45. DuBois, *The Philadelphia Negro*, 123.

## 4

Housing

The September 1913 issue of the prestigious journal *Annals of the American Academy of Political and Social Science* was devoted to the topic of "The Negro's Progress in Fifty Years." Written by well-trained black and white scholars, journalists, and social workers, the articles explored employment, education, politics, and housing. Professor George E. Haynes's article on "Conditions Among Negroes in the Cities" was one of the most significant in the monograph. A recent Ph.D. graduate from Columbia University, where he had studied blacks in New York City, Haynes pointed out that since the Civil War a steady stream of blacks had moved into the cities. Since many of the black migrants were poor, they were confined to the worst housing in run-down neighborhoods. But because of discrimination in many cities, the relatively few blacks who could afford better housing found it very difficult to obtain, and they usually were forced into the same run-down areas that housed the poor. In city after city, this Negro district had less effective police and fire protection and lacked such essential services as street lights, paved streets, and sanitary facilities. For the most part, playgrounds were nonexistent, and the public schools located in the area compared poorly with schools in white neighborhoods. Professor Haynes wrote that the "red light district" was usually in or near the black area. His important article highlighted the fact that "this separation in all areas of life in the city means that a distinct Negro world is growing up, isolated from the white world." This total separation was occurring in a number of cities, both North and South, including Louisville.

New York has its "San Juan Hill" in the West Sixties, and its Harlem District of over 35,000 within about eighteen city blocks; Philadelphia has its Seventh Ward; Chicago has its State Street; Washington its North West neighborhood, and Baltimore its Druid Hill Avenue. Louisville has its Chestnut Street and its "Smoketown"; Atlanta its West End and Auburn Avenue.[1]

---

1. George E. Haynes, "Conditions Among Negroes in the Cities," *Annals of the American Academy of Political and Social Science*, XLIX (September, 1913), 105–20, quote is on p. 109.

I.

Haynes was correct that areas of high black concentration in Louisville were indeed denied adequate city services, but significantly, he overstated the case of Louisville having a "distinct Negro world" completely isolated from the rest of society. The black ghettos around Chestnut Street and "Smoketown" were not established by 1910. Certainly, from the end of the Civil War to the early 1900s, the majority of Afro-Americans moving to the city were poor, and therefore limited to certain areas. But during that time all blacks were not forced to live in one specific area. In the 1880s, for example, several whites called for an ordinance restricting blacks to a designated "colored district," which suggests that blacks were living all over the city at that time. A letter to the Louisville *Times*, signed "Pro Bono Public," said that allowing blacks to occupy quarters all over Louisville marred the beauty of the city and lowered property values. It suggested that blacks be relegated to the far west end of town, a suggestion that would be echoed repeatedly over the years. Blacks often complained about the discriminatory high cost they paid to live in areas outside of the central part of town. Though lacking specific figures, both the Indianapolis *Freeman* and the New York *Freeman* said that blacks "paid enormous rental charges," often double the rate charged whites, and that Irish landlords were the worst offenders. One black told a reporter that he had to pay more than half of his monthly salary of $25 for an old house that had only two rooms and a kitchen.[2]

The U.S. Census materials and the Louisville city directories reveal clearly that blacks lived throughout the city during 1880–1917. (Most of Louisville's housing was located east and west of the downtown area; First Street divided east from west. An exception was the south part of town where wealthy whites lived.) The city had several clusters of black neighborhoods—the California District, Smoketown, and one or two areas near the center of town—but far more significant is the fact that blacks and whites often lived on the very same streets, and that some streets which had more blacks than whites in one given year did not necessarily become all-black streets. A close look at several streets will demonstrate a pattern repeated throughout the city (see map 1). Walnut Street, more than thirty blocks long, running east to west, had only a few blacks living at the east end in the late 1880s. (This, in fact, would be the case for most of the twentieth century.) Starting at the 100 block of West Walnut and going

2. Louisville *Times*, November 13, 1885; New York *Freeman*, June 27, 1885, September 18, 1886.

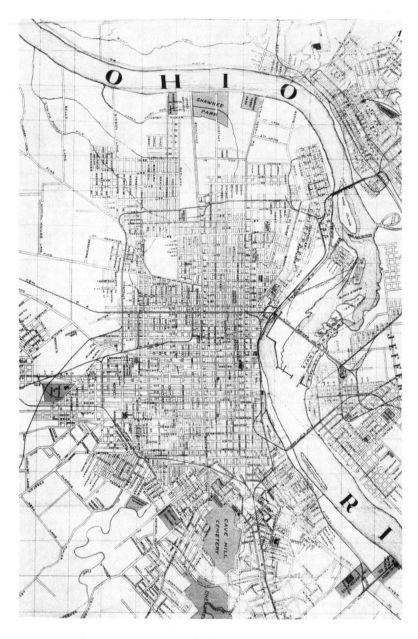

Map 1

Mendenhall's New Index Map of Greater Louisville, Kentucky, 1906. C. S. Mendenhall, Cincinnati, Ohio, 1906.

Map 2

Mendenhall's Index Map, showing the center of Louisville, 1906.

west, black housing was interspersed with white businesses. Then, blocks 200–900 were all black, while the 1000 block was racially mixed. Blocks 1100–1500 seemed to alternate back and forth between white and black, but often both races lived on the same block. In the 1880s and 1890s, no blacks lived on West Walnut from block 1500 to 2800, the far western edge of development at that time. By 1900 the racial makeup of West Walnut began changing: blacks were completely scattered throughout blocks 900–2000, and blocks 900—1200 were totally black. Yet the 1915 city directory indicates that whites did not leave the West Walnut area entirely. The housing pattern on Chestnut Street was similar. In the early 1880s, no blacks lived on the eastern part of the street but were scattered throughout the first eight westend blocks only. By 1886 a few blacks had moved into the first few houses on the 900 block. Yet, this did not signal a white exodus from the block. On the contrary, whites rented homes that were previously occupied by blacks. For example, in 1893 the first homes in the 900 block (901, 903, 905, 906, and 907) were once again occupied by whites after housing black residents for several years. By 1915 whites were still living on West Chestnut.[3]

It must be admitted, however, that this analysis of integrated housing in Louisville can be viewed too optimistically. Despite the fact that some blacks lived near whites, a closer look reveals that the races were usually segregated within an area (see map 2). For example, in 1886 physician Henry Fitzbutler and attorney N. R. Harper were neighbors on West Madison. Their closest neighbors were blacks. All of the whites lived on the other side of the street or were separated from blacks by vacant houses. Prominent black leader William H. Steward lived on several different streets during his life, but his neighbors were always black. In 1886 he lived at 108 West Walnut, close to several white businesses. All of his immediate neighbors, in houses 100–109, were black. House 110 was vacant and a white family lived in 111. This pattern persisted when Steward moved elsewhere. William Spradling, one of the wealthiest Afro-Americans in the city, lived at 911 West Chestnut. All of his neighbors in the 900 block were black.

Even more so than black professionals, poor blacks lived near white businesses, livery stables, and the city's many whiskey and tobacco fac-

3. A number of sources were consulted to determine where blacks lived in Louisville: City directories from 1870 to 1930; the published volumes of the U.S. Census from 1870 to 1930; and the original manuscript census of Louisville for 1870, 1880, and 1900. The manuscript census for 1890 was destroyed by fire.

tories. As in the 1870s, white saloons and vice joints were often located close to black neighborhoods. Moreover, many whites who did live in these neighborhoods were far from desirable citizens: in many instances the whites living in the same tenements as blacks were listed as madames. A number of these women lived on Pearl Avenue, otherwise an all-black street. At 313 Pearl, for example, there lived a white man and five madames; at 336 Pearl, above a saloon for whites, were six madames. Probably even more madames than those listed in official records were living in black neighborhoods but some were too modest to list their true occupations.

Other whites living in the same tenements or next door to blacks were usually very poor and could not afford to move. Quite often these people were old and had lived on the street when no blacks were present. They were the only whites left. For instance, Newton Street grew progressively black in the 1880s. By 1890 the only whites remaining were Paul and Bernardian Pulsford. By 1892 he was dead and she remained there alone. Several years later she too was gone, presumably deceased.

Many of the blacks listed as residents of integrated neighborhoods lived in the all-black alleys adjacent to white streets. This, of course, was a carryover from antebellum days when free blacks and slaves often lived in close proximity to whites. After the war, some blacks still lived in the homes of their employers, but more often they lived in the nearby alleys. Many blacks who worked in the center of town lived in alleys simply because it was the best they could afford. In fact, it is rare to find an alley in Louisville, even in the extreme east or west ends, where blacks did not live. For example, in the early 1890s all of the residents on Second Alley, which ran from Thirtieth to Thirty-Ninth Street in far west Louisville, were black. No blacks lived on any of the streets close to Second Alley. Most of the people living on Second Alley were domestics and laborers who worked for the whites in that area.[4]

As the occupations of the black residents of Second Alley indicate, a majority of the blacks who lived in white areas were not "neighbors" but employees. Another reason why blacks could live in white neighborhoods relates to race relations in Louisville. Whites were aware that blacks were excluded or at least segregated from them in most aspects of city life and that social equality between the races did not exist. With racial segregation well entrenched in all other areas of black-white relations, there was

---

4. An important book on alley life is James Borchert, *Alley Life in Washington: Family, Community, Religion, and Folklife in the City, 1850–1970* (Urbana, 1980).

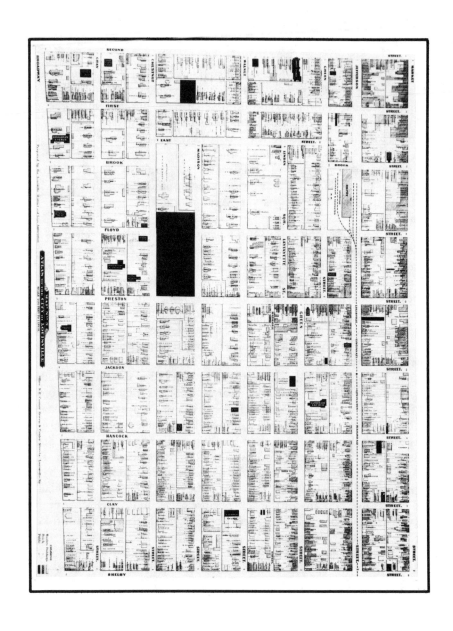

Map 3
East End Streets

Atlas, City of Louisville, 1876. Prepared and published by the Louisville Abstract and
Loan Association, 1876.

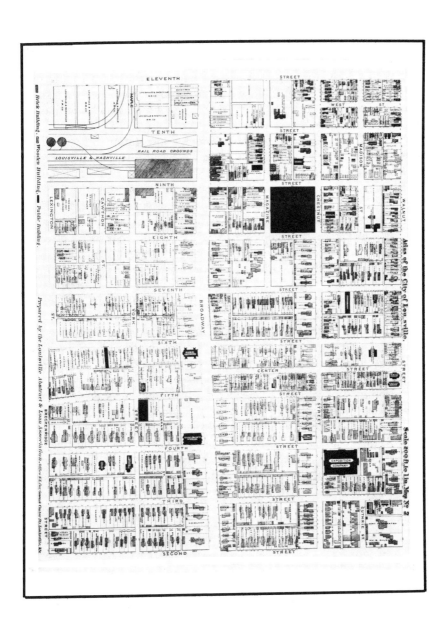

Map 4
West-End Streets

Atlas, City of Louisville, 1876.

little need for rigid segregation in housing. The whites advocating residential segregation in Louisville were those who competed with blacks for employment and housing, not the upper-class whites who knew that the gulf between themselves and blacks could not be altered.[5]

While it is true that there was residential integration in Louisville, it is also true that most blacks lived in the center of town. Moreover, data on Louisville's twelve wards between 1870 and 1920 show not only that blacks were concentrated in wards close to the business district, but also that more and more blacks were moving there. Blacks comprised no more than 5 percent of the residents in the wards located on the outskirts of town (1, 2, 3, and 12). Blacks comprised 15–25 percent of the residents of wards 4, 5, 6, 7, 8, and 11. But the highest number and percentage of blacks were found in wards 9 and 10—the center of town (see table 6).

Most scholars agree that prior to World War I Afro-Americans did not live in areas resembling the black ghettos of the second half of the twentieth century. Beginning in the 1880s in Cleveland and in many other northern cities, Afro-Americans were clustered in certain areas, but they were intermixed in significant proportions in many other places in the city. One reason for this was that practically all northern cities were experiencing an influx of Europeans between the years 1880 and 1910. Because these immigrants were poor, they lived in the same areas as blacks. This was especially true of the Irish. "Irish and Negroes lived in the same neighborhoods, not because of any mutual toleration but because of accessibility to their jobs, similar levels of economic status, and employment on the same types of unskilled and domestic service jobs," explains a scholar about the origins of the black ghetto in Cincinnati. Blacks in Richmond and in cities further south were also concentrated in clusters with a few scattered throughout the city. The few blacks who lived in the West knew nothing about ghettos, according to Professor Douglas H. Daniels. Blacks in San Francisco lived in neighborhoods containing practically all of the ethnic groups found in that multiracial city.[6]

---

5. Rabinowitz, *Race Relations in the Urban South*, 113; Thomas L. Philpott, *The Slum and the Ghetto: Neighborhood Deterioration and Middle-Class Reform, Chicago, 1880–1930* (New York, 1978), 118.

6. The quote comes from Paul J. Lammermeier, "Cincinnati's Black Community: The Origins of a Ghetto, 1870–1880," in John Bracey, August Meier, and Elliott Rudwick (eds.), *The Rise of the Ghetto* (Belmont, Calif., 1971), 26; Kusmer, *A Ghetto Takes Shape*, 12; Gerber, *Black Ohio*, 289; Zane L. Miller, *Boss Cox's Cincinnati: Urban Politics in the Progressive Era* (New York, 1968), 14–15; Rabinowitz, *Race Relations in the Urban South*; Daniels, *Pioneer Urbanites*, 75.

Table 6

Black Percentage of Total Population of Wards 9 and 10, 1870–1920[a]

	1870	1890	1900	1910	1920
Ward 9:					
Blacks	2,162 (28%)	3,558 (34%)	4,635 (42%)	4,038 (41%)	3,887 (45%)
Whites	5,668	6,806	6,490	5,738	4,686
Ward 10:					
Blacks	2,225 (20%)	4,884 (33%)	6,587 (44%)	7,999 (58%)	8,385 (69%)
Whites	9,161	9,868	8,648	5,746	3,784

[a] U.S. Bureau of the Census, *Negro Population in the United States, 1790–1915* (Washington, D.C., 1918), 106. Zane Miller, "Urban Blacks in the South, 1865–1920: The Richmond, New Orleans, Louisville, and Birmingham Experience," in Leo F. Schnore (ed.), *The New Urban History* (Princeton, 1974), 190.

II.

In January 1910 the Indianapolis *Freeman* ran a feature on "Negro Homes in Louisville," highlighting the residences of the city's elite blacks. The article pointed out that the Chestnut Street area—the area cited by Haynes—was extremely popular with black professionals and businessmen. The homes visited by the reporter had all of the modern conveniences found in the homes owned by whites. Moreover, a few of the more affluent blacks had three-story homes decorated in the most popular styles. Some of these homeowners had imported furniture, oriental rugs, expensive lamps, and the like, and were vying with their neighbors for the distinction of having the most elegant home. The reporter, after visiting some seventy-five of these homes, recognized horse trainer William Walker as having "the most brilliant and richly furnished home." But the reporter was quick to note that the new $30,000 home being constructed by saloon-owner Tom Cole stood an excellent chance of surpassing all black homes in the city.[7]

7. Indianapolis *Freeman*, January 22, 1910.

Most blacks did not live in fancy homes or nice neighborhoods. The same newspaper article reported that most black homeowners lived in small, modest cottages. Yet these blacks were fortunate, for the overwhelming majority of Louisville's Afro-Americans lived in even smaller apartments and tenements. As a rule the apartments that blacks rented were congested and dilapidated, lacking modern bathroom facilities. The same, of course, was true for the dwellings of poor whites, but the city did provide them with free public bathhouses, something not available to blacks before 1910. Furthermore, most of the buildings were firetraps. Throughout the entire period of 1870–1930 fires caused a tremendous amount of property damage in the areas of high black concentration. Yet it would be the mid-1920s before a fire station opened in the black neighborhood in the west end, and a decade later before one was established in the east end. The city provided fewer municipal services in black neighborhoods than elsewhere. Unpaved streets, the absence of sewers, and the presence of litter characterized too many of the city's all-black neighborhoods. Health officials consistently ignored sanitation in the black community, obviously never realizing that blacks could carry infectious diseases into the businesses and homes of their white employers. Indeed, the lack of adequate sanitation and sewage drainage coupled with overcrowded conditions led to higher rates of death and infant mortality for blacks and to a greater susceptibility to diseases like tuberculosis and pneumonia. According to the U.S. Census, far more deaths occurred from contagious and infectious diseases among blacks than whites.[8]

Several times in the early 1900s the city's black leaders called for housing reforms and the adoption of minimum building standards for tenements. However their pleas fell on closed ears. Some action finally resulted in 1908 when a joint committee of several white organizations formed the Tenement House Commission and used its influence to bring the housing crisis to the attention of city officials. The city council unanimously approved funding for the Tenement House Commission to conduct an exhaustive survey of tenement conditions and to make recommendations for a new housing code. After consulting with experts all over the country, the commission chose Janet E. Kemp, a professional investigator who had done similar work in New York City, Cleveland, and Baltimore, to head the survey and to write the report. Originally, Miss Kemp

---

8. *Eleventh Census*, "1890: Vital and Social Statistics," 21, 251–57, has an excellent discussion of neighborhoods in Louisville.

was to limit her investigation to only the east-end district that bordered the downtown area (see map 3), but she quickly discovered that tenements were spread all over town and that they were not limited to only one group of residents but housed poor blacks, whites, and immigrants.[9]

Kemp's study is a revealing description of the conditions under which Louisville's poor lived. Although the report was not limited to a discussion of black housing, most of her examples of the worst conditions were drawn from black tenements. Repeatedly throughout the report, Kemp vividly described numerous instances of blacks living in places hardly fit for animals. It was not uncommon for poor blacks to live in basements that had little light and inadequate ventilation. Thomas L. Philpott, in his study *The Slum and the Ghetto*, gives an example of what it was like to live in the basement of a tenement: "The streets, in effect, drained into their living quarters, and when sewers backed up, they spilled swill into the cellar residences. The offscourings of the privy vaults oozed into the soil, seeped through the thin walls and floorboards, and left a scum inside the flats." [10] Some blacks lived in large tenement houses that had been constructed for single families but were now occupied by eight to ten families. The "Tin House" on Pearl Street—so named because the entire structure was covered with tin—was a typical black tenement cited in the study. Thirty-one families lived in the thirty-seven rooms of the "Tin House." Most of those rooms lacked cross-ventilation. Sanitary provisions for the thirty-one families were "four ill-kept privy compartments over one common vault, which was constantly overflowing."

Kemp recommended tearing down a black tenement on Ninth Street called "The World's Fair." The structure had one-room apartments that extended from the street to the rear of the lot. The building's primary defect was its lack of ventilation. Each room received air only from the door and window opening on the porch at the front of the room. "The World's Fair" had no halls or interior stairways, so the only entrance to the upper stories was an outside stairway. Probably the worst place visited by Kemp was an apartment on Brook Street occupied by a woman, two men, and two dogs. They lived in two cellar rooms, four-and-one-half feet below street level. The ceiling in the apartment was barely six feet high. The floor of the apartment was covered with rags, refuse, and decaying vegetables. "The odors that filled the rooms were nauseating and were distinctly per-

9. Janet E. Kemp, *Report of the Tenement House Commission of Louisville* (Louisville, 1909).
10. Philpott, *The Slum and the Ghetto*, 39.

ceptible from the street before entering the apartment," the report said.

The Tenement House Commission Report said that many poor blacks kept their homes clean and attempted to improve the physical conditions of their neighborhoods. Special mention was made of blacks living in the "Coke Alley District" on Clay, Caldwell, Hancock, and Breckinridge Streets because this area had a higher percentage of clean rooms, yards, and toilets than other poor areas in Louisville. Yet the Coke Alley District had few water hydrants, and filthy cisterns served as the main source of water. Kemp said:

One look into the murky depth of a Coke Alley cistern is enough. The black, oily fluid, frequently dotted with bubbles indicating decomposition and fermentation, is unfit for any household use, . . . yet ninety-five of the ninety-nine apartments inspected in this district had no other water supply provided for their use.

Kemp's survey of housing conditions could have been far more critical for blacks were living in small shacks and the like all over the city in areas that were not included in the final report. Furthermore, she acknowledged that the data from several neighborhoods were omitted from the final report because conditions were too bad! "If the 100 block of East Jefferson Street . . . had been included in the study, the percent of houses in bad repair would have been materially higher; but this block was purposely omitted because the houses are too dilapidated to fairly represent the conditions found in the poor sections in the city." After reading the horrible conditions described in the report, one wonders what the situation must have been like on East Jefferson Street.

The findings of the Tenement House Commission received wide circulation and provided the basis for a new tenement law. The new ordinance, which went into effect in June 1910, placed limitations on using basements and cellars as residences. All ceilings, even in basements, had to be at least nine feet tall. Though it was vague on specifics, the new law called for adequate ventilation and a clean water supply for residents. The law also instructed the health department to place a limit on the number of people living in a single apartment. Despite all of the work of the commission and the strong endorsement of city officials, the new law, like the old one, was not enforced. The Kemp Commission had cited "The World's Fair" as one of the most hazardous tenements in Louisville and had recommended demolishing the structure. Yet in 1912, two years after the new law went into effect, "The World's Fair" was still housing blacks when the chimney fell off, seriously injuring two people. A reporter commented that "the house had been notorious for years. Some of the rooms were hot beds for tuberculosis and other contagious diseases, yet the place is kept open." [11]

Instead of demanding that landlords repair their tenement houses or close them, city officials blamed blacks for the conditions found in their neighborhoods. The Board of Health reported in 1910 that the high death rate in black neighborhoods resulted from a "general want of knowledge in respect to proper sanitary and hygienic precautions." Several years after the enactment of the new tenement law, the 1913 health report clearly indicated the racial views of its authors.

On Pearl Street there are two large negro tenements popularly known as the "Tin House" and "Cave Hill." These places have been remodeled and repaired so as to bring them within the law, but the tenants are of a low, degraded class of negroes, who recognize neither moral nor civil law. They live in unbelievable filth. Repeatedly the Tenement House Inspector visits these houses, orders them to clean up, and personally superintends the cleaning. Within a few weeks another inspection reveals conditions almost as bad.

Among the white tenements much greater success has been met along this line. The tenants seem to realize how much more comfortable they are since their homes are repaired and cleaned, and have been striving to reach a higher standard of cleanliness. [12]

Kemp's study revealed that a higher percentage of blacks lived in unfit houses and deteriorating neighborhoods than native or foreign-born whites. Blacks comprised 53 percent of the residents of these dwellings compared to 32 percent native whites and 15 percent foreign whites. Yet, ironically, even Kemp proved unsympathetic to the plight of black tenants. She said, on the one hand, that it was distressing to see a large number of whites accepting such horrible living accommodations. On the other hand, she dismissed the fact that a much higher percentage of blacks lived in substandard dwellings. "Negroes," she explained, "take such conditions with a sort of come-day-go-day, happy-go-lucky philosophy and make merry at their discomforts." It is obvious that while reformers like Kemp could accurately describe the conditions they observed, their conclusions, and hence their recommendations, were constrained by their racial prejudices. Perhaps these reformers were concerned when black conditions affected the city as a whole, but unconcerned about helping blacks for humanitarian reasons. [13]

11. *Law of the Tenement, City of Louisville* (Louisville, 1910); *Survey*, XXIII (December 18, 1909), 391–94; Indianapolis *Freeman*, April 6, 1912.

12. Louisville Board of Aldermen, *Annual Reports, City of Louisville, 1905* (Louisville, 1905), 426: idem., *Annual Reports, City of Louisville, 1910*, 507; idem., *Annual Reports, City of Louisville, 1913*, 444–45.

13. Kemp, *Tenement House Commission*, 77. Lilian Brandt, a white social worker in

Four years after the completion of the Kemp study, investigative reporter Robert T. Berry of the *Courier-Journal* tried to find the most densely populated block in Louisville. Before starting his assignment, Berry met with social workers who described to him several areas where whites lived under extremely bad conditions. His own investigation revealed that a black area in the east end, bordered by Clay and Shelby Streets on the east and west, and Fehr and Jefferson Streets on the north and south, was the worst area by far. (Although this was primarily a black neighborhood, a handful of white immigrants—Irish, German, Italian, Russian, and Greek—lived there too.) All of the houses had narrow passageways. There were no back yards, no grass, no trees, "nothing save small brick pavements and stairways to the upper floors." The area had 83 buildings containing 447 rooms. About 500 people were listed as living in the block. But, returning to the area late one evening, Berry quickly discovered that the actual number of people living in the block was considerably higher: "Men lie prone on cots and bits of bedding thrown on floors. Children are huddled into the arms of parents; men and women, ten a dozen, fifteen of them in a single room. Their night clothes are the same they wear on the streets during the day." [14]

While inside the homes during the day, Berry noticed that sickness and disorder were the norm. He found a woman suffering from paralysis, another woman and a small child both ill with pneumonia, several cases of typhoid fever, and many severe cases of rheumatism. Berry commented on the "strange co-mingling of stifling odors" found in many of the homes. This resulted from the dampness, the breath of many sleepers in poorly ventilated rooms, and the almost continuous fires. The women cooked during the day and dried clothes on the same fires at night. Yet, after presenting his moving description of the human tragedy found in the Clay Street area, Berry concluded with a familiar comment. He said the residents had a carefree attitude toward life. Much happiness abounded among them. In fact, since there were no playgrounds or parks, the children played merrily in the streets and gutters.

An additional burden for Louisville's black poor was that their neigh-

---

St. Louis, did an excellent job of depicting most of the hardships suffered by blacks. Yet she too was a product of her time and stereotyped blacks and minimized their suffering. "A nickel's worth of bananas and watermelon will content a Negro for a day. For this reason, although poverty is palpably great and widespread among the Negroes here, it probably does not mean so much as one would at first view suppose." See Brandt, "The Negroes of St. Louis," 203–304.

14. *Courier-Journal*, October 5, 1913.

borhoods continued to be a haven for criminals. Reporter Robert Berry noted the high number of criminals in the block he investigated: "Saloons and disreputable houses bob up in the neighborhood, among negroes especially, and agents are at work to foster and encourage the use of drugs, cocaine in particular." Moreover, criminal activities were carried on openly in black neighborhoods. Opium could be purchased at numerous "joints" between Liberty and Broadway. Houses of prostitution abounded throughout the area, with most of them catering to whites. According to one account, anyone walking through the black district at night stood a good chance of being accosted by pimps and prostitutes. Gambling was widespread, with many poolrooms, stores, and residences equipped with gambling paraphernalia.[15]

Louisville witnessed several drives against crime in the early 1900s. White civic leaders, church leaders, and black organizations would investigate crime and finally, with enough publicity, get the police to act. The most exhaustive attempt to end the red-light district occurred in 1907 under the interim administration of Robert Bingham. That July, hundreds of whites and blacks were arrested and about 300 gambling games halted. Several weeks later the police conducted a series of drug raids, netting 200 people, most of whom were blacks, involved in selling cocaine, opium, and other narcotics. Most of the people were convicted in police court, while others without visible means of support were forced to leave town. Yet even this effort did not end crime in black neighborhoods, especially in the district from Seventh to Fourteenth Streets and Jefferson to Broadway. Black neighborhoods continued to be hounded by crime and vice because law enforcement officials directed their attacks primarily on the easily identifiable "black shadies"—drug pushers, numbers runners, gamblers, pimps, and prostitutes—leaving untouched the undesirable whites who frequented the black district.[16]

Despite its high crime rate, by 1910 Louisville's black community offered numerous services and activities. Many of the leisure-time activities of Afro-Americans were centered around Tenth and Chestnut Streets, an area containing the Western Colored Library, the YMCA, ice cream stands, and several theaters. But starting in 1915 the main attraction in the area became the Kentucky Pythian Temple, billed by the Knights of Pythian as "The Finest Hotel and Office Building Owned and Operated by Colored People in the World." The knights specialized in bringing live entertain-

15. *Ibid.* See also *Report of the Vice Commission of Louisville, Ky.* (Louisville, 1915).
16. *Courier-Journal*, July 15, 1907, February 1, 1908; *Evening Post*, August 5, 1907.

ment to the Temple, with the Rathskeller becoming popular for its "up-to-date and modern cabaret." Throughout the decade dances were held practically every Friday and Saturday night in the large banquet hall. According to a local black newspaper, teenagers attended these dances and many of them became intoxicated from the whisky that was readily available. So much activity occurred at the Temple that several pimps and prostitutes moved into the area, hoping to attract new business.[17]

West Walnut Street was even more exciting than Tenth and Chestnut. A score of pool halls and night spots were prominently located along the street, plus several barber and beauty shops, ice cream stands, three theaters, the two finest black-owned restaurants in Louisville, and four public halls. Unfortunately, the black "shadies" worked in the Walnut Street area as well. Several ice cream stands served as fronts for gambling. Also, Charles "Cocky" Reed, a "bad man with several killings to his credit," sold narcotics in the area for more than a decade. Reed was eventually given a three-year sentence in federal prison and fined $3,000, a sum he paid before leaving the courthouse.[18]

III.

It is not surprising that many blacks sought housing outside the areas of high black concentration. As mentioned earlier, a few blacks in the early 1900s did purchase homes west of the downtown district on such streets as Magazine, Madison, Chestnut, and Walnut (see map 4). These blacks, primarily ministers, teachers, and businessmen, cited high crime in the downtown area and a desire to live in nice homes and neighborhoods that received adequate city services as their reasons for moving into integrated neighborhoods. According to the Indianapolis Freeman, this movement of blacks escalated between 1908 and 1910. The paper predicted that Chestnut Street was destined to become the center of Afro-American life since blacks were rapidly purchasing all available property from Tenth to Twentieth Streets. Indeed, as the city directory reveals, by 1915 this entire section of West Chestnut was all black.[19]

17. Richardson (ed.), The National Cyclopedia, 194–95; Indianapolis Freeman, November 20, 1915; Crisis, XXI (January, 1920), 132.
18. Roscoe C. Grant (ed.), The 1921 Louisville Colored Business, Professional, Religious, and Educational Directory (Louisville, 1921); Louisville Leader, February 26, March 28, December 24, 1921.
19. Indianapolis Freeman, May 2, 1908, October 9, 1909, January 22, 1910. C. K. Caron, Directory of Louisville, 1915 (Louisville, 1915), 1647–48.

Local whites realized that blacks were moving in sizeable numbers into the city's west end. In many cities, organized efforts by whites prevented blacks from purchasing property in certain areas,[20] but similar attempts in Louisville had failed. City officials and civic leaders showed little interest in the matter, assuming that the cost of housing would largely dictate where blacks could live. In Louisville, therefore, the movement to enact an ordinance to prevent blacks from moving into white neighborhoods was led by the lower-middle-class whites, the very people who feared that blacks would overrun their neighborhoods. This group ultimately convinced city officials of the seriousness of the matter and of the need to do something. They also let it be known that they would campaign against any alderman who sympathized with blacks.

On November 14, 1913, W. D. Binford, the superintendent of the mechanical department of the *Courier-Journal* and *Times*, gave an address before the Louisville Real Estate Exchange advocating the passage of a residential segregation ordinance. Binford began by saying: "There is no problem so grave, nor one fraught with so much danger to property values as the gradual influx of the negro into blocks or squares where none but whites reside. It is not necessary for me to inform you that this menace has cost the city many thousands of dollars in taxes, to say nothing of the loss of propety owners." He explained that many whites rented instead of buying a home for fear of becoming trapped next to black neighbors. "Why should this migratory movement of whites from 'pillar to post' to avoid contact with a negro as a neighbor be continued when there is a remedy for such a condition?" Binford asked. His most crucial point, and one that other advocates of residential segregation would use, was that blacks moved into white neighborhoods for mercenary reasons only. Binford explained that blacks who moved into white areas expected to receive a "prohibitive bonus" from the white residents if they offered to leave the neighborhood. A segregation ordinance, he said, would prevent blacks from moving into white neighborhoods and would be a "protection to the property owners in Louisville who have sacrificed so much in the past from the effects of the negro's presence." Binford piously concluded that a residential segregation ordinance would be good for race relations.[21]

The initial reactions of local whites to Binford's suggestion of a residential segregation ordinance were varied. Two members of the Real Estate Exchange disapproved of such an ordinance, while two other mem-

20. For tactics used by whites in another border city to prevent blacks from moving into their neighborhoods, see Brandt, "The Negroes of St. Louis," 224–25.
21. *Courier-Journal*, November 15, 1913.

bers agreed with Binford that Louisville needed such a statute. The *Courier-Journal* took a neutral position, but two other local daily papers, the *Times* and the *Post*, supported the idea. In an editorial, the *Times* reported on the disastrous effect of blacks moving into white neighborhoods.

There are many sections of the city where property values have deteriorated almost 50 percent through the influx of colored people. Some of these neighborhoods, notably portions of West Walnut and West Chestnut Streets, were not only peopled exclusively by whites at one time, but were among the most fashionable portions of the city. Negroes who could afford it began buying homes in these sections a number of years ago, and with their entry the whites took their departure.[22]

Binford's call for a segregation ordinance encouraged whites who lived in districts bordering black areas to begin working for legislation to prevent the integration of their neighborhoods. They formed neighborhood associations and urged their councilmen to enact a segregation law. Their efforts led to action by the city council and the introduction of a segregation ordinance on December 16, 1913. City councilmen voted 21–0 in favor of the ordinance on March 17, 1914, and then sent the measure to the Board of Aldermen. The aldermen unanimously passed the measure and sent it to Mayor John Bushemeyer, who signed the residential segregation ordinance on May 11, 1914.[23]

The practice of enacting residential segregation ordinances to prevent blacks from moving into white neighborhoods began in border and southern cities in 1910. Baltimore passed the first one in December 1910, but a month later the Maryland Supreme Court declared it unconstitutional. Baltimore officials enacted a second segregation ordinance on April 7, 1911, and the court struck it down in June 1913. City legislators then introduced a third segregation ordinance; the court, instead of ruling on the constitutionality of the ordinance at that time, decided to postpone its decision until after the United States Supreme Court ruled on the Louisville ordinance. In 1912, Winston-Salem and Mooresville, North Carolina, passed residential segregation ordinances. The North Carolina Supreme Court, in April 1914, declared the Winston-Salem ordinance unconstitutional. Yet other cities continued to pass similar ordinances. In 1913 alone, Madisonville (Kentucky), Birmingham, Atlanta, Richmond, Norfolk, Roanoke, and Asheville set up housing restrictions for blacks. By 1916, St.

22. Louisville *Times*, May 11, 1914; Roger L. Rice, "Residential Segregation by Law, 1910–1917," *Journal of Southern History*, XXXIV (May, 1968), 184.
23. Charles H. Parrish, Albert E. Meyzeek, and J. B. Colbert (eds.), *The History of Louisville Segregation Case and the Decision of the Supreme Court* (Louisville, 1918), 3–7; Louisville *Times*, March 19, 1914; Indianapolis *Freeman*, April 11, 1914.

Louis, Dallas, and several other cities in Texas and Oklahoma had joined the segregation movement. Real estate dealers and whites living in districts bordering on black neighborhoods in St. Louis had been trying since 1910 to pass such an ordinance, and advocates of residential segregation voted in a new city charter that called for direct legislation. As expected, the first ordinance approved under the new charter for St. Louis called for residential segregation.[24]

The promoters of the Louisville segregation ordinance hoped to avoid the flaws of other ordinances by embodying the concept of equal protection in the Fourteenth Amendment by applying their measure equally to whites as well as blacks. The first three sections of the ordinance prohibited blacks from moving into predominantly white neighborhoods and whites from moving into black neighborhoods. Section four said that the ordinance did not affect the location of residences in Louisville made before May 11, 1914. But if a house became vacant after that date, only members of the race last living in the house could move into it. Sections five and six discussed the procedure to be followed when building new homes. In essence, these sections prohibited blacks from constructing homes in white areas and vice versa. Section seven instructed the city's building inspector to prepare a map of all the blocks in Louisville, designating which blocks were reserved for each race. The last section stated that anyone violating the ordinance would be fined no less than $5 nor more than $50 for each day of occupying property in violation of the ordinance. Louisville officials hoped that their carefully worded segregation ordinance would become a model for other cities desiring to segregate the races.[25]

Black Louisvillians rallied around the issue of housing segregation and successfully fought the ordinance through the courts. The eventual overturning of the ordinance led to the expected result of opening more neighborhoods to middle- and upper-class blacks. Yet many of these blacks had always escaped the worst housing by living on certain blocks in the western section of Magazine, Chestnut, and Walnut Streets. However, nothing

24. *Crisis*, XV (December, 1917), 69. For a view of residential segregation in Baltimore, see W. Ashbie Hawkins, "A Year of Segregation in Baltimore," *Crisis*, III (November, 1911), 27–30. For residential segregation in St. Louis see *Survey*, XXXV (February 26, 1916), 627, and (March 11, 1916), 694; see also Lawrence O. Christensen, "Black St. Louis: A Study in Race Relations, 1865–1916," (Ph.D. dissertation, University of Missouri-Columbia, 1972), chap. 9. For additional information on residential segregation laws, see *Survey*, XXXIII (October 17, 1914), 72.

25. *Eleventh Biennial Compilation of General Ordinances of the City of Louisville, 1915* (Louisville, 1916), 548–52.

altered the fact that poor blacks continued to live in congested, crime-ridden areas. Indeed, throughout the 1920s, Louisville's civic leaders called for housing reforms and conducted additional "drives on crime" to rid the black community of thieves, drug addicts, pimps, and prostitutes. These efforts were futile. Tragically, the deplorable conditions described in the Kemp Report of 1909 still existed fifteen years later. As a 1924 survey of black tenement housing explained:

> Typical tenement conditions are four frame structures facing . . . on Thirteenth and Maple and Malt Alley. These are old two story buildings. They contain three apartments, of two rooms each. They are thirty inches apart with windows facing each other. Only those apartments on the ends have sufficient light so that lamps do not have to be burned all day. Each apartment contains a family of from three to nine or ten persons, the four houses containing over 100 people, for which four common outdoor toilets in the backyard are provided.[26]

Another report, published toward the end of the decade, echoed this finding: "Louisville has a large downtown area, with fair conditions in housing facing the streets and extremely unsanitary and unhealthful conditions in alley houses. Satisfied or ignorant families live in houses not fit for work animals; children are familiar with vice before they start to school; and unattached men and women who work in tobacco factories lodge with families in rooms." [27] Despite these two vivid reports, city officials refused to adopt any new housing measures. Maybe they were discouraged, realizing that all previous tenement reforms had failed. Another reason for their lack of action might have been the persistent belief that the leading causes for the deplorable conditions in the tenements were the laziness and lack of cleanliness of the tenants themselves.

26. Haven Emerson and Anna Phillips (eds.), *Hospitals and Health Agencies of Louisville, 1924, A Survey* (Louisville, 1925), 42–43.
27. Thomas Jackson Woofter, *et al.*, *Negro Problems in Cities* (New York, 1928), 103.

5

Community Life

The rapid growth of Louisville after the Civil War put a tremendous strain on existing institutions trying to solve social problems. Local churches, active in community work before the war, continued to promote moral and religious uplift. The magnitude of the problems in the city, however, made it necessary for other institutions besides the church to tackle urban problems. Local government officials and white civic leaders responded by establishing orphan homes, sanatoriums, reform schools for delinquent girls and boys, kindergartens for the children of working mothers, and Young Men's and Young Women's Christian Associations as places of learning and recreation.

Urban progressives in Louisville established settlement houses to help improve living conditions in tenement housing districts and to aid rural and foreign whites to make the transition to life in the city. This was, of course, part of a much larger national movement which saw the growth of settlement houses all across the United States in the 1890s. Mrs. Gross Alexander established the city's first settlement house, Louisville Wesley House, in 1893 in an area dominated by poor foreign immigrants. Mrs. Alexander and her associates provided the residents of the area with free legal aid, a branch library, and religious instruction on Sunday. In 1896 the work of the Louisville Neighborhood House began in an abandoned saloon in a neighborhood of Jewish immigrants. Archibald A. Hill started the work with financial backing from Miss Lucy Belknap and the Jewish Federated Charities of Louisville. Hill organized a playground, a library, a kindergarten, a pure milk station, and had public baths constructed. The directors of the Louisville Neighborhood House agitated for a juvenile court and truancy laws, labor laws to protect women and children, and housing reform.[1]

Through the efforts of local government officials, civic leaders, charity organizations, and churches, white Louisvillians had numerous social

1. Robert Woods and Albert Kennedy, *Handbook of Settlements* (New York, 1970), vi, 89–90; Francis M. Ingram, "The Settlement Movement in the South," *World Outlook*, XXVII (May, 1937), 13.

and welfare institutions by the 1910s, including the Catholic Orphan Society, Children's Free Hospital, Home of the Innocents, Children's Protective Association, Jennie Cassaday Rest Cottage, the Salvation Army, Union Gospel Mission, and King's Daughters Home for Incurables. These institutions cared for the sick, sheltered the homeless, and fed the hungry. All of these institutions refused services to Afro-Americans.

But under Louisville's polite racism, and often because of genuine humanitarian concern, whites aided blacks in sustaining several institutions that served the Afro-American community. "There are a number of institutions of this nature (doing charity work) in Louisville supported largely by Negroes," wrote a black educator to Professor W. E. B. DuBois, "but not one that I know of supported entirely by them. The white people in this community are very friendly, and give generously to charity, regardless of race or creed." Another correspondent also praised local whites for supporting black institutions: "These organizations are doing much good, and while maintained and managed by colored people are largely and generously supported by white people." [2]

It must be noted, however, that long before whites started contributing to black welfare causes, local blacks had started and sustained their own institutions. Largely because of white indifference after the Civil War, blacks through their churches conducted schools, opened institutions to care for the sick and homeless, and aided newcomers in their transition to city life. Afro-Americans continued and expanded these activities in the 1880s and 1890s, when white racism reached a peak and very few black causes could rely on support or even sympathy from whites. Some black institutions in Louisville started receiving white support around the turn of the century, meaning that blacks had maintained these institutions by themselves for twenty-five to thirty years in most cases. Moreover, the church, the most important black institution, received little or no white support. It is true that several local churches did receive small donations from whites, but the vast majority were completely independent and conducted a variety of programs for their people. That Louisville blacks were able to start and sustain a college, a hospital, an orphanage, and several other important institutions is remarkable when the overall poverty of their community is considered. Their institutions could not rely on large endowments from a handful of wealthy philanthropists; instead it took hundreds of blacks contributing small amounts to keep their institutions afloat.

2. W. E. B. DuBois (ed.), *Efforts for Social Betterment Among Negro Americans*, Atlanta University Publications, no. 14 (Atlanta, 1909), 47.

Afro-Americans in communities all across the country saw the necessity of creating or expanding institutions during the late-nineteenth century. In some of the northern cities, such as Cleveland, blacks argued about the merits of establishing separate institutions, fearing that they might be contributing to their own segregation. But in Louisville, and most surely farther south, blacks were under no illusions about being accepted in white institutions. Therefore, they worked consistently to keep their institutional life thriving. Whether in the North, South, East, or West, by the early 1900s black communities of all sizes were imbued with a sense of self-help and a spirit of togetherness.[3]

I.

The church sustained black folk during slavery and the early days of freedom and continued to provide valuable assistance during the last decades of the nineteenth century. By 1900 Louisville had about sixty-six black churches, mostly Baptist, and not all of them were involved in a social gospel. But the largest Baptist churches and a few other denominations were consistently involved in supporting the institutional life and lending their voices to numerous civil rights causes.

Led by three able ministers over the years and a host of community leaders, Fifth Street Baptist was the best example of a total church in Louisville. The first pastor, Henry Adams, served thirty-three years, his successor, Andrew H. Heath, pastored for fourteen years, and John H. Frank followed with fifty-three years of service. An enduring period of stability of leadership enabled Fifth Street to remain free of much of the internal dissension that too often occurred when churches selected new ministers. In the early 1870s, the church's trustees unanimously agreed to set out boxes of clothing for the poor of the community, regardless of whether they attended the church. They also agreed to pay for funerals for poor members, and during the Depression of 1873 the church started giving financial aid to destitute members. In June 1876, the church increased from $1 to $3 per week the amount to be given to some of the poor. This amount compared favorably with the weekly wages paid to laborers at that time. The church viewed taking care of its members during harsh times as an important part of its mission. Moreover, Fifth Street sacrificed having a

3. Kusmer, *A Ghetto Takes Shape*, 124; Mary C. Terrell, "Society Among the Colored People of Washington," *Voice of the Negro* (April, 1904), 150–56.

large bank account in order to aid its members. Repeatedly in each quarter, Fifth Street's bank account showed only a small balance after the church had paid expenses and given to the poor.[4]

Fifth Street was also involved in other philanthropic work. Like most black churches, Fifth Street gave annually to support "the missionary cause in Africa." The church held annual fundraising drives for the black orphanage, the old folks home, and the local college. For several years, the church awarded a college scholarship, preferably to one of its members but open to the community at large. In spite of all its efforts, the church still acknowledged that too many people were not being reached at all. Therefore, in October 1888 a committee was organized "to canvass the neighborhood looking for non-regular members, new members, and to look after the sick and administer to their temporal and spiritual wants."[5]

Most of the other Baptist churches could not compete with the program of Fifth Street, but they nevertheless made important contributions to the Afro-American community. Such churches as Green Street, Calvary, and Zion had large congregations who were attracted to the churches by the dynamic pastors. Rev. Charles H. Parrish of Calvary, William Craighead of Zion, and D. A. Gaddie of Green Street were active in all movements against discrimination, gave liberally to local welfare institutions, and used their large congregations to extract political patronage. These three men were outstanding role models for their church members. All of them were born slaves and had struggled to receive an education. They preached constantly of the value of hard work. Moreover, they provided decades of strong leadership for their churches. Parrish pastored for forty-six years, Craighead for forty-nine, and Gaddie for thirty-nine.[6]

In a remarkable show of unity, Louisville Baptist churches and their counterparts throughout the state formed a joint organization and established a college. In 1866, Rev. Henry Adams of Fifth Street called for a convention of black Baptist ministers. The men attending the convention

4. George A. Hampton, *History of Fifth Street Baptist Church* (Louisville, n.d.); Parrish (ed.), *Golden Jubilee*, 281; Minutes of Fifth Street, January 3, 1870, June 14, October 11, 1876, May 9, 1883.

5. Minutes of Fifth Street, December 18, 1872, August 26, October 13, 1874, July 17, 1878, November 9, 1881, October 31, 1888.

6. *History of Calvary Baptist Church, 1872–1958* (Louisville, 1958); Parrish (ed.), *Golden Jubilee*, 174; John Miles (ed.), *Calvary Baptist Church* (Louisville, 1969); *Zion Baptist Church, 1878–1953* (Louisville, 1953), 2–4; Minutes of Green Street, September 17, 1872, November 10, 1911; Indianapolis *Freeman*, July 20, 1901. See the *Leader*, June 24, 1936, for the story of Rev. John H. Perdue who pastored Emmanuel Baptist Church for forty-one years.

organized the General Association of Negro Baptists in Kentucky, and they called for the establishment of a school to train young men and women in Christian work. They agreed to ask their respective church members to contribute five cents monthly toward the start of the school. The first substantial steps toward organizing the school occurred in 1869 when the General Association obtained a charter and purchased Fort Hill in Frankfort as the site for their school. But the leaders of the General Association, upon close inspection of the property, decided that it was inadequate for their needs and quickly sold Fort Hill. William H. Steward, the leading layman in the General Association and the state's leading black, then selected a location in Louisville on Kentucky Street between Seventh and Eighth Streets for the school. The organization purchased the two-and-one-half-acre tract, including two large brick buildings, for $13,800.[7]

Their school, Kentucky Normal and Theological Institute, finally opened November 25, 1879. Founders of the school believed the problems confronting the race could be solved by mutual confidence, unity, industry, education, and morality. They adopted ambitious goals for their school: to build character; to prepare young blacks for service to God, country, and the race; to meet the demand in Kentucky for a higher level of studies for blacks than that found in common schools; to train ministers to lead the people; to prepare women to care for the sick and helpless; and to develop the bodies as well as the minds of their students.[8]

Kentucky Normal offered theological training, elementary and secondary education, college courses, and specialized training for women. Like most black schools of its day, Kentucky Normal also offered industrial training to help fill the shortage of skilled black workers. This was, of course, also a way of attracting donations from white businessmen. Under its charter, Kentucky Normal received the right to be the only black institution in the state to offer degrees in law and medicine. Therefore, in the mid-1880s Louisville National Medical College and Central Law School became affiliated with the school. For years the law school was under the direction of local attorney Albert S. White. It was usually very small, and unfortunately it never ranked with the better Negro law schools in the country. The medical school, one of five all-black medical schools in the

7. A number of sources discuss the founding of Kentucky Normal and Theological Institute. See Simmons, "What the Colored People Are Doing," 85–90; Elisha W. Green, *Life of Rev. Elisha W. Green, One of the Founders of the Kentucky Normal and Theological Institute* (Maysville, Ky., 1888); Marrs, *Life of Marrs*, 122–29; Richings, *Evidences of Progress*, 55.

8. *State University Catalogue 1883–84* (Louisville, 1883).

nation during this time, was much better organized. Dr. Henry Fitzbutler founded and directed the program of the medical school, which fortunately had a spacious two-story brick building and was able to offer courses in bacteriology, histology, and pathology. Normally, the medical school had five teachers and fifteen students. By the early 1900s it had awarded eighty-three medical degrees. After the establishment of the law and medical schools, the founders of Kentucky Normal changed the name of the school to State University, a name they believed better expressed their varied program.[9]

As was the case with most black institutions, State University had a weak financial base which led to weak academic programs. Financial support for the operation of the college came from the General Association, white missionary societies, and tuition and fees paid by the students. Student fees, which averaged $100 a year in the 1880s, were insufficient to operate the school. Whites connected with Walnut Street Baptist Church and Southern Baptist Theological Seminary gave small yearly donations and formed an advisory board to help State University solicit additional funding. Grants from the American Baptist Home Mission Society proved critical to the operation of the school. The society gave $1,500 a year during the school's first three years and increased its yearly grant to $2,500 in 1882. Also, the school's administrators and trustees raised money. Nevertheless, throughout its existence the school limped along, barely able to pay its expenses. Without needed funding, most of the university's programs, except industrial training, suffered. Indeed, though calling itself a university, for all practical purposes the school was little more than a normal school in which students acquired the rudiments of an education.[10]

State University, despite its limitations, was important to black Louisville. It was their own institution, something they had created. Furthermore, State University trained many of the future black leaders of Louisville and Kentucky. For a number of years only Berea College and State University offered college training to black Kentuckians, and the adoption

9. *Ibid.*; W.E.B. DuBois (ed.), *The Health and Physique of the Negro American*, Atlanta University Publications, no. 11 (Atlanta, 1906), 95–96.

10. Indianapolis *Freeman*, September 11, 1909; *28th Annual Announcement of State University and 20th Announcement of Louisville Medical College* (Louisville, 1908). The records of State University have largely been preserved, see Department of Archives and Records, University of Louisville. W. E. B. DuBois (ed.), *The College Bred Negro American*, Atlanta University Publications, no. 15 (Atlanta, 1910), 12, 22. DuBois was very critical of State University. He noted that the school had only eighteen students in grades four through eight, and one hundred in grades nine through twelve. He concluded that both the thoroughness and the quality of the work were poor.

of the Day law in 1904, prohibiting blacks and whites from attending the same school, left State University as Kentucky's only college for blacks.[11] The quality of the education might have been poor, but for blacks it was State University or nothing. As one visitor to the school's campus noted, "I forgot about the grotesqueness of the surroundings when learning how these poor people had shouldered a debt of $13,000 in buying the building; how they kept up the running expenses of the school without encroaching on what they had 'laid down' for the payment of the property; how they organized a band of 'jubilee singers' to lift at the wheel, and so on."[12]

The Baptists were not alone in attempting to uplift the race. The Methodist ministers often took the lead in racial movements. It was no coincidence that the streetcar demonstrations of 1870–1871 were led and sustained by members of Quinn Chapel AME. Starting with that incident, Quinn Chapel gained a reputation for being a strong champion of racial causes. Through the years, blacks from all over the city, including non-churchgoers, turned to that church whenever a crisis developed. Another Methodist church, Center Street CME, was served by a succession of well-educated ministers who devoted time to civic work. For example, Rev. Charles H. Phillips, a graduate of Central Tennessee College and Meharry Medical College, became pastor of the church in November 1891. During his short tenure of twenty-two months in Louisville, Phillips worked unceasingly on numerous community activities. He preached to fraternal orders, devoted time to local school affairs, and worked closely with the organizers of State University. It was largely due to his efforts that the Afro-American community agitated for a house of refuge for young girls arrested on misdemeanor violations. He, like many of the city's black ministers, also served on the statewide Anti-Separate Coach organization.[13]

Broadway Temple AME Zion Church rivaled Fifth Street Baptist in the makeup of its members and its varied program. By the dawning of the

11. Kentucky State Normal and Industrial Institute for Colored People, offering elementary and secondary training, was established in Frankfort by the Kentucky State Legislature in 1886. It was not until 1931 that Kentucky State became an accredited four-year college. Many of the first instructors at the school had received training at State University. See Kentucky Commission on Human Rights, *Kentucky's Black Heritage* (Frankfort, 1971), 39–40; *Berea College* v. *Kentucky*, 211 U.S. 245.

12. The quote comes from Nobel Lovely Prentis, *Southern Letters* (Topeka, 1881), 10–11. Indianapolis *World*, October 22, 1892, contains a highly complimentary view of State University.

13. Charles H. Phillips, *From the Farm to the Bishopric* (Nashville, 1932), 101–24; Walters, *My Life and Work*, 38–39.

new century, Broadway Temple could boast of having many of the younger black professionals and businessmen as members. These successful blacks showed their commitment to improvements for the entire race by sponsoring welfare programs and by contributing regularly to the orphanage and St. James Old Folks Home. Broadway Temple could also be proud of the succession of strong dynamic men who pastored the church before moving up the ranks in the church hierarchy. George Clement, the best known of the group, served Broadway Temple for several years in the early 1900s. He left to assume the position of editor of the AME Zion national newspaper, *The Star of Zion*. Elected bishop, Clement returned to Louisville in 1916 and became one of the few blacks capable of communicating effectively with the white establishment.[14]

Two other ministers, Rev. Leroy Ferguson of the Church of Our Merciful Savior and Rev. E. G. Harris of Plymouth Congregational, were close associates of white leaders and wielded enormous influence in the black community. Whites found Ferguson's social gospel acceptable: he stressed the middle-class virtues of thrift, industry, and determination as essential for uplifting the race. He had harsh words for black parents who allowed their children to enter saloons and other "dens of sin" in the city. Ferguson, well known in philanthropic circles, received several donations to his church from Andrew Carnegie. Rev. Harris came to Louisville in 1893 and started a number of social programs. In the early 1900s, he purchased three tenement houses which he leased out. His most ambitious plan, however, was a settlement house which he began raising money for in 1910 and completed seven years later. But what probably most attracted blacks, especially middle- and upper-class ones, to Plymouth Congregational was Harris's influence in the "right places." Over the years he aided blacks in getting jobs as teachers and as servants in the homes of wealthy whites.[15]

Although Harris and Ferguson were highly respected and active for years (Harris, for example, remained at his church for more than four de-

14. Indianapolis *Freeman*, December 25, 1915. Broadway Temple has preserved numerous scrapbooks and pamphlets. See *Souvenir Program, Twenty-fifth General Conference AME Zion Church, Broadway Temple, Louisville, Kentucky, May 1916* (Charlotte, N.C., 1916); *Centennial Celebration, Broadway Temple*; Jesse B. Colbert (ed.), *General Conference Handbook of the 25th Quadrennial Session of the AME Zion Church held in Broadway Temple, Louisville, Kentucky, May 3–21, 1916* (Louisville, 1916).

15. Indianapolis *Freeman*, January 28, October 21, November 25, 1911; George F. Bragg, *History of the Afro-American Group of the Episcopal Church* (Baltimore, 1922), 236; *Brief History of Plymouth Congregational Church* (Louisville, n.d.). Several interviewees

cades), their congregations were small in comparison with the city's other prominent black churches. Neither the Church of Our Merciful Savior nor Plymouth Congregational had more than 200 members at any one time. Most blacks complained that the services at both churches lacked emotionalism. Furthermore, both Harris and Ferguson were not regarded as great exhorters. Undoubtedly, many less-educated blacks felt uncomfortable worshipping with the black professionals who dominated the two churches.[16]

Louisville's single Catholic church for Negroes, St. Augustine, had even fewer members. At no time from its inception in the 1860s to 1920 did more than 120 people claim affiliation with the church. Nevertheless, the Catholic church developed several programs to aid its largely poor black members. No doubt, white Catholic officials started many programs at St. Augustine to keep blacks from being a part of these activities at white parishes. From its location at Fourteenth and Broadway, St. Augustine ran a small house to care for indigent blacks, especially senior citizens. The church offered a parochial education to Catholic children. Concern about the high crime rate and juvenile delinquency in its area led the Catholic church to establish the House of the Good Shepherd for girls. With the permission of juvenile authorities or a girl's parents, church officials placed wayward girls in the House of the Good Shepherd and instructed them in citizenship, cooking, and sewing. By the early 1900s, the house was caring for about 105 girls a year, saving many of them from spending time in the city jail, a breeding ground for criminals.[17]

Second in importance to the churches in black community life were the lodges. During 1870–1910, "the golden age of Negro secret societies," many well-developed organizations that were popular in black communities throughout the United States proliferated in Louisville. By 1900 there were at least 67 lodges with 7,535 members. Blacks established these lodges primarily to exploit the economic and recreational pos-

mentioned that Rev. Harris was very influential in getting appointments for blacks who followed him: Lyman T. Johnson, interview with author, Louisville, January 3, 1976; Parrish interview, January 5, 1976; William H. Perry, Jr., interview with author, Louisville, May 20, 1976.

16. Bragg, *History of the Afro-American Group of the Episcopal Church*, 236. Plymouth had 114 members in 1904 and 174 in 1908. For financial information on Plymouth Congregational, see "The Annual Report of Plymouth Congregational Church" (Louisville). Indianapolis *Freeman*, January 28, 1911.

17. Indianapolis *Freeman*, September 25, 1909; John T. Gillard, *The Catholic Church and the American Negro* (Baltimore, 1924), 58, 178, 201.

sibilities available through them. To many blacks fraternal societies signified the apex of self-help and racial solidarity. Moreover, these societies often gave blacks invaluable business training and provided the foundation for insurance companies, banks, and other commercial enterprises.[18]

The Masons, the Odd Fellows, the United Brothers of Friendship, and the Knights of Pythians were the leading fraternal orders in Louisville's black community. Freemasonry had the longest history among blacks in America: Prince Hall established African Lodge No. 459 in 1784 when he received a warrant from the Grand Lodge of England after being denied a chapter by white Freemasons in Massachusetts. Louisville blacks founded a chapter in 1850, but Freemasonry only began to grow in the city after being officially incorporated in the state in 1866. For a time the Louisville lodges were under the jurisdiction of the Ohio Masons. But in 1875, they broke free and this started the unprecedented growth of black Masons in Louisville and throughout Kentucky. By the early 1900s, there were fifteen lodges in Louisville alone and a total of forty-eight in Kentucky.[19]

The Masons assigned themselves worthy functions: purchasing property, caring for sick members, watching over the families of deceased members, and building men of good character. During a time when health and life insurance policies were rare for everyone, the Masons' way of aiding members during illnesses and deaths proved to be an important benefit. All of the lodges, large and small, set aside money in case their members suffered hard times. Like many other organizations in the Afro-American community, the Masons strived to build the character of the race by providing role models for the young. They took seriously the oath that all Masons pledged: to be honest and sober at all times. And, as part of their strong belief in uplifting each other, Masons were expected to aid any fellow Mason in times of need. Throughout the late nineteenth century, the Masons purchased small pieces of property in Louisville. They did this to have a meeting place and a recreational center, and above all as a symbol of black financial success through cooperation.[20]

Several members of the Center Street AME church formed Louisville's

18. Edward M. Palmer, "Negro Secret Societies," *Social Forces* XXIII (December, 1944), 209–10.

19. *Ibid.*, 208; W. H. Grimshaw, *Official History of Freemasonry Among the Colored People in North America* (New York, 1903), 231; Weeden, *History of the Colored People*, 54; W. E. B. DuBois (ed.), *Economic Co-Operation Among Negro Americans*, Atlanta University Publications, no. 12 (Atlanta, 1907), 109–14.

20. Grimshaw, *Official History of Freemasonry*, 231. DuBois (ed.), *Economic Co-Operation*, 110, reported that by 1907 Kentucky Masons owned property valued at over $40,000.

first order of black Odd Fellows in June 1867. They first called themselves the United Sons of Independence but changed their name to Odd Fellows after receiving literature and aprons from white Odd Fellows. The white Odd Fellows, however, refused to accept the blacks as members in their order. Therefore, with the aid of black Odd Fellows from Cleveland, Louisville blacks organized eight Odd Fellow lodges, which in turn formed the Grand United Order of Odd Fellows in order to pool their resources to purchase property. They first bought a two-story building for $2,500. In 1885 the Grand Order purchased a three-story lodge for $10,000. It was destroyed five years later by a tornado. But the Odd Fellows responded by raising $17,000 to finance the construction of a three-story structure that included a music hall, banquet rooms, storefronts for businesses, and recreational rooms. Besides acquiring property, the Odd Fellows emphasized benevolent endeavors, giving to the orphan home, and supporting racial uplift movements.[21]

Surprisingly, the United Brothers of Friendship started in Louisville and grew into a national fraternal order, ranking in size with the Masons and Odd Fellows. In 1861 Marshall W. Taylor, a common laborer, and several other men formed the United Brothers to provide impoverished blacks with decent burials. During the Civil War their work was expanded to caring for the sick. Taylor's group received a charter in 1868 and formed a state grand lodge. Seven years later the United Brothers had spread from Kentucky to Missouri, Arkansas, Iowa, Texas, and Indiana. By the 1890s the order claimed to have over 200,000 members, making it the largest black fraternal order in the country. With its national headquarters in Louisville, the order and the Sisters of the Mysterious Ten, the female affiliate of the United Brothers, purchased property in the downtown area. Although some fraternal orders acquired property primarily for social reasons, the United Brothers never strayed from its initial purpose. The order opened a refuge for widows and orphans and gave small donations to State University and other institutions. With money flowing in from lodges all over the nation, the United Brothers built a $20,000 hall in Louisville for its golden jubilee anniversary in 1911.[22]

Of the more prominent lodges in Louisville, the Knights of Pythians was undoubtedly the one devoted more to recreational activities than to

21. Weeden, *History of the Colored People*, 42; Indianapolis *Freeman*, April 26, 1890, December 12, 1891. J. J. C. McKinley, *Grand United Order of Odd Fellows in America* (Louisville, 1893); DuBois (ed.), *Economic Co-Operation*, 116–20.

22. William H. Gibson, *The United Brothers of Friendship and Sisters of the Mysterious Ten* (Louisville, 1897); Indianapolis *Freeman*, December 10, 1910, August 12, 1911.

good works. Founded in 1864 in Washington, D.C., the Knights of Pythians first came to Kentucky in the 1880s. Like the other fraternal orders, the Pythians paid sickness and death benefits, but from its start in Louisville the order was far better known for its annual parades and frequent social activities. Appropriately, the Knights of Pythians built the most elegant structure ever owned by a black fraternal order in Louisville. For a decade in the early 1900s Kentucky's 128 Pythian lodges raised money for the construction of Kentucky Pythian Temple. Completed in 1915 at a cost of $130,000, the Temple was viewed as a landmark of black cooperative achievement. Located at Tenth and Chestnut Streets, an area rapidly becoming the heart of the black district, the Temple stood seven stories tall and included five business rooms, a theater, twelve offices "suitable for colored men to carry on their business enterprises," fifty-two sleeping apartments, an amusement hall, a kitchen, dining room, pool room, and elevator. As one observer commented, "practically everything one wants to buy can be secured under the roof of this magnificent temple."[23]

Churches and fraternal orders conducted many needed social activities, but they also tended to divide rather than unite the Afro-American community. Two churches in particular, the Episcopal Church of Our Merciful Savior and Plymouth Congregational, attracted blacks who believed they gained prestige by being associated with churches that were not Baptist or Methodist. According to Rev. Homer E. Nutter, one of the leading black clergymen in Kentucky and a pastor for over fifty years, many blacks attended these churches but maintained their affiliation with Baptist churches. In Louisville the most prestigious black church was always Fifth Street Baptist. The church boasted of having a few black "old families" (free blacks from antebellum days) as members and of attracting a majority of the black elite who migrated to the city. William H. Steward, several members of the medical profession, and two of the city's best-known lawyers, William H. Wright and Albert S. White, headed the list of influential blacks who attended the church. In the early 1900s at least fourteen school teachers also attended the church. Also, faculty and students from State University who were from out of town made Fifth Street their church while in Louisville.[24]

Like the churches, the lodges were often class conscious. Through the

23. Richardson (ed.), *The National Cyclopedia*, 194–95; Indianapolis *Freeman*, November 20, 1915; *Crisis*, XXI (January, 1920), 132.

24. Rev. Homer E. Nutter, interview with author, Lexington, July 3, 1976; Hampton, *History of Fifth Street Baptist Church*; Parrish (ed.), *Golden Jubilee*, 281.

lodges the city's upper and middle classes interacted, though the leadership positions were naturally held by the elite. William H. Steward twice served as Worship Master of the Grand Lodge of Kentucky Masons. Physician John A. C. Lattimore rose to positions of leadership in the Knights, the Masons, and the United Brothers. School principal John McKinley, the most widely known Odd Fellow in Kentucky and the author of the *Grand United Order of Odd Fellows in America*, held the post of Grand Secretary of the Kentucky Odd Fellows for seventeen years. Another school principal, William H. Perry, was a thirty-third degree Mason and secretary of the Grand Lodge Chapter for seven years. Perry also served as Grand Champion of the Knights of Pythians.[25]

A small group of blacks in Louisville attempted to isolate themselves socially from the rest of the black community. This elite, often called the "Four Hundred," boasted that their education, close contact with whites, occupations, indeed their entire life-style, elevated them above other Negroes. This black elite often set the tone for the entire race. "Though the upper class is relatively small in numbers," wrote Gunnar Myrdal, "it provides the standards and values, and symbolizes the aspirations of the Negro community; being the most articulate element in the community, its outlook and interests are often regarded as those of the community at large."[26]

In Louisville, Washington, Charleston, New Orleans, and several other cities, a majority of the black elite were light-skinned. To be sure, skin color alone was not enough to insure admission to the upper class, but as John Dittmer points out, it was an important symbol of success. From the antebellum days when Washington Spradling and several other mulatto children were freed by their white fathers, Louisville's elite Negro group was

25. Weeden, *History of the Colored People*, 47; W. D. Johnson, *Biographical Sketches of Prominent Negro Men and Women of Kentucky* (Lexington, 1897), 27; Perry interview.

26. Influenced by the work of E. Franklin Frazier, most scholars agree that about 5 percent of the Afro-American urban community were elite. This group had more economic security than other blacks, usually owning their homes. The source of their wealth was either inheritance or work as professionals and entrepreneurs. Between 20 and 30 percent of the blacks were middle class, some owning their homes, but most renting. They were usually small businessmen, skilled workers, or ministers. This group was very intent on bettering its lot, especially that of their children. By far the largest percentage of blacks were members of the lower class. Their lives were classic examples of the struggle to survive. Being very susceptible to economic hard times, they had little hope of climbing the economic and social ladder. Myrdal, *An American Dilemma*, II, 689–708; St. Clair Drake and Horace Cayton, *Black Metropolis: A Study of Negro Life in a Northern City* (2 vols.; rev. ed.; New York, 1962), II, 526–64; E. Franklin Frazier, *The Negro in the United States* (rev. ed.; New York, 1961), 273–305; Dittmer, *Black Georgia*, 59–60; Kusmer, *A Ghetto Takes Shape*, 93–104.

dominated by light-skinned persons. Of Louisville's three leading blacks before 1917, William H. Steward and Albert E. Meyzeek, both descendants of free blacks, were light-skinned, while Charles H. Parrish, an ex-slave, was extremely dark. Practically all of the women in the exclusive clubs were light-skinned, even though they claimed that Negroes with dark complexions were welcomed as members. It is safe to assume that in Louisville before 1917, and before the rise of the new business leaders, skin color played more of a role in determining status and class ranking among blacks than it would later on.[27]

A few Louisville blacks gained admission to the Four Hundred because they were servants of influential whites. Black porters who worked in banks or at city hall had considerable prestige and were viewed as members of the upper class. So were the head waiters who worked in the best restaurants and hotels. A few black servants were considered the trendsetters in the elite circle. As one contemporary explained, "I can tell you of fine people who were servants in the homes of the wealthy here in Louisville and who were as polished and dignified as they could be. . . . They had acquired culture from contacts with whites." For example, Albert Hathaway, the chauffeur for the Ballard family, was a member of the Four Hundred; he and his wife attended social functions, gave parties, and participated in community projects.[28]

Some scholars have observed that blacks relied more on education than occupation to determine class position. With the narrow occupation range available to blacks, education was used to mark off social divisions within the same general occupation level.[29] The importance of an education was apparent in Louisville, for a degree from a college spelled rapid admission into the ranks of the elite. By 1915 Louisville was the home of black professionals with degrees from Fisk, Howard, Tuskegee, Hampton, Wilberforce, Berea, Meharry Medical College, and state universities in Indiana, Illinois, Ohio, and Michigan. Fisk was the out-of-state institution best represented in Louisville, with enough graduates in 1911 to form a Louisville Fisk Club. That year a local newspaper reported that the city would eventually have even more Fisk graduates because the six Central High

27. *American Baptist*, May 21, 1886. This weekly religious newspaper was published in Louisville by William H. Steward. Lucy H. Smith (ed.), *Pictorial Directory of the Kentucky Association of Colored Women* (Louisville, 1945); Dittmer, *Black Georgia*, 62; Blassingame, *Black New Orleans*, 152–57.

28. Blanton interivew; Indianapolis *Freeman*, June 19, 1909; *Leader*, March 5, 1921.

29. Drake and Cayton, *Black Metropolis*, II, 515; E. Franklin Frazier, *Black Bourgeoisie* (rev. ed.; New York, 1962), 23; Carter G. Woodson, *The Negro Professional Man and the Community* (1934; rpr. New York, 1969).

graduates attending Fisk were doing well in their studies. Of course, a substantial percentage of Louisville's black elite were graduates of State University or affiliated with the institution as teachers or members of the board of trustees.[30]

Having the right life-style was undoubtedly the single most important ingredient to becoming a member of the elite. Upper-class blacks spent considerable time and money on furnishing their homes and showing them off to friends and neighbors. The black press devoted much attention to describing the style of furniture and the modern conveniences found in these fine homes.

> One of the most beautiful homes in the city is that of Misses Lucy and Eva Duvalle, located on West Chestnut Street. It is a two-story brick of modern structure, stone trimmings, and always newly painted. The interior is charming and beautiful. The double parlors, dining and reception rooms are handsomely furnished in old mahogany style. Every room in the house is attractive. The entire home is cheerful and comfortable.[31]

Louisville's Four Hundred were famous for their lavish dinner parties. The black press delighted in detailing the six-course meals. In 1910 visiting members of the National Association of Colored Women were served a seven-course luncheon at the home of Mrs. Stephan Bell. For the occasion, Mrs. Bell hired a caterer from Indianapolis (nearly 200 miles from Louisville), four waiters, and a group of musicians. The young ladies forming the receiving party wore long, white satin dresses set off by a display of pearls and diamonds. Finally, the local correspondent for the Indianapolis *Freeman* described a whist party given by Mrs. Lavinia Cooper, the widow of a funeral director, as the most brilliant one ever held in Louisville.

> The lawn was lavishly decorated and brilliantly illuminated with light and color that had an effect which rivaled in gorgeousness the oriental festivals. The guests retired to the dining hall at 8 o'clock. There the eyes grew weary of gazing on beautiful flowers, rich gold-threaded tapestry, beautifully lighted candelabra, marble statuary and tropical plants that beggared description. Covers were laid for a score of guests. The service was all that the most fastidious could desire. Those that had won favors at whist upon the lawn now found a more intellectual duty to perform, when called upon to respond to the various toasts inscribed upon their cards.[32]

30. Wesley interview; Indianapolis *Freeman*, October 17, 1905, July 1, 1911; Lewis, "Louisville and Its Afro-American Citizens," 265.

31. Indianapolis *Freeman*, May 2, 1908, June 19, 1909, January 22, 1910.

32. *Ibid.*, July 16, 23, 1910, December 19, 1911.

Though often informal, many social activities were significant because of the unity they brought to the Afro-American community. Parades and celebrations, like the one held on Emancipation Day, involved the entire community. Mass meetings were held in public parks or at churches to celebrate every victory against Jim Crow. Also, as a way of maintaining a sense of "family," the churches had annual picnics and excursions or a special homecoming day where all the members would eat and socialize together.

All classes of blacks attended sporting events. According to the New York *Freeman*, the first black baseball team was formed in Louisville in 1887. By the early 1900s there were several professional baseball teams, varying in degree of expertise and skill. These teams played each other and baseball clubs from other cities. Without a doubt, the leading team was the Louisville Giants, which existed for over two decades. The Giants drew large crowds of spectators, averaging between 3,500 and 4,000 on Sundays. The team's manager, Ed Lancaster, proudly pointed out that blacks owned and directed every aspect of the team and that "a white man has nothing to do with it." As part of their concern for the community, the Giants would occasionally contribute part of their proceeds to local charitable institutions.[33]

By 1915 basketball was well on its way to overtaking baseball as the most popular sport. The YMCA and the various settlement houses formed teams and challenged each other to games that were, according to the local press, well attended. State University and Central High fielded basketball teams which created great interest within the community. Indeed, as in a later period (roughly from the late 1950s to the mid-1970s) when Central High dominated basketball in hoop-crazy Kentucky and was the center of attention, the fans figuratively lived and died with the successes and failures of their teams.

Though social distinctions existed among their parents, younger blacks broke down social barriers by attending the same parties and spending time together in the city's notorious pool halls and chili parlors. As in other cities in the early 1900s, dancing was very popular among young Louisvillians. Not surprisingly, the community's leading ministers denounced the "dance craze" afflicting the young, warning that it would lead to immoral lives. Also, to their dismay, many teenagers frequented the pool halls. One of them, Blyden Jackson, the son of a school teacher, remembers spending all of his spare time in the pool halls. Regarding the activities of the young,

33. New York *Freeman*, January 22, 1887; Indianapolis *Freeman*, May 22, 29, June 12, 1909.

a newspaper reporter concluded with disgust: "If one-third of the money that passes through Chili Parlors on Sunday nights could be distributed among . . . the YMCA, the Orphan Home and other charitable institutions [they] would soon be able to erect handsome buildings and would be better prepared to carry on the work." [34]

Central High School, more than any other institution or activity, united black Louisville. Blacks equated Central with academic excellence, discipline, and fine teaching. Thomas Jesse Jones, in his national survey of black schools, paid a compliment to Central: "A well-organized city school. . . . The teaching force and equipment are considerably above average." Blacks looked to Central for recreational activities, as the school's athletic teams, singing groups, and debating society provided entertainment for the entire community. The annual Thanksgiving football game pitting Central against a key out-of-state rival was always well attended, as were the annual school play and commencement ceremonies. Practically every black (or so it seemed) had an affiliation with the school, either as graduates, as parents of students, or as employees. Identity in the black community was in part derived from being a Central graduate, and each graduating class was associated with a certain event.[35]

Segregation usually meant inferiority to blacks, but such was not the case with Central High School. Central's building and facilities were certainly inferior to the white high schools', but the dedication of the teachers enabled them to offer a top-quality education. The heavy dose of Afro-American history and culture (the school celebrated Negro History Week each year with plays, poetry, singing and speakers, all open to the public) dished out in classes and assemblies helped blacks gain an important measure of self-respect. Louisville blacks attended different churches, maintained loyalty to numerous fraternities, sororities, social clubs, and cliques. But they had only one high school. Central High was unquestionably the pride of the black community and would remain so for decades.

II.

Through their churches and lodges, black Louisvillians established institutions to care for the sick and the homeless of their own community.

34. Indianapolis *Freeman*, March 5, April 9, 1910, October 28, 1911; Blyden Jackson, interview with author, Chapel Hill, N.C., August 1, 1979; Blanton interview.

35. Jackson interview; Blanton interview; Parrish interview; Thomas Jesse Jones, *Negro Education: A Study of the Private and Public High Schools for Colored People in the United States* (2 vols.; Washington, D.C., 1917), II, 272.

Practically all of these institutions were started by blacks, but they came to depend on whites for the bulk of their financial support. Not surprisingly, most of these institutions had white advisory board members who gave substantial financial contributions and who greatly influenced the programs of these institutions.

Several black churches joined forces in 1877 to raise money for an orphanage. In January 1878, the orphan home committee leased an abandoned army hospital and opened the Colored Orphan Home, the first welfare institution established by black Louisvillians. Later that same year, the orphan home was moved to a much larger and nicer structure at Eighteenth and Dumesnil Streets, a site donated by the American Missionary Society.[36]

At its inception, the Colored Orphan Home received financial support and materials from black churches and organizations. The Ladies Sewing Circle made the orphanage its special project by contributing to the building fund, making clothes for the children, and donating furniture, blankets, and sheets. Several other women's clubs held a special day for the home each year during which ladies baked cakes and pies for residents of the orphanage. Most of the larger churches and fraternities gave annual contributions. Fifth Street Baptist Church was especially generous to the orphanage. In February 1890 the church took up a collection to buy a carpet for the home. Several months later, the church appropriated money to put a new roof on the home. For three decades the Colored Orphan Home was supported only by the Afro-American community. Obviously the institution could have used more support; the home lacked adequate facilities and accommodations and desperately needed more paid workers. In 1909 the board of directors of the home selected Rev. E. G. Harris as its president, hoping that he could convince whites to contribute. His selection was an immediate success. One of Harris's strongest supporters, James B. Speed, gave $500 in 1910, an amount greater than the total white contributions up to that time. And over the next few years a number of whites contributed regularly and were responsible for the institution eventually receiving a yearly grant from the Louisville Welfare League. All of this was accomplished at a price: the board became dominated by whites.[37]

36. Weeden, *History of the Colored People*, 20–22; Gibson, *Progress of the Colored Race in Louisville*, 72.

37. Weeden, *History of the Colored People*, 20–22; Indianapolis *Freeman*, December 10, 1910; W. D. Weatherford (ed.), *Interracial Cooperation* (Atlanta, 1921), 66; W. H. Slingerland, *Child Welfare in Louisville* (Louisville, 1919), 48; Minutes of Fifth Street, July 17, 1878, February 19, April 16, 1890.

Exactly ten years after starting the Colored Orphan Home, the churches founded St. James Old Folks Home. Again, Fifth Street Baptist provided financial support and leadership to the institution, holding annual concerts to raise money and making contributions to the home a regular part of the church's quarterly budget. Despite such efforts, the institution was forced to close in the mid-1890s under a pile of debts. Several women's groups then started working to reopen the home. How and where the women obtained the money to reopen the institution is unclear, but by the end of the decade the group (with some aid from the churches) not only had reopened St. James but also had purchased a large house and property valued at $10,000 as the new site for the home. Within five years, the women had paid off the entire mortage. Through the support of these women, St. James Old Folks Home remained in existence until 1920. The home's patrons were rightfully proud of their accomplishment. One of them, in a letter to DuBois, said unashamedly: "The institution is owned and controlled exclusively by colored people, and we owe not a cent on it. It is the only institution of its kind in the city that is strictly and unconditionally owned by colored people."[38]

Equally as beneficial to the black community as the homes for orphans and senior citizens was the start of a hospital. Louisville General Hospital admitted blacks but gave them inferior service in a Jim Crow section of the hospital. Louisville National Medical College was equipped to handle only minor emergencies, since it had no beds. Doctor Ellis D. Whedbee came to Louisville in the mid-1890s from Washington, where he had served as assistant resident physician at Freedmen's Hospital. Once in Louisville, Whedbee found himself barred from local medical institutions and handicapped by the lack of trained black nurses. In close cooperation with Doctors W. T. Merchant, Solomon Stone, E. S. Porter, and William H. Perry, Whedbee began a campaign in 1897 to raise capital to open a hospital for blacks. The Red Cross Hospital and Nurse Training Department opened in November 1899 in a rented house on Sixth Street, remaining at that location until the founders purchased a much larger facility on Shelby Street in 1905.[39]

38. Weeden, *History of the Colored People*, 24, DuBois, (ed.), *Efforts for Social Betterment*, 74; Minutes of Fifth Street, November 9, 1881, February 8, 1882, March 12, 1890.

39. Bertha J. Whedbee, "History of Red Cross Hospital and Sanatorium" (April 1, 1948); Red Cross Minute Book, "Articles of Incorporation of Red Cross Hospital, November 18, 1902"; Mary E. Dean, "History of Red Cross Hospital" (February 15, 1976). These sources on Red Cross Hospital can be found at the Department of Archives and Records, University of Louisville; *Courier-Journal*, January 3, 1930.

Red Cross immediately met a vital need in the black community. The hospital operated a free clinic that offered preventive treatment, because the doctors were determined to fight the spread of debilitating diseases and to reduce infant mortality. Realizing that most blacks were too poor to pay for medical care, the directors of Red Cross provided services at 75 percent of the cost charged by other hospitals. The hospital attracted additional black physicians to Louisville. In 1896, one year before the campaign began that resulted in the establishment of Red Cross Hospital, Louisville had twelve black doctors; by 1910 there were forty.[40]

The nurse training program was an important feature of Red Cross Hospital. William H. Perry, who was also the principal of an elementary school, developed the department and set up a three-year curriculum that required young women to take several courses in nursing, to work in clinics, and to assist in minor operations before becoming nurses. Miss Mary E. Merritt, a graduate of the nurse training school at Freedmen's Hospital in Washington, became closely associated with the nurse training at Red Cross and dedicated the remainder of her working life (until 1945) to instructing young women. The work of Merritt and Perry was invaluable: nearly all of the first black nurses in Kentucky received their training at Red Cross since it was the only hospital in the state that accepted black women in its nurse training program.[41]

After starting the hospital, the black doctors appealed to a number of local whites for financial assistance. These whites, specifically Mr. J. B. Speed and Miss Lucy Belknap, both from wealthy Louisville families, responded by forming the Red Cross Club and the Red Cross Advisory Board. Members of both groups paid off the mortgage and financed several renovations of the hospital building. Their support was crucial for it was not until 1920 that the state began giving an annual appropriation to the hospital. From the beginning, local whites not only gave money but also provided Red Cross with beds, blankets, and furniture.[42]

Even with this much needed white support, Red Cross Hospital could not meet the many needs of the large black population. The hospital was usually filled to capacity. Persons needing immediate attention often had

40. Whedbee, "History of Red Cross Hospital"; Louisville *Leader*, August 7, 1912; Dr. John H. Walls, interview with author, Louisville, September 26, 1978.

41. *Courier-Journal*, February 8, 1942; Whedbee, "History of Red Cross Hospital."

42. *Courier-Journal*, April 19, 1928, February 8, 1942; *Leader*, March 10, 1928; Louisville *Herald*, July 25, 1922; "Red Cross Hospital Report for Year Ending December 31, 1916" (Louisville, 1917) in Archives Department, University of Louisville; DuBois (ed.), *Efforts for Social Betterment*, 88.

to be turned away, and patients were sometimes dismissed earlier than good practice would dictate because of the urgent need for bed space. Equipment in the operating room and the nurse training department was substandard, and doctors did without the modern apparatus found in white hospitals. In short, despite white support, Red Cross remained too small to serve Louisville's nearly 50,000 blacks as well as blacks from nearby counties.[43]

When they started Red Cross Hospital, the doctors considered it a temporary measure and looked forward to the day when they could practice in all hospitals in the city. But as time passed and segregation in medical care persisted, they grew weary and bitter about being restricted to Red Cross, especially since it was so inferior to white hospitals. The whites affiliated with the hospital acknowledged that Red Cross was inferior, but they never went on record to urge city leaders to admit black doctors and patients to the city's many medical facilities. Instead they simply continued donating money to Red Cross Hospital. Despite black pleas for change, it would be the 1950s before black doctors were allowed to practice in all of the hospitals in Louisville.[44]

III.

During the same years that they started the orphanage, old folks home, and hospital, the leaders of the Afro-American community also labored to end the problems that they believed were caused by idle young people and newcomers to the city. Long-time black residents of Louisville found the newcomers, especially the poor from rural areas, a source of embarrassment and blamed them for much of the race problem. Black leaders believed that the less fortunate of the race would improve morally from contact with a Christian environment, so they established a YMCA and several settlement houses. It was also hoped that they would acquire a few basic work skills and qualities of good citizenship while at these institutions. Most of the settlement houses were not open long because they lacked workers, funding, and well-developed programs. The more successful ones, the YMCA and especially the Presbyterian Colored Missions and Plymouth Settlement House, received financial support from whites.

43. Haven Emerson and Anna Phillips (eds.), *Hospitals and Health Agencies of Louisville, 1924, A Survey* (Louisville, 1925), 90–91.
44. Indianapolis *Freeman*, June 1, 1912; *Courier-Journal*, January 5, 1925, May 21, 1926; *Leader*, May 10, 1924; Walls interview.

In 1885 school teacher Albert Mack started a one-man campaign for a YMCA to provide an alternative to the "dens of sin" found in black neighborhoods. All alone, he entered gambling dens to "rescue young men." After convincing some of them to follow him, he then appealed to the Odd Fellows for the use of their lodge for weekly meetings. As interest continued to increase, he sought the support of the local white YMCA officials and a number of black leaders. In 1892 the black group, led by William H. Steward and school principal Albert E. Meyzeek, who would devote most of his long life to working with the poor Negro boys of the city, solicited funds from the white YMCA and purchased an old building at 942 West Walnut Street.[45]

Though understaffed, the YMCA did provide several important services to the Afro-American community. It did become an alternative to the pool halls, for hundreds of youths came to view the YMCA as an ideal recreation center. Once the young men were there, Albert Mack, Meyzeek, and other volunteer workers attempted to interest them in church work, conducting Sunday School classes and Bible training sessions. In fact, the entire program of the YMCA centered around moral improvement and Christian uplift. YMCA officials started basketball and baseball teams and other organized activities. A small reading room was opened, since blacks were denied access to the public library. Black women's groups and clubs used the YMCA's facilities for recreational activities and meetings. (A YWCA would not open until the 1920s.) In an attempt to prevent homeless black men from being arrested on vagrancy charges or from succumbing in the inclement weather, the YMCA often gave these men temporary shelter at a cheap price or, as was most often the case, gratis.[46]

Mrs. Bessie Allen, perhaps the most active of Louisville's many black social workers, started a nonsectarian Sunday School in 1902. A graduate of State University, Mrs Allen worked as head of the newly created Colored Division of Probation Work. Through her job she came into contact

45. Indianapolis *Freeman*, December 27, 1890, January 17, 1891. For years, local Negro leaders claimed that they started the first YMCA in the country for blacks. But according to the *Freeman* of October 18, 1890, that distinction rightfully belongs to Norfolk, Virginia: "Norfolk was the first to organize a full work of the YMCA; the first to throw open its doors to the public, the first to have a reception room, the first to be recognized by the International Committee and the first to employ a general secretary." Additional information on the early years of the YMCA can be found in Ben Horton, "Life and Achievements of Albert Ernest Meyzeek," *Kentucky Negro Journal* (1958); Letter from O.S. Kline to Albert E. Meyzeek, March 6, 1906; The deed to the YMCA building was signed by Meyzeek and is in the YMCA office at Tenth and Chestnut Streets.

46. Indianapolis *Freeman*, March 14, April 11, 1914.

with many young delinquents and was convinced of the importance of religious instruction in promoting child welfare, vocational training, and morality. Her program operated only on Sundays for several years until she received financial assistance from local white philanthropists. With their backing, she purchased a building at Ninth and Magazine Streets, named it Booker T. Washington Community Center, and began offering domestic science courses for girls and woodworking and shoe repairing classes for boys. She started a Daily Vacation School during the summer to keep children occupied and off the streets. During the Christmas season Allen solicited articles from department stores to provide gifts for poor children.[47]

But the heart of Mrs. Allen's work at the Booker T. Washington Center was always religious instruction. As a way of rewarding faithful attendance at Sunday School, Allen organized a marching band. She provided each member of the band with a uniform and a musical instrument, and it was not long before the band became widely known in Louisville, particularly for marching in parades. Playing in her band became an honor ardently sought by many black children. Over the years a number of well-known musicians received their start in her marching band, including Johan Jones, Helen Humes, Dicky Wells, Bill Beason, and Russell Bowles. "Mrs. Allen's Marching Band," as it was popularly called, was an idea conceived to keep the children occupied and to teach them about religion; yet it had a much broader impact.[48]

Perhaps the most comprehensive and best program for black youths was directed by a white man, Rev. John Little. In every survey of black settlement houses in the United States, his was consistently rated as one of the best. His settlement houses offered industrial training and met the need for social services in the eastern part of town. Most of the other social workers concentrated their programs around Tenth and Chestnut Streets in the west end. Little enjoyed solid financial backing and overwhelming support from the white community, something that the black churches and institutions so desperately needed but lacked. The story of his institution is significant because it clearly shows the kind of training that progressive whites of the early 1900s thought best for the Negro. Simply put, John Lit-

47. Mrs. Ann Allen Schockley (daughter of Bessie Allen), interview with author, Nashville, August 26, 1979; *Leader*, October 9, 1909, January 24, 1914, August 27, 1921; *Courier-Journal*, March 17, 1944; *The Booker T. Washington Community Center and Newsboys Improvement Association* (Louisville, 1919); National Urban League *Bulletin*, IX (January, 1920), 18.

48. Schockley interview; Louisville *Times*, August 4, 1979.

tle's settlement houses conformed to, and maybe set the tone for, the Louisville way of uplifting Afro-Americans.

In 1897 Little, along with members of the Student's Missionary Society of the Louisville Presbyterian Seminary, decided to organize a Sunday School program for blacks. While knocking on doors in black neighborhoods, Little was appalled at what he saw: unclean homes, many prostitutes and criminals, and the absence of formal, and even informal, institutions working for positive community change. He noticed that tuberculosis was rampant in certain deplorable black tenement houses. Little said he found "poverty, ignorance, and sickness" in the overwhelming majority of the black homes he entered. After the first Sunday School class, he decided to concentrate his efforts on instructing blacks in "simple things like how God in making the world, had provided many things which they used daily." Little converted a former gambling and lottery office into a black settlement house, called Hope Mission Station, in the hope that it would serve to improve the moral and health standards of the black community.[49]

Little's settlement house opened in February 1898 on Hancock Street with a properly modest program. Little stressed the importance of a clean body, knowledge of Jesus Christ, and organized games. Hope Mission was so well received by east-end blacks that Little established a second settlement house, Grace Mission Station, in "Smoketown" in April 1899. Grace Mission, located on the corner of Hancock and Roselane, was about a mile from Hope Mission. Both settlement houses became known as the Presbyterian Colored Missions or John Little's Missions.[50]

With the aid of white volunteer workers, he started vocational programs for blacks. Sewing classes were held six days a week and also in the evenings to accommodate the many women wanting to learn how to sew. The missions also offered cooking and canning classes. Besides teaching the women how to prepare various dishes, the cooking instructors stressed the importance of cleanliness while cooking and the importance of a balanced diet. Little was proud that a large number of black women who had been trained at his missions found employment as servants. Meanwhile, boys took courses in basketry, carpentry, shoe repairing, and tailoring. Little asserted that many graduates from his mission classes obtained skilled

49. John Little, *The Presbyterian Colored Missions* (Louisville, 1909); Miriam Gaines, "The John Little Missions of Louisville, Kentucky" *Southern Workman*, LXII (April, 1933), 161–70; *Courier-Journal*, February 8, 1948.

50. Little, *Presbyterian Colored Missions*, 3; John Little, *Hope Versus Hope* (Louisville, 1939), 14.

jobs, made furniture for their homes, and repaired their own shoes and clothing.[51]

The Presbyterian Colored Missions worked to improve personal hygiene and health among blacks. Hope Mission opened the first public bathhouse for blacks in Louisville. It was open on alternating days for males and females, and towels and soap were furnished free of charge. In 1913, five showers and toilets were installed at Hope Mission Station for blacks to use since many of them lived in places without bathrooms. A clinic was held periodically at both missions to give physical examinations to all children and adults served by the institution. Several local doctors donated a portion of their time to ensure better health among the children. An eye, ear, and throat specialist fitted children with glasses and removed diseased adenoids and tonsils, while two surgeons performed other minor surgery when needed.[52]

Recreational activities became an important feature of the Presbyterian Colored Missions. Little said that playgrounds at the institutions provided recreation for black children under Christian supervision and helped increase attendance at religious services. He noted that many first acquaintances with black children took place at the playgrounds and these recreational contacts carried over to the church and vocational work. The missions organized several clubs and sponsored baseball and basketball teams for black teenagers. For many teenagers and adults, the missions became social centers where games, parties, and meetings could take place.[53]

Religious training remained an important part of the total program of the Presbyterian Colored Missions. The missions had Sunday School classes and a summer Vacation Bible School. Little hired his first black worker in 1906, Rev. G. W. Nicholas, as pastor of the missions. Nicholas, Little, and the other religious workers founded Grace Presbyterian Church on May 8, 1910. Many blacks in the Hancock Street area attended Grace Presbyterian Church but few of them became members. Only thirty blacks joined the church between 1910 and 1912. This obviously disappointed

51. Little, *Presbyterian Colored Missions*, 5–10; Weatherford (ed.), *Interracial Cooperation*, 66; see "Annual Report of the Presbyterian Colored Missions for 1913," Presbyterian Colored Missions Papers, Archives Department, University of Louisville, 2.

52. Board Minutes, Presbyterian Colored Missions, March 2, 1911; see also, "The Presbyterian Colored Missions After Twenty Years of Service," typed memo, Archives Department, University of Louisville, 3; "Annual Report of the Presbyterian Colored Missions for 1913," 3.

53. "Annual Report of the Presbyterian Colored Missions for 1913," 2; Little, *Presbyterian Colored Missions*, 12; Weatherford (ed.), *Interracial Cooperation*, 55; "Enrollment of the Missions, 1913–1914," Archives Department, University of Louisville.

Little; Nicholas resigned as pastor in the summer of 1912 (probably under pressure) and Little began an immediate search for a black minister with charisma to pastor the foundering church. Little decided that Dr. William H. Sheppard was the black preacher he wanted. Sheppard, a native of Virginia and a well-known minister of the Southern Presbyterian Church, had been a missionary in the Belgian Congo for ten years and had written a book, *Pioneers in Congo*, about his experiences in working with Africans. He received a number of awards for his work and was one of the few blacks, and the only Presbyterian minister, invited to join the Royal Geographical Society of London. Sheppard accepted Little's offer to become pastor of Grace Presbyterian.[54]

Church attendance and membership at Grace Presbyterian increased steadily during Sheppard's tenure. He was installed at the church on September 15, 1912, and the weekly attendance quickly rose from under 100 to 143 a week. During Sheppard's first year as pastor, sixty new members joined the church. Little noted that Sheppard's arrival brought renewed interest in the church choir, Bible training classes, and other church activities. Sheppard gave Little what he wanted: increased black participation and enthusiasm for the institution's religious activities. He served as pastor of Grace Presbyterian Church until his death in 1927.[55]

The Presbyterian Colored Missions eventually received more financial support than other black institutions. But at first, Little lacked financial support and struggled to keep Hope and Grace Missions open. In October 1899, the Presbytery of Louisville agreed to give a yearly donation to the missions. Eleven years later Little received a much needed financial boost when the Presbyterian Church, U.S.A., and the Reformed Church were persuaded to support his work. Because of this solid financial backing, the Presbyterian Colored Missions had modern facilities. Both settlement houses occupied rented quarters during their first years of operation, but a five-room structure was purchased to house Grace Mission in 1902. Hope Mission remained in rented quarters until 1911, when a nearby factory under construction was purchased for $11,500. The mission modi-

54. "Annual Report of the Presbyterian Colored Missions for 1913," 2; for biographical information on Sheppard, see William Sheppard, *Pioneers in Congo* (Richmond, n.d.). In an article entitled "From Darkest Africa to Darkest Louisville," the *Courier-Journal*, June 22, 1913, mentioned Sheppard's plans to come to Louisville.

55. Board Minutes, Presbyterian Colored Missions, October 14, 1912, June 11, 1913, March 31, 1914; see also "Annual Report of the Committee of Colored Evangelization of the Presbyterian and Reformed Churches," for the year ending March 31, 1914, Archives Department, Louisville University.

fied the building plans to convert the structure into a combination church, vocational plant, and recreational center. Equally important to the smooth operation of the missions was the staff in charge. Little and his wife were the only full-time workers for the first years of the venture, but by the early 1900s there were a couple of full-time workers at both missions, and by 1915 there were eight full-time employees and a black minister. Furthermore, the missions always enjoyed more than enough volunteer workers; in 1909 there were fifty, and by 1915, ninety. Little said that his volunteer workers came from "Louisville's best white families." They were ministers, doctors, lawyers, social workers, teachers, and businessmen. A number of students from the local seminaries and the Baptist Women's Missionary Training Union also regularly volunteered their time to work in the settlement houses.[56]

Although he dedicated his life to race improvement, John Little was, perhaps unavoidably, a man of his times in his attitude toward blacks. At best, he was paternalistic, at worst, a racist. Throughout his writings and in the articles in which he was quoted, Little referred to blacks as ignorant and altogether lacking such qualities as cleanliness and punctuality. He believed that his work "instilled refinement in their nature." Little certainly derived pleasure from his view that black people had existed in a very dismal state before his settlement houses came to rescue them. Whites praised Little for what he had accomplished and agreed that blacks had lived in an endless cycle of poverty and ignorance before he opened his settlement houses. An article by Miriam Gaines centered on the theme that Little and his white workers "have met the needs of a desperately ignorant and poverty stricken community." Louise J. Speed made the astonishing claim that black parents were irresponsible before Little opened his missions and began giving moral and religious training to their children. Continuing her praise of Little's work, Speed said,

The change in the outward deportment of the pupils is that most noticeable to the average observer. Clothes have taken a turn for the better, cleanliness is fast be-

56. See "Sources of Income from April 1, 1914, to March 31, 1915," Archives Department, University of Louisville; Little, *Hope Versus Hope*, 4, 14; "Resolutions Adopted by the Executive Committee of the Presbyterian Colored Missions, January 11, 1949, in Memory of John Little," *Crisis* XXXIX (February, 1930), 60.

Hope Mission remained adequate for the increasing number of blacks who used its facilities. Grace Mission, however, became too small and in the early 1920s Little initiated a building fund for a new structure. Little received contributions from many sources, and in November 1929 the $106,000 Grace Mission opened with its spacious auditorium, gymnasium and work area.

coming the order of the day, the decorums of life are gradually making their way into regions once barren or barbarous—and when recently a small boy was found who against all parental traditions and training persistently refused to drink a beer or carry it for others, a white stone was set for the parting of the ways.[57]

Bad feelings existed between Little and black ministers who pastored churches in the vicinity of the two missions. Not surprisingly, he noted that "there was at first intense hostility on the part of the ignorant colored ministers to the efforts of the white people to give religious instruction to the colored children." Little never took steps to cultivate a friendship with the "ignorant colored ministers" or to use them in his work. In fact, Little steadfastly refused to use blacks as workers in his settlement houses even though several of his former students were doing community work in other parts of the city. Before 1933, the only black workers used by Little were the Reverends Nicholas and Sheppard, and their function was to increase black participation in the religious activities of the institution. Finally in 1933 a black physician and nurse began working in the baby clinic at the missions.[58]

It is impossible to know all of the reasons why Little directed the settlement houses from 1897 until his death in 1948. One thing seems clear: he was not interested in producing black leaders or blacks who could duplicate his work. Little spoke with pride of the progress students at the institution made in vocational training and of the high number of servant girls the missions trained. He believed that Negroes could learn simple manual tasks but that they were incapable of running an institution such as he had established or of uplifting themselves. In one of his pamphlets, Little wrote that his program for blacks could be duplicated in other communities if enough money was provided to operate the institution, *and* if a southern white man was chosen to direct the work.[59]

57. Little, *Hope Versus Hope*, 6; Gaines, "The John Little Missions," 163; Louise J. Speed, "The Evolution of a Kentucky Negro Mission," *Charities and the Commons*, XVII (September 21, 1907), 727. Investigators were usually critical of the work going on in black institutions. They, however, praised Little's work. See *Annual Report of Welfare League, 1922* (Louisville, 1922), 50–51; Slingerland, *Child Welfare*, 96–97.

58. Little, *Presbyterian Colored Missions*, 13–15.

59. *Ibid.*, 15. See Thomas L. Philpott, *The Slum and the Ghetto: Neighborhood Deterioration and Middle-Class Reform, Chicago, 1880–1930* (New York, 1978), 300–320, 341. Philpott explains that the white social workers in Chicago barred blacks from all of the settlement houses they established for immigrants. But in the years 1900–1916, with Chicago's black population increasing rapidly, they felt compelled to open settlement houses for blacks. These segregated institutions emphasized manual training for blacks. The white social workers, Philpott concludes, desired to uplift blacks to their proper place in society, which of course was not the same level as whites.

Despite Little's assertion that only a white man could duplicate his performance, Louisville had a very successful black-run settlement house. Rev. E. G. Harris, the most civic-minded of Louisville's black ministers, established a settlement house as an extension of his ministry. Desiring to "reach the unreached," Harris started planning for his settlement house in 1910 and it was incorporated in 1914. Between 1914 and 1917 Harris raised enough money from white supporters and the Welfare League to build a $20,000 structure. Plymouth Settlement House, completed in the fall of 1917, was hailed by Harris as an ideal facility for conducting numerous activities. The first floor had an office and an auditorium, the second had classrooms, a dining room, and kitchen, and the third floor had dormitory rooms. Yet for all his good intentions, Harris planned his institution with the same limited concept as his white counterpart, John Little. He would teach blacks simple skills and make them ideal workers in the homes of whites.[60]

Plymouth Settlement House prided itself on offering a "wholesome environment" for blacks. Harris allowed bazaars, concerts, plays, receptions, and parties to be held in the auditorium. Motion picture shows became regular events. Harris and his workers organized a Boy Scout troop, clubs for girls, and basketball teams. During the summer, the institution provided games and activities for approximately 300 children. Bible classes and other religious activities were stressed. Harris claimed that his Community School, which was held on Sundays, reached blacks who had never before attended church.[61]

Plymouth Settlement House became best known for its program for black women. Harris ran an employment bureau which specialized in placing black females in domestic jobs. His program offered courses in cooking, sewing, and handicrafts—activities designed, so Harris said, to improve their skills as housekeepers. Harris's settlement house taught black women to be efficient in the domestic sciences, so "that our people may be more reliable, polite, and competent workers." In addition to finding employment for black women, he provided them dormitory rooms in which to live. The minister charged these women $1.75 a week for a "neat and well-furnished" room where they could spend their evenings relaxing and reading instead of getting into trouble in "chili parlors or dance halls."[62]

Like most black institutions in Louisville, Harris's settlement house

60. *Brief History of Plymouth Congregational Church*; *Courier-Journal*, July 9, 1917.
61. Nancy H. Duncan, "A Study of the Plymouth Settlement House Neighborhood" (M.A. thesis, University of Louisville, 1965).
62. *Ibid.*; *Annual Report of Welfare League*, 1922, 48.

relied on whites for financial support. Colonel P. H. Callahan, Mrs. J. B. Speed, and Mrs. W. R. Belknap were members of the advisory board and made large contributions for the construction of the settlement house. These whites and the other members of the advisory board lobbied successfully for the inclusion of the Plymouth Settlement House in the Welfare League, which gave a yearly donation of $3,500. This financial backing enabled Harris to hire two full-time and several part-time workers. Viewed cynically, a few whites undoubtedly supported Harris's work because he provided an important service for them, namely, the training of young black women to work in their homes. As one investigator noted: "There is an increasing number of employers who entrust the recommendation of their help entirely to the Free Employment Bureau of Plymouth Settlement House. Through this bureau 191 girls found employment . . . and have given eminent satisfaction."[63]

Black women established many community organizations and clubs of their own. Without a doubt, some of these organizations were elitist in makeup, with membership being a status badge. Yet the various clubs concentrated on goals that were designed to improve the entire race morally, physically, and financially. The role of black Baptist women in the development of State University, for example, was instrumental to the growth of the college. They formed the Baptist Women's Missionary Convention and the Baptist Women's Educational Convention. These two groups raised scholarship money for girls, assisted in the paying of salaries to teachers, and built a girl's dormitory. Various women's clubs donated beds and sheets to the Colored Orphan Home, the St. James Old Folks Home, and the Red Cross Hospital. Of special concern was the well-being of children. Women helped establish and direct playgrounds in black neighborhoods. The Georgia A. Nugent Improvement Club, formed in the 1890s, sponsored kindergarten training classes and eventually opened a day nursery. A second day nursery was begun in 1905 by the Loyalty Charity Club. Children were fed and cared for from seven in the morning to six in the evening for five cents a day. By the early 1900s, Louisville had dozens of black women's clubs working in a number of different areas.[64]

Several women stand out for the numerous activities they promoted

63. Duncan, "Plymouth Settlement House," 5; *The 90th Year, Welfare League* (Louisville, 1921), 86.

64. Indianapolis *Freeman*, September 11, 1909, October 21, 1911; Smith (ed.), *Pictorial Directory*. For additional information on women's clubs in Louisville, see Mrs. Mary V. Parrish (ed.), *Fourth Statistical Report of the National Association of Colored Women* (Louisville, 1914).

in the black community. Besides doing probation work and directing the Booker T. Washington Community Center, Mrs. Bessie Allen served as the only black on the Tenement House Commission, conducted several symposiums on child welfare, and formed the Newsboys Improvement Club, an organization of young men and women who met weekly to discuss community projects and problems. In 1909 a group of white and black leaders, aware of the inadequacy of the Colored Orphan Home, founded the Kentucky Home Finding Society for Colored Children. They believed that something had to be done for neglected black children besides placing them in jails or reform schools or institutionalizing them in the orphan home. They selected Mrs. Allen to direct the day-to-day operation of the Finding Society, a position she would hold for more than three decades.[65]

Miss Nannie Helen Burroughs also worked effectively on a number of different projects. A native of Virginia, she came to Louisville around 1900 to attend the Eckstein Norton Institute, a school established by Rev. Charles H. Parrish. After graduating, Miss Burroughs remained in Louisville and started a program to meet young women arriving in Louisville on the trains and to direct them away from the city's vice areas. Miss Burroughs took the lead in helping the various women's clubs to consolidate their efforts and unite with the National Association of Colored Women. She eventually left Louisville for Washington, where she started the National Training School for Women and Girls. This institution, with its emphasis on the "3 B's"—Bible, bath, and broom—offered training in domestic science, clerical and secretarial skills, farming, and printing in a Christian environment for twenty years. Several Louisville black women were trustees of the school.[66]

From its inception in the early 1900s, the Louisville affiliate of the National Association of Colored Women worked primarily in education, health care, and child welfare. With a membership consisting of the city's leading black women, the organization was often successful in getting a hearing before the school board and local government officials. The Louisville affiliate also corresponded with women throughout Kentucky and aided them in forming branches of the National Association. Mrs.

65. Indianapolis *Freeman*, October 15, 1910; Slingerland, *Child Welfare*, 31–39. Most of the records of the Kentucky Home Finding Society are in the possession of Mrs. Schockley in Nashville.

66. Nannie H. Burroughs Papers, Manuscript Division, Library of Congress, Washington, D.C.; Lewis, "Louisville and Its Afro-American Citizens," 261–62. See Evelyn Brooks Barnett, "Nannie Burroughs and the Education of Black Women," in Sharon Harley and Rosalyn Terborg-Penn (eds.), *The Afro-American Woman: Struggles and Images* (Port Washington, N.Y., 1978), 99–105.

Mary V. Parrish and Mrs. Mamie Steward, both wives of prominent leaders, rose to positions of leadership in the national organization, and, along with Miss Burroughs, they were instrumental in the Thirteenth Annual Convention of the National Association being held in Louisville in 1910.[67] The clubs formed by Louisville's Afro-American women were invaluable. They clearly show the many efforts by black women to uplift their sisters and their deep concern for the children of the community. Club women also provided young women with role models. Moreover, because black women were rarely chosen to head organizations that were dominated by men, having their own clubs provided them with important training for positions of leadership. As the historian Gerda Lerner has correctly concluded, "The work of black club women contributed to the survival of the black community. . . . They were concerned with education, self and community improvement, but they always strongly emphasized race pride and race advancement."[68]

From the 1880s to 1917 black Louisvillians formed a number of institutions and organizations to serve the race. Living in a hostile white world, Afro-Americans did what they could to combat racial discrimination. But instead of devoting all of their energies to trying to solve the never-ending racial problems, they worked to build a better and richer life for themselves. Most black institutions suffered from a lack of money; some from a lack of workers. But considering that these institutions depended on black support, it is remarkable that an institution like St. James Old Folks Home lasted as long as it did. Too often scholars have spoken of disorder in the black community, of the lack of an effective program for meaningful change, and of all black talent being exhausted in just trying to survive. But the construction of an institution like State University, which took considerable planning and years of earnest saving, shows the vision of black leaders and their dedication to bettering themselves and their community.

Since very few activities of the black minority were totally free of the dominant group, it is not surprising that whites exerted influence in black

67. W. E. B. DuBois (ed.), *Some Efforts of American Negroes for Their Own Social Betterment*, Atlanta University Publications, no. 3 (Atlanta, 1898), 41; *idem., Efforts for Social Betterment*, 62; An important source is the Mary Church Terrell Papers, Manuscript Division, Library of Congress, Washington, D.C., which contains a number of pamphlets on Kentucky women's organizations. For example, see *Kentucky Federation of Colored Women's Clubs, 1916, 1917* (Louisville, 1919).

68. Gerda Lerner, "Early Community Work of Black Club Women," *Journal of Negro History*, LIX (April, 1974), 162; *idem.* (ed.), *Black Women in White America: A Documentary History* (New York, 1972), 450–59.

institutions. Despite the fact that they had started their own institutions, black leaders looked more and more to whites for economic stability. Such institutions as the Colored Orphan Home and the Red Cross Hospital had white advisory board members who gave financial support and lobbied for donations for these institutions in the Louisville Welfare League. In fact, by the 1920s the Welfare League had replaced both blacks and individual whites as the chief contributor to Negro institutions. In 1920 the Colored Orphan Home received $3,144 from the League and only $700 from other sources; Plymouth Settlement House received $3,300 from the League and $138 from individual contributors.[69] In other words, after sustaining their institutions during the 1880s and the Depression of the 1890s, blacks, for whatever reasons, allowed whites to take over the financial responsibilities of many of their institutions in the early 1900s.

Although whites claimed that they gave to black institutions to aid the black community, the two institutions receiving the largest contributions from whites had programs that provided services to whites. The Presbyterian Colored Missions received the largest donations; they had programs that taught black women to become better personal servants and that taught black men manual skills. Similarly, Harris's Plymouth Settlement House was built entirely on white contributions; he enrolled black females in domestic science classes and placed many of them as servants in white homes.

Whites contributed to black institutions in part to insure that blacks would not demand equal access to their institutions. The actions of whites in Louisville were similar to those of their counterparts in northern cities. Historians have noted that in some northern cities, notably Chicago, whites supported black hospitals, YMCA's, and Phillis Wheatley Associations because they did not want blacks admitted to white institutions. In Louisville, the central white YMCA helped upgrade the black YMCA instead of allowing blacks admission. Similarly, the white advisory board members of the Red Cross Hospital gave contributions that enabled the health facility to remain in existence and thus thwarted the push for the admission of black doctors into white hospitals. In sum, whites supported black institutions in part out of paternalism, in part out of genuine philanthropy, and in part because they desired racially segregated institutions.

---

69. *The 90th Year, Welfare League,* 86.

## 6

Black Leaders

Booker T. Washington was the best known and most influential black in the United States at the turn of the century. From 1895, when he made his famous address in Atlanta before the Cotton States and International Exposition, to his death in 1915, Washington had unprecedented influence. A word from him often meant an appointment or rejection for black patronage seekers. His support or disapproval could bring financial contributions or economic collapse to a black college. Nevertheless, a significant number of black leaders in northern cities such as Chicago and Boston were openly antagonistic to Washington; they disapproved of his trusting attitude toward conservative white leaders and his practice of silencing black opposition. Black leaders in the South, who had less opportunity to denounce racism but who were well aware that whites at best would only support an education for blacks that made them "useful" to whites, tended to agree with Washington or at least to refrain from openly challenging his program.

In Louisville there was rarely any visible or vocal opposition to Washington. Yet, not all of the black leaders agreed totally with his ideology. In fact, one reason Washington was so successful was that all could find something they agreed with in his message. Louisville leaders, for instance, concurred with Washington on the importance of industrial education for blacks. They also wanted the economic power that Washington talked about for the race, and they believed in self-help. On the other hand, local black leaders saw the necessity of higher education for blacks. They believed that some needed improvements would come from the judicious use of the ballot. Louisville black leaders saw no inherent contradiction in supporting both Washington and his leading critic, the Harvard-trained black educator W. E. B. DuBois. To them, Washington, a man of action, had great prestige and influence and a realistic program. DuBois, a highly respected intellectual, pointed out the potential of the race and made them realize, to use his phrase, that they must protest "in season and out of season, that young black boys need an education as much as young white boys." Overall, it is clear that black leaders in Louisville, and probably in many other places with similar racial problems, adopted only those positions advocated by Washington that clearly coincided with their own racial philosophies and special needs.[1]

Like black leaders all over the nation, several prominent Louisvillians corresponded with Washington, seeking his advice on how best to deal with whites. William H. Steward, a vice president in the Washington-dominated National Afro-American Council, kept the Tuskegeean informed on the developments of the black fight against disfranchisement and segregation in Kentucky. In a February 1904 letter to Washington, Steward relayed the good news that a proposal to disfranchise black voters had failed in the Kentucky legislature. Steward attributed this to the activities of a committee he headed that "has been working quietly at the matter for some time." However, in the same letter to Washington, Steward lamented that very little could be done to prevent the expulsion of black students from Berea College.[2] The Rev. Charles H. Parrish served as president of Eckstein Norton Institute, a school that mirrored Washington's program of industrial education. He occasionally wrote to Washington for advice, especially on how to raise money. Washington gave him encouragement and more: in June 1908 Washington traveled to Louisville to give a speech that raised several hundred dollars for the school.[3]

In addition to supporting the philosophy of Washington, Louisville's black leaders shared several other characteristics too. Most of them had migrated to the city in early adulthood and lived in Louisville for the remainder of their lives. They were usually professionals—ministers, educators, doctors, and lawyers. Their jobs were flexible and gave them time to pursue civil rights causes. Additionally, because they were involved with civil rights and their activities always received coverage in black newspapers, Louisville's leaders were well known in Afro-American communities throughout the nation. Finally, and maybe most important of all, Louisville's Negro leaders prior to 1917 worked closely with influential whites. There were, to be sure, one or two exceptions, but the leaders with the most

1. Spear, *Black Chicago*, 56; Kusmer, *A Ghetto Takes Shape*, 114. See Louis R. Harlan, *Booker T. Washington: The Making of a Black Leader, 1856–1901* (New York, 1972), and Louis R. Harlan, *Booker T. Washington: The Wizard of Tuskegee, 1901–1915* (New York, 1983).

2. Letter from William H. Steward to Booker T. Washington, February 3, 1904, Booker T. Washington Papers, Manuscript Division, Library of Congress, Washington D.C. See also Steward to Washington, August 9, 1910; Washington to Steward, August 14, 1910.

3. Letters from Charles H. Parrish to Washington, May 16, 1903, August 9, 1907, June 30, 1908; Washington to Parrish, April 23, 1908; *Courier-Journal*, June 20, 1908.

influence were close associates of whites and were praised by whites for providing blacks with sensible leadership.[4]

I.

As racial conditions steadily worsened during the 1880s and 1890s, black leaders realized the importance of maintaining, if not expanding, their relationships with sympathetic whites. Louisville's white establishment had always spoken out against racial violence. Henry Watterson, Basil Duke, Bennett H. Young, and others said that their city was different from other southern cities, with far fewer racial problems, and that it was their obligation to keep Louisville that way. Milton H. Smith of the Louisville and Nashville Railroad said that whites should help blacks by giving generously to their educational programs. So not surprisingly, local black leaders found a few white leaders responsive to their desires to prevent conditions from deteriorating further. Louisville's leading black during Reconstruction, Horace Morris, had been adept at gaining white support. Consistently, he urged blacks to work hard but to go slow when demanding political and social equality. At the same time he reassured whites of the loyalty and trustworthiness of blacks. Whites appointed him to several patronage positions in Louisville and strongly endorsed his appointment to the Treasury Department in Washington. During the Garfield Administration he would become the first black to hold the position of steward at the Marine Hospital.[5] Like Morris, succeeding black leaders would often minimize the necessity of social equality and urge blacks to be hardworking, frugal, and sober—qualities that whites found quite acceptable for blacks. On one occasion, black spokesman George W. Brown, a restaurant owner, publicly denounced C. F. Adams, a black newspaper editor, for urging blacks to demand political and social equality. After labeling Adams a troublemaker, Brown reminded blacks of the importance of maintaining good relationships with white allies.

4. The following sources were used to determine Louisville's black leaders: (1) newspapers; (2) books published in the late 1800s and early 1900s containing biographical sketches of prominent Afro-Americans; (3) the membership lists of black institutions, organizations, and important clubs; (4) the Booker T. Washington Papers for the names of Louisville blacks who corresponded with Washington; (5) several interviewees who mentioned the names and reputations of prominent blacks.

5. *Daily Union Press*, December 23, 1865; *Daily Commercial*, April 2, 1870; Weeden, *History of the Colored People*, 42.

I mention these things to show how dependent we are upon the white people after all, and the utter folly of courting their ill-will. These white haters had better stop and see if their course is best even for themselves. I do not believe there is a colored man in the city who has a place worth keeping that does not owe it to a white man, . . . and those who have businesses of their own are no less dependent.[6]

This practice of maintaining close ties with whites is perhaps best il- lustrated by the experiences of State University's first president, William J. Simmons. Born a slave in Charleston, South Carolina, Simmons even- tually became well educated and one of the best-known blacks of his day. In 1865, while attending a white Baptist church in Bordentown, New Jer- sey, he expressed a desire to become a minister, and the church paid for Simmons to attend the Theological School of Madison University, where he graduated in 1870; he continued his education at Howard University, receiving the A.B. degree in 1873. Simmons pastored several black churches, including the First Baptist Church of Lexington, Kentucky, be- fore accepting the presidency of the fledgling Baptist college in 1880. As president of State University, Simmons cultivated the friendship of white Baptists in Louisville and called on those he knew in Pennsylvania, New York, and New Jersey for financial support. He secured grants from the American Baptist Home Mission Board of New York, white philanthro- pists, and the white General Association of Kentucky Baptists. Simmons supplemented his State University salary by working as an agent for the American Baptist Home Mission Society and by traveling throughout the South, speaking to black Baptists on behalf of the white organization.[7]

Simmons was the black leader of Louisville during the 1880s. His po- sition as president of State University gave him influence in black Baptist circles in Kentucky and the rest of the South. He founded the National Baptist Convention and served as its president from 1886 to 1890, mak- ing him well known across the country. Along with fellow Louisvillian William H. Steward, Simmons founded a Baptist newspaper, *The Amer- ican Baptist*, which circulated in black communities throughout the coun- try. In the mid-1880s Simmons was elected president of the Colored Press Association, and in 1888 he published *Men of Mark*, a book of biograph- ical sketches about famous black Americans.

Simmons was also adept at keeping white supporters while speaking out against overt injustices. Like other black leaders, he decried discrim-

6. *Commercial*, May 3, 1881. On one occasion, C. F. Adams led a protest against the Cincinnati Southern Railway, *Courier-Journal*, November 29, 1881.

7. For biographical information on Simmons, see Simmons, *Men of Mark*, 38–63; In- dianapolis *Freeman*, February 2, 1889, November 5, 1890.

ination on the railroads where blacks were often denied first-class treatment. He urged that blacks be selected to juries so that the race could receive an impartial hearing before the law. But instead of denouncing whites in sharp terms, he pleaded with them to live up to their own creed of giving everyone, including blacks, a fair chance to succeed or fail in this country. In 1886, as chairman of the State Convention of Colored Men of Kentucky, he was allowed to address the state legislature, the first time an Afro-American was given that opportunity. This was Simmons's big chance. Throughout his speech, Simmons reminded whites that Kentucky's 272,000 blacks had always been loyal to them: "Our mothers washed your linen and nursed you, our fathers made the soil feed you, and kept the fire burning in your grate." In a tone that Booker T. Washington would become famous for, Simmons spoke of the destiny of blacks being linked with whites in Kentucky and the "New South." He hoped that all fair-minded whites would give blacks a hearing:

As Kentuckians, we meet you with the feelings and aspirations, common and peculiar to those born and surrounded by the greatness of your history, the fertility of your soil, the nobility of your men and the beauty of your women. We come, plain of speech, in order to prove that we are men of judgement, meeting men who are desirous of knowing our wants.[8]

Simmons's philosohy for blacks found widespread approval among local whites. Although president of a liberal arts college, he recognized the utility of vocational skills for blacks. He preached that above all young black men and women needed moral training. He published articles such as "Industrial Education: A Plea for the Young Men of the Race" and "What the Negroes Are Doing in Kentucky" to encourage blacks to better themselves and to inform whites that blacks were indeed making progress. On one occasion Simmons appeared with Henry Watterson at Zion Baptist Church. Throughout his speech, Watterson proclaimed a desire to see blacks elevated to a respectable level in society. But he cautioned that this could only be accomplished by hard work, by the right kind of education, and by blacks remaining in the South. Simmons praised Watterson for his words of encouragement and his commitment to the race's advancement. Then he talked at length about the progress made by Afro-Americans since the end of slavery. Whether out of sincerity or expediency, he won the praise of local whites by urging blacks to break with the Republican party. He repeatedly pointed out that educational gains for blacks were made under Democratic administrations. Simmons said that Republicans were uncon-

8. Simmons, *Men of Mark*, 49–50.

cerned about the Negro. "We must," he informed blacks, "cultivate new friends."[9]

In the summer of 1890 Simmons shocked State University's board of trustees by resigning as president and establishing his own school, Eckstein Norton Institute. By this time he had become more convinced than ever that industrial training rather than higher learning should be emphasized for blacks. With a large donation from L & N Railroad executives Eckstein Norton and Milton Smith, and promises of additional support from Louisville businessmen, Simmons purchased property twenty-nine miles from Louisville in Bullitt County near the L & N line. The school opened in mid-September 1890. Its motto—"Education of the hands, head, heart, and mind"—expressed an idea that was receiving widespread attention in black schools throughout the South. Simmons established a business department at Norton, offering courses in bookkeeping and office skills, but the pride of the institution was the industrial department which included training in carpentry, blacksmithing, farming, painting, dressmaking, tailoring, and cooking. Simmons hoped to establish a branch school in Louisville where blacks could be trained as competent, trustworthy domestic servants. But in November 1890, only a few weeks after opening the school, Simmons died, the victim of a heart attack.[10]

Prominent Louisville whites believed in the school established by Simmons. As Professor August Meier explains, white businessmen and philanthropists "who had no exalted ideas of Negro equality, but felt a sense of noblesse oblige and wanted a supply of trained labor available for the industrialization of the South, saw in industrial education a 'practical' method of educating Negroes, glibly phrased in terms of thrift, industry, morality with which they were so much at home." Railroad executives Smith and Norton encouraged Simmons's assistant, Rev. Charles Parrish, to remain at the school and continue the work. They assured Parrish of their support. Indeed, throughout its twenty-one-year existence, the Eckstein Norton Institute relied almost totally on support from Milton Smith, the Norton family, and a handful of Louisville businessmen. The L & N Railroad built a railroad station at Cane Spring for the school and pro-

9. *Ibid.*, 47–48; New York *Freeman*, March 20, December 13, 1886; see Simmons, "What the Colored People Are Doing," 85–90.

10. See August Meier, "The Vogue of Industrial Education," *Mid-West Journal*, VII (Fall, 1955), 241–66. See also, *Circular of Information for the Twenty-first Annual Session of Eckstein Norton Institute* (Cane Spring, Ky., 1911); Richings, *Evidences of Progress*, 218–20; Raymond J. Randles, "A Biography of the Norton Family," (M.A. thesis, University of Louisville, 1961).

vided the students and faculty with free transportation to Louisville for the school's graduation ceremonies and annual picnic.[11]

Parrish was Simmons's protégé. Like Simmons, Parrish was an ex-slave. A native of Lexington, he came to Louisville with Simmons in 1880 and enrolled as a student at State University. After graduating in 1886, Parrish accepted the pastorship of Calvary Baptist Church and maintained his ties with State University by serving as secretary and treasurer of the college, guardian of the young men, and professor of Greek. Along with Simmons, Parrish and several other faculty members resigned from State University to accept positions at Norton Institute.[12]

After the death of Simmons, Parrish became Louisville's leading black minister. He often appeared before the mayor or aldermen as leader of a protest. His church held rallies on behalf of black causes. In the early twentieth century, Parrish organized the Louisville branch of the National Association for the Advancement of Colored People (NAACP) to fight the residential segregation ordinance through the courts. Parrish, however, like Simmons, was always careful to maintain the fragile equilibrium of speaking out yet not alienating his white supporters. In fact, Parrish was well aware that the main proponents of the housing ordinance were low- and middle-class whites and not his white associates. Moreover, by the 1920s, when a younger more militant group of blacks joined the NAACP and denounced the city's white leaders, Parrish resigned from the NAACP to devote time to the Commission on Interracial Cooperation, an organization with a more moderate approach to racial problems. All of the organizations and institutions with which Parrish was affiliated relied on white community leaders for direction and financial support. A board of white businessmen advised Parrish during his years at Norton Institute and during his presidency of State University (1918–1931). His church was one of several in Louisville to receive donations from whites and to rely on these "friends of the church for advice."[13]

Instead of harping on racial discrimination, Parrish blamed blacks for most of their problems and shortcomings. He deplored the life-style and activities of lower-class blacks and constantly condemned them for frequenting saloons and gambling joints. Parrish was confident that racial

11. Meier, "Vogue of Industrial Education," 246; *Courier-Journal*, May 18, 1902; *Circular of Information for Norton Institute*, 26–27.

12. Simmons, *Men of Mark*, 1059; Charles Alexander, *One Hundred Distinguished Leaders* (Atlanta, 1899), 63; Johnson, *Biographical Sketches*, 22–23.

13. For a list of Parrish's white friends, see the Simmons University Scrapbook, Archives Department, University of Louisville. For information on influential whites in Louisville, see Alvin Seekamp and Roger Burlingame (eds.), *Who's Who in Louisville 1912* (Louisville, 1912).

problems could be solved; that whites would eventually accept educated, property-owning blacks as equals. He agreed with Booker T. Washington and other leaders who believed that whites of goodwill were friends of the race and wanted to see an end to racial problems. As he once told a black fraternal order, "get property, get it in all parts of the city, and the good white people of Louisville will see that you are protected. You hear talk of breaking up of colored societies, the taking away of their names—that is down South. Kentucky's white people will never permit such a thing in Kentucky." [14]

White Louisvillians spoke highly of Parrish and rewarded him with positions on interracial boards and within the local Republican party. The *Courier-Journal* viewed him as a "negro leader," noting that "since he has been in Louisville he has been involved in all movements to improve the condition of the negro." Even the city's Democratic mayors respected Parrish and consulted him about racial matters. In a break with local custom, Parrish was often welcomed in the homes of prominent whites, and according to his son, he often attended meetings and banquets at hotels that normally refused services to blacks. A staunch Republican, Parrish served as a delegate to the Kentucky Republican Convention for nine consecutive years. He also served as a member of the executive board of the Republican Committee of Jefferson County. [15]

In the areas of influence and prestige, only William H. Steward matched Parrish. Born a free black in 1847 in Brandenburg, Kentucky, Steward came to Louisville as a youth to attend the school operated at First African Baptist Church by Rev. Henry Adams. While a young man, Steward developed long-lasting friendships with influential whites. These relationships first began when he worked as a messenger and purchasing agent for the L & N Railroad, a position he held for several years. In 1877 Steward resigned from the L & N and accepted a position as the first black letter carrier in Louisville. Steward's mail route proved to be an ideal one: he delivered mail in the district occupied by wealthy whites, and this enabled him to maintain ties with L & N executives and to acquire new white friends as well. [16]

14. Indianapolis, *Freeman*, April 8, 1911. See Charles H. Parrish, "Educational Development Among Negroes of Kentucky," Louisville *Times*, December 31, 1909 (silver anniversary ed.).

15. The quote comes from the *Courier-Journal*, November 27, 1927; see also *Courier-Journal*, July 17, 1924; Parrish interview; Richardson (ed.), *The National Cyclopedia*, 172; Louisville *Herald-Post*, December 6, 1925.

16. Simmons, *Men of Mark*, 603–604; Blanton interview; Alexander, *One Hundred Distinguished Leaders*, 64.

In addition to making white friends during his early years, Steward became prominent in black Baptist circles. Steward, often called the "pioneer of colored Baptists in Kentucky," selected the site for State University, handled the purchasing of the property, and gave contributions at critical times to keep the school in existence. He lured William J. Simmons to State University and served the university as interim president whenever a vacancy occurred in that office. From the 1870s and 1880s until his death in 1935, Steward held a variety of positions, including secretary of the Kentucky Baptist Convention, secretary of the General Association of Negro Baptists of Kentucky, and chairman of State University's board of trustees. He also edited *The American Baptist* for fifty-six years. The paper was the official organ of the American National Baptist Convention, the General Association of Negro Baptists of Kentucky, and all of the small district associations in the state.[17]

His black connections were important, but Steward owed much of his influence and prestige in Louisville's black community to his close relationship with Louisville's leading white businessmen, educators, and politicians. Like Horace Morris, Steward was named to the Colored School Board of Visitors, and over the years he helped numerous blacks, including members of his family, secure teaching positions. When the Republicans held office, Steward helped select blacks for patronage jobs. In the 1920s, when city officials finally decided to hire blacks as policemen and firemen, all of the applicants had to be approved by Steward before being hired. Steward drew the praise of whites for his efforts. The Louisville *Herald-Post* acknowledged that "Steward has been a factor in every movement in the city looking at the improvement of the colored people and of the city generally during his long and useful life, and is probably better known to more white people of the city than any other colored man now living."[18]

Steward, like Parrish, believed that many of the problems encountered by blacks resulted from their own shortcomings. He deplored their lack of morality and unity and condemned black men for not attending church. Speaking to the members of the Dexter Avenue Baptist Church in Montgomery, Alabama, he said, "Where are the boys and men? The girls are cared for while the boys are left to the dogs. You make one standard of morality for women and one for men, but we should bear in mind that

17. St. Joseph *Herald*, January 26, 1896; Baltimore *Afro-American*, November 6, 1897; Blanton interview; *Courier-Journal*, July 27, 1922; William H. Steward Scrapbook, Louisville.

18. Blanton interview; *Herald-Post*; Ohio Falls *Express*, September 29, 1894.

no country nor race can rise higher than its component parts." To him a lack of unity was a major black problem, a problem for which whites were not responsible: "We need to be united. Our people can take from a fellow, but they can never add anything to him. We are great Bible students, but we forget that the Bible says 'To him that hath, it shall be given, and him that hath not, it shall be taken away even that which he hath.'" [19] When working with young people at Fifth Street Baptist Church, where he was superintendent of the Sunday School for over fifty years, Steward preached a gospel of abstinence, honesty, and hard work. He said this would lead to the end of racial discrimination.

You represent the future of the negro in this country, and if you go wrong then you will find that the race will not rise. I want you young boys to be manly, to discontinue smoking cigarettes, be true, have good manners, and by all means do not learn to gamble, and avoid drinking whisky and beer. I am proud to tell you boys that there is for you a bright future right here in the South, it is not necessary to leave this country. Your color will not keep you back in this age if you are qualified, for in this age fitness and character must win. You boys and girls must not think that you can go to the North and find social equality for that does not exist anywhere; you must build your own social circles and lift up your own girls.[20]

As editor of *The American Baptist*, Steward became the most powerful black layman in church affairs in Kentucky and probably in the nation. Yet he remained active in the secular world through his Masonic positions (Worship Master of the Grand Lodge of Kentucky, and High Priest of Enterprise No. 4) and his actions on behalf of the Republican party.

Knowing that both Steward and Parrish were men of genuine ability and strong personality and that they both courted the same influential whites, it is not surprising that some bitterness existed in their relationship. Much of their disagreement centered on William J. Simmons, whom Steward hired as president of State University and who was closer to Parrish than to Steward. Throughout Simmons's tenure at the school, he and Steward differed sharply on who should run the school and how. Steward was convinced that Simmons and Parrish started Norton Institute to destroy State University. Therefore, after their departure Steward closely guarded the school and tried to insure that everyone affiliated with it was completely loyal to him. He was able to do this because he held two powerful positions, secretary of the General Association and chairman of State

19. Newsclip from the Steward Scrapbook.
20. Newsclip, Nashville *American*, from the Steward Scrapbook.

University's board of trustees. Because of these positions, he virtually chose all of the presidents who served the school. In the early 1900s, the president died and Steward took over as interim president. Parrish, realizing that his school would never match State University in enrollment and influence, made known his desire to fill the vacancy. The Indianapolis *Freeman* noted that a feud developed in the General Association with Parrish pitted against several other candidates. The General Association wanted a well-known and dynamic leader as president. They finally agreed on Dr. J. R. L. Diggs from Virginia, and Steward reluctantly agreed. Diggs, who had been active in the militant Niagara Movement, a forerunner of the NAACP, proved too radical for Steward's way of thinking. Fortunately for Steward, Diggs grew tired of the bickering and left after only two years. Steward then mustered all of his support to get Dr. William T. Amiger selected as president. Amiger died in 1915, after serving seven years; from 1915 to 1918 Steward prevented Parrish from being elected but lacked the influence to have any of his own candidates chosen. By 1918 Parrish was the moderator of the General Association, a position that rivaled Steward's in influence. The mere fact that Parrish had been elected moderator signaled Steward's declining influence, and in that same year, Parrish was chosen president. The final blow occurred when Parrish, with the full support of the Association, changed the name of the State University to Simmons University.[21]

Steward and Parrish worked closely, though often separately, with school principal Albert Ernest Meyzeek. The son of a white Canadian and a black, Meyzeek was born in Toledo, Ohio, in 1862 but was reared in Toronto, Canada. His maternal grandfather, John Lott, while living in Madison, Indiana, in the 1850s had aided blacks in their escape from slavery. When Indiana authorities learned of his activities, Lott was forced to flee to safety in Canada along the same route he had sent many slaves. From childhood Meyzeek was told stories of his grandfather the black abolitionist and his Canadian relatives, who were of French Huguenot stock. When Meyzeek was a teenager, his family moved to Terre Haute, Indiana, where he was valedictorian of his class at the predominantly white Terre Haute Classical High School. After receiving degrees from Indiana State Normal School for Teachers and Indiana University, Meyzeek went to Louisville in the early 1890s and passed the competitive examination given school principal candidates. Thereafter, he served as principal of Central

21. Indianapolis *Freeman*, January 3, June 16, 1906. This writer learned of the conflict between Steward and Parrish from an interview with Rev. Homer E. Nutter, July 3, 1976. As a student at State University, Nutter gained the friendship and confidence of both men.

High and several elementary schools. He quickly became active in Louisville's black community. For example, he started a campaign for a black library, since the race was denied admission to the main public library. After several years of work, his library committee opened a library in temporary quarters on Chestnut Street near Tenth. A permanent building was constructed and finally opened on October 29, 1908. Most of the construction capital came from a fund for black libraries started by Andrew Carnegie. The Western Colored Branch Library met with such success that Meyzeek had little difficulty in persuading white library officials to open a second branch in the east end of town. The Eastern Colored Branch, also a Carnegie-endowed building, opened January 28, 1914. Meyzeek served continuously on the YMCA's executive committee, even mortgaging his home to help finance the purchase of a lot for the YMCA. He also served as a probation officer in an attempt to combat juvenile delinquency among lower-class blacks.[22]

Unlike Steward and Parrish, Meyzeek rarely consulted with whites and was quick to denounce discrimination. Nicknamed the "Old War Horse," he has been described as "a dynamic person, a fearless man who advocated bold approaches."[23] It was well understood that black school employees were to remain free of controversial issues. Meyzeek ignored this unofficial rule and assumed a leadership role in numerous confrontations with the white establishment. Though it is difficult to determine whether the school board was tolerant or if it just purposely ignored his actions, he was never fired despite being reprimanded on four different occasions for his civic activities and for publicly denouncing discrimination. In meetings with the white school board members, it was not uncommon for Meyzeek to criticize their handling of the black schools, often getting into heated discussions with them. Meyzeek took pride in the role he played in

22. For biographical information on Meyzeek see "Life History of A. E. Meyzeek," an interview conducted for E. Franklin Frazier, *Negro Youths at the Crossways* (Washington, D.C., 1940) and in the possession of Dr. Charles H. Parrish, Jr.; Horton, "Life and Achievements of Meyzeek," 25–26; "The Record of Albert Ernest Meyzeek," *Negro History Bulletin*, X (May, 1947), 186–97; *Courier-Journal*, July 26, 1962; Indianapolis *Freeman*, December 26, 1908.

By 1914, blacks in Louisville could boast of having the first black branch library in the country and the only black community in the United States with two library branches. See the following sources on Louisville's black libraries: John Wilkins, "Blue's Colored Branch: A 'Second Plan' That Became a First in Librarianship," *American Libraries*, VII (May, 1976), 256; *Colored Branches of the Louisville Free Public Library* (Louisville, 1915); Rachel Harris, "The Advantages of Colored Libraries," *Southern Workman*, XLIV (July, 1915); Indianapolis *Freeman*, January 8, 1910, January 24, February 7, 1914.

23. Lyman T. Johnson interview.

Louisville and had contempt for the passive attitudes of other black school teachers and principals. "I am counted as a radical in this town and do more civic work than any other principal in town," he informed an interviewer in the 1930s.[24]

Meyzeek's willingness to speak out against discrimination aided blacks in their struggles for civil rights. Few black protest movements were attempted without his backing. Though outspoken, Meyzeek knew just how far to push the white establishment; he never called for social equality, but emphasized improving black life through education and character development. He always argued effectively that as taxpayers blacks were entitled to decent city services and quality schools. No one in Louisville matched Meyzeek in the duration and the intensity of his fight for black rights. At the age of ninety-two, he complained after the Brown Decision of May 1954 that the school board was not moving fast enough to end school segregation. He protested discrimination in Louisville until his death in 1963 at the age of 101.[25]

Steward, Parrish, and Meyzeek worked with Negro ministers, lawyers, and doctors on many different issues. In Louisville, as in most cities, black ministers were significant leaders. Their social programs were of inestimable benefit to the community, but most ministers fell short when it came to openly challenging discrimination and race hatred. Although black ministers have historically been viewed as free of white control, evidence in Louisville suggests that several leading black ministers were so closely tied to white financial strings that they were hampered in their criticism of racism. Parrish's attitude toward whites was typical of the other leading ministers. None of Rev. E. G. Harris's many worthwhile projects could have succeeded without the support of several well-established white families. Although concerned about the plight of local blacks, Harris refused to participate in any of the confrontations that blacks had with city officials. Rev. John Frank, the pastor of the most prestigious black church in Kentucky for fifty years, an activist in a score of race movements, admitted that he looked to whites for support. "I think white people owe us something more than a word of commendation. Fifth Avenue has been and is a community asset of outstanding value. . . . Upon such a consideration, I should not be viewed as presumptuous in asking help of our white friends

24. "Life of Meyzeek," interview for Frazier, Negro Youths at the Crossways; Lyman T. Johnson interiew; Perry interview.
25. Lyman T. Johnson interview; Omer Carmichael and James Weldon, The Louisville Story (New York, 1957), 48.

and neighbors regardless of their religious faith or political persuasion."[26]

Another minister, William H. Craighead, pastored Zion Baptist Church for forty-nine years and served on State University's board of trustees. During his long tenure in Louisville, he participated in many black movements, often serving as a fund raiser to aid black causes. His willingness to aid the poor and newcomers to Louisville attracted many of them to his church. By the early 1900s Zion Baptist had a membership of over 2,000, making it one of the largest black churches in Kentucky. Craighead believed that whites were largely responsible for the positive gains blacks had made since the Civil War. He spoke of how his mother, a former slave, had acquired culture from contact with whites. To his large congregation, Craighead preached that paternalistic whites aided blacks.

There was a time when the Negroes and whites were a bit uncertain about their attitudes toward one another. That has passed and today the colored people realize and appreciate the help and encouragement they receive from white people. For instance, the great Baptist Theological Seminary is continually sending us much needed advice and training.

Before the war in Kentucky our ancestors lived under the direct supervision of their white owners and obtained unusual training in behavior and religious thought. This unique closeness of the races has enabled us to advance as we have in a relatively short time.[27]

Since that was the predominant attitude, it is not surprising that a number of the ministers took very conservative positions when dealing with the white establishment lest they offend their white supporters. Perhaps most significant for the Afro-American community, these ministers undercut the self-help philosophy they preached to the race by constantly soliciting whites for advice and financial support.

In contrast to the attitude prevalent among ministers, Louisville's black doctors were more outspoken on racial matters. They were excluded from white hospitals and had practically no relationship with white doctors.

26. *Brief History of Plymouth Congregational Church; Courier-Journal,* July 9, 1917; Louisville *Post,* May 29, 1923. Rev. Theodore Ledbetter, who succeeded Harris as pastor at Plymouth Congregational, remembers Harris as a "con man." Harris would go to the meat market and buy rabbits and other small game and take it to the homes of his white patrons, claiming that he had just returned from a successful hunting trip and wanted to present the game as a present. Several days later Harris would return again, this time asking for a favor. Rev. Theodore Ledbetter, interview with author, Washington, D.C., August 27, 1979. Frank was quoted in the *Courier-Journal,* October 31, 1927. Indianapolis *Freeman,* September 16, 1911.

27. *Courier-Journal,* July 20, 1937; *Zion Baptist Church, 1878–1953,* 2–4.

They depended entirely on a black clientele for their livelihood and therefore felt fewer constraints against protesting racial injustices. The city's first black doctor proved to be the most outspoken, and he surely was too radical for the Stewards and Parrishes. After arriving in Louisville in 1871, Dr. Henry Fitzbutler quickly became the leading advocate for improvements in black education, calling on the state to increase its funding for Negro schools. Local black leaders who were more knowledgeable about race relations told Fitzbutler to go slow. He ignored their advice. In 1874 he drafted a letter at the Negro Education Convention sharply criticizing Kentucky's segregated schools. Fitzbutler was also something of a political maverick. In the 1880s he ran for the school board several times, becoming the first black to campaign for an elective post in Louisville. Although a Republican, he constantly threatened to bolt the party unless blacks received better treatment.[28]

In 1879 Fitzbutler established a newspaper, the *Ohio Falls Express*, as an organ for black opinion on political and social issues. In his newspaper he condemned segregation and racial discrimination in Louisville and the accommodating positions of William H. Steward and other black leaders. His newspaper was a valued enterprise. Lasting twenty-two years, it was far and away the longest running nineteenth-century newspaper in black Louisville.[29]

Though not rivaling Fitzbutler in racial activism, most Negro doctors did participate in movements designed to improve the welfare of blacks. Dr. John A. C. Lattimore, for example, had a well-deserved reputation as a "race man." A graduate of Meharry Medical College in Nashville, Lattimore came to Louisville in 1901. He felt that Louisville blacks were receiving little consideration from city officials because of their blind loyalty to the Republican party. So unlike most of his fellow blacks, he joined the Democratic party. He helped organize the Negro Outlook Committee to combat police brutality. Obviously a joiner, Lattimore was elected to leadership positions in several fraternities and was one of the strongest backers of both the Louisville NAACP and the Urban League. Additionally, he worked to improve health conditions in the black community. According to the Indianapolis *Freeman*, his work on behalf of poor blacks

28. For biographical information on Dr. Fitzbutler, see *Journal National Medical Association*, LXIV (September, 1952); Leslie L. Hanawalt, "Henry Fitzbutler: Detroit's First Black Medical Student," *Detroit in Perspective*, I (Winter, 1973); AME *Christian Recorder*, March 6, 1873.

29. Unfortunately, the *Ohio Falls Express* was not preserved. A few copies of the paper can be found in the William H. Steward Scrapbook. I. Garland Penn, *The Afro-American Press and Its Editors* (Springfield, Mass. 1891), 316–19, mentioned the paper.

earned him the title "Doctor of the town." Yet he somehow found the time to build a lucrative private practice and to make profitable investments. The *Freeman* noted in January 1911 that "Dr. Lattimore has bought two more pieces of property on Fifteenth Street." [30]

In most cities a sizeable number of the black leaders were attorneys. Because they knew first-hand the injustices the race suffered before a white legal system and because they desired patronage jobs or the chance to run for elective offices, attorneys were often quick to complain and rally the race to combat discrimination. In Louisville, however, the leading attorneys were too dependent on patronage jobs to fully denounce discrimination. On one occasion, when blacks flexed enough political muscle to get attorney Nathanial R. Harper on the Republican ticket as a candidate, he withdrew when offered a job by Republican officials who did not want a black on the ticket. Another example was the career of attorney William H. Parker. A native of Louisville and a graduate of State University, Parker was largely unsuccessful in establishing a private legal practice in the early 1900s. So he started a newspaper, the *Columbian*, which collapsed and was revived only during political campaigns. In his paper, Parker supported candidates who offered him patronage jobs. In April 1910 Parker called himself a staunch Republican while trying to be appointed as private messenger to a local white, H. H. Thatcher, who was a member of the Panama Canal Commission. After being denied the appointment, Parked called on blacks to support him in an independent party movement. He had few followers.[31]

The role of black journalists as race leaders in Louisville is difficult to assess since most of their newspapers are lost to history. From 1870 to 1915 Louisville had at least eight different Afro-American newspapers, but only a few extant copies have been preserved from two of them. Moreover, with the exception of Steward's *American Baptist* and Fitzbutler's *Ohio Falls Express*, the newspapers were in existence for short periods of time, rarely lasting a year. Throughout the country Afro-American journalists kept their black readers informed about injustices and tried to stir the race into action. The black press also tried to instill desirable qualities in the race. Indeed, the editorial page of the *American Baptist* usually stressed themes of

---

30. Biographical information on Dr. Lattimore can be found in Thomas Jackson, "Biographical Sketches on Kentucky Negroes," project completed for the Works Progress Administration, Washington, D.C., 1940; Indianapolis *Freeman*, August 31, 1907, January 14, 1911, June 24, 1913.

31. New York *Freeman*, May 16, 1885; Indianapolis *Freeman*, December 12, 1896, August 31, 1907, December 26, 1908, September 25, 1909, March 5, August 8, 1910, January 7, July 29, 1911, December 25, 1915.

racial improvement and other ideas consistent with the philosophy of Steward.[32]

Interestingly, newspaper editors who came to Louisville from elsewhere and attempted to challenge the moderate philosophy of Steward and the ministers found black Louisville a hostile environment. Around 1908 a young woman news reporter from Washington, D.C., Miss J. S. Young, bought an interest in the Kentucky *Standard*, a paper that had been around for some time and had made at best only a minor contribution. As editor, Miss Young was very outspoken on a number of issues; she was especially critical of local black leaders who advised the young to learn skills that would enable them to become good workers. "Are we to forever tamely submit to the prevailing idea that the Negro must be educated as 'hewers of wood and drawers of water' for the more favored race, or shall we make a plea for the same kind of education every other race enjoys, telling them among us who elect, and whose minds are so inclined, to hew wood and draw water to their hearts' content," Miss Young wrote. Her paper's circulation failed to increase and within six months after arriving she left for greener pastures.[33]

Roscoe C. Simmons had a similar experience. A former editor of the Memphis *Sun* and the New York *Age*, Simmons came to Louisville in late 1915 to publish the Louisville *News*. He protested segregation and the unbelievable humiliations it caused blacks. He concluded that the primary reason for black mistreatment was the lack of strong black leaders willing to stand up to whites. In the summer of 1916, Simmons declared that Louisville needed new black leaders and that he would run for the state legislature from the city's Tenth Ward. However, he soon realized that he stood no chance of winning, since he did not even receive black support. By election time in November he had left Louisville.[34]

II.

In his assessment of the career and power of Booker T. Washington, Professor Louis Harlan concludes that blacks had very little to do with

---

32. The best source for information on Afro-American newspapers in Louisville is Penn, *The Afro-American Press and Its Editors*, 120–22, 316–19, 368–76, 410–13. Additional information can be found in Penelope L. Bullock, *The Afro-American Periodical Press, 1838–1909* (Baton Rouge, 1981), 167–68; *AME Church Review*, V (October, 1888), 187.

33. Kentucky *Standard*, February 14, 1909; Indianapolis *Freeman*, March 19, 1910.

34. Indianapolis *Freeman*, February 19, August 5, November 11, 1916.

making him the Negro leader. Whites selected Washington because he was "safe"; because Washington, better than any other black spokesman, could reassure both the North and South that race problems could be resolved along the lines that whites thought appropriate. As Harlan explains, when considering the realities of the world in which Washington operated, and realizing that any outburst of protest on his part would have cost him white support, Washington's style of leadership could not have been any different. "If by 1895 he had become a 'white man's black man,' considering his background it is hard to see how he could have been anything else."[35]

When looking at Louisville's black leaders it is difficult to disagree with Harlan's theory that whites appointed black leaders primarily because they were safe. Furthermore, the moderate positions they assumed on racial problems were understandable given the reality of life in Louisville. Steward and Parrish were leaders during the height of racial hatred, when southern blacks were being disfranchised and lynched in alarming numbers and northern blacks were being segregated in areas previously open to them and victimized by rioting whites. Conditions in their city were deteriorating, though not as greatly as further South. Yet Louisville blacks knew what awaited them if they dared move too quickly. Like Booker T. Washington, they knew that some whites were willing to keep racial violence under control. Moreover, instead of continuously denouncing discrimination, Louisville's black leaders urged blacks to make their community a desirable place to live, stressing the importance of education, frugality, and morality for the race's advancement. By doing so, they were comforting whites by shifting most of the responsibility for the hardships of segregation onto blacks themselves instead of onto white society.

Even Albert Ernest Meyzeek, the most controversial of the local black leaders, shared the belief that black self-help would lead to the desired changes in society. As principal of Eastern Elementary School he instructed students in the virtue of thrift by encouraging them to take whatever money they could afford, place it in a savings account, and allow the money to accumulate interest undisturbed for a year. Meyzeek also initiated domestic science courses for his elementary students after noticing that newspaper advertisements often read "white servants preferred." He concluded that greater efficiency among blacks would ensure positions for them in domestic service. These efforts to improve the race show that Meyzeek, like his fellow black leaders all over America, fervently believed in the American ideal of fairness despite the reality of racial prejudice. The lead-

---

35. Harlan, *Booker T. Washington: The Making of a Black Leader,* 227—28.

ers' own lives should have convinced them of the futility of their efforts to achieve equality. Meyzeek, for example, was as well educated as any white principal, yet he received a much lower salary. Despite his impressive educational credentials, he was still only a "negro principal." He and the other black leaders had to believe that conditions would improve for the race or otherwise all of their teachings and actions would have had no meaning.

Meyzeek and other black leaders worried that the lack of refinement among lower-class blacks might result in setbacks for the entire race. Throughout these years many white Louisvillians called for the exclusion of blacks from the streetcars. They claimed that blacks misbehaved on the streetcars and that black men often offended white women. In early 1910, after repeated white complaints, several black leaders grew concerned that the expulsion of blacks from the streetcars might become a reality. They met with streetcar officials and civic leaders and assured them that black behavior would improve and that blacks would avoid sitting next to whites. The leaders then organized a meeting at the YMCA to enlighten the Afro-American community about the informal policy agreed upon with the streetcar companies. The meeting was well attended, and those there heard Meyzeek, the Old War Horse, say

> When talking with influential men on behalf of the negroes . . . we were continually faced with the argument that the negroes do not behave themselves on the streetcars. We were forced to admit this. . . . I have seen—and so have you—members of our race get on cars and talk in a loud and boisterous manner, yelling to one another from either end of the car. We have in measure succeeded in placing the negroes of the city on probation, and one overt act will cause us to lose all the ground we have gained.

Parrish then spoke to the black crowd. After agreeing with Meyzeek's comments, he then explained how they should act on the streetcar:

> Don't hold malice because your white neighbor would rather not sit next to one of your race, and if possible avoid sitting by a white woman. Above all, be polite. Many a negro has successfully held a position he was not qualified in experience to hold because of his politeness. Be careful of your conduct, and let no one wrong bring on another. Suffer in humility rather than resent a slight at the cost of the entire negro population of the city.[36]

The pleas of Meyzeek and Parrish tell much about the racial climate of the day and the limited room Afro-American leaders had for negotiation and change. By the turn of the century, racial hatred had increased

36. *Courier-Journal*, February 14, 1910; Indianapolis *Freeman*, February 29, 1910.

and the color line was broadly drawn throughout American society. Black leaders tried everything—allying themselves with influential whites, encouraging blacks to better themselves, and even blaming blacks for the problems—to improve race relations and to prevent a further deterioration in the status of the race. That conditions failed to improve was not their fault (or Booker T. Washington's as some of his critics charged), but it was an indictment of the racism in America, an irrational racism that relegated blacks to an inferior position and then ignored all of their efforts to improve and their significant accomplishments.

## 7

Political Activity

Louisville's black leaders sharply disagreed with Booker T. Washington's public statements that blacks should remain aloof from political activity. They believed that the right to vote was one of their most cherished possessions. Moreover, they believed it would be through politics that many needed changes would take place, that only by petitioning and protesting to local and state officials would their concerns receive attention. Additionally, a number of black leaders viewed themselves as candidates for political offices or at least patronage jobs.

Between 1880 and 1917 blacks were repeatedly frustrated in their political activities. Too often they were manipulated and abused by the Republicans and ignored or condemned by the Democrats. Supporting the minority party meant that few political plums could be harvested by Afro-Americans. More important, the Republican party, wanting to secure white support, downplayed its role as the Negro's party. On the two occasions when the Republicans controlled city government, they refused to hire blacks for jobs other than menial labor. Moreover, they consistently refused to endorse or support blacks as candidates, even when a black had fairly gained the Republican nomination. As Howard Rabinowitz explains, the Republican party was caught in a dilemma. Republicans could not win without the Negro vote, "but such support ironically made it increasingly difficult to attract the white voters indispensable for the final victory. Thus for white Republicans, . . . the Negroes had to be disciplined and kept in their place lest they prove detrimental to the larger goals."[1]

Unfortunately for blacks, the Democratic party was not a realistic alternative, even though a few blacks joined the party and urged others to do likewise. Led by "Boss" Whallen, the party continued its practice of ignoring and insulting Afro-Americans. On several occasions the more respectable Democrats took steps to discipline him. Yet they too were unconcerned about blacks. It is true that Louisville's Democrats were never

1. Rabinowitz, *Race Relations in the Urban South*, 287–88. See also Callcott, *The Negro in Maryland Politics*, 75–80.

as virulent in denouncing blacks as their southern counterparts, but they were just as adamant in their refusal to include blacks. Under their polite racism the Democrats preferred simply to leave blacks alone. That way they could claim that they were different from other southerners; that in their city blacks maintained their right to vote. This was a political luxury Louisville and Kentucky Democrats enjoyed because of their superior numbers and the weakness of the opposition. Nevertheless, on the few occasions when the Republicans had a realistic chance of winning, the Democrats, led by "Marse Henry" Watterson of the influential *Courier-Journal*, secured their victory by arousing the racial fears of whites.

That blacks in Louisville (and throughout Kentucky) were never elected to office and rarely appointed to local and state positions is strikingly different from the experience of blacks in many other places in both the North and South. In this regard the performance by blacks in Louisville was much worse than elsewhere, especially in comparison with cities of roughly the same size. In Cincinnati and Cleveland, blacks were consistently elected to the Ohio legislature from 1877 to 1916. Nor was it uncommon for Negroes to be elected to the city councils in other cities in Ohio. In Indianapolis, a city with a much smaller black population than Louisville, several Negroes were elected on the Republican ticket to the state legislature in the 1880s. The Democrats of Indianapolis even attempted to woo the Negro vote. One Democrat in particular, Thomas Taggart, was elected mayor in the 1890s with the support of blacks. He responded by giving more blacks city jobs, especially in the police and fire departments (something Louisville blacks had been agitating for since the 1870s but were unsuccessful in attaining until the mid-1920s).[2]

In other border and southern cities, blacks also made political gains far beyond those achieved by Louisville blacks. For a number of years, blacks ran, though without success, for the city council of Baltimore. Finally in 1890 a young attorney won, and for the next twenty-five years an Afro-American would serve on the Baltimore city council. Blacks held office in Richmond for several years after the end of Reconstruction. In Tennessee a dozen blacks served in the state legislature in the 1880s, though this practice did come to an end in 1889. Blacks were particularly effective in Nashville, a city much like Louisville in its population and number of black businesses. Nashville blacks flirted with political independence, and this led white politicians to be more responsive to black concerns. During the 1870s and 1880s, the city had an all-black fire station. In Nashville,

2. Gerber, *Black Ohio*, 212–30; Thornbrough, *The Negro in Indiana*, 293–313.

Raleigh, and several other cities, blacks were appointed as policemen and as justices of the peace.[3]

I.

"The Republican party is the deck, all else is the sea," a phrase made famous by Frederick Douglass, accurately describes the philosophy of Louisville blacks in the late nineteenth century. Blacks were loyal to the Republican party during these years even though the party lacked influence and patronage, and even though Republican leaders, in an attempt to attract more support, tried repeatedly to project an image of being primarily concerned about the white business community and only secondarily about blacks. For blacks, supporting the Republican party was synonymous with race loyalty. After the Civil War, a Negro Democrat was looked upon with suspicion, as having somehow sold out the race. Though not Democrats, some blacks were on friendly terms with Democratic leaders. For instance, William H. Ward, after campaigning unsuccessfully for marshall of the city court on the Republican ticket in 1877, was hired by the Democratic administration as chief janitor of city hall. Madison Minnis, William H. Gibson, and several other black politicians received minor positions and boasted of their friendships with Democratic leaders. But none of these men claimed affiliation with the party. Doing so would have cost them dearly in the Afro-American community. Since black support was not essential for success the Democrats were often content to buy off the few blacks aspiring to hold office by offering them minor jobs at city hall.[4]

A number of local blacks formed Republican clubs to ensure that the race remained loyal to the "party of Lincoln." Realizing that their chances of winning were slim as long as the Democrats remained united, the Republicans hoped that respectable showings at the polls would at least lure more party supporters. They needed a solid black vote as a base of power from which to grow. The black Republican clubs attempted to keep all blacks behind the party by reminding the race of the Republicans' good

3. Callcott, *The Negro in Maryland Politics*, 58, 153; Rabinowitz, *Race Relations in the Urban South*, 294–96; Joseph H. Cartwright, *The Triumph of Jim Crow: Tennessee Race Relations in the 1880s* (Knoxville, 1976), 101–18; Lamon, *Black Tennesseans*, 11; Wynes, *Race Relations in Virginia*, 39–45.

4. *Commercial*, May 3, 1881; *Courier-Journal*, July 10, 1887; Gibson, *Progress of the Colored Race in Louisville*, 53; Weeden, *History of the Colored People*, 6, 42.

deeds. Although the party was most often out of office, local Republican officials found small ways to reward their black supporters. They secured small jobs through patronage from Republican administrations in Washington, D.C.; they aided black newspapers, especially during election years; and they assisted a number of the club members who were involved in illegal activities. Organizations such as the Colored Republicans Vigilance Committee, the Colored Political League of Voters, and the Race Protective Association existed for decades. Political scientist Martin Kilson notes that blacks in these political clubs were involved in a patron-client relationship with white Republicans. They attempted to explain their actions by saying they were benefiting the race when in reality they were benefiting only themselves.[5]

Getting out the vote and keeping blacks loyal to the Republican party were the primary functions of black political clubs in Louisville. These clubs and Republican officials tried to intimidate Negro candidates and frighten blacks away from the dangerous waters of political independence. White Republicans would try to bribe a rebellious black candidate for public office to remain in the party with promises of better treatment for the race. Personal appeals, favors, or jobs would also be offered. If these approaches failed, members of a black political club would visit and explain to the black candidate that his candidacy was hurting the black community. If he continued, the political club would denounce him publicly, calling him a tool of white Democrats. On election day, the political club would get out the vote, using a variety of tactics to ensure an overwhelming rejection of the militant black. These tactics were resorted to on several occasions in the 1880s when Dr. Fitzbutler campaigned for the school board and other elective positions. It is likely Fitzbutler would have lost anyway, but the opposition from black political clubs increased his loss by a much wider margin, which discouraged others from trying for political office. Lawyer Nathaniel R. Harper occasionally flirted with the idea of running independently of the Republic party, but he was easily swayed with the offer of a job to quit the race and support the white Republican candidate.[6]

5. Martin Kilson, "Political Change in the Negro Ghetto, 1900–1940's," in Nathan Huggins, *et al.*, *Key Issues in the Afro-American Experience* (2 vols.; New York, 1971), II, 171–74. For information on the different black political clubs, see the Indianapolis *Freeman*, March 7, 14, 21, 1896, June 19, 1909, September 17, 1910, September 9, 1911, April 26, 1913; *Courier-Journal*, October 7, 1919.

6. *Commercial*, December 6, 1883; New York *Freeman*, June 12, July 31, August 14, 1886.

A split in the Democratic party in 1887 provided the Republican party with an opportunity to gain control of city government. A number of Democrats and civic leaders, disgusted with Whallen's corrupt domination of local government, convinced former mayor Charles Jacob to challenge Whallen's handpicked candidate, William B. Hoke. The Republicans decided to enter a candidate for the first time. Their selection of Samuel Avery, the son of millionaire B. F. Avery, proved to be an ideal one since he was widely respected in the business community. As election day drew nearer, Avery and the Republicans were confident of winning since a number of prominent civic leaders openly endorsed his candidacy. In addition, the Republicans were assured of receiving a solid black vote. Fearing that the black vote might tip the balance of power, Whallen resorted to a number of illegal tactics—arbitrarily arresting blacks, asking senseless questions of prospective black voters, and outright violence—to keep them from voting. But to the surprise of practically everyone, the "reform Democrats" used the same methods. The election turned into a disaster for the Republicans, with Jacob garnering 11,339 votes, compared to 5,987 for Avery, and 3,325 for Hoke. Avery was especially galled when he learned that he received only 15 percent of the black vote. Indeed, the reform Democrats had bought some black votes and had used Whallen-like intimidation to keep others from the polls. One of the first acts of the new mayor was to remove Whallen as head of the police force.[7]

The civic leaders who had backed Jacobs were so dismayed by his party's illegal tactics that they wanted immediate reform in Louisville. A call went out for the use of secret ballots at all elections, and Louisville became the first city in the nation to adopt the Australian ballot. But this did not eliminate political corruption. It simply meant that buying someone's vote involved a greater sporting chance. As Abraham Flexner recalls, "Bribery was common, especially bribery of the Negro voter. Many a time I have seen a worker take a Negro by the arm and walk with him to an alley and present him a bill—a dollar, two dollars, and on rare occasions more. The voter's preference was marked on a ballot either by himself or by the party worker. It was deposited in a box, a practice which led to ballot stuffing on a huge scale."[8] Political corruption did not end in Louisville, but more and more whites became disgusted with the Democrats and were willing to give the Republicans a chance.

    7. Yater, A History of Louisville, 132; Courier-Journal, November 25, December 7, 1887.
    8. Flexner, I Remember, 33; Krock, Myself When Young, 212; Arthur M. Schlesinger, The Rise of the City, 1878–1898 (New York, 1933), 393–94.

The first Republican victory in Louisville occurred in 1894. A coalition of party regulars, dissident Democrats, and members of the American Protective Association, a nativist organization opposed to immigration and Catholics, elected a Republican to Congress. Almost immediately thereafter, Dr. Henry Fitzbutler took the lead in forming a black political organization called the R. B. Elliott Club, named in honor of Robert Brown Elliott, a prominent black politician from South Carolina who had recently died. As a spokesman for the club explained, their aim was "to elect men to office in the Republican party who are willing to accord to colored Republicans every political right as citizens, to the end that the general condition of the race might be bettered and the good of the community enhanced." The *Commercial* speculated that the Democrats had helped form the Elliott Club to undermine black support for the Republican party. Several black leaders, including William H. Steward, shared that suspicion and refused to join the new organization, noting that the militant blacks might hurt their party's chances in the upcoming election.[9]

In July 1895 members of the Elliott Club were selected as delegates from the Tenth Ward to the City and County Republican Convention. They favored Nathaniel R. Harper as their candidate to the state legislature. Traditionally, the Republican party allowed the delegates from each legislative district to select their own candidates to the legislature and then all of the delegates at the convention would select the party's candidates for posts in city and county governments. After learning that Harper would be nominated as the candidate from the Tenth Ward, the Republican election officials met and changed the rules for selecting candidates: no longer would the delegates from the wards select their own candidates; instead, prior to the regular convention, a mass meeting of all delegates would be held to choose the party's candidates for the legislature. When a reporter asked the election officials why a mass meeting was being held before the regular convention, one official candidly replied, "We have a good chance to win this fall, and we don't intend to throw a vote away." Learning of the rules change, the black Republicans met and pledged their support for Harper. They threatened to bolt the party and establish an independent organization if the delegates failed to nominate Harper. Democrat Henry Watterson of the *Courier-Journal* delighted in talking about the disagreement between the Republicans and blacks: "Harper is becoming a problem for the Republican bosses. They want to get rid of him for they fear a black will hurt the ticket. [They are] trying to think up a way to dispose

9. Yater, *A History of Louisville*, 132–33; *Commercial*, July 25, 1895.

of him quietly." Harper, a struggling lawyer, was offered a job of speaking to black voters on behalf of Republican candidates during the fall campaign if he withdrew his candidacy. He promptly accepted the offer.[10]

The black Republican delegates who had supported Harper's candidacy were outraged over his withdrawal. Dr. Henry Fitzbutler, an unsuccessful candidate on several occasions, and C. B. Preston issued a statement condemning Harper. "By a preconcerted arrangement with the Republican City and County Committee, Mr. Harper withdrew from the race upon the promise of remunerative employment during the campaign and the six delegates who have always supported him . . . feel that he has not acted honorably." Fitzbutler and Preston wanted it known that Harper would not be representing the blacks of Louisville and Jefferson County in any speeches he made to black people in Kentucky since he had entered into a corrupt deal which they had not and would not have sanctioned.[11]

Even without the endorsement of the Elliott Club, the Republican party gained control of the city council in November 1895. In early January 1896 the mayor died, and the city council chose George Todd as Louisville's first Republican mayor, With their party firmly in control, black leaders urged the mayor to hire blacks as policemen and firemen and to appoint Negro Republican workers to high-level patronage jobs. Todd refused to consider their requests, saying that during his administration, "Negroes will have to stay in their place."[12]

Unfortunately for blacks, Todd kept his word. The "party of Lincoln" did very little for its black supporters when in control of city government in 1896–1897. In the early 1890s, the Democrats had enacted laws consolidating the various city government departments under two boards, thereby controlling more than 1,000 jobs. They then proceeded to appoint blacks to janitorial positions at city hall and other municipal buildings. As mayor, the Republican Todd also refused to hire blacks for white-collar jobs, relegating them to janitor work and appointing only one

10. *Courier-Journal,* July 15, 19, 25, 1895. The *Commercial* was silent about the entire controversy between blacks and the Republicans. Indeed, throughout the campaign the Republicans were fearful that the "negro question" would be raised. Their leader, George Todd, counseled all party workers to avoid public debates with the Democrats for "it will give the Democrats an opportunity to spring the negro question and the force bill legislation." See the George Todd Papers, especially "The Republican Campaign of 1895," Filson Club, Louisville.

11. *Courier-Journal,* August 21, 1895.

12. Indianapolis *Freeman,* February 1, 1896; Yater, *A History of Louisville,* 132–33; see also James T. Wills, "Louisville Politics 1890–97" (M.A. thesis, University of Louisville, 1966).

black to a highly visible, though low-paying, position on the City-County Republican Committee. His only other gesture toward his black supporters was an appropriation of $500 to maintain the Louisville Negro Exhibition at the Tennessee Exposition. What was occurring in Louisville was also happening in another border city. That same year, Baltimore elected a Republican mayor. Upon taking office he promised blacks several new positions, yet assured whites that they would not be replaced. Blacks were hired as janitors, street cleaners, and messengers. No blacks were considered for white-collar positions or any position that required contact with the white public.[13]

Mayor Todd's lack of positive action to help the black community upset black Republicans. The Elliott Club consistently denounced Todd and urged blacks to abandon the party unless changes were made. Todd and party leaders were undaunted by the blacks; he further alienated the Afro-Americans by allowing the formation of the High Class Republican Club. As its name suggests, the club was an exclusive organization designed to keep blacks from taking part in the selection of Republican candidates, to prevent a recurrence of incidents like the one centering around the nomination of Harper in 1895. A $20 initiation fee and $10 annual dues were required to become a member. The club selected all of the Republican candidates for the November 1897 election.[14]

But as the election approached, Todd realized that without the black vote he stood little chance of remaining in office. In an attempt at fence-mending, he met in late August with a group of black leaders at the home of William H. Steward. At the meeting, Steward reassured the mayor of black loyalty to the Republican party. He also presented Todd with a list of blacks who should be considered for patronage positions. Within a matter of days after the meeting, the Republican party announced the appointment of Steward as a judge of registration and election in the Fifteenth Precinct of the Ninth Ward. Steward, the first black to hold such a position in Kentucky, was to oversee and verify the voter registration for the fall election. The immediate impact of Steward's appointment was to rally a few disgruntled blacks behind the Republican banner.[15]

13. Wills, "Louisville Politics," 109–10; P. T. Risdale, *A Political Guidebook of Louisville,* 1897 (Louisville, 1897), 94; Callcott, *The Negro in Maryland Politics,* 94.

14. Wills, "Louisville Politics," 110; see also the George Todd Papers. *Courier-Journal,* November 24, 1929, has an obituary on Todd that details his political career.

15. *Courier-Journal,* August 29, 1897; *Post,* October 22, 1897. A copy of the certificate that Steward received as a judge of registration can be found in the William H. Steward Papers.

As a result of the poor treatment they received from the Republicans and the violence they suffered from the Whallen-controlled Democrats, fewer blacks voted in 1897 than had voted in the previous mayoral race. Though not directly in control of city government for several years, Whallen had remained a powerful force behind the scenes. Both mayors Jacob and Todd had failed to dismantle the Whallen machine in city government largely because the police and fire departments remained loyal to him. This became quite evident to the surprised Republicans on election day November 2, 1897, a day marked by voter fraud and police abuse of blacks. Whallen once again seized control of city government. Whallen's candidate, postmaster George Weaver, won over incumbent mayor Todd by only 2,728 votes out of 40,000 cast. The headline of the *Commercial* expressed Republicans feelings about their narrow defeat: "Rankest Fraud in History of the City; Ninth and Tenth Wards Stolen Bodily." The paper noted that black voters in wards all over town were intimidated by the police and were often prevented from voting. In the Ninth and Tenth Wards the polls opened at noon, instead of early in the morning. Blacks were further delayed from voting by having their registrations slowly checked. When the polls closed in the Ninth and Tenth Wards many blacks were still waiting in line to vote. Todd stated that 4,500 Republicans were prevented from voting while 2,000 votes were cast by Democratic repeaters.[16]

Without a doubt, violence kept some blacks from the polls, but others stayed away because they felt that was the most effective means of protesting against both parties. Fitzbutler's group did not actively campaign, and another group, the Negro Republican Club, claimed that it was organized *not* to vote. According to a story that appeared in the *Courier-Journal* about a year after the November 1897 election, the Negro Republican Club was formed shortly after Todd was sworn in as mayor. It was comprised of sixty-eight men, all of whom had campaigned for the Republican party and had expected patronage positions. "When patronage was denied, they decided to sit out the next election." As a reporter explained, "The by-laws of the club were to the effect that, as the Republican officers had done nothing for the members of the club, they had pledged themselves to remain away from the polls." It is impossible to state with complete accuracy the effect these two organizations had on black voting. But as one contemporary political observer noted regarding the 1897 election, blacks cast 1,343 fewer votes in the Ninth and Tenth Wards,

16. *Commercial*, November 3, 4, 1897. For a different view of the election, see *Courier-Journal*, November 3, 4, 1897.

where these groups were strongest, than they did in the previous mayoral race. If the R. B. Elliott and Negro Republican Clubs had any support elsewhere in the city, it is conceivable that they might have been the determining factor causing the Republicans to lose the close race.[17]

The decade of the 1890s was a crucial point in the history of black involvement in Louisville politics. Republicans gained power. Unfortunately, the Republicans followed the example of the Democrats and refused to appoint blacks to high-level positions. Yet, after being rebuffed by the Republican leaders, blacks still remained in the party of Lincoln. One obvious reason, of course, was the continued refusal of the Democrats to make any overtures to gain black support. A second important reason was the extreme popularity among blacks of the head of Kentucky's Republican party, William O. Bradley. In 1895 Bradley became the state's first Republican governor. Under his administration, blacks received a number of "firsts": a black was appointed to be director of the Negro division of the State Asylum; blacks were appointed to the State Agriculture Board, to the board of trustees of the State Colored Normal School, and to a lumber inspection team at the State Prison. Furthermore, local attorneys Nathaniel Harper and Albert S. White received small patronage jobs. Bradley consistently urged the legislature to allocate additional funds for Negro education. Finally, his administration established a black normal school in Paducah, in the far western part of the state.[18]

Governor Bradley spoke fearlessly on controversial issues. As he told a Louisville gathering of blacks, "I have never been afraid of the bugbear of 'social equality.' " He called for the repeal of the Separate Coach Law, and reminded blacks that the Democrats had enacted the law. "For twenty-seven years after the war had ended there was no separate coach bill on the statute books, until in 1892 the Democratic party of Kentucky enacted such a measure, and now . . . a Kentucky negro cannot ride from point to point in the State except in the Jim Crow car, while a negro from any other state in the Union may pass across the State in a Pullman's palace." He consistently denounced the lynchings of blacks in his state, warning that all members of a lynch mob would be prosecuted. On one occasion he re-

17. *Courier-Journal*, November 9, 1898; P.T. Risdale, *A Political Guidebook of Louisville, 1897* (Louisville, 1897), 94.
18. See the voluminous newspaper clippings in the William O. Bradley Scrapbooks, Special Collections, University of Kentucky, Lexington. See Johnson, *Biographical Sketches*, 11–14. Johnson explained that Governor Bradley was such a champion of Negro rights that it was appropriate to include him in a book on Afro-Americans.

fused to turn over a black man accused of the brutal rape slaying of a young white girl to Graves County officials because he believed the man would not receive a trial.[19]

Perhaps influenced by Bradley's success with the black vote, and because of his need for additional support from other than traditional Democratic strongholds, state senator William Goebel became the first Democratic candidate for governor to appeal to blacks for support. Under Kentucky law, Bradley could not succeed himself, so he campaigned enthusiastically for the Republican candidate, William S. Taylor. Goebel, one of the most controversial figures in Kentucky politics, emerged from the Democratic convention of 1899 with the nomination of a bitterly divided party. Throughout the campaign he attempted to secure the black vote for the November general election. He pointed out that he had never resorted to a cry of "nigger domination" to win an election. Since he also needed the support of lower-class whites, Goebel hedged on his view of the separate coach law. But finally in a speech in Louisville he was cornered and had to state his position: Goebel favored the segregation law, but wanted a statute passed giving blacks equal accommodations on the railroads. He said it was an injustice for black women to share coaches with uncouth white men who drank and smoked. Black leaders rejected Goebel's position and remained with their party. Their vote proved crucial. Taylor defeated Goebel by 2,383 votes; 193,714 to 191,331. The results of the election were challenged by Goebel. Throughout the month of January 1900, the state capitol was in a turmoil as the legislators tried to determine the outcome of the election. On January 30, 1900, Goebel was shot. The Democratic-dominated General Assembly met, and on the very next day swore in the dying Goebel as governor. After his death, Lt. Governor J. C. W. Beckham was then sworn in as governor.[20]

Despite Goebel's strategy, Louisville's Whallen-led Democratic party remained unconvinced of the necessity to court the black vote. Once back in power Whallen took steps to entrench his position. At voter registration time before the mayor's race in October 1901, blacks were closely questioned and their right to register challenged. Many blacks, fearful of the police, stayed away from the polls. Moreover, in an attempt to combat the

19. See the following newspapers for speeches by Governor Bradley to blacks: *Courier-Journal*, October 20, 1899; *Bluegrass Bugle*, October 28, 1899; Lexington *Leader*, December 9, 1899; Kentucky *Standard*, December 16, 1899; Tapp and Klotter, *Kentucky, Decades of Discord*, 396.

20. Tapp and Klotter, *Kentucky, Decades of Discord*, 435; *Courier-Journal*, August 24, September 8, 9, 17, 19, October 3, 27, November 3, 1899.

solid black Republican vote, the Democrats encouraged a number of black "shadies" to form Negro Democratic clubs. These blacks willingly aligned themselves with the racist Whallen for it meant less trouble from the policemen as long as they did Whallen's bidding. Throughout the registration period, Skeets Johnson, a black underworld figure, prevented blacks from registering in the east-end wards. Despite well-documented evidence attributing several criminal acts to Johnson, the police refused to arrest him. These Negro thugs, as much as anything else, kept many blacks from viewing the Democrats as a respectable party.[21]

In 1905 a number of prominent civic leaders, tired of corrupt politicians controlling their city, formed a political party to challenge "Boss" Whallen. Like civic and business leaders elsewhere in that dawning age of urban progressivism, they called for honest and businesslike efficiency in city government. Unfortunately, they cared little for blacks, viewing them as easily corruptible and thus a negative influence on politics. In May 1905, the Louisville Grand Jury condemned Democratic politicians and the close link between the underworld and city government. Shortly thereafter several civic groups formed the Fusion party and named an entire slate of candidates for the November election. Violence began with the start of voter registration in October. This time several prominent whites, including former Confederate hero Basil Duke, were the victims of Whallen's thugs. Not surprisingly, given the incidents of ballot stuffing and police intimidation under Whallen's rule, the Fusion candidates lost in the November election. Some scholars have concluded that election day November 7, 1905, was the rowdiest day in Louisville's history.[22]

The Fusionists refused to accept defeat. They easily raised the funds needed to contest the election in court. After a year of gathering evidence, their case was heard in the Jefferson County Chancery Division. Despite clear evidence of election day fraud, the judges validated the returns. The Fusionists pressed on, and in May 1907 the Kentucky Court of Appeals, in a 5–2 decision, reversed the lower court and declared the election null and void and ordered the offices vacated. Governor J. C. W. Beckham named Robert W. Bingham as interim mayor. During his four months in

21. For examples of election rigging, see the Louisville *Evening Post*, October 2, 4, 26, 30, November 2, 1901. For the activities of black Democratic clubs, see Letters to Mayors of Louisville, Filson Club, Louisville.

22. George Metcalf, "The Fusion Movement in Kentucky 1905–07" (M.A. thesis, Murray State University, 1969); Louisville *Herald*, October 4, 5, 1905; *Courier-Journal*, October 7, 1905; Thomas D. Clark, *Helm Bruce, Public Defender: Breaking Louisville's Gothic Political Ring, 1905* (Louisville, 1973).

office, Bingham attempted to destroy the Whallen machine by firing all policemen above the rank of captain, closing gambling establishments, enforcing Sunday closing laws, and running known criminals out of town. Bingham supervised the special election in November 1907 which the Republicans won, electing James F. Grinstead as mayor.[23]

Once back in control of local government, the Republicans showed a lack of understanding of the failure of the Todd administration in the mid-1890s and continued to treat their black supporters with disdain. Though they now controlled over 1,200 jobs, the Republicans hired blacks only as street cleaners, janitors, and porters. Rev. E. G. Harris headed a delegation of ministers who met with the Republican-dominated city council to ask for the appointment of more blacks to patronage positions. Mayor Grinstead responded by appointing William H. Parker, the editor of the *Columbian* and an active party worker at this time, as elevator conductor at city hall. Four other men also received positions: Dudley Edwards, a blacksmith, was appointed a street inspector; William Leonard, already a janitor, was named head janitor of city hall; and two doctors, P. R. Peters and W. T. Merchant, received nominal salaries to examine sanitation conditions in Negro neighborhoods. Like all of his predecessors, Grinstead refused to hire blacks in positions that dealt with the white public or even to consider blacks as policemen or firemen. The black leaders were obviously disappointed. They had expected far more. But in reality, as long as the Democratic party remained closed to them, and as long as they lacked a political organization that the Republicans could not take for granted, there was little that they could do because they lacked the political leverage to demand more.[24]

Not only did the Republicans refuse to appoint blacks, but they also continued to deny party backing to Afro-Americans running for office. In April 1909, lawyer-businessman William H. Wright announced his candidacy for the state legislature from Louisville's Tenth Ward. Just as in the cases of Fitzbutler and Harper in the 1880s and 1890s, the party refused to support Wright, telling him that it was still too early for a black to run for office. When Wright refused to withdraw from the race, several blacks from Republican clubs came to him with the usual offers. Wright ran any-

23. Metcalf, "The Fusion Movement," 66–70; see the *Louisville Election Cases, 1905–1907* (8 vols.; Louisville, 1907). These sworn testimonies provide an excellent view of voter fraud, ballot stuffing, and intimidation of black voters in Louisville.

24. Indianapolis *Freeman*, March 28, June 16, November 21, 1908, September 25, October 23, November 13, 1909. For similar problems in other cities, see Spear, *Black Chicago*, 119; Katzman, *Before the Ghetto*, 175–207; Osofsky, *Harlem*, 159–79.

way, but he lost the election because black voters led by the political clubs supported the white Republican candidate.[25]

The party's attitude toward black candidates was clearly revealed during the election of 1913 for the state legislature. Lee Brown, a graduate of Eckstein Norton and a reporter for the Louisville *News*, announced his intentions to run for the seat from the Tenth Ward. The party was so sure that their white candidate would win that they totally ignored Brown. They were therefore shocked when he won by thirty-one votes. Brown's victory in the primary made him the Republican candidate against the Democrats in the November general election. As the election approached, Brown was opposed by the Republican party and their black political clubs. The Louisville correspondent for the Indianapolis *Freeman* said that Brown would win anyway because the black residents of the Tenth Ward wanted a member of their race elected to office. However, in a district where blacks comprised 75 percent of the voters, Brown lost to a white Democratic candidate. Brown bitterly attributed his defeat to a lack of support from the Republican party and the failure of blacks to vote a straight Republican ticket.[26]

Brown's defeat was indicative of the tremendous hold the Republican party had on the city's conservative black leaders. It is understandable that the black political clubs, largely engaged in illegal acts, could easily be coerced to help defeat Brown. But the Republican officials also convinced the more respectable black leaders that any changes, even the election of one black to office, would upset the delicate nature of race relations in their city and would lead to increased problems because the Democrats would resort to an outcry of "nigger domination." In the cases of William H. Wright and Lee Brown, both men were established citizens, neither was a radical. All they wanted was a measure of recognition for the race. But the Republican party was not prepared to give blacks even this small concession. Undoubtedly, if the Republicans had supported black candidates the Democrats would have used that against them; but in their anxiety over close elections, the Democrats accused the Republicans of being "the negro's party" anyway. Republicans refused to support black candidates not only because of what the Democrats might say but because they feared losing the many patronage positions held exclusively by whites.

The election of 1909 proved that the Democrats were still willing to use race as an issue, and that despite the Republicans' lukewarm attitude

25. Indianapolis *Freeman*, May 8, June 29, July 3, 1909.
26. *Ibid.*, August 16, November 8, 1913; *Courier-Journal*, November 15, 1913.

toward blacks, they remained vulnerable to attack. After a two-year absence from office, the Whallen machine was determined to regain city hall. This could best be achieved by playing on the racial fears of the voters. From the beginning of the campaign, when the Democratic chairman proclaimed "that all whites should get behind the Democrats as the white man's party," to election day, the Democrats charged that a Republican victory would lead to "nigger domination." Throughout the month of October, William O. Head, Whallen's candidate for mayor, aroused white audiences by informing them that in Cincinnati, Ohio (105 miles away), a black man had married a white woman. Head told his audiences that the Republicans might make interracial marriage legal in Louisville, to which the crowd predictably replied in a heated tone, "We will have nothing like that in Louisville." Candidate Head tried to keep the immigrant groups in the Democratic camp, informing the Irish that the Grinstead administration fired white construction workers, replacing them with blacks. "It means that taxpaying white men have been deprived of jobs for the benefit of non-taxpaying Negroes. What was this done for? Simply to keep the Negro in line to vote for the Republican party." [27] When speaking to the German community, Head emphasized that the Republicans were placing blacks above whites in employment: "The other day I passed where some old men were working on the streets and I noticed that a negro was bossing them and was cussing one of the men. Now, do you want that condition of affairs to continue in this city?" Finally, he informed his alarmed audiences that something terrible was sure to happen since many blacks were armed with razors, knives, and guns, all with the approval of the Republicans. [28]

The Democratic attack on blacks put the Republicans on the defensive. At a large Republican rally (where the races were segregated), U.S. Senator William O. Bradley, instead of denouncing the racist diatribes of the Democrats, attempted to reassure white Republicans that their party opposed social equality. As governor a decade earlier he had expressed no fear of social interaction between the races, but now Bradley said, "some of the Democrats seem distressed about negro equality. They have my earnest sympathy. The Anglo-Saxon race, that is the white race, is the greatest race that ever lived on the face of the earth." Bradley's comments

27. See the *Courier-Journal* for all of October 1909, especially October 1, 2, 10, 16; Indianapolis *Freeman*, September 4, 11, 18, October 2, 9, November 27, 1909. See also the *Evening Post* for October 1909. The *Evening Post* ridiculed the Democrats and said that their cry of "nigger domination was fostering racial hatred."

28. *Courier-Journal*, September 15, 1909.

brought loud applause from white Republicans but little response from blacks. In a patronizing way, he then told blacks that since being set free by the Republicans and under Republican leadership, blacks had made some advances and they had a right to be proud of their race. Mayor Grinstead, speaking after the senator, made a similar address. He received a loud roar of approval from the white Republicans when he defended his policy of hiring blacks only as common laborers and not as policemen and firemen.[29]

With tactics usually associated only with Deep South politicians, the Whallen forces constantly charged blacks with assaulting white women and robbing wealthy whites. A series of stories appeared in the *Courier-Journal* and the *Times*, accusing the Republican party of being lenient toward black criminals. On November 1, the day before the election, the *Courier-Journal* reproduced a letter that allegedly had been sent by the Young Men's Colored Republican Club to blacks in other cities, urging them to move to Louisville after the Republican victory "where people of our color will be on equality with any damn white person." The nonsensical letter was the capstone of the Democratic hate campaign. Louisville's voters returned the Democrats to power with Head narrowly defeating Grinstead by 1,500 votes.[30]

Once back in power, the Democrats kept their promise to white voters. They refused to hire blacks in city government even for the usual menial jobs reserved for blacks. They segregated the races at the city jail and workhouse. Furthermore, the Whallen forces relied on racial tension to elect John Bushemeyer as mayor in 1913. Bushemeyer continued the policies of his Democratic predecessors. Several attempts were made to segregate the city's streetcars. In January 1916, Louisville State Senator Charles H. Knight introduced a bill in the legislature requiring all companies operating streetcar lines to furnish separate accommodations for the races. After streetcar company representatives from several cities protested the measure, Knight changed his bill so that it applied only to the state's first-class cities. (Louisville was the only designated first-class city in Kentucky). Knight's bill passed the Senate but was defeated by the full legislature. After this defeat, Mayor Bushemeyer suggested that in Louisville whites should fill the streetcars from the front and blacks from the back. "Custom," the mayor said, "is much more effective than man-made laws and both races have a personal obligation to society . . . to observe an un-

29. *Ibid.*, October 2, 1909.
30. *Ibid.*, November 1, 2, 3, 1909.

written 'Jim Crow' law." Blacks refused to observe the Jim Crow seating arrangement. However, a number of whites took Mayor Bushemeyer's suggestion seriously about an "unwritten Jim Crow law": they refused to allow blacks to sit next to them on the streetcars and they assaulted blacks for sitting in the front part of the streetcar. Bushemeyer's administration also enacted the Louisville Residential Segregation Ordinance that prohibited blacks from moving into white neighborhoods.[31]

II.

In one significant aspect, Louisville (and Kentucky) blacks were treated differently than blacks in other border and Deep South states. Although the Democratic party, and even the Fusionist reformers, berated blacks and viewed them as a corrupting influence on politics, no attempts were made to disfranchise them. In 1890 Mississippi disfranchised its black voters. Thereafter, disfranchisement of blacks spread to South Carolina in 1895, Louisiana in 1898, North Carolina in 1900, and Alabama in 1901. By 1902, in the neighboring state of Virginia, a number of Republicans agreed with the Democrats that blacks should be eliminated as voters. As Charles Wynes explains, "There were some Republicans of the lily-white faction . . . who favored a convention and disfranchisement of the Negro on the grounds that only by removal of the colored voter from Republican ranks could the party make itself respectable in the eyes of the mass of white Virginians." So the disfranchisement of blacks became a reality in the Old Dominion. By 1910 all the former Confederate states and the new state of Oklahoma had disfranchised the black voter. In Maryland, a border state that resembled Kentucky by being controlled by the Democrats yet having a strong Republican party, the Democratic party tried on several occasions to disfranchise blacks. All of their attempts failed, not because of a sense of fair play by the majority party but because of a number of political realities. First, Maryland's ratio of black voters fell "well within the tolerance range," fluctuating between a high of 22.5 percent in 1870 and 17.9 percent in 1910. Second, Maryland blacks were led by a number of strong leaders who effectively pressed the concerns of blacks before government officials. Third and most important, a sizable immigrant popu-

31. Indianapolis *Freeman*, November 27, 1909, March 18, 1911; *Crisis*, XII (March, 1913), 221; *Courier-Journal*, January 20, April 8, 1916; Louisville *Times*, January 28, 1916; Louisville *Post*, March 7, 9, 1916.

lation voted against disfranchisement attempts because they were fearful that such a law would eventually affect them as well.[32]

Kentucky whites refused to even propose a disfranchisement law. Beyond a shadow of a doubt, the Democratic party was supreme in Kentucky. From the end of the Civil War to the mid-1890s, the party was rarely challenged in local, state, and federal elections. The Republicans finally won in the 1890s only because of bickering among the Democrats. The same was true in the early twentieth century whenever the Republicans were victorious. One reason whites often switched and voted Republican was their assurance that the Republicans would not upgrade the status of blacks. Since the Republicans agreed with the Democrats on the limited role of blacks in politics, there was no need to disfranchise Kentucky's blacks. The Republicans appointed them to the same minor positions that were reserved for them under Democratic administrations. Furthermore, the Republicans refused to support black candidates, preferring to see a white Democrat win instead of a black Republican. They also refused to hire blacks as policemen and firemen, important symbols of the white establishment. Simply put, because of the solid white opposition from both political parties, Louisville blacks were no threat to the status quo. Though they looked to politics to improve their condition, this proved to be a false hope. In fact, as in so many areas of race relations in Louisville, whites could enjoy a sense of being tolerant and generous by allowing blacks to vote. They did not infringe on the Afro-Americans' most sacred of rights—the right to vote. Whites realized that as long as blacks were mistreated by the Republicans and despised by the Democrats their voting would accomplish very little.

32. Rayford Logan, *The Betrayal of the Negro* (New York, 1965), 346; Wynes, *Race Relations in Virginia*, 57; Callcott, *The Negro in Maryland Politics*, 101–61.

## PART III

The "New Negro": 1917—1930

INTRODUCTION

Most students of blacks in urban America agree that a change in leadership occurred around 1915. Prior to that time, the black leadership (led by Booker T. Washington) had relied on white support for power and prestige in the black community. But with increased black migration to the city and with white racism confining blacks to certain neighborhoods, black entrepreneurs multiplied. They not only provided services to blacks but also relied on the large Afro-American population as their principal source of power. As August Meier has explained: "It was a newer rising group of men that formed the backbone of the entrepreneurial and professional group that depended on the Negro market, and that they in time . . . came to constitute not only the economic elite, but the social elite of the Negro community."[1]

Although it is difficult to pinpoint when the change in leadership occurred in Louisville, two significant events happened in late 1917 that led to a new group of blacks being more vocal and forceful in their demands for changes. In early November the U.S. Supreme Court overturned the Louisville Residential Segregation Ordinance, and toward the end of that month the Republican party swept back into power. The court case, one of the early significant victories of the NAACP, convinced local blacks that they could successfully challenge discriminatory laws. Though the local branch of the NAACP would occasionally be inactive, from this time forward black leaders, especially several newcomers, would view it as a powerful vehicle for racial justice and would always turn to the NAACP during a crisis. To be sure, the Republicans had controlled city government before and little had changed for Afro-Americans. But younger blacks, well aware of previous mistreatments suffered by the race at the hands of their party, were more determined to press the Republicans for changes and not to accept, as their elders had, the party's excuses for refusing to hire blacks in visible positions. As their own actions would show, the young leaders

1. August Meier, "Negro Class Structure and Ideology in the Age of Booker T. Washington," *Phylon*, XXIII (January, 1962), 260–65. See also Meier, *Negro Thought in America*, 152–56.

were willing to switch parties or run as independents to force the Republicans' hand. Louisville's black leaders after 1917 were optimistic that positive changes could occur, but they were firmly convinced that they had to take the initiative in race relations instead of relying on the better element of whites for desired changes.

The court decision and the Republican victory occurred on the eve of the "New Negro" period, a time when black businesses were looked to for racial development. This ideology of supporting and promoting black businesses was very important in Louisville because one of the principal catalysts for change in black leadership in other cities was absent. Many border and northern cities experienced huge black population increases that formed the base of support for new black leaders. But in the decade of 1910–1920, Louisville's Afro-American population declined as blacks left for the industrial jobs in the North. Nevertheless, Louisville's new black leaders stressed the essential role business enterprises would play in transforming the status of blacks. They repeatedly said that blacks could expect to be mistreated when patronizing white establishments, and that only by going to black-owned businesses would they be treated with respect. A young journalist explained another reason to "shop black" at the opening of the black-owned Mutual Shoe and Clothing Store in 1921: "The opening of this business means that the door of opportunity is open to young men and women of the race for employment commensurate with their training and elevation."[2] Black businesses would most surely provide jobs, especially in white-collar positions.

2. *Leader*, March 12, 1921; see the *Leader*, February 9, 1924, June 6, 1925, for long editorials on the need for blacks to support black businesses.

## 8

A Change in Leadership

Most of Louisville's new black leaders were born in the last two decades of the 1800s, a time of extreme racial polarization. Unlike the black leaders who reached maturity in the decades after the Civil War, these young men found few optimistic trends in race relations. Indeed, Louisville's new leaders were under few illusions about whites willingly breaking down racial barriers. During their lives they had witnessed an acceleration of the building of barriers. Significantly, unlike the established group of black leaders, most of the young leaders were aware that while it was often beneficial to work with whites on some matters, for the most part whites were only interested in limited gains for blacks. Therefore, most of the new leaders had few white allies and were far less dependent on whites than the group led by Steward and Parrish. The new leaders would often harshly criticize city officials for the continuation of racial discrimination and violence in a city that claimed to be more progressive than the Deep South in its handling of racial problems.

I.

Journalists I. Willis Cole and William Warley were the most outspoken among Louisville's new leaders. Cole was a native of Memphis and a graduate of LeMoyne Junior College. He came to Louisville as a Bible salesman during the summer of 1915. Finding the city to his liking, he decided to remain and start a weekly newspaper and publishing company. Cole's newspaper, the *Leader*, was launched in November 1917 and quickly became the leading black newspaper in the city. Like most successful black newspaper editors of his day, Cole strongly protested discrimination, constantly informing his readers of insults blacks received when patronizing white businesses and urging blacks to boycott white establishments whenever possible. He believed that blacks received few political plums because they remained tied to the Republic party instead of being political independents. Cole was not blind to the dangers created when black leaders fought among themselves: "Negroes will never amount to anything," he declared, "until the leaders among them stop so much bickering, and throw into the waste basket their personal differences." [1]

Cole maintained that the *Leader*, "the voice of the minority," aided blacks by speaking out on racial issues and by providing jobs. In 1921 he noted that his business employed "more members of the race than any other publishing house in Kentucky." Cole utilized college graduates in all phases of his business, and several future publishers and printers received valuable training from him. But like most black newspapers, desperate for revenue, the *Leader* contained many advertisements that undermined Cole's emphasis on black pride; these advertisements told blacks that to become beautiful and accepted in the right circles they needed to straighten their hair and lighten their skin. [2]

Journalist William Warley was an even more visible protester in early-twentieth-century Louisville. Warley, a native of Louisville and a graduate of Central High School and State University's Law School, founded the *News* in 1912 and used the paper to denounce segregation and racism. In 1914 Warley led a black boycott against the National Theater's policy of restricting blacks to the gallery and the back entrance, a policy also followed by other local white-owned theaters. After several months of urging blacks to boycott the establishment and ridiculing those blacks who accepted such humiliations by publishing their names in his newspaper, Warley's group won a partial victory when the management of the National Theater allowed blacks to enter from the main street and to have accommodations in the first balcony. Warley championed many black causes in Louisville, including the fight against the residential segregation ordinance. Not surprisingly, his outspoken opposition to segregation, and particularly the manner in which he denounced blacks who he thought were too cautious, often put him at odds with the traditional black elite who relied on a more conservative approach and friendship with whites to bring about results. Perhaps the Louisville *Times* was correct when describing Warley as a "man ahead of his time . . . thoroughly dissatisfied with the status quo. His attitude earned him the enmity of some elements in the black community." [3]

    1. The quote comes from the *Leader*, April 2, 1927. Biographical information on Cole was obtained from the following sources: *Leader*, October 29, 1921, August 30, 1927, March 11, 1950; *Courier-Journal*, February 20, 1950; Rosa Cole (widow of I. Willis Cole), interview with author, Louisville, May 25, 1976.
    2. White interview; *Leader*, March 12, 1921, September 28, 1929. During its peak in the 1930s, Cole's paper employed twenty people.
    3. Warley's paper, except for a few copies, has not been preserved. Quite often, how-

Warley was one of the few local black leaders who consistently criticized Booker T. Washington. During the 1890s and the first decade of the
1900s, Washington subsidized a number of black newspapers, thereby
controlling a sizeable portion of the black press. There were always, of
course, a handful of black editors, like William Monroe Trotter of the
Boston *Guardian* and Harry Smith of the Cleveland *Gazette*, who persistently denounced Washington's conservative approach. Although Warley
appeared during the twilight of Washington's career, the educator was still
held in high regard. This, however, did not intimidate Warley who repeatedly said that Washington was out of step with the race when he urged
blacks not to protest discrimination but merely to build better communities of their own. Moreover, he rebuked Washington for saying that
Trotter had hurt the race in his interview with President Wilson. Instead,
Warley applauded Trotter for talking frankly to the president about racial
matters.[4]

In many ways Warley lived a tragic life. For speaking out against segregation, especially the residential segregation ordinance, Warley was dismissed from his job at the Post Office. Over the years, he became bitter
and convinced that local blacks did not appreciate his sacrifices on their
behalf. In 1929 in an emotional editorial, Warley denounced the entire
black leadership in Louisville, saying that he alone was fighting racism and
that he was tired of working on behalf of a race that did not understand
or appreciate him. He threatened to end his fight for Negro businesses and
Negro rights because the great majority of blacks were selfish and totally
unconcerned about aiding others. There was no doubt that Warley was an
extremely difficult man to work with; he had trouble keeping competent
workers and often had to produce his newspaper alone. The *News* collapsed several times and never enjoyed as large a circulation as Cole's
Leader. According to black Louisvillians who knew him, Warley's problems were compounded by a drinking problem which grew much worse in
the 1930s and 1940s, leaving him virtually bankrupt. On several occasions Warley compromised his principles and accepted token positions in

---

ever, Cole reprinted Warley's editorials. See *Leader*, September 29, 1923; Ralph J. Bunche,
"A Brief and Tentative Analysis of Negro Leadership," research memorandum prepared for
the Carnegie-Myrdal Study of the Negro in America, September, 1940, 20–21, 63; Louisville *Times*, September 25, 1961. For Warley's fight to desegregate the National Theater, see
the following: *Crisis*, VIII (March, 1914), 221; Indianapolis *Freeman*, January 24, 31, February 21, 1914.

4. August Meier, "Booker T. Washington and the Negro Press," *Journal of Negro History*, XXXVIII (January, 1953), 67–90; *Crisis*, IX (November, 1914), 17, (February, 1915),
174–75.

Republican administrations in order to earn a living. But he would always resign, denouncing the Republicans. The consequences of his independence and his acerbic pen were often unpleasant. On three different occasions in the 1920s black gangs destroyed his printing office after he had criticized his race for remaining loyal to the Republican party.[5]

When Warley was in his right mind, he and Cole worked together effectively for black rights. The two editors did not limit their activities to local racial problems for they realized that from their position in Louisville they could speak out far better than black leaders in small Kentucky towns. In addition, both editors felt an obligation to be active throughout the state since their papers were read everywhere in Kentucky. Together they strongly protested the lynchings that occurred and the "legal lynchings" when accused blacks had no chance of a fair trial in court. On April 7, 1926, three black men were arrested in Madisonville, in the western part of the state, for allegedly raping a white woman. Several months earlier in Lexington, a black had been convicted of raping a white woman in a trial that lasted sixteen minutes. Fearing that the court in Madisonville would act in a similar manner, Cole and Warley wrote articles condemning the justice system in Kentucky and calling for fair trials for the three men. Warley wrote: "Outdone by Mississippi, Georgia, and other states South when it comes to making Negroes charged with certain offenses pay the extreme penalty outside the courts, Kentucky bids to outdistance them all in the double standard of laws, the mockery of it, when the Negro is involved, through speedy trials, which fall little short of legalized lynchings."[6]

Despite the risk of bodily harm from irate whites who read his editorials, Warley went to Madisonville to investigate the incident. His findings indicated that the men were not guilty. Warley and Cole then launched a fund-raising drive in Louisville that netted $500 for the defense of the men. The rape trial began in Madisonville in late April in a climate of extreme racial tension, but Warley's and Cole's editorial denouncements had already led Kentucky officials to take steps to ensure that no lynching occurred. At the trial one of the men, Columbus Hollis, "confessed" to being involved in the crime, saying that the other two, Bunyan Fleming and Nathan Bard, forced him to hold down the victim while they raped her. Of

5. Letter from I. Willis Cole to Robert Abbott, editor of the Chicago *Defender*, May 13, 1929, NAACP Papers, Manuscript Division, Library of Congress, Washington, D.C.; *Leader*, December 16, 1922, August 16, 1924, January 23, 1932; White interview.

6. See "Kentucky Libel Case," NAACP Papers, Manuscript Division, Library of Congress, Washington, D.C.; Louisville *News*, May 22, 1926; see also *News*, October 2, 1926.

course, after hearing this evidence the all-white jury found the two men guilty of rape. In his newspaper, Warley explained that the evidence against the two men was extremely weak, that the victim, Miss Nell Catherine Breithaupt, never identified them as her attackers and that Hollis had been pressured into making false accusations against them. As Warley pointed out, Bard and Fleming testified that Hollis lied after being paid by the deputy sheriff to do so. The deputy sheriff did admit to giving Hollis two dollars, saying it was for tobacco. Warley, convinced of a conspiracy against Bard and Fleming, asked sarcastically, "Can anyone imagine a white man giving a Negro $2 to buy tobacco while in jail when that Negro had just confessed to aiding in the rape of a white girl?" The court sentenced Bard and Fleming to death and Hollis to twenty years in prison.[7]

With the urging of Cole and Warley, the Louisville NAACP tried desperately to save the lives of Bard and Fleming. They appealed to the Kentucky Court of Appeals and then to the U.S. Supreme Court on behalf of the convicted men. After the Supreme Court refused to hear the case, the NAACP had the execution postponed while they urged the governor to commute the sentence. But all attempts to save the men failed. Bard and Fleming were hanged in Madisonville on November 24, 1927. Despite the death of the two men, both Cole and Warley were praised for their efforts. Indeed, had it not been for them, a lynching might have occurred and the trial would have been even more of a mere formality than it was. In a negative way, the white establishment acknowledged Cole's and Warley's roles in the case: both editors were charged with violation of the "criminal syndicalism" and the "sedition" sections of the Kentucky statutes for denouncing justice in Kentucky and the judge in Madisonville. They were tried in Madisonville in October 1926 and were convicted and fined $250 each.[8]

Cole and Warley could rely on a number of young community leaders for support in racial causes. One of these men, Wilson Lovett, grew increasingly impatient with established black leaders like Steward and Parrish. Before coming to Louisville, Lovett had received commercial training at Dickinson College in Carlisle, Pennsylvania, and had worked in the business office at Tuskegee Institute for several years. His experience at Tuskegee shaped his attitude toward old black leaders:

7. *News*, April 24, May 1, October 2, 1926, March 5, August 20, 1927; *Courier-Journal*, May 20, 1926.

8. For additional information on the Bard-Fleming case see the numerous newsclips in the Louisville NAACP Papers; also see "Kentucky Libel Case" and "Cole-Warley National Defense Fund," NAACP Papers. The National NAACP paid the fine for Cole and Warley.

I had the natural feeling at Tuskegee that the men in authority were not my superiors essentially though practically they were. I remember quite definitely my feelings. There was a Council there which had control over everything. Young men came there and got in a rut. Unless they were extremely brilliant or pulled some wires they stayed put, living monotonous suppressed lives. If for any reason a man was called before the Council, he would go to pieces for fear he would lose his job. He had to conform to Tuskegee policy. I said to myself, "I'll be damned if these men will ever pass judgment on me."

Finally I decided to leave and left without a job in the world and only $2.50 in my pocket. Sometimes it is necessary for a man to assert himself in order to maintain his self-respect. I thought insurance had possibilities.[9]

Lovett arrived in Louisville in 1911 as an agent for Atlanta Mutual Insurance, and in a very short time had developed close ties with the city's few successful black businessmen. In December 1920, a group headed by Lovett opened the First Standard Bank of Louisville, the first black-owned bank in Kentucky. Lovett served as its first president.[10]

Lovett wrote a column for Cole's paper in which he discussed a wide range of topics from business opportunities for blacks to race relations. A constant theme in his writings was the importance of unity, of Afro-Americans supporting the businesses found in their community. Lovett criticized older black leaders who believed that desired changes would become a reality through the goodwill of whites. He proclaimed that blacks would only be respected by whites when they asserted themselves in such areas as politics. Where most black leaders usually worked closely with or at least spoke of the good work being done by the black church, Lovett was extremely critical of the institution, saying that the Negro church upheld the status quo by unconsciously believing "white is right."[11]

In 1920 Lovett led black opposition to a million-dollar bond proposal that called for the upgrading of the University of Louisville. In a series of letters to John L. Patterson, dean of the College of Arts and Sciences at the University of Louisville, Lovett explained that he would encourage blacks to vote against the bond issue unless blacks received some benefits from the bond, such as admission to the university. When Lovett's recommendations were ignored by the school's officials, he rallied blacks to defeat the bond issue. The proposal was defeated by 4,000 votes. It was clear that

9. "Life History of Wilson Lovett," interview conducted for Frazier, Negro Youths at the Crossways.

10. For biographical information on Lovett, see Leader, August 23, 1924.

11. Ibid., May 14, 1921, February 9, May 10, 1924, February 5, 12, 1927.

blacks had supplied the crucial margin, for their precincts returned a plurality of 12,000 negative votes.[12]

During the same November campaign, Lovett ran for a seat on the Louisville Board of Education. He announced his candidacy after Robert E. Woods, the former postmaster who had sharply curtailed black appointments to the Post Office, decided to run as an independent. Lovett, a Republican, was bitterly denounced by local party officials. They told him to withdraw from the race "for the good of the party" because if he won the Democrats would use the threat of "nigger domination" in the next election. Lovett refused to withdraw. But on election eve local white political leaders reached an agreement which insured Lovett's defeat: the racist Woods withdrew from the race and the white-controlled Republican party endorsed the Democratic candidate. This was a victory of sorts for Lovett since he achieved his goal of defeating Woods.[13]

Arthur D. Porter was another new black leader and successful businessman. A native of Bowling Green, Kentucky, Porter moved to Louisville to attend Central High School. After graduating, he went to Cincinnati and received training as an embalmer. He then returned to Louisville and gained experience in the funeral business by working for the Watson Funeral Home and the James H. Hathaway Funeral Home. By 1908 Porter had opened his own business on Fifteenth Street, and by the early 1920s he was the city's leading black funeral director. Though not as outspoken as Cole, Warley, or Lovett, Porter gained a reputation in the black community as a "race man" who was deeply concerned about the injustices that blacks suffered and who was committed to bringing about change. Easily one of the most respected leaders in the black community, Porter's opinion was sought on all racial matters. And while Porter attempted to maintain friendly relationships with the city's older black leaders, he let it be known that they did not speak for him.[14]

From the arrival of Henry Fitzbutler in the 1870s to the time of John A. C. Lattimore in the early 1900s, a number of physicians had been im-

12. For Lovett's letters on the bond issue, see the NAACP Papers, Box C-285; see also letters from the Louisville NAACP to the National Association, November 11, 18, 1920, NAACP Papers.

13. *Crisis*, XXIII (January, 1921), 117–18; (February, 1921), 175. For Lovett's view of black involvement in politics in Louisville, see Charles H. Parrish, Jr., "Politics," typescript, 1938, Charles H. Parrish, Jr., Papers, Archives Department, University of Louisville.

14. Mrs. A. D. Porter (widow of A. D. Porter), interview with author, Louisville, May 26, 1976; Indianapolis *Freeman*, December 17, 24, 1910.

portant members of the city's black leadership. Dr. A. C. McIntyre, though only in Louisville for a decade, helped the local NAACP during its early stages by serving as branch president for three successive terms. Dr. John Walls, however, probably had a greater impact on improving health conditions and aiding civil rights causes than any of the new doctors. A native of Mason, Tennessee, and a graduate of Meharry, Walls came to Louisville in February 1918. His practice convinced him that far too many poor people were doing without vital health services. Therefore, with the help of Rev. E. G. Harris, who donated space at Plymouth Settlement House, Walls started a "Well Baby Clinic" to aid mothers in caring for their children. He convinced his fellow black doctors to work at the clinic on a rotating basis. He eventually opened another clinic on the east end of town and received money from several churches to provide free milk for babies.[15]

From the 1920s through the 1960s, Dr. Walls was actively involved in virtually all civil rights activities by local blacks. Though not as flamboyant as some of the other leaders, he was nevertheless widely respected. He was especially effective in meetings with white city officials as a representative of the black community. Along with his wife, Murray, a school teacher at Central High School, Walls consistently demanded that as taxpayers blacks had a right to use the main branch of the public library, downtown facilities, and other public services. As president of the black doctor's organization, the Falls City Medical Association, he championed the right of black physicians to use the city-owned hospitals.[16]

II.

As these more outspoken young leaders gained influence in Louisville, several new leaders emerged who preferred to work with the older Negro leaders and with influential whites. These more moderate new leaders, though seeking racial progress, wanted to keep the lines of communication open between themselves and white leaders, and they were reluctant to adopt any position that would offend their white supporters. They were even more cautious than Steward and Parrish, who would occasionally denounce racial prejudice in sharp tones, always knowing where to draw

15. Walls interview.
16. Mrs. Murray Walls, interview with author, Louisville, September 26, 1978. See the many newsclips in the collection of Mr. and Mrs. Walls that discuss their numerous activities in civil rights.

the line. These more moderate new leaders believed that most of the goals of Cole and Warley were unrealistic, that blacks should seek small concessions whenever they met with whites. When the more militant young leaders called for an independent political party as a tool to recruit black candidates and gain patronage positions, the more moderate new leaders simply urged the two established parties to appoint more blacks to the same old positions. When the young militants denounced the ousting of blacks from the parks and sought access to all of the parks, the other black leaders called for Negro parks.

George Clement was a new leader who became a close associate of Parrish and Steward. Clement was a graduate of Livingstone College of North Carolina and pastored several AME Zion churches including Louisville's Broadway Temple from 1899 to 1904. In 1916 he was elected bishop and chose Louisville as the headquarters of his diocese, which included Kentucky, Tennessee, Ohio, Michigan, and part of North Carolina. When Clement returned to Louisville he was appointed by whites to numerous boards, most notably the Commission on Interracial Cooperation (CIC). Clement sincerely believed in the work of the CIC and its theory that cooperation between white and black civic leaders would ameliorate race relations. Clement sounded remarkably like older black leaders when he emphasized the importance of education and hard work as the true path to black progress.[17]

The CIC also provided an important forum for its director in Louisville, Rev. James Bond. A native Kentuckian and a graduate of Berea and Oberlin Colleges, Bond spent a great portion of his life pastoring churches throughout the South. During World War I he accepted a position with the Kentucky State YMCA as Secretary of Colored Work. Bond concentrated his YMCA activities in Louisville, and his outstanding performance with that organization made him the logical choice to head the Kentucky branch of the CIC in 1919. Bond organized affiliates of the CIC in sixty Kentucky counties. But his efforts in promoting good race relations were most effective in Louisville where Bond had the backing of white newspapers, businessmen, and civic leaders.[18]

17. George Clement, Jr., (son of Bishop Clement), interview with author, Louisville, May 24, 1976.
18. Roger M. Williams, *The Bonds: An American Family* (New York, 1972), 25–71; J. Max Bond (son of James Bond), interview with author, Washington, D.C., August 20, 1979; Mrs. Thomas Bond (daughter-in-law of James Bond), interview with author, Louisville, May 27, 1976. Bond and Clement came from two of the most prominent black families in Kentucky. Horace Mann Bond, the well-known black educator, was a son of James Bond. Julian Bond, the current Georgia legislator, was the son of Horace Mann Bond and the grandson

As director of the CIC, Bond wrote a weekly column in white news-papers, advising blacks to become educated and trained as a means of combating discrimination. He was confident that well-qualified blacks would eventually find jobs in industry. Bond felt that it was useless to ar-gue for integration, that segregated institutions were the best blacks could hope for given the racial climate in Kentucky. He therefore worked for the establishment of Lincoln Institute after blacks were ousted from Berea College, insisting that above all blacks needed skills and higher education, even in a segregated form. He also called for the start of Louisville Mu-nicipal College for Negroes in the late 1920s because he realized that ad-mission to the University of Louisville was impossible. His philosophy was that blacks should press for their rights for an education, for decent jobs, and for other rights as taxpayers while being prepared to accept less than they desired. He believed that it was far better for blacks to receive only half of their goal and to have whites and blacks on good terms, than for blacks to be successful in achieving certain demands at the price of in-creased white resentment.[19]

How could Bond call himself an advocate of black rights and yet be so willing to compromise his positions? When looking at his life, it is un-derstandable why he consistently advocated such an approach. Bond barely made a living pastoring churches. The only economic security he enjoyed was as director of the Kentucky CIC, a position that encouraged, if not demanded, Bond to take a more sanguine view of race relations. So white Louisvillians still controlled a segment of the black leadership.

The circumstances surrounding the million-dollar bond issue that was defeated November 2, 1920, give a vivid example of how Louisville's more moderate black leaders could remain loyal to whites even when it was not in the best interest of their race. Old leaders Steward, Parrish, and Harris and new leaders Clement and Bond supported the bond to aid the all-white University of Louisville. In a statement printed in the *Herald*, this black group explained that they deplored any circumstances which would make the improvement of educational facilities for the white people of the city

of James Bond. Rufus Clement, a son of Bishop Clement, was president of Atlanta Univer-sity. Bishop Clement's wife was the first black woman named "Mother of the Year" in the United States. Several of the children and grandchildren of Bond and Clement received ad-vanced degrees and held important positions in education, business, and government. The two families were related through marriage, with J. Max Bond marrying a daughter of Bishop Clement.

19. J. Max Bond, interview; Mrs. Thomas Bond interview. See *Leader*, June 9, 1923, for an article by Bond on race relations in Kentucky. Also see *Courier-Journal*, May 11, 1924, for Bond's call for interracial goodwill.

a race issue that would align blacks against whites, thus fostering racial bitterness and hatred. Their primary reason for supporting the bond issue, however, was that they did not want to lose their white supporters: "We note that generally speaking, the white people who have in the past been our best friends, sympathizing with us in our struggles, helping us in our churches and in our schools and lending a helping hand along all lines— are the promoters in the bond issue. . . . It would not be to our advantage to break with these white friends." [20]

The more militant young leaders, led by Lovett, bought space in the *Evening Post* to respond to this letter. Lovett's group noted that their opposition to the bond was not prompted by any desire to heighten black-white antagonism. It "is merely a matter of principle that we do not desire to pay taxes from which we get no benefit." The new leaders concluded that they too valued their white friends and appreciated white contributions to black organizations, but noted that individual whites had made voluntary contributions to blacks while the million-dollar bond proposal was a tax levy which would be a compulsory obligation upon all citizens. [21]

Both the militant and conservative black leaders attempted to maintain an alliance with Harvey Burns, an alleged underworld figure. A native of Louisville with only an eighth-grade education, Burns eventually opened a funeral home, saloon, and several ice cream stands. During the 1920s the Republican party relied on Burns to get out the black vote on election day and to keep disgruntled blacks from voicing their complaints about the party too loudly. In return, Burns was hired as the city's undertaker and, more importantly, according to newspaper accounts, city officials allowed him to operate several illegal activities in the black community. In 1920 police officers Miles Pounds and James E. Graham resigned from the police force under pressure from Republican officials after using excessive force in arresting Burns and several other blacks for gambling. As a rule, nothing happened to policemen who exercised undue force in arresting blacks. In addition, the charges against Burns of gambling and resisting arrest were dropped. Three years later Burns and eleven men were arrested for gambling at his bar on Ninth Street. For a second time the police court dismissed the charges. [22]

Burns was very influential in the black community. Just like white ward heelers, Burns gave money to the needy, helped black newcomers to find

20. *Herald*, October 20, 1920.
21. *Evening Post*, October 29, 1920.
22. *Courier-Journal*, June 26, 1920; *Post*, October 22, 1923; *Leader*, May 23, November 7, 1931.

employment and housing, and intervened on behalf of many blacks accused of minor crimes. Indeed, one definite advantage he had over the more respectable black leaders was his ability to get blacks out of jail. Also, though black leaders warned young people to stay away from the vice areas controlled by Burns, they like practically everyone in the community respected and in some instances were awed by "bad men" like him. Stories were told about the exploits of Harvey Burns, of his influence at city hall, and that he owned an expensive automobile, wore fancy clothes, and lived by his own standards. One of the tragedies of racism and the black community has been that too often underworld figures have been held in high esteem, especially by the young. Racism too often relegated educated or hard-working, self-sacrificing blacks to low-paying, low-status jobs. Meanwhile, the "bad men" had the respect of the white police officers and they possessed many of the tangible symbols of success (money, cars, clothes) in white society. When Louisville's respectable leaders died, the black community turned out in large numbers to pay their final respects. The crowd at Burns's funeral in November 1931 probably exceeded that of any black leader. The *Leader*, which so often had criticized Burns and the police department for allowing his illegal activities to go unchecked, wrote that "the Auditorium of Calvary Baptist Church was too small to hold the hundreds of friends and citizens who wished to pay their final respects to Harvey Burns." [23]

III.

In a research memorandum prepared for the Carnegie-Myrdal Study of Negro Life in America, Ralph Bunche stated that black leadership was predominantly a local phenomenon; that even on the local level the influence of black leaders seldom filtered down to the masses. Bunche claimed that black leaders did not emphasize the problems that were most important to the masses. [24] Like the older leadership group, most of Louisville's new black leaders concerned themselves primarily with ending racial discrimination in public accommodations, seeking equal employment opportunities and a better allocation of school funds, and generally improving conditions in the Afro-American community. They were also very concerned about white violence upon blacks. As Bunche wisely pointed out, the achievement of some of the goals of this elite group would have

23. *Leader*, March 19, 1927, May 23, 1931; *Post*, November 4, 1925.
24. Bunche, "A Brief Analysis of Negro Leadership," 125.

principally benefited those blacks who had obtained college degrees or had the money to enjoy leisure-time activities. But ending police brutality and other white violence against blacks would surely have aided the black masses since in the vast majority of instances they were the ones who bore the brunt of such injustices. Improving schools and employment opportunities would also have benefited lower-class blacks. Black leaders' concern about health conditions also was an indication of their desire to end problems that primarily affected the poor. Indeed, contrary to what Bunche stated, Louisville's new black leaders did work diligently for the welfare of all blacks, if for selfish reasons. As businessmen who depended on the Afro-American community for their livelihood, they knew that they would profit from improvements in black employment and life-style.

Nevertheless, Bunche correctly noted that in many cities the established black leadership did not appeal to the local black masses. Many plain folk turned to charismatic leaders, such as Marcus Garvey, who exhibited a flashy style, open contempt for established black leaders, and who told lower-class blacks that they were important in their own right. Information on Garvey's influence in Louisville is scant. The *Leader* noted in 1921 that Louisville had a branch of Garvey's Universal Negro Improvement Association which had more than 500 members and was headed by Rev. Noah W. Williams, pastor of Quinn Chapel AME. Garvey spoke to an overflow crowd at a black fraternal hall in Louisville in 1923. The Rev. Parrish was on the program, and editor Cole introduced Garvey. That Parrish and Cole appeared publicly with Garvey was significant, considering that in many cities the black leadership viewed Garvey as a threat to their control over the black community and refused to have any association with him.[25]

Although the more militant group of new leaders were far more aggressive in denouncing racial discrimination than the old leaders (and surely more than the moderate new leaders), they were in many respects like the old leaders in their belief that the puritan ethic of hard work leads to success. They repeatedly urged young blacks to develop right habits as the first step toward bettering their lot. They too were concerned about crime and vice in Negro areas. But, unlike older leaders, the more militant new leaders never minimized racial discrimination as the primary cause of the ills

25. *Leader*, June 25, 1921, November 10, 1923. Garvey's newspaper, *Negro World*, has only an occasional reference to the Louisville branch. For example, on August 22, 1925, the paper mentioned that the choir of the Louisville UNIA would be singing in Cincinnati. The Louisville branch was rarely mentioned in the newspaper's section called "Summary of the Branches" which might indicate that the branch experienced long periods of inactivity.

suffered by the race. They never shifted the ultimate blame for segregation onto blacks themselves.

In a time when black leaders all over the country were becoming more aggressive in demanding changes, the presence of conservative young leaders in Louisville was very significant. Though they claimed that their approach kept racial violence to a minimum, the facts, especially regarding police brutality, indicate otherwise. What they did accomplish, however, was to keep the black community divided about which approach to adopt—theirs or the one advocated by the more radical blacks. Because of their close relationship with whites, the approach of moderate blacks received the widest hearing and the most favorable comments. These black leaders gave the illusion, as much as white civic leaders did, that Louisville had few racial problems; that blacks were better treated there than elsewhere. By relying on influential whites, and by convincing the race that the conservative way was the only realistic approach to gaining civil rights, these new leaders did help blacks make improvements in a few areas, but only under the terms dictated by the white establishment. Although it is strong indictment, the more moderate new leaders most certainly contributed to the continuation of Louisville's polite racism during the years after 1917.

## 9

Employment and Enterprise
Continuity and Change

Black Louisvillians experienced a great disparity in employment opportunities from 1917 to 1930; they were very good times for some, continued bad times for others. Several business enterprises, especially insurance companies, that relied on the city's 50,000 blacks for support enjoyed tremendous growth. For black workers, especially those in industry, discrimination continued to keep them in the lowest paid and least secure positions. To be sure, a few employment gains were made, and because of political pressure a few blacks were hired in new positions in city government. Most of these breakthroughs, however, were token positions for one or two blacks intended to placate the protesters. The great majority found that positions other than menial labor were still closed to them. By 1930 blacks remained underrepresented as skilled workers and overrepresented as common laborers and domestics. The Depression wiped out many of the gains black workers had managed to make during the previous thirteen years.

I.

Most of the jobs available to blacks during these years differed very little from those held by their mothers and fathers in the 1880s and 1890s. In fact, several sons followed in the footsteps of their fathers and became waiters at the Galt House or Pendennis Club, or became chauffeurs for wealthy white families whom their fathers had served as coachmen. Positions such as chief janitor, elevator operators, and messengers at city hall were still actively sought by Negro politicians.[1] The U.S. Census for 1920 shows that blacks still dominated the employment category of "domestic and personal." A little over 90 percent of the city's janitors, porters, servants, and waiters were black. As they had since the end of the Civil War,

1. *Courier-Journal*, November 6, 1917, January 1, 1918; Louisville *Times*, September 28, 1923; Blanton interview; Lorenzo J. Greene and Carter G. Woodson, *The Negro Wage Earner* (Washington, D.C., 1930), 111.

black women continued to be employed as servants, working in hotels, restaurants, laundries, and private homes. Of the city's 3,987 laundresses, 3,721 or 93 percent were black; of 4,389 servants, 3,128 or 71 percent were black.[2]

Discrimination kept many avenues of employment closed to blacks and closed others that had been open to them. By 1920 there were no black conductors on the L & N and other railroads operating in Louisville, a contrast with the nineteenth century when blacks had held this skilled job. Local government officials still hired blacks only as laborers, consistently refusing to consider them for other jobs. In 1920 Louisville city government employed almost an equal number of black and white common laborers (283 blacks and 285 whites), but all of the clerks, stenographers, policemen, and firemen were white. To the dismay of blacks, the Post Office was limiting the number of Negro postal workers by the early 1920s. According to the Louisville branch of the NAACP, the number of black mail carriers declined sharply from a high of forty employed in 1910.[3]

Except for teaching at the black schools or working as nurses at Red Cross Hospital, few jobs other than domestic service or common labor were open to Afro-American women. Being hired as telephone operators (one out of 616) or saleswomen was out of the question. Black women were still viewed by white employers as a source of cheap, exploitable labor. They continued to comprise more than half of the women tobacco workers, who, as a rule, were still paid by how much they produced. But the few black women who received straight salaries were paid 25 to 35 percent less than whites regardless of experience or expertise. Blacks also worked in the clothing industry. According to reports from the Women's Bureau of the U.S. Department of Labor, black women worked the longest hours for the least pay under deplorable conditions in the overalls, feathers, and wool industries. Tragically, the reports conducted in the 1920s read just like reports of conditions for working women decades earlier, indicating that little if anything had improved.[4]

2. *Fourteenth Census*, "1920: Population," IV, 1132–35.
3. *Fourteenth Census*, IV, 1134. On discrimination at the Post Office, see letters from the Louisville NAACP to the National Association, November 11, 18, 1920, and Board Minutes of the Louisville NAACP, April 17, 1925, NAACP Papers.
4. U.S. Department of Labor, Women's Bureau, *Negro Women in Industry in Fifteen States*, Bulletin no. 70 (Washington, D.C., 1929), 15. See also Women's Bureau, *Women in Kentucky Industries*, Bulletin no. 29 (Washington, D.C., 1923). For a comparison with earlier working conditions, see *Report of the Commission to Investigate the Conditions of Working Women in Kentucky* (n.p., 1911); Greene and Woodson, *The Negro Wage Earner*, 152, 283–85; *Crisis*, XVII (November, 1918), 12, 16. There is little doubt that the managers

The World War I years were a most significant time for Afro-American workers in industry. In Louisville and elsewhere, black leaders and concerned organizations like the National Urban League had been cautiously optimistic that the labor shortage caused by the start of the war would lead to blacks gaining a permanent foothold in industry. As a result of the curtailment of European immigration, the buildup in war-related industries, and the labor shortage, blacks found opportunities in many of the industrial northern cities. Somewhere between 300,000 and 1,000,000 blacks left the border and southern states for jobs in Gary, Chicago, Cleveland, Detroit, and elsewhere. Within the U.S. Department of Labor a special Negro Division of Labor was created to try to minimize potential problems and to ensure that blacks were fully utilized by the various war-related industries. The National Urban League held a conference for white employers and black migrants, informing both of the advantages to be derived from a joint effort. During the war years, blacks occupied vital positions in virtually all of the war-related industries: automobile and truck production, iron and steel production, and meat-packing.[5]

It would be easy to exaggerate the role of blacks in industry during the war. But as Allan Spear points out, in Chicago black industrial workers "were concentrated in the least skilled, least desirable jobs; their opportunities for advancement were severely limited; they were subject to periodic layoffs; and they had little hope of obtaining white collar jobs." In a recently completed study of black workers from the Civil War to the present, the historian William H. Harris clearly shows that during World War I blacks were used almost exclusively as unskilled workers in industry: "In short, no fundamental change took place between black workers and white employers during the war. Employers simply experimented with the use of black labor during the emergency." Harris also points out that even during the war, very few employment opportunities in industry were open to Afro-American women. Given the limited advancement into industry made by blacks, it was inevitable that after the wartime crisis had passed, most of them would be dismissed from their jobs. As a border city, Louisville had thousands of blacks drifting into the city during the early 1920s on their way to the South after having lost their jobs in the North.[6]

---

of tobacco factories preferred black women over white women. See an advertisement by the Atlas Tobacco Company in the Louisville *Herald*, January 11, 1920.

5. John Hope Franklin, *From Slavery to Freedom: A History of Negro Americans* (3rd ed.; New York, 1967), 473–74.

6. Spear, *Black Chicago*, 166; William H. Harris, *The Harder We Run: Black Workers Since the Civil War* (New York, 1982), 61–65; *Annual Report of Welfare League, 1921* (Louisville, 1922), 52–53; *Post*, June 28, 1923.

Blacks experienced a similar fate in Louisville's industries. To be sure, gains were made during the war years, but as a survey of the Industrial Foundation of Louisville pointed out, most companies refused to hire blacks even during the war crisis. Officials from the Louisville Urban League held countless meetings with employers, trying to convince them to hire a few blacks. A few companies did employ blacks but used them primarily as helpers and janitors, not in such skilled positions as machinists, mechanics, electricians, toolmakers, engineers, diesinkers, pattern makers, or core makers. Furthermore, skilled blacks found that instead of fully utilizing their trades, they were often employed as sandblasters or furnace tenders, jobs which whites found unappealing when other positions were available.[7] In the final analysis, during World War I blacks did enter industry but this did not constitute a real break with past discrimination, for blacks continued to be employed in marginal or undesirable occupations and excluded from most other jobs.

With such an attitude prevailing during the war, it is not surprising that little progress was made in breaking down the color barrier in industrial employment in Louisville during the 1920s. As was the case elsewhere in the nation, when white men returned from the war, blacks were pushed out of jobs or moved from skilled to unskilled positions. In 1925 the Louisville Urban League found that almost all blacks employed in industry worked as laborers; that only a few were employed in the steel mills and foundries, positions that paid $15–$25 a week, the highest industrial wages in the city. "It is the low wage scale for colored workmen in Louisville that constitutes the basis for most of our industrial troubles," concluded the 1925 Urban League report. The League conducted another study in 1929 which only substantiated the earlier findings. A majority of industries still did not employ blacks, and those that did saw them merely as a source of cheap, unskilled, and semiskilled labor. The Urban League estimated that most black industrial workers made $16 a week, or at least $4 to $10 less than white workers performing the same jobs.[8]

Blacks made no appreciable gains with organized labor during the 1920s. Scholars Sterling Spero and Abram Harris indicated that labor or-

7. J. Harvey Kerns, *A Survey of the Economic and Cultural Conditions of the Negro Population of Louisville, Kentucky, and a Review of the Program and Activities of the Louisville Urban League* (New York, 1948), 17–34; Atwood S. Wilson, "The Vocational Opportunity and Education of Colored Pupils at Louisville" (M.A. thesis, University of Chicago, 1934); Yater, *A History of Louisville,* 173–82.

8. "The Urban League Report of 1925," *Opportunity,* IV (February, 1926), 72; "Louisville Urban League Report for 1929," National Urban League Papers, Manuscript Division, Library of Congress, Washington, D.C.

ganizers worked only "half-heartedly" in Louisville to unionize black un-skilled tobacco workers. Thomas L. Dabney of the National Urban League estimated in 1928 that only 474 of the nearly 20,000 organized workers in the city were Negroes. Dabney reported that union after union failed to try to bring blacks into their organizations. For instance, the Carpenters' Union No. 64 was unconcerned about blacks because there were "only a few good colored carpenters in the city, so that the local does not have to worry about them. If they were a menace, the whites would pay some at-tention to them." In the tobacco industry, where there were plenty of black workers, most of them remained unorganized; of 1,400 union members, only 100 were black.[9]

Dabney's report pointed out that the vast majority of Louisville's 474 organized blacks were in segregated unions. They formed their own or-ganizations of bricklayers, carpenters, hod carriers, and waiters. The Hod Carriers and Common Laborers Union No. 86 was the largest with 156 members. Despite the presence of unions, black workers were incapable of exerting much influence in Louisville. As long as white unions refused to stand with the black unions, blacks could do very little. White contrac-tors would not employ Negroes as hod carriers or bricklayers on the same jobs with white union men even though blacks were members of a union. The Louisville branch of the National Association of Colored Waiters, re-alizing its weakness, adopted a very passive platform. Strikes were out-lawed. The union simply aimed to show its members how to be good workers and to provide them with recreational activities.[10]

Black laborers were especially susceptible to economic slowdowns. Even during the "good times" of the early 1920s, when a number of local businesses were expanding, some 15,000 workers were occasionally idle in Louisville. Without union protection and being relegated to the most insecure jobs, blacks comprised a sizable number of the city's unemployed throughout the decade. Job prospects for workers grew even worse by the late 1920s. Such large employers as Ford Motor Company, Standard San-itary Company, International Harvester, the Louisville Railway Com-pany, and even city government had to drastically reduce their work force and lower the salaries of those employees still on the job. Yet by January 1930 a number of Louisville observers were optimistic. They believed that

9. Sterling D. Spero and Abram L. Harris, *The Black Worker: The Negro and the La-bor Movement* (New York, 1931), 323–24; Thomas L. Dabney, "Louisville, Kentucky: A Summary of Industrial Conditions, Organized Labor and Negro Labor," National Urban League Papers.
10. Dabney, "A Summary of Industrial Conditions."

the worst was over; that because of Louisville's diversified work force, their city would not be greatly affected by the nationwide depression. A writer in the *Herald-Post* reported that the Standard Sanitary Company had recalled 3,500 workers and Ford Motor 1,200 workers, and that all of the city's factories would soon be operating at full capacity. The local press even predicted that the construction industry would improve in 1930. Several national studies of unemployment concluded that employment prospects looked bright in Louisville, especially with the reopening of a few local distilleries to produce "medicinal whisky." The National Urban League, which usually painted a grim picture of job opportunities, said that prospects for blacks were much better in Louisville than in Richmond, another border city.[11]

All of these hopes proved to be unfounded, for conditions in Louisville grew steadily worse. The building industry, instead of recovering, collapsed as new construction came to a halt. The city's leading financial institution, The National Bank of Kentucky, collapsed and led to the ruin of other financial institutions and businesses. Many of the businesses that had resumed operations in January 1930 were shut down by the middle of the year.[12] J. A. Thomas, the executive secretary of the Louisville Urban League, said that black unemployment increased from 12.1 percent in 1930 to 37.2 percent in 1932, while white unemployment rose from 9 percent to 23.5 percent. League officials noted that blacks were not only being laid off in industry, but that black women, who were often the sole breadwinners of their families, were losing their service jobs as well. Writing in *Opportunity*, a spokesman for the Urban League asked, "Are Negro women losing to white women in domestic service?" The anonymous Urban League official said that want ads in the daily newspapers indicated that whites were preferring white household workers. "White servants," his own inquiry revealed, "are regarded as being more tractable, more willing to work long hours, more apt to sleep in, and generally more satisfactory than the traditional Negro servant." No firm evidence exists to confirm or dispute his contention that black women were being replaced by whites. It is probably safe to assume that during the economic crunch many white families

11. See the articles on the front pages of the *Herald-Post* and *Courier-Journal* for the first week of January 1930. See also the *Herald-Post*'s editorial of January 5, 1930; Robert F. Sexton, "Kentucky Politics and Society: 1919–1932" (Ph.D. dissertation, University of Washington, 1970), 213; National Urban League, *Unemployment Status of Negroes: A Compilation of Facts and Figures Respecting Unemployment in One Hundred and Six Cities* (New York, 1931), 5; *Opportunity*, IX (July, 1931), 218.

12. *Herald-Post*, June 8, 1930; Sexton, "Kentucky Politics and Society," 211–12.

did without their household servants entirely, which led to increased woes for blacks.[13]

As a solution to black unemployment in the cities, the National Urban League conducted a Vocational Opportunity Campaign. Urban League workers throughout the country compiled and disseminated information on employment prospects in certain vocations, pleaded with white employers and unions "to give qualified Negroes a chance," informed the white public of the consequences of limiting employment opportunities for blacks, and encouraged young black people to train for future employment even though job prospects looked dismal at the present. The League issued statements saying that the entire community had to become involved, that something had to be done to increase work and vocational training programs for blacks and to provide them with adequate training facilities.[14]

Albert E. Meyzeek directed the Louisville Urban League's Vocational Opportunity Campaign. He met with local black ministers and encouraged them to speak to their congregations on the importance of vocational training. He addressed the black Parent-Teacher Association on the need for more vocational courses in the public schools. Meyzeek and Urban League officials met with several of the city's largest employers and urged them to hire some of Louisville's unemployed black workers. To conclude the vocational campaign, they invited all interested citizens to attend the Urban League's Conference on the "Economic Problems Arising for Negroes Caused by Changing Industrial Conditions and Unemployment." The efforts by Louisville's Urban League to improve employment and vocational opportunities for blacks failed. With white unemployment increasing in Louisville, the Urban League stood little chance of convincing the general public to take measures to decrease black unemployment. Meyzeek, in a letter to the National Urban League executive officers, summarized the problem faced by the Louisville Urban League when conducting its vocational campaign: "Because the quest of improving the Negro's economic status is still considered controversial by so many people, it was impossible to send speakers to local (white) civic clubs. Likewise, a program over Radio Station WHAS, in which Mayor Harrison was

13. *Fifteenth Census,* "1930: Unemployment," I, 400–402; *Courier-Journal,* April 19, 1931; National Urban League, *Unemployment Status of Negroes,* 21; *Opportunity,* VIII (April, 1930), 120.

14. *Courier-Journal,* April 19, 1931; Nancy J. Weiss, *The National Urban League 1910–1940* (New York, 1974), 257.

[to be] the principal speaker, was cancelled by the station director." The historian Nancy Weiss noted that because of the Depression, the Urban League's nationwide Vocational Opportunity Campaign accomplished very little. She concluded that the campaign was ultimately an appeal from the Urban League to blacks to not give up on the American system.[15]

Despite the vocational campaign and other efforts by the Urban League, employment opportunities for blacks in Louisville remained depressed throughout the 1930s. World War II would finally bring some of the gains that the League and others had been advocating for twenty-five years. During World War II, Negroes would find jobs as machine operators, factory foremen, chemists, buffers, painters, welders, and clerical workers on federal projects. However, blacks would face discrimination in most of Louisville's industries just as they had during World War I. A survey conducted by the Louisville Urban League in 1941–1942 of black employment in twenty large industries in Louisville and nearby Indiana found that these industries were receiving government contracts totaling $200 million dollars. Out of a total work force of 25,000 workers, only 1,564 were blacks, and they were largely concentrated in the menial jobs. Ten of these industries used blacks only as janitors and porters; six others employed them as semiskilled operators; two industries did not employ blacks at all and the managers refused to consider their employment in any capacity.[16]

II.

In bold contrast with the worsening employment situation experienced by black workers and the ever-present discrimination they faced was the impressive rise in the number of businesses that succeeded because of the strong financial backing they received from all segments of the Afro-American community. Indeed, the most significant change in black Louisville after 1917 was the growth of independent business enterprises. As the *Leader* proudly pointed out in 1924, "Yesterday as it were, we had a few

15. "1931 Louisville Report on the Vocational Opportunity Campaign," National Urban League Papers; Weiss, *The National Urban League*, 258.

16. J. A. Thomas, "The Negro Wage Earner in Kentucky," unpublished paper, Louisville Urban League, March, 1942, 7–8; Kerns, *The Louisville Urban League*, 23. For examples of job discrimination against blacks in Louisville during World War II, see Records of the Committee on Fair Employment Practice for Region V, Boxes 690–93, National Archives, Washington, D.C.

restaurants and barbershops, an undertaking establishment or so. Today we have two banks, four insurance companies, two hotels, . . . two building and loan associations, six real estate companies, three drug stores, eight undertakers, two photographers, fifteen groceries, four newspapers, three architects, . . . three movie houses and buildings for our business and professional men." [17]

The city's new leaders repeatedly stressed the point that blacks would remain in "economic slavery" as long as they were dependent upon whites for important services, such as insurance and banking. Insurance companies were important to the well-being of the entire community since most blacks lacked coverage against accidents, disasters, and death. Black leaders envisioned banks loaning money to help stimulate yet other business activities. To ensure that Afro-Americans realized the importance of these businesses, the new leaders coined slogans praising banks and insurance companies as crucial for the race's progress. They labeled anyone in the community who did not support these enterprises as traitors to the race. Surprisingly, given the animosity between the two groups, the city's old black leaders agreed with the younger leaders on the importance of black-owned businesses and helped to launch the necessary financial institutions.

By the 1920s blacks had established financial institutions and other businesses in a number of cities. Even more impressive than Louisville was Nashville, where in the early 1900s blacks formed two banks. By the time of the Great Depression, Nashville had black-owned publishing houses, insurance companies, and a score of other business enterprises. In Richmond were four banks, nine insurance companies, and a number of realty associations. With Atlanta leading the way, blacks in Georgia had thirteen banks and insurance companies, including the second largest insurance company in black America, Atlanta Mutual. Then there was Durham, North Carolina, the black "business capital of the world," and the home of the largest black business, North Carolina Mutual Life Insurance Company. With the exception of Chicago, most of the insurance companies and banks were located in southern and border cities. Blacks in northern cities opened places of amusement, hotels, restaurants, and a few realty associations. Throughout the North and South, blacks agreed with Louisville blacks on the desirability of their own independent enterprises. [18]

17. *Leader*, May 10, 1924.
18. Lamon, *Black Tennesseans*, 173–87; Dittmer, *Black Georgia*, 43–49. For information on black businesses in Richmond, see Raymond Gavins, *The Perils and Prospects of Southern Black Leadership: Gordon Blaine Hancock, 1884–1970* (Durham, 1977), 45–46;

The growth of black insurance companies was stimulated by the discriminatory rates that white insurance companies charged blacks and the arrogant way white companies acted toward black customers.[19] In the early 1900s, a number of large white companies, greatly influenced by Fredrick L. Hoffman's *Race Traits and Tendencies of the American Negro* which purported that blacks were extremely bad risks, felt justified in charging blacks higher premiums if they accepted blacks at all. For years the local Afro-American press urged blacks to quit supporting the white companies and to buy policies from the out-of-state fraternal organizations and small insurance companies that had representatives in Louisville. In 1906 a group of the city's leading black men—William H. Steward, Rev. Charles H. Parrish, Rev. John H. Frank, and several physicians—formed a life insurance company, giving it a most unusual name: the Cave Dwellers Life Association. Their objective was to provide mutual protection for the members of their insurance group, to provide life insurance benefits at a minimum price, to invest their funds, and, of course, to uplift the race. This company remained small, being very selective in its membership. Meanwhile, the vast majority of blacks continued to be insured by white companies or did without insurance.[20]

It took an assault incident in 1910 to fully arouse the black community against white insurance companies. W. O. Christianburg, an agent for the National Sick, Accident, and Life Insurance Company, was charged with assaulting eleven-year-old Grace Jackson at her home on Esquire Street. Christianburg admitted in court that he occasionally "fooled around" with the black girls on his route, but denied that he forced himself on Grace Jackson. The court dismissed the charges against Christianburg, and his insurance company refused to fire him. After this incident black leaders initiated a boycott of white insurance companies, and several out-of-state black companies began to pursue Louisville black clients more vigorously. The Atlanta Mutual and Standard Life Insurance Company developed such a thriving business that its agent, Henry E. Hall, managed two office rooms and had several agents and stenographers

---

Gerber, *Black Ohio*, 309–19; Kusmer, *A Ghetto Takes Shape*, 192–95; Spear, *Black Chicago*, 181–86.

    19. Walter B. Weare, *Black Business in the New South: A Social History of the North Carolina Mutual Life Insurance Company* (Urbana, 1973), 22.

    20. Carter G. Woodson, "Insurance Among Negroes," *Journal of Negro History*, XIV (April, 1929), 211–20; Weare, *Black Business in the New South*, 16, 98; Indianapolis *Freeman*, June 2, 1906, November 25, 1911.

working under him. Kentucky's white insurance companies, with their business decreasing in the black community, backed the adoption of a bill that prohibited Atlanta Mutual and other out-of-state black insurance companies from operating in the state. The law required all out-of-state insurance companies to deposit $100,000 with the state, a sum much too high for small black insurance companies.[21]

In response to this effective ban on the activities of external black insurance companies, Henry Hall and lawyer-businessman William H. Wright took steps to organize a local company. Hall was undoubtedly the right person for the task. A native of Henderson, Kentucky, and a graduate of Hampton Institute, he had been working for two decades promoting insurance ventures in Kentucky. In 1900 he had worked as an agent in Henderson for an insurance fraternal organization with headquarters in Lynchburg, Virginia; he eventually became the organization's manager for the entire state of Kentucky. Several years later he formed his own insurance company, which he sold to the much larger Atlanta Mutual. Now with Atlanta Mutual unable to continue in Kentucky, Hall and Wright interested several black businessmen in their new company and also received some financial support from Bennett H. Young, a local white lawyer who often contributed to black causes. They organized the Mammoth Mutual Company in 1914 and applied for a license. The state insurance department, however, rejected their license request. They immediately filed a suit against the Kentucky Insurance Department and appealed their case to the Kentucky Court of Appeals after losing in their first court hearing. The Kentucky Court of Appeals granted Hall and Wright a license and Mammoth opened for business July 12, 1915.[22]

Mammoth had a modest but promising beginning. The entire work force consisted of one clerk and a dozen field representatives, and the company had only $10,000 in total assets. Nevertheless, Hall and Wright knew that their business venture would be successful because while waiting for the insurance license, they received pledges of support from black fraternal orders and most of the black churches in the city. By December 1, 1915—not quite six months after receiving a license—Mammoth Mutual Company had written more than $800,000 in insurance policies in Louis-

21. Indianapolis *Freeman*, September 3, 1910, December 24, 1912; *1915–1965, 50th Anniversary Mammoth Life* (Louisville, 1965), 4, 51.

22. Indianapolis *Freeman*, October 14, 1914; *Leader*, March 7, 1925; M. S. Stuart, *An Economic Detour: A History of Life Insurance in the Lives of American Negroes* (New York, 1940), 150.

ville and throughout Kentucky. Black businessmen, schools, fraternal orders, and religious denominations in the state endorsed the company. Ministers became Mammoth's best agents and friends, as they preached from their pulpits the value of having insurance and then sold policies to their church members. Mammoth's agents wrote 80,000 policies in Kentucky during the company's first five years of existence.[23]

This strong financial backing enabled Mammoth to purchase a three-story brick building in 1917; only eight years later Mammoth built a six-story building, at a cost of $377,000, for its burgeoning business. As an indication of how good local business had become, Mammoth retained the three-story building and used it only for Louisville insurance business. Mammoth, established as a mutual company, became a legal reserve stock company in 1924 after a successful statewide stock sale. Company officials issued $100,000 in stock. When the stock was oversubscribed within ninety days, the officials increased the capital stock to $200,000. All of the stock was purchased by the end of 1924. That same year, Mammoth had total assets of $223,255 and liabilities of $19,464.[24]

Other black businessmen quickly followed Hall and Wright and established other insurance companies and financial institutions in Louisville. G. P. Hughes, J. E. Smith, and W. F. Turner, all former employees of Mammoth Mutual, organized the Domestic Life and Accident Insurance Company in June 1920. Domestic Life received a charter in September 1921 to operate as a legal reserve life insurance company. Even though Domestic Life never achieved the same level of success as Mammoth Mutual, the company did prove that blacks in Louisville and Kentucky could support more than one insurance company. Domestic Life first operated out of rented quarters in the Knights of Pythians' building at Tenth and Chestnut, but by 1924 it had purchased its own facility at 601 West Walnut Street, directly across the street from Mammoth Mutual. The *Courier-Journal* of June 7, 1924, reported that Domestic Life had issued 51,981 policies, a total of $5,828,548 worth of insurance, in less than three years. The total income of Domestic Life, as reported in the *Courier-Journal*, was $428,344.02. Benefits totaling $130,019.07 had been paid to policyholders, while $202,969.41 had been paid in salaries. Domestic Life sold insurance throughout Kentucky and even ventured into Ohio. Domestic Life used the methods of Mammoth Mutual to appeal to the black public for

23. *Leader*, March 7, 1925.
24. See the *Courier-Journal*, June 17, 1924, for a special "Homecoming Section" that highlighted businesses and institutions in Louisville; Stuart, *An Economic Detour*, 152.

support, informing them that their company provided much more than just insurance for blacks: it strengthened the race and provided jobs.[25]

Black leaders took great pride in their insurance companies. The insurance company buildings were pointed out to visitors in Louisville as signs of the race's progress. Cole regularly used his newspaper to invoke the virtues of black insurance companies: "The promotion and operation of insurance companies changed conditions among Negroes in Louisville. It changed the look of the whole town. It made an oasis out of a desert, opened the door of hope and opportunity to the black boy and the black girl, and put a new idea into their heads." The insurance companies, especially Mammoth, were quick to realize that the continued goodwill of the race was essential for business success. Mammoth's directors consistently gave business to other black enterprises. As Cole proudly pointed out (he owned a printing establishment), Mammoth used Negro businesses for practically all of its printing needs. In 1923 the company spent $3,000 on advertising, printing, and stationery, with all but $300 going to blacks. Each year the company held a reception to thank the black community for its support, and all of the ice cream and other refreshments were purchased from black stores.[26]

Within six months after establishing their insurance company, the executives of Domestic Life opened First Standard Bank. As Walter Weare explains, "A Negro bank obviously complemented the insurance company as a depository for its funds and an outlet for its investments." Black-owned banks were important to Afro-American communities. White banks seldom financed businesses or homes for blacks. If they did, they commonly charged blacks a much higher interest rate. The black community made First Standard an immediate success: during its first seven months the bank secured deposits of $114,127.71. By 1924 the total deposits reached $375,000, with close to $500,000 in resources. The bank's officials claimed that their institution helped advance the race by providing loans totaling more than $300,000 to Negro businesses and by raising black self-confidence and the estimation of blacks in the eyes of whites. As Wilson Lovett, the bank's president, explained: "In the final analysis the primary function of a Negro bank is to provide working capital and credit which makes business development possible, while at the same time rendering service to the community both by helping to teach habits of thrift

25. *Souvenir Magazine*, I (October, 1939), 20; *Opportunity*, I (October, 1923), 311; *Leader*, August 20, 1921, September 13, 1924; *Courier-Journal*, June 17, 1924.
26. *Leader*, February 9, 1924, August 5, 1927.

and making small loans to individual colored men and women who might not otherwise be given assistance at larger and older established banking institutions."[27]

Shortly after starting Mammoth Mutual, William H. Wright made an abortive attempt to organize a bank. Two years later, with the financial backing of twenty-three business associates, Wright successfully organized Mutual Savings and Realty Association. Wright appealed to the black community to support Mutual Savings: "The Mutual Savings and Realty Association is for the Masses and the Classes; Large Enough to Protect All of Us and Small Enough to Know Each of Us; Lift as You Climb: Savings, Business, and Integrity, Honesty and Efficiency; The Need for the Mutual." Wright's savings company obviously received support from Louisville's black community for the total amount of deposits increased steadily, rising from $300 in March 1917 to over $28,000 in August 1920. The growth of Mutual Savings encouraged Wright to organize the American Mutual Savings Bank. American Mutual received a license from Kentucky in December 1921 and began operating February 18, 1922, with Wright as president.[28]

In Louisville's black community, Wright and his business associates controlled American Mutual Savings Bank and Mammoth Mutual, while Lovett and his associates controlled First Standard Bank and Domestic Life. Lovett's group also invested in property, opened a realty company, and organized two loan companies: the Standard Building and Loan Association and the Parkway Building and Loan Association.

The new banks and savings and loan companies showed their gratitude to the black community for its support by sponsoring community projects, and giving donations to charities. During its first year of operation, First Standard Bank had a free movie for children every Saturday at the Lincoln Theater.[29]

Louisville's two black banks were in existence for almost a decade. Their eventual failure resulted from the collapse of their depository bank, the National Bank of Kentucky. Long the leading financial institution in Louisville, the National Bank of Kentucky came under the control of James B. Brown in the early 1900s. By the late 1920s Brown sought consolida-

27. Weare, *Black Business in the New South*, 82; Lovett was quoted in the *Leader*, May 14, 1921; see also the *Leader*, February 9, May 10, 1924; *Opportunity*, I (October, 1923), 311; *Crisis*, XXI (December, 1920), 86; *Courier-Journal*, June 17, 1924, February 5, 1925.

28. *Leader*, January 5, 1921, May 3, 1924; *Courier-Journal*, June 17, 1924.

29. *Leader*, January 5, February 21, 1921, May 3, 1924.

tion with other financial institutions to offset the more than $9 million debt he had incurred through his other business enterprises. (For instance, under Brown's ownership the Louisville *Herald-Post* lost $5 million in five years before finally collapsing.) In 1930 Brown merged his holdings with Caldwell and Company of Nashville. With both of their companies near bankruptcy, Roger Caldwell and Brown had deceived each other into agreeing to the partnership. Caldwell's company collapsed first in October 1930, taking along the National Bank of Kentucky and about 120 other banks. One scholar has noted that the National Bank of Kentucky was the most important national bank to close in 1930.[30]

Both the First Standard Bank and the American Mutual Savings Bank closed immediately after the collapse of the National Bank of Kentucky. After a series of meetings, the two black banks merged, forming the Mutual Standard Bank, and reopened in late January 1931. However, confidence in all banks was extremely low. Despite pleas from the bank's officials, blacks rushed to withdraw the few dollars remaining in the bank, thus severely crippling Mutual Standard's attempt to remain open. In May the bank's officials took the inevitable step of closing Mutual Standard and placing it under the control of the Kentucky Banking Commission for liquidation.[31]

The closing of Mutual Standard Bank was a great blow to Louisville's black leadership. They consoled themselves with the knowledge that white ineptness caused the bank's failure. In later years, when reflecting on the collapse of the bank, they pointed out that during the Depression the insurance companies they owned had remained open despite having to pay unusually large claims resulting from the increase in illnesses and deaths. Here was proof positive of their business acumen.

In addition to financial institutions, the 1920s saw the start of a number of enterprises that provided leisure-time activities for blacks. Restaurants, which had been common in black Louisville in the 1870s and 1880s, made a comeback in the 1920s. For several years prior to 1920 several white businessmen had run movie houses that catered exclusively to blacks. In 1919 a syndicate headed by a Philadelphia black, E. C. Brown, opened a theater in Louisville which became an immediate success. A year later, several local black businessmen opened the Lincoln Theater. Editor Cole

30. John B. McFerrin, *Caldwell and Company: A Southern Financial Empire* (Chapel Hill, 1939), 126–40; *Herald-Post*, June 8, 1930; Sexton, "Kentucky Politics and Society," 211–12.

31. *Leader*, October 22, December 13, 1930, January 10, 24, February 21, December 5, 1931.

called on the race to support black theaters: "Go to the Lincoln; your own playhouse under absolute Colored Management." Several of the black theaters would stay in business until the 1960s. The complaints of the ministers and civic leaders attest to the thriving saloons and pool halls operated by Harvey Burns and other blacks. According to the press, these establishments were found on practically every block in black Louisville.[32]

Throughout the 1920s the Afro-American community gave strong support to black businesses. After witnessing the satisfaction that most blacks obviously derived from seeing black-owned enterprises flourish, practically all of the local businessmen appealed for support in racial terms. For example, Jordan and Son informed blacks that they sold "the best ice cream for the least money," and that "we are a Race Firm and deserve the patronage of our people."[33]

The argument can be made that Louisville's black community as a whole did not profit from these successful business enterprises, that the success was enjoyed by only a few black businessmen. It is true that despite their assertions about providing job opportunities for the race, all of the black banks and insurance companies employed no more than 200 people, thus barely affecting the dismal job market for Louisville's 50,000 blacks. But in the final analysis, Afro-American leaders did aid the community by establishing financial institutions that would provide loans to black businesses and consumers. These institutions were formed when racism was overt and rampant, when whites viewed blacks as barbaric or childlike. Black businesses gave most Negroes a sense of accomplishment and a spirit of hope for the race. They could never equal white enterprises, given the handicaps that black businessmen faced (remembering that their support came from the poorest paid workers in the community). But the mere existence of black businesses speaks volumes about the race's pride, talent, and determination to succeed.

32. Associates of Louisville Municipal College, *et al.*, *Study of Negro Business in Louisville* (Louisville, 1940); *Courier-Journal*, July 10, 1919; *Leader*, January 15, 1921.

33. For examples of advertisements by black businessmen, see Jessie B. Colbert (ed.), *General Conference Handbook of the 25th Quadrennial Session of the AME Zion Church held in Broadway Temple, Louisville, Kentucky, May 3–21, 1916* (Louisville, 1916). For a listing of black businesses and the services they provided, see Grant (ed.), *The 1921 Louisville Colored Directory*.

## 10

The Louisville NAACP
Triumphs and Failures in Civil Rights

The years from 1917 to 1930 witnessed not only the start of successful black businesses but also the emergence of a new and more aggressive civil rights movement. The "New Negro" period after World War I was more than a time when blacks coined slogans and opened mom-and-pop stores. It was a time when Afro-Americans became better organized and more assertive in denouncing legal discrimination, disfranchisement, and violence. Many blacks began to seriously question the wisdom of continued loyalty to one political party. It was during this time that the groundwork was laid for the modern black civil rights movement.

The National Association for the Advancement of Colored People (NAACP) was the bulwark of the movement. Shocked by the ever-widening racial conflict, a group comprised of white intellectuals and social workers and a handful of black educators, journalists, and ministers gathered in New York in 1909 and founded the NAACP. White members of the organization came from New York or New England and prided themselves on being the "new abolitionists." A few of them, most notably Oswald Garrison Villard, the grandson of William Lloyd Garrison, had blood ties to the abolitionists who denounced slavery before the Civil War. Well-known blacks connected with the organization included Mary Church Terrell, Bishop Alexander Walters, W. E. B. DuBois, and newspaper editor Ida Wells-Barnett. The founders of the NAACP stressed that their organization would be interracial. They believed that whites would bring prestige and money to the organization; organizational integration would also promote the concept of interracial understanding.[1]

The NAACP established legal and publicity departments at its New York headquarters to aid Afro-Americans in securing their rights, to inform the public of injustices against blacks, and to publicize black achievements. The legal department studied disfranchisement laws, resi-

---

1. Charles F. Kellogg, *A History of the National Association for the Advancement of Colored People, 1909–1920,* (Baltimore, 1967), 26, 118.

dential segregation ordinances, and other discriminatory statutes in order to develop test cases in the state and federal courts. The first important victory of the NAACP was won in June 1915 when the Supreme Court ruled the "Grandfather Clause" unconstitutional. This was a device used to keep blacks from voting. As editor of the NAACP publication *The Crisis*, DuBois also headed the publicity department. *The Crisis* contained information on successful black enterprises, on black social, cultural, and educational accomplishments, and on discrimination and racism.[2]

Branches of the NAACP were organized in New York, Boston, Chicago, and Philadelphia, and concerned people in other cities were encouraged to form NAACP affiliates. The NAACP established requirements for membership and carefully investigated local groups before granting them admission to the association. The national office instructed affiliates on the methods to be used to achieve the goals of the organization. The local branches became critical to the success of the NAACP. They fought racial discrimination, agitated for black political, social, and educational rights, helped secure fair trials for blacks accused of crimes, and brought potential test cases to the attention of the national office. It was the job of the local branches to watch over the general welfare of the black population in their area. In 1914 Louisville's black leaders organized a branch of the NAACP to fight the Louisville Residential Segregation Ordinance.[3]

The NAACP was the most effective civil rights group in Louisville. In addition to challenging the residential ordinance, the NAACP protested the existence of the Ku Klux Klan in the 1920s. Although no lynchings occurred in their city, the local branch denounced all instances of mob rule in Kentucky. The organization was responsible for many changes that blacks had been working toward for years. Often the Commission on Interracial Cooperation (CIC) would be given credit for racial progress when the young people of the NAACP had actually initiated the action. The primary reasons for the NAACP's aggressiveness in Louisville were its leaders—Warley, Cole, and Lovett—and the fact that, unlike NAACP branches in most cities, the Louisville affiliate was an all-black organization. However, a number of serious problems haunted the organization, including a lack of unity and a shortage of funds.

2. *Ibid.*, 65, 206, 210.
3. *Ibid.*, 60–61, 117–39; Ralph J. Bunche, "The Programs, Ideologies, Tactics, and Achievements of Negro Betterment and Interracial Organizations," research memorandum prepared for the Carnegie-Myrdal Study of the Negro in America, June, 1940, 45.

I.

Immediately after the residential segregation ordinance was introduced at the Louisville city council meeting on December 16, 1913, a group of black leaders, called together by Rev. Charles H. Parrish, met and formed a temporary NAACP branch to monitor and urge the defeat of the ordinance. The members of this ad hoc NAACP branch selected William H. Steward to meet with the mayor in an attempt to persuade him to reject the ordinance if it reached his desk. A steering committee, composed of the Reverends Charles H. Parrish, William T. Amiger, and C. B. Allen, was assigned to monitor the actions of the city council. Parrish was selected president of the organization.[4]

The Louisville NAACP (which did not receive formal recognition from the national headquarters until August 1914) tried to prevent passage of the segregation ordinance in a variety of ways. Immediately after the city council referred the ordinance to the revision committee of the general council, Parrish asked the committee to hold a public hearing before making a decision. The revision committee agreed, and a debate on the segregation ordinance was held March 18, 1914. Parrish, Steward, Allen, and Meyzeek spoke against the ordinance, while a group of white businessmen spoke in favor of it. After the debate, black leaders asked various white clubs and organizations to oppose the segregation ordinance. They printed a circular that contained their arguments against residential segregation and distributed it to influential whites. Parrish met with representatives from several women's clubs and received assurances from them that they would pressure the mayor into vetoing the ordinance. Parrish also appeared before the white Ministerial Alliance, which responded by passing a lukewarm resolution that "no injustice be done the colored citizens." Steward, well known by white businessmen, appeared before the Louisville Board of Trade to try to persuade them to go on record opposing the ordinance.[5]

Despite all of their statements and proclamations that they were "friends of the Negro," Louisville's white civic leaders proved to be unsympathetic to the black agitation against residential segregation. Although they had not initiated the proposed ordinance, the white elite refused to speak out against it or to use their influence with the mayor or the

---

4. Parrish, Meyzeek, and Colbert (eds.), *The Louisville Segregation Case*, 3–7; Louisville *Times*, March 19, 1914; Indianapolis *Freeman*, April 11, 1914.

5. Parrish, Meyzeek, and Colbert (eds.), *The Louisville Segregation Case*, 4–8.

city council to prevent it from becoming law. Not surprisingly, all of these attempts by blacks failed to halt the enactment of the residential ordinance. The board of aldermen allowed Rev. Allen and Rev. Parrish to speak before they voted unanimously in favor of the ordinance; they then sent the measure to the mayor, who signed it on May 11, 1914, despite the numerous pleas and petitions by blacks.[6]

NAACP officials at the national office in New York had closely followed these events in Louisville, hoping to find a test case to end residential segregation ordinances. At their board meeting in January 1914, several members had expressed interest in fighting Louisville's proposed ordinance. However, no word of the events in Louisville was mentioned at the NAACP board meetings for several months. But the board minutes of July 7, 1914, reveal that immediately after the Louisville mayor signed the ordinance, the NAACP took steps to become involved officially in the Louisville case. May Childs Nerney, executive secretary of the NAACP, William Pickens, and Joel E. Spingarn went to Louisville to give formal recognition to the Louisville NAACP and to aid in the fund-raising efforts already started by local blacks. J. Chapin Brinsmade of the NAACP's legal department visited Louisville. While there he attended a mass meeting at which $200 was raised to retain local counsel to fight the ordinance. On July 5, Pickens and Spingarn spoke at Quinn Chapel AME to a crowd of more than 800 about the harmful effects of the segregation ordinance and the reasons it should be overturned. Spingarn and Pickens were elated over the black response. Reporting to the national office about the July 5 meeting in Louisville, Spingarn said, "The colored people are thoroughly organized as a branch of the Association to fight segregation." [7]

While members of the NAACP were deciding how best to attack the segregation ordinance, two blacks were arrested for living on white blocks. Police officers arrested John Miller after the city's building inspector filed a complaint alleging that Miller moved into a white block after the ordinance went into effect. The police court fined Miller $5. On August 15, 1914, Arthur Harris moved into a house at 630 South Nineteenth Street, a block where ten whites and two blacks resided. Harris was arrested August 23. His case was heard by the Jefferson Circuit Court, a state court, rather than Louisville's Police Court. Nevertheless, the court found Harris

6. *Ibid.*, 8.

7. Board Minutes, NAACP, January 6, February 3, July 7, 1914, NAACP Papers. *Crisis*, VIII (August, 1914), 168; Indianapolis *Freeman*, July 11, 25, 1914.

guilty of violating the city's residential law, fined him $20, and ordered him to move from the white block.[8]

By November 1914 the NAACP had developed a test case to challenge the Louisville ordinance. In that month William Warley, a member of the Louisville NAACP, purchased a lot from Charles Buchanan, a white real estate dealer who oppposed the segregation ordinance. The lot, located on Pflanz Avenue, was in a white block. The wording of the contract between Buchanan and Warley had been carefully drawn up by the NAACP. Warley wrote to Buchanan, "It is understood that I am purchasing the above property for the purpose of having erected thereon a home which I propose to make my residence, it is a distinct part of this agreement that I shall not be required to accept a deed on the above property or to pay for said property unless I have the right under the laws of the state of Kentucky and the city of Louisville to occupy said property as residence." Buchanan agreed to Warley's terms, but on December 1, 1914, Buchanan's lawyer, Clayton C. Blakey, a member of a prestigious white firm, filed suit in Jefferson Court to test the validity of the ordinance. To avoid the charge of collusion, Warley asked City Attorney Pendleton Beckley to represent him. The NAACP had developed an unusual case to challenge the validity of the Louisville segregation ordinance: a white man, backed by the NAACP, called for the outlawing of the ordinance; a black man, represented by the city attorney, claimed to be fighting to uphold the ordinance.[9]

As anticipated by the NAACP, the Kentucky courts upheld the constitutionality of the Louisville segregation ordinance. The Jefferson Circuit Court dismissed Buchanan's suit in April 1915. The Kentucky Court of Appeals heard arguments on the ordinance in May 1915, and on June 18, 1915, the court unanimously agreed with the ruling of the Jefferson Circuit Court. The Court of Appeals said that the ordinance was a proper exercise of the police power of Louisville's city legislators. They could adopt reasonable measures for the public welfare in view of the public policy of Kentucky to secure the separation of the races. A residential segregation ordinance such as the one adopted in Louisville, the Court of Appeals concluded, did not violate the rights guaranteed individuals by the Fourteenth

8. *Courier-Journal*, August 28, 1914; *City of Louisville v. Arthur Harris*, Jefferson Circuit Court, see Spingarn Papers, Manuscript Division, Library of Congress, Washington, D.C.

9. See *Buchanan v. Warley*, 245 U.S. 60, 1; Parrish, Meyzeek, and Colbert (eds.), *The Louisville Segregation Case*, 10–11.

Amendment. Shortly after the ruling of the Kentucky Court of Appeals, Arthur B. Spingarn, chairman of the NAACP's legal committee, announced that the Louisville segregation ordinance would be appealed to the U.S. Supreme Court and that Moorfield Storey, president of the NAACP, would assist Blakey in the case.[10]

The U.S. Supreme Court first heard *Buchanan* v. *Warley* on April 10, 1916. At that time, however, only seven justices heard the case (one justice had just died and another one was ill). On April 17, Chief Justice Edward D. White announced that the case had been returned to the court's docket for reargument before a full court. It was exactly one year later when the court again heard arguments by Clayton Blakey and Moorfield Storey, representing Buchanan, and Pendleton Beckley and Stuart Chevalier, representing Warley, over the validity of Louisville's segregation ordinance. Beckley and Chevalier quoted freely from the Supreme Court's ruling in *Plessy* v. *Ferguson* and the *Berea College Case* to remind the justices that other laws separating the races had been upheld by the court. They argued that the Louisville segregation ordinance applied equally to whites and blacks; yet the briefs they filed with the court clearly indicated that the purpose of the ordinance was to prevent blacks from moving into white neighborhoods. Beckley and Chevalier argued at one point that "the ordinance will only affect that relatively small percentage of . . . Negroes, who to gratify their new-born social aspirations, seek to move into white neighborhoods." "Moreover," they asked, "can it be that a Negro has the constitutional rights, which cannot be restricted in the slightest degree, . . . to move into a block occupied by white families . . . simply to gratify his inordinate special aspirations to live with his family on a basis of social equality with white people?" The ordinance must be upheld, the city attorneys concluded grimly. Not to do so would spur racial antagonism and the destruction of white property.[11]

Blakey and Storey countered that Louisville's segregation ordinance restricted the right of citizens to buy and sell property, thereby depriving them of income without due process of law. They pointed out that the ordinance, while it sought to preserve the semblance of equality by forbidding whites from living in black areas, actually rested on the assumption

10. Rice, "Residential Segregation by Law," 187.
11. Portions of the briefs are quoted in *Crisis*, XIV (June, 1917), 62; see also Rice, "Residential Segregation by Law," 191. The *Post*, December 28, 1914, which favored the ordinance, claimed that city attorney Stuart Chevalier had been active throughout his career on behalf of blacks. "He has worked for liberal appropriations for colored children, and has assisted all municipal efforts to improve housing conditions among our colored people. Mr. Chevalier has earned the right to consider himself a friend of the Negro."

that whites would not wish to live in black neighborhoods. Even if the ordinance had applied equally to both races, it would still be unconstitutional because "the Constitution cannot be satisfied by any such offsetting
of inequalities and that a discrimination against one race is not [a] whit
less a discrimination because in some other matter a discrimination is made
against the other race." In summary, Blakey and Storey argued that the
Louisville segregation ordinance destroyed the fundamental rights guaranteed by the Fourteenth Amendment.[12]

On November 5, 1917, Justice William R. Day delivered the unanimous opinion of the Supreme Court, overturning the Louisville segregation ordinance: "The assignments of error in the court attack the ordinance upon the ground that it violated the Fourteenth Amendment of the
Constitution of the United States, in that it abridges the privileges and im-
munities of citizens of the United States to acquire and enjoy property, takes
property without due process of law, and denies equal protection of the
law." Day explained that the Fourteenth Amendment had been created
specifically to protect blacks in cases involving federal rights; however, the
broader purpose of the amendment was to protect all persons from discriminatory legislation by the states. Even though the Louisville ordinance
claimed to promote peace by preventing race conflict, that aim could not
"be accomplished by laws or ordinances which deny rights created and
protected by the Federal Constitution."[13]

The NAACP and those opposed to segregation ordinances were elated
over the Supreme Court's decision. Buchanan, the victor, and Warley, the
vanquished, both praised the court. Moorfield Storey, obviously pleased
with the court's decision, said: "I cannot help thinking . . . [that] it is the
most important decision that has been made since the Dred Scott case, and
happily this time it is the right way." The NAACP told all of its branch
groups to celebrate the organization's victory in the Louisville segregation
case. "This victory alone justified the existence of the NAACP, and all the
effort and money that have been put into it." Blacks in Louisville, Baltimore, Richmond, and St. Louis responded by holding victory rallies. In
Louisville, a crowd of 400 gathered for a rally at the Broadway Temple
AME Zion Church where they heard some of the principal figures talk
about their involvement in the case. Finally, writers in a number of leading
journals expressed their pleasure with the court decision in the Louisville
case. A *New Republic* author hoped that the favorable ruling would lift
the morale of all groups and individuals working for improvement in the

12. *Crisis*, XIV (June, 1917), 67–69.
13. *Buchanan* v. *Warley*, 245 U.S. 60.

status of blacks. He optimistically concluded that Jim Crow streetcars and other forms of segregation would end.[14]

The local white press expressed either displeasure or gave no comment at all on the court's decision. The *Courier-Journal* simply stated that the Supreme Court, in a unanimous opinion, ruled that compulsory separation of the races in residential districts violated the Constitution. The *Evening Post* and the *Times*, both supporters of the segregation ordinance, were disappointed with the Supreme Court's decision. An editorial in the *Post* called for "reasonable segregation" since residential segregation ordinances violated the Constitution. For an entirely different reason, a writer in the *Harvard Law Review* was disappointed with the Supreme Court's narrow ruling in the case. The writer pointed out that the court did not remove any of the burdens of discrimination that were placed on blacks; the only constitutional right violated by the ordinance, so the court said, was the right to buy and sell property as guaranteed by the Fourteenth Amendment.[15]

Fighting the residential ordinance through the courts resulted in more housing for blacks, but not in integrated neighborhoods. As had been the case for decades, very few blacks found housing in the eastern part of the city except in "Smoketown," the area around Shelby and Hancock Streets. In the decade following 1917, blacks moved further west on Chestnut, Jefferson, Madison, and several other streets, but only to Thirtieth Street. To make sure that blacks knew exactly where their area ended, the whites living west of Thirtieth changed the names of the streets to clearly differentiate their neighborhoods. At Thirtieth Street, Walnut became Michigan, Chestnut became River Park, Madison became Vermont, and Jefferson became Lockwood. As one long-time black resident of Louisville explained, "Whites wanted to make it absolutely clear where the black folks' neighborhood stopped and theirs began."[16] Indeed, whites made no secret

14. Storey was quoted in William B. Hixson, *Moorfield Storey and the Abolitionist Tradition* (New York, 1972), 142; NAACP *Branch Bulletin* (November, 1917), 1; Board Minutes, NAACP, November 12, 1917; letter from Mrs. W. Nola King, secretary of the Louisville NAACP, to James Weldon Johnson of the national office, November 20, 1917; letter from Dr. A. C. McIntyre, president of the Louisville branch, to May Childs Nerney, November 8, 1917; William H. Baldwin, "Unconstitutional Segregation," *New Republic* (January 19, 1918), 345–46; *Literary Digest* (November 24, 1917). *Crisis*, XV (January, 1918), 134–35 reprinted the views of newspapers throughout the nation that praised the Supreme Court's ruling in the Louisville case.

15. *Courier-Journal*, November 6, 1917; Louisville *Times*, November 5, 1917; *Evening Post*, November 5, 6, 1917; *Harvard Law Review*, XXI (1917–1918), 476–78.

16. Martha Minnis, interview with author, Louisville, July 8, 1979; Benjamin D. Berry,

of their desire to keep blacks from moving west of Thirtieth Street. One speaker addressing a hostile white crowd at the formation of a neighborhood association said their goal should be to make "a Negro living in the West End . . . as comfortable as if he was living in Hell." [17]

The NAACP had become involved in the residential segregation case to help end housing discrimination. But after the ordinance was overturned, several white organizations were formed to prevent blacks from "invading" their neighborhoods. The most notable of these organizations was the West Louisville Civic Club. Working closely with several attorneys, this Civic Club designed a ninety-nine-year contract that said any property sold or transferred to a black would automatically become the property of the Louisville Board of Education. Very few whites, however, signed the restrictive covenant. Ironically, the West Louisville Civic Club was so successful in spreading rumors of the black invasion that most whites feared signing any contract that might lead to their being trapped in a Negro neighborhood.[18]

White harassment of blacks proved to be far more effective than restrictive covenants in preventing blacks from moving into white neighborhoods. If they did move into a white area, blacks had their windows smashed and received threatening phone calls and vicious letters warning them to leave immediately. In October 1925 C. G. Sayles, a porter in the mail room of the L & N Railroad, purchased a home at 1051 South Thirty-Second Street. Several weeks later another black family bought the house next door. Both families received letters containing threats to burn their homes. Within several days, both homes were damaged by dynamite, yet both families refused to leave the area. On Thanksgiving Day their homes were dynamited a second time. This time Sayles was better prepared and fired five shots at his fleeing assailants. The local NAACP offered its assistance. The group posted a $100 reward for information leading to the arrest and conviction of the bombers and demanded police protection. Mayor Huston Quin, whose firm had helped in the residential segregation case, agreed to give police protection to the black families. Therefore, both families were able to remain in the area. Unfortunately, most blacks moving into white neighborhoods did not receive publicity nor police protection. For instance, whites repeatedly resisted all efforts by blacks to move north of Jefferson Street into the Portland area. Blacks venturing into this

---

"Plymouth Settlement House and the Development of Black Louisville, 1900–1930," (Ph.D. dissertation, Case Western Reserve University, 1977), 58.

17. *Leader*, July 2, 1927.
18. *Ibid.*; Jackson interview; Parrish interview; *Courier-Journal*, October 12, 1925.

area, especially after dark, risked bodily harm. The experiences of blacks in Louisville were like those experienced by Afro-Americans elsewhere. Even after *Buchanan* v. *Warley*, explains a historian of blacks in Georgia, Afro-Americans could only move into undeveloped areas or residential sections that whites no longer wanted.[19]

Though the repeal of Louisville's ordinance did not end housing discrimination, winning the case was without question one of the most important victories for the NAACP during its formative years. The triumph overturned residential ordinances in Baltimore, St. Louis, Birmingham, Richmond, Norfolk, and other cities. It gave the NAACP the needed momentum both to continue fighting racial injustices and to increase its membership. Before the court decision of November 1917, the NAACP had 85 branches and 9,866 members. Louisville had only 89 active members. After the court decision, a national membership drive was held which resulted in 35,888 new memberships and 32 new branch organizations. Only the Washington, D.C., branch with 2,553 new members brought in more than Louisville's 1,431 new members. Before the start of the membership drive, Louisville ranked twenty-sixth out of eighty-five branches; after the campaign, Louisville had become the fifth largest NAACP branch.[20]

II.

For several years after 1917, the Louisville NAACP was an effective watchdog over the rights of Afro-Americans. A highly racist and inflammatory film, *The Birth of a Nation*, came to Louisville for a week's engagement in November 1918.[21] The NAACP wired Republican mayor George W. Smith, urging him to ban the film. Members of the local branch met with the mayor and expressed their displeasure with the film and informed him of the potential racial problems the film could cause. With en-

19. *Courier-Journal*, November 27, 1925; Board Minutes, Louisville NAACP, November 17, 1925; Dittmer, *Black Georgia*, 13–14.

20. Kellogg, *NAACP*, 135; NAACP *Branch Bulletin* (November, 1917), 2, (February, 1918), 5, (July, 1918), 21–22; *Crisis*, XVI (June, 1918), 75; A. E. Meyzeek to John Shillady, secretary of the association, May 2, 1918; Walter White, of the national office, to Wilson Lovett, May 7, 1918; William Warley to Shillady, May 19, 1918.

21. D. W. Griffith, the director and producer of the film, was a native of Oldham County, Kentucky, and spent his formative years in Louisville. For several years he worked in the city's theaters as an usher or stagehand; Robert M. Henderson, *D. W. Griffith, His Life and Work* (New York, 1972), 1–57.

couragement from the NAACP, Mayor Smith stopped *The Birth of a Nation* after the film had been shown for two days. One of the reasons he gave was a Kentucky law of 1906 that made it unlawful to present plays that were based "upon antagonism alleged formerly to exist between master and slave or that excite race prejudice."[22]

The mayor's action to shut down the presentation of the film differed markedly from the decision of his predecessor, Democrat Mayor John Bushemeyer. In 1915 *The Birth of a Nation* had come to Louisville and Mayor Bushemeyer, claiming to find nothing objectionable in the film, had allowed its showing. But Mayor Smith had been elected with the solid backing of blacks, and he was well aware of the determined effort demonstrated by the NAACP in ending residential segregation as well as its increasing and increasingly vocal membership. The Louisville NAACP was elated over stopping the film; their city was one of only eight where the film was banned between 1915 and 1918.[23]

The Louisville NAACP attempted to investigate and protest all acts of violence against blacks. In 1920 the branch helped settle a conflict between black residents of Highland Park, a Louisville suburb, and white soldiers from Camp Taylor, a nearby army base. After receiving numerous complaints from blacks who were harassed by the soldiers, NAACP officials conducted an investigation and presented a list of wrongdoings by the soldiers to the commander of Camp Taylor. The army officials, impressed with the report of the NAACP, agreed to keep the soldiers out of the Highland Park area. Also in 1920, the branch protested to city authorities until the police finally arrested a white man and held him without bond for the brutal killing of a black youth. The branch hired a criminal lawyer to help with the prosecution of the case, but the accused man committed suicide in his jail cell several days before the start of his trial.[24]

In the early 1920s, the Louisville NAACP began a decade-long struggle against the resurgent Ku Klux Klan. In cities all over America, frustrated lower- and middle-class whites who opposed the rapid changes occurring in society and who were most definitely afraid that blacks were moving into their neighborhoods joined the KKK. At its height of popu-

---

22. *Laws of Kentucky, 1906* (Frankfort, 1907), 315.

23. The association kept a file on the protest over *The Birth of a Nation*. See NAACP Papers, Series C, Boxes 301 and 302, for the letters and telegrams between the Louisville branch and the NAACP headquarters about the film; *Courier-Journal*, November 17, 20, 1918; NAACP *Branch Bulletin* (December, 1918), 63; *Crisis*, XVII (April, 1919), 283.

24. Lee Brown of the Louisville branch to Walter White, August 9, 1920; Lovett to White, September 11, 1920; Brown to James W. Johnson, November 11, 1920, Brown to White, March 21, 1921, NAACP Papers. Krock, *Myself When Young*, 196–97.

larity in Louisville, the Klan claimed to have 3,000 members, and a number of the city's respectable citizens, including policemen, government employees, businessmen, and ministers, were linked to the organization. One minister in particular, Rev. E. W. Parkes of the Portland Avenue Baptist Church, was outspoken in defense of the Klan. According to Parkes, 90 percent of the men in his congregation belonged to the Klan. Rev. Parkes, however, eventually quit the Klan, citing their race hatred and his concern that the Klan would take over Louisville as his reasons. To support his contention about the Klan's growing influence in Louisville, Parkes identified several prominent Republicans and high-ranking police officers who had recently joined the Klan. To the dismay of blacks, none of the people named by Parkes denied his charges.[25]

Louisville city officials banned Klan demonstrations and membership drives only after the NAACP vehemently protested their existence. At first, Mayor Smith tried to apologize for the Republicans and police officers who joined the Klan, saying that they had received undue pressure from their associates to join and describing the Klan as little more than a fraternity. After a visit from NAACP representatives, however, Smith halted Klan activities and promised to use "every lawful means to prevent and suppress its growth in our community." Several Klan meetings and parades were held in the early days of the administration of the next mayor, Republican Huston Quin. After hearing complaints from the NAACP, the mayor prohibited all Klan activity and ordered the police to raid the Klan's headquarters. During the remainder of Quin's term, Louisville Klansmen held meetings in nearby New Albany, Indiana. Throughout the decade, the slightest act by the Klan resulted in quick action by the NAACP. In 1928 Jefferson County officials gave the Klan permission to hold a meeting at the Jefferson County Armory, but a protest by the NAACP resulted in the officials' rescinding of the permit.[26]

From its inception the NAACP devoted considerable energy to investigating lynching and to calling on local, state, and national officials to prohibit these outrages. Members of the Louisville branch investigated ev-

25. Kenneth T. Jackson, *The Ku Klux Klan in the City 1915–1930* (New York, 1967), 38, 65, 240–44. All of the Louisville newspapers commented on the growth of the Klan; see *Leader*, June 9, 1923, June 21, 1924, January 24, 1925; *Herald*, October 20, 1922, March 11, July 4, 1923; *Courier-Journal*, June 16, 17, 1924, October 30–November 5, 11, 14, 1928; Kentucky *Irish-American*, October 8, November 19, 1921, August 30, 1924, June 4, 1927, January 14, October 27, 1928.

26. *Herald*, February 27, June 5, July 4, 1923; *Leader*, September 1, 1928, June 1, 1923; *Courier-Journal*, June 16, 1924; *Opportunity*, VI (October, 1928), 315; Mayor Smith was quoted in Jackson, *The Klan in the City*, 87.

ery lynching that occurred in Kentucky during these years and wrote reports on the tragedies, sending copies to Kentucky officials and the national NAACP office. The branch even concerned itself with lynchings
occurring in other states. For instance, after receiving word of a lynching
in Georgia in 1918, Wilson Lovett sent a telegram to the national office
suggesting that the NAACP organize parades to protest the repeated occurrences of lynchings. After thanking Lovett for his concern, the national
office decided against his suggestion, explaining that the new sedition laws
might be invoked to suppress the NAACP.[27]

Mob rule remained a constant concern of the Louisville NAACP, and
it tried to get state officials to go on record against all outbreaks of lawlessness. The group praised Governor Augustus Stanley for his actions in
preventing a mob from hanging a black man in Murray in 1917. While
fighting the Louisville Residential Segregation Ordinance, the branch
campaigned for an antilynching and mob bill. Their efforts bore fruit in
1920 with the passage of "an act to suppress mob violence and prevent
lynching; providing for punishment of persons violating the provision of
the act, and for the removal of officers permitting a prisoner to be injured
or lynched by a mob." As the local NAACP pointed out to the national
office, this measure passed without a dissenting vote, making Kentucky the
first state to pass such a law. Officials of the Louisville NAACP stated on
numerous occasions that their efforts resulted in white Kentuckians being
aware of the horrors of mob rule and had led to a few instances of blacks
receiving fair trials.[28]

Unfortunately, however, fighting racism all over Kentucky caused the
Louisville branch to overextend itself. Officials of the group traveled
throughout the state at their own expense to inform blacks and concerned
whites on how best to challenge discrimination. As executive secretary in
the early 1920s, Lee Brown helped organize branches in ten cities.[29] The
arrest and trial in Madisonville of Columbus Hollis, Bunyan Fleming, and
Nathan Bard (the case in which Cole and Warley were convicted of sedition) became the most celebrated undertaking of the Louisville NAACP
during the 1920s. This case, however, had a detrimental effect because the

27. *Crisis*, XII (September, 1916), 219. Telegram from Lovett to Shillady, May 20, 1918;
letter from Shillady to Lovett, May 31, 1918, NAACP Papers.
28. Kentucky Senate Bill no. 143, February 20, 1920; Letter to James W. Johnson from
Kentucky State NAACP, March 25, 1920, NAACP Papers; *Crisis*, XIII (March, 1917), 226–
27; *Independent*, LXXXIX (January 22, 1917), 40.
29. For information on Kentucky's other NAACP branches, see NAACP Papers, Series
G, Box 77.

litigation proved to be extremely costly, nearly bankrupting the Louisville branch. The trial and appeals left the branch $4,000 in debt, a debt that remained outstanding for several years. The debt affected morale and prevented the NAACP branch from supporting litigation in other areas of deep concern to black Louisvillians.[30]

While the Louisville branch devoted most of its effort to opposing mob violence and discriminatory laws, it also focused attention on black employment. This was significant since too often the NAACP was more concerned with obtaining rights for middle- and upper-class blacks to attend the theater or dine in restaurants while ignoring the pressing problems of poorer blacks. From the start, the Louisville branch investigated instances of job discrimination and complained about the lack of black employees in city government. During World War I, city officials relented to the pleas of the organization and hired six black women, but placed them in the sanitation department as street cleaners. The NAACP protested this racial slight to black women, pointing out that no white women were assigned the "disgusting task of sweeping manure off the downtown thoroughfares." After this uproar by the NAACP, city officials assigned the women to other positions. In the early 1920s, executive secretary Lee Brown often visited businesses and industries in hopes of persuading employers to hire Afro-Americans as clerks and skilled workers. The branch investigated working conditions for blacks at the Post Office and complained about the postmaster limiting the number of black postal employees. In cooperation with several other groups, the NAACP tried to convince city authorities to hire blacks as policemen and firemen, and to convince the Board of Education to upgrade a black to the position of assistant superintendent of the public schools.[31]

However, by the late 1920s the NAACP was devoting less and less time to employment, leaving that area to the local Urban League and CIC. This was an unfortunate decision, though a realistic one. Members of the other two groups knew whites personally and were therefore in a better position to meet and discuss the hiring of blacks. Yet these two groups, with their more moderate blacks, were too often less willing to fully press the main concerns of the race.

    30. I. Willis Cole to James W. Johnson, January 3, 1929; Johnson to Cole, February 4, 1929, NAACP Papers.
    31. Letter from A. C. McIntyre to Shillady, October 10, 1918, NAACP Papers; *Crisis*, XVI (October, 1918), 293; Kellogg, *NAACP*, 296; Letter from Archie Bensinger, president of the Federated System of Bakeries of Kentucky, to Lee Brown, April 10, 1920; Board Minutes, Louisville NAACP, November 17, 1925, NAACP Papers.

The Louisville branch of the NAACP played an instrumental role in the black struggle for change during the years 1917–1930. Through the efforts of the organization, the residential segregation ordinance was overturned, Kentucky became the first southern state to take a more stringent step to end mob rule, and blacks won a number of victories ranging from the banning of the *Birth of a Nation* and the prohibition of parades and open membership drives by the Klan, to being hired in a number of city government positions. Yet despite the presence of the NAACP, Louisville's covert and overt racism prevailed. For instance, after overturning the discriminatory housing ordinance, blacks still could not live where they desired. Restrictive covenants and violence were used to maintain lily-white neighborhoods. Housing discrimination remained so widespread that very few blacks would live west of Thirtieth Street before the 1950s. Additionally, despite the efforts of the NAACP, the 1920s saw "informal segregation" continued on the streetcars, with blacks being relegated to Jim Crow seats at the back and excluded from the hotels, restaurants, and places of amusement. In summary, white racism in Louisville during the 1920s often effectively neutralized the activities of the NAACP.

Internal fighting also often hindered the activities of the local NAACP. Repeatedly, the organization was wracked by dissension, usually with young leaders pitted against the old leaders or ministers against other professionals. Individual factions had the NAACP so divided that the national office had to disband and completely reorganize the Louisville branch in July 1915 before the court fight against the residential segregation ordinance could be continued.[32] The first conflict after the segregation case pitted the president, Dr. A. C. McIntyre, against the executive board. Several board members wanted to be president and resented the fact that McIntyre had held the post for three consecutive terms (1916–1918). They

32. At the July 15, 1915, meeting of the NAACP, May Childs Nerney reported on her most recent trip to Louisville, in which she found the affiliate in chaos: "The branch was utterly disorganized by factions, the treasury empty, the churches antagonistic, the present executive committee in bitter disagreement with the former executive committee of the branch, and a general attitude of suspicion because money already collected had not been accounted for in a business-like manner." Miss Nerney reorganized the branch and appointed a Committee of 100 to raise four hundred dollars toward the expenses of fighting the segregation case. The Committee of 100 represented several important elements of Louisville's black community—churches, schools, fraternal orders, and women's clubs—and, led by such leaders as Steward, Parrish, and Meyzeek, they raised five hundred dollars in less than three weeks to help pay the lawyer's expenses and court costs. After reorganization by Miss Nerney, the Louisville branch was free of serious internal conflicts during the remainder of the segregation case. See Board Minutes, NAACP, July 12, 1915; *Crisis*, X (November, 1915), 198, 243–44.

accused McIntyre of failing to notify them when elections would be held, thereby insuring that only his supporters would attend the meeting. The final blowup between McIntyre and the board occurred in December 1918 when, without authorization from the board, McIntyre withdrew $100 from the branch's treasury to pay his expenses to the NAACP's annual meeting in New York. Members of the executive board—Parrish, Steward, Meyzeek, Lovett, and Warley—were outraged by McIntyre's actions and ordered him to return the $100 or face legal action. McIntyre refused to return the money, telling the board members "so help me God, I will go as the delegate to New York and not one cent of this money will I return." The executive board filed charges and had McIntyre removed from the presidency, but his departure took some of his supporters from the ranks of the NAACP.[33]

The next split developed between the city's old and new leaders. For several years both groups had maintained an uneasy alliance in the NAACP. Parrish and Steward, of course, had started the branch and served regularly on the executive board. In November 1920, immediately after the successful defeat of the University of Louisville's bond proposal, Wilson Lovett used Steward's and Parrish's support for the bond as a reason to have the two venerable leaders removed from the NAACP's executive board at the branch's election. Parrish and Steward then resigned from the NAACP and began devoting their efforts to the CIC.[34]

Bitter in-fighting often led to periods of inactivity, often at a time when the NAACP desperately needed a consistent program with well-defined goals. In fact, the most serious criticism that could be made against the NAACP was that it was a crisis-oriented organization. The branch was formed in response to the segregation ordinance. After turning the ordinance around, the NAACP met irregularly during the 1920s and usually only in response to instances of overt racism. For example, after fighting against the growth of the Klan from 1920 to 1923, the branch virtually disbanded until the enactment of a park segregation ordinance in late June 1924. The organization protested the ordinance for several months, and then stopped meeting until November 1925, when a bombing occurred at the homes of two black families who lived in a white neighborhood. After that incident, the organization did little until April 1926 when Cole and

33. A. C. McIntyre to the national association, November 21, 1918; Meyzeek, Steward, Lovett, Warley, and Parrish to the association, December 30, 1918; telegram from Steward, Warley, and Lovett to the national office, January 4, 1919; Lovett to White, January 4, 1919, NAACP Papers.
34. Lovett to the national NAACP, November 11, 18, 1920, NAACP Papers.

Warley convinced the NAACP to become involved in the Bard-Fleming case.

Maybe most of the NAACP's problems resulted from being a voluntary organization. The NAACP was forced to rely on a few people donating their time and talent to racial causes. When the organization was at its best, during the residential segregation ordinance litigation and the first years thereafter, the NAACP could be a potent force. But by the late 1920s, after the Madisonville rape trial, the NAACP was a pale replica of what it had once been. Fortunately, in the long run the NAACP would remain a fixture in Louisville, and after being dormant in the 1930s would spring to new life in the 1940s.

## 11

Black Political Insurgency

The young leaders active in the NAACP formed the Lincoln Independent Party (LIP) in August 1921 and urged black voters to renounce their loyalty to the Republican party. The founders of the LIP explained that under the present Republican administration, the black community had become a haven for political corruption and crime. Furthermore, they were thoroughly dissatisfied with race relations and the meager political patronage given blacks. They concluded that the race would continue to receive poor treatment as long as Afro-Americans maintained their abiding loyalty to one party. For the November 1921 elections, the LIP announced a full slate of candidates. Their break with the Republican party was censured not only by party officials but also by the city's conservative black leaders. Indeed, the members of the LIP received verbal and even physical abuse for conducting a third-party campaign. Not surprisingly, they were easily defeated at the polls. But the importance of the LIP lies in the fact that it was an organized form of black opposition to the political status quo, and it ultimately caused city officials to be more responsive to the concerns of the Afro-American population.

Several additional factors accounted for the political insurgency of the young leaders and the strong opposition they received from the older conservative leaders. The young leaders had reached maturity during a time when the Republican party had backed away from championing the rights of the Afro-Americans. Young black leaders were not tied to the Republican party by sentiment; in fact, calling the Republicans the "party of emancipation" or the "party of Lincoln" was nothing more than political rhetoric. However, many of Louisville's older black leaders had a vested interest in the Republican party; that they opposed the LIP came as no surprise. The formation of a viable independent political party indicated to the white establishment that the older leaders were losing their influence in the Afro-American community. David Gerber's description of Ohio blacks is reflective of the Louisville situation: "The challenge of the young men, therefore, posed a threat to the political power of their elders, who were already struggling to preserve their influence in a rapidly changing political environment."[1]

Many blacks who were genuinely concerned about progress remained loyal to the Republican party only because they thought a vote for the LIP would ultimately aid the Democrats. In the years from 1917 to 1930, when young blacks were calling for a break with the Republicans, the Democratic party still denounced blacks. In campaign after campaign, Democratic election officials publicized the number of registered black voters to arouse white citizens against the threat of Negro domination. In 1921, of the slightly more than 25,000 registered black voters, 99 percent were Republicans, while only 57 black voters claimed affiliation with the Democratic party. "These startling figures," the Democrats warned Louisville's white citizens, "emphasize the solemn duty of every white person to register in October and to vote in November. . . . There are in this city 10,000 white men who did not register last year, and 26,000 white women who did not register. There are almost enough unregistered white women to cancel the entire negro vote." The Democrats claimed that in urban areas no more than 82 percent of the people eligible to vote actually did so. The Democrats alleged that local blacks ultimately wanted to have political domination over whites and therefore a higher percentage of them had registered.[2]

In 1923 Kenrick Lewis, Democratic campaign chairman, produced statistics allegedly proving that numerous blacks were illegally registered. In three selected all-black precincts, no black Democrats were registered, compared to 611 Republicans. This led Democrats to assume that someone had tampered with the registration records. The *Post*, a strongly partisan Democratic paper, ran a series of articles attacking the high number of blacks registered as Republicans and called on white men and women to register and vote as Democrats to restore honesty in Louisville. The *Post* said that blacks had helped Republicans steal every election in Louisville since 1917 and that white Democrats could prevent this from continuing by watching blacks on election day and by coming out in large numbers to vote.[3]

Such attacks by the Democrats on the credibility of black voters in-

1. Gerber, *Black Ohio*, 398–99.

2. *Campaign Book of Facts Published by Democratic Campaign Committee, 1921* (Louisville, 1921); *Keynote Address Delivered by W. O. Harris, Democratic Candidate for Mayor* (Louisville, 1921).

3. *Courier-Journal*, October 18, 1919, October 5, 6, 1921, October 9, 1923, May 18,

sured that a great majority of Afro-Americans remained Republican until
the Great Depression. City registration books for 1927 show that Louisville had 24,150 black Republicans and 223 black Democrats. The registration books for 1931 list 25,760 black Republicans, 545 black Independents, and only 129 black Democrats.[4]

Two significant political changes occurred in Louisville after the
Democratic victory in 1913. Shortly after spearheading the election, John
Whallen died. He had been the Democratic boss for thirty years. By the
next mayoral race the party was badly split into several factions. While the
Democratic machine was crumbling, the Republican party found a strong
leader in Chesley Searcy. On November 12, 1917, one week after the Supreme Court overturned the Louisville Residential Segregation Ordinance, the Republican party swept into office. They would control Louisville to the time of the Great Depression. Therefore, the anger blacks felt
toward the political situation during the 1920s would be directed primarily at their own party.

A solid black vote was crucial to the success enjoyed by the Republican party from 1917 to 1931. According to the *Leader*, by the early 1920s
blacks comprised 45 percent of the city's registered Republicans. But once
in office, the Republicans turned deaf ears to black demands for an increase in patronage positions and the hiring of blacks as clerks and other
white-collar positions. Indeed, in early 1918 Republican officials made
much of the naming of a black as the elevator operator at city hall, the type
of job blacks had been given since the Civil War. Furthermore, the Republicans continued to refuse to support blacks as political candidates. In
1919 the party prevented William Warley's bid for election to the state
legislature. As mentioned in chapter eight, the party helped a Democrat
win a seat on the school board in 1920 instead of supporting the candidacy of Wilson Lovett.[5]

Worse still, several Republicans attempted to expand segregation
practices. In January 1918, Alderman William H. Ziser introduced a bill
calling for segregation of the races on the city's streetcars. The bill caused
such an outcry from the local NAACP that it was quickly defeated. Two

1924, May 14, 27, 1926, October 12, 1927. See the *Post* for the entire month of October
1923, especially October 1, 2, 3, 4, 8, 9, 15, 22; see also September 28, 1923.

    4. *Courier-Journal*, November 4, 1927; Ernest M. Collins, "The Political Behavior of
the Negroes in Cincinnati, Ohio, and Louisville, Kentucky" (Ph.D. dissertation, University
of Kentucky, 1950), 79–81.

    5. *Leader*, October 15, 1921; *Courier-Journal*, November 6, 1917, January 1, 1918.
A similar situation could be found in Cleveland, Ohio, during these years. See Kusmer, *A
Ghetto Takes Shape*, 177.

months later another Republican introduced a similar bill. Again, the black protest was so overwhelming that the city council killed the measure by a unanimous vote, with the alderman who introduced the legislation refusing to cast his ballot. After the defeat of the second Jim Crow streetcar bill, the *Courier-Journal*, a pro-Democratic newspaper, took delight in the situation: "The Republican administration under the rules of the General Council must wait a year before another 'Jim Crow' law aimed at the negroes on the streetcars can be introduced. . . . Two defeats mean that no similar bill can be introduced in the General Council for a year."[6]

By defeating the segregation measures, the Republican administration may have appeared to be far more concerned for blacks than the Democratic administrations had been. But the Democrats owed nothing to blacks; in fact, they had often won their elections by appealing to the racist fears of white voters. The Republicans relied heavily on black support, so the fact that such racist legislation was even considered revealed in part how some Republicans actually viewed blacks. Consistently throughout the 1920s, the Republican party retreated on discriminatory practices only when the young blacks of the NAACP launched an effective protest campaign.

Several incidents in 1921 led to a break between Louisville's young black leaders and the Republican party. In the spring, signs appeared in the public parks designating specific areas for blacks. The mayor, an ex-officio member of the Board of Park Commissioners, had the signs removed only after a strong protest was registered by Cole and Warley. Later that summer, blacks attending the state fair were restricted to the hot dog stands and toilet facilities designated "For Colored People." Lovett, upset with these new segregation attempts, announced his candidacy for the state legislature. Announcing was one thing. Gaining the support of the Republican politicos was another. Despite the fact that Lovett received the endorsement of many black groups, the Republican party instituted a legal suit that led to Lovett being disqualified on the grounds that one of his petitioners was ineligible since he was a registered socialist.[7]

Several young leaders met after Lovett's disqualification and formed the LIP. The organizers of the party said they were tired of being mistreated by both political parties. "This condition of political slavery has placed us in the very unenviable position of being owned by the Repub-

6. *Courier-Journal*, January 27, 1918; *Evening Post*, March 6, 1918; *Crisis*, XV (March, 1918), 245, XVI (May, 1918), 233.
7. *Leader*, January 29, April 9, July 30, August 6, September 3, 10, 17, 24, 1921; *Herald*, September 5, 1921.

licans and hated by the Democrats," A. D. Porter explained. Lovett said his decision to run on the LIP ticket was based on the belief that "colored people ought not be represented by underworld characters and ought to have a voice in city administration. The most important fact being that Republicans were getting almost 100% support by colored people and received absolutely no return except vice privileges for the operation of rooming houses, gambling joints, etc." For the November general election, the LIP announced a slate of candidates for office, headed by Porter for mayor, Lovett for the state legislature, Cole for the state senate, and Warley for magistrate. The party adopted the following platform:

1. We want absolute equality of opportunity.
2. We want racial representation at the forum where laws are made to tax our property.
3. We want a proportional share of the emoluments of official preferment.
4. We owe no allegiance to either political party.
5. We can neither be bought or bluffed.[8]

This political rebellion led to increased bitterness within the black elite. In a long editorial in the *American Baptist*, Steward warned that black involvement in independent movements would foster racial animosity. He called on blacks to remain with their party, citing the numerous gains blacks had made under Republican administrations. He implied that the Democratic party was underwriting the upstart LIP, and that the leaders of the new party had sold out the race. Several blacks employed in patronage jobs echoed Steward's sentiments and charged that Lovett and company were mere self-seekers. A small black weekly, the *Kentucky Reporter*, edited by R. T. Berry, printed 10,000 copies of an article, "Yes, Sold Out Again," denouncing the LIP leaders. The paper was distributed free in the black community. As Cole noted, it was obvious that the Republican party had paid for the publication since Berry normally printed 500 copies and had trouble selling them. Only three or four black ministers applauded the black leaders for forming an independent party, while the more established ministers joined in condemning the move. Cole dismissed the black ministers' criticism with contempt: " 'Tis true politics makes strange bed mates and when Boss Searcy and money speaks to some of our colored brothers, be they preachers or pimps, religion takes a back seat."[9]

The formation of the LIP led to physical violence against the party

8. Lovett was quoted in Charles H. Parrish, Jr., "Politics," typescript, 1938, Parrish Papers. *Leader*, September 24, 1921, December 24, 1937, March 11, 1950.

9. *Leader*, September 10, 17, 24, 1921; *American Baptist*, August 27, 1921. Editor Cole attacked the black ministers in *Leader*, October 8, 1921.

members. A group of black hoods began disrupting their meetings. On the night of October 1, 1921, three blacks were arrested for disturbing a LIP strategy meeting. But instead of being locked up at the police station, the three men sat in the waiting room until their bond had been posted. The *Courier-Journal* admitted that allowing the men to remain in the waiting room until released on bond was "a departure from the usual practice." At an LIP meeting several nights later, a black opponent of the party fired a shot into the crowd that had gathered to hear several of the black candidates speak. As if on cue, the police appeared at the meeting immediately after the firing of the shot and began dispersing the crowd. They ordered members of the party to leave the area, claiming that their presence had caused the disturbance. As the LIP candidates left the area, a group of black men and women threw rocks and eggs at them. According to newspaper accounts, the men disrupting the meetings were members of the Protective Aid Society which had headquarters at Ninth and Cedar in a building owned by the notorious underworld leader Harvey Burns.[10]

LIP leaders were subjected to additional abuse as election day drew near. A black mob damaged Warley's office. Vandals ransacked Porter's funeral home on three different occasions. Porter finally asked the police for protection for his family after shots were fired into his home, but the police refused to help him as long as he remained a candidate for office. On election day a group of black hoods with clubs and guns stormed Porter's funeral home. "Negroes were breaking out the plate glass of his large front window, destroying the furniture and fixtures and tearing up his high priced books and valuable papers," the *Leader* noted. The mob then destroyed Warley's printing press. Lovett himself was assaulted while waiting to vote. The police refused to arrest his assailant but arrested Lovett for disturbing the peace.[11]

Opposed by white newspapers, white politicians, older black leaders, and the black underworld, the LIP was easily defeated. In his race for mayor, Porter received 274 votes to 63,332 for the Republican candidate and 56,199 for the Democratic candidate. All of the party's other candidates lost by nearly the same margin as Porter. Yet they believed they had actually made a better showing, because Republican henchmen had dumped some of their votes in the Ohio River. Editor W. E. B. DuBois of *The Crisis* applauded the effort of the LIP and noted that the party had probably been cheated out of most of its votes: "The party was credited with 274 votes at the polls but as they were not represented at the count-

10. *Leader*, October 1, 1921; *Courier-Journal*, October 2, 7, 1921; Porter interview.
11. *Leader*, November 12, 1921; Porter interview; Parrish, "Politics."

ing of the ballots and were beaten away from the polls by the police, this probably does not represent one-tenth of the actual votes cast." Regardless of the number of votes actually received, the men of the LIP realized beforehand that they had no chance of winning. Their aim had been to show blacks and the political parties that some changes were long past due. Indeed, their efforts frightened the Republican party. The Republicans marshalled all of their resources to crush the rebellious blacks. Chesley Searcy later admitted to Lovett that the Republican party spent a considerable sum of money during the campaign to insure the overwhelming defeat of the LIP.[12]

In an attempt at fencemending, black patronage holders, older leaders, LIP members, and Harvey Burns held a peace meeting several months after the vicious campaign. All of the speakers representing the old leaders and patronage holders urged reconciliation and the return of solid black support for the Republican party. Warley was the last speaker. Characteristically, he claimed to be unable to say anything worthwhile to a group that had applauded "such truckling, pussy-footing, and self-serving speeches." He then continued his attack on the Republican party: "The local Republicans have not had the time to make any Negro appointments but have had time to vote in a Negro park and name it after an Indian, have had time to close up Negroes in business and let the same business conducted by white men in Negro districts run on, have had time to beat a Negro woman and shoot a Negro man." Warley demanded that changes be made before he returned to the Republican party.[13]

The creation of the LIP with its threat of political independence did lead to positive changes for black Louisville. For the first time, the Republican administration began to hire blacks for clerical and white-collar jobs in city government. As far as black leaders were concerned, an even more significant step was the willingness of the GOP to hire blacks as policemen and firemen, a policy change blacks had been seeking for more than fifty years. In early 1923, the Quin administration announced that a fire station would be constructed at Thirteenth and Broadway and would be manned by blacks. Immediately thereafter, city officials, with the assistance of young and old black leaders, conducted a search to find the "right type" of men to become the city's first black firemen. Eleven men were selected and all of them successfully passed the written and physical examinations. At the opening of the fire station on September 29, 1923, Fire

12. Parrish, "Politics"; Collins, "The Political Behavior of the Negroes," 163; *Crisis*, XXIII (January, 1922), 119.
    13. *Leader*, January 21, 1922.

Chief Arnold Neueschwander announced that one of the black men would assume the post of captain after the men had finished a probationary period.[14]

City officials also relied on advice from black leaders when selecting the first black police officers. Fearful that whites would resent blacks in such an important and visible position, city officials decided that the first blacks on the force would be plainclothes detectives. Moreover, the four officers chosen were assigned to the city's black neighborhoods. Black leaders were far from satisfied with this arrangement and pressed on until 1928 when twelve black uniformed officers were hired and assigned to various districts throughout the city. Nevertheless, black leaders still had to compromise because for several years black police officers were prohibited from wearing their uniforms to and from work.[15]

Despite the positive changes, a fragile alliance existed between the young black leaders and the Republican party, one that could easily be shattered. Ironically, the blacks blamed most of the problems on Huston Quin, whom they had strongly supported for mayor. A native of Louisville and a graduate of the University of Louisville Law School, Quin had all the right connections. He first practiced law with the prestigious firm of Helm and Bruce. From 1908 to 1912, Quin served as the assistant city attorney. With Clayton Blakey, Quin formed a law partnership in 1913. It was his partner, Blakey, who served as legal counsel to the NAACP in the residential segregation case. When *The Birth of a Nation* first came to Louisville, the NAACP contacted Quin and he agreed to do whatever he could to stop the film from being shown. Blacks were very appreciative for all of his actions on their behalf. In both his successful appellate judge race in 1918 and his mayoral race in 1921 he received huge majorities of votes from the city's Negro wards.[16]

Blacks expected much of Quin as mayor. When the expected changes did not occur, the young blacks were quick to denounce him. Editors Cole and Warley became his sharpest critics, accusing him of being apologetic about the growth of the Klan. A number of young black leaders were very upset by his inaction after Warley was assaulted. In 1922 J. H. Scales, the secretary of the Republican League, struck Warley in the face and called

14. Louisville *Times*, September 28, 1923; *Post*, September 28, 29, 1923; *Courier-Journal*, October 9, 1923.

15. For information about the hiring of blacks as policemen and in other positions in city government, see the *Leader*, November 24, 1923, January 1, March 3, 1928, October 26, 1929, July 13, 1930, April 25, 1931; Chicago *Defender*, February 16, 1929.

16. For biographical information on Quin, see W. T. Owens (ed.), *Who's Who in Louisville* (Louisville, 1926), 141.

him a "damned Nigger," for his outburst against the party. Scales was not arrested or removed from the party, and the mayor refused to comment on the matter. Blacks also vehemently denounced the mayor for his position on park segregation and for the increased number of police attacks on black citizens that occurred during his administration. Not all of these criticisms of Quin were justified. Just because a number of reprehensible incidents happened during his administration did not necessarily mean he was directly responsible. It is possible that Quin and the other Republican mayors in Louisville were trying to hold rather disparate—even contradictory—interest groups together, which meant that their behavior was not always consistent or favorable to blacks.[17]

A case in point was the police brutality against blacks which continued, if not increased, during the Republican administrations of the 1920s. Unfortunately, police brutality had always been a part of black life in the city. Yet on the surface the early 1920s should have been different: blacks were being hired as policemen; the city had mayors who were friends of the race; Afro-Americans were involved in politics and getting a hearing at city hall; and the NAACP, Urban League, and Commission on Interracial Cooperation were all very active. But as James Bond, the director of the CIC and a person usually given to viewing white actions in the most positive light, explained, "The fact is that the beating and shooting up of Negroes by police seems to have become so common under the present administration in Louisville that it has developed into a kind of sport or pastime and is written up by the reporter in much the same way that a chase of a rabbit through the city would be written up." City officials ignored black complaints of police abuse except in very rare instances. In August 1923 a number of black motorists complained about the treatment they received from certain traffic policemen, especially from the officer working at Fourth and Walnut Streets in the afternoon. He was extremely rude and often used the derogatory term "nigger" when shouting at blacks. Several blacks obtained his badge number and reported him to police officials. Nothing happened. As the *Leader* headlined two months later: "Big Cop at Fourth and Walnut Still Abusing Negroes."[18]

Police brutality reached new heights whenever the police had diffi-

17. For the details of the assualt on Warley, see the *Leader*, June 2, 1922. In a letter to the author, July 15, 1980, Professor August Meier made this important point about the continuation of violence during a time when the leaders of the Republican party might have been genuinely concerned about improving conditions for blacks.

18. *Leader*, August 25, September 15, October 20, 1923, September 20, 1924.

culty apprehending suspected rapists and murderers. In August 1924, twenty-one-year-old Charles Gassaway was detained by the police since he resembled a murder suspect. The next morning word leaked out that Gassaway had been killed for attacking several policemen. The coroner's investigation revealed that he had been brutally beaten and shot at least ten times. Much of Louisville was in an uproar. Even the Kentucky *Irish-American*, which often ridiculed and castigated the black community, called the shooting a "brutal murder." "There can be no apology for that crime, for crime it is. . . . We are told that he attacked four policemen in a station house surrounded by other policemen, and that the four were unable to overpower him, and two shot him five times because they were afraid for their lives. . . . In all the history of cities in this country, no one ever heard of a case where a man was shot to death in a station house, and an unarmed man at that." In defense of the officers involved, the police department said that Gassaway was extremely dangerous and was responsible for eight unsolved murders in Louisville. The police officers were exonerated, but as *Irish-American* concluded, "all the camouflage and press agent work . . . will not explain or absolve the present Republican administration from the fact that a brutal and uncalled for murder was perpetrated by police officers right in a police station." [19]

According to a letter in the *Courier-Journal*, at least seventeen blacks were killed by policemen during the 1920s.[20] Although this figure cannot be substantiated, several instances of outright murder undoubtedly occurred. The police officers in all of the cases pleaded self-defense and were exonerated, even in cases where the victim was an unarmed youth. Blacks witnessed several of the shootings, but the courts still refused to indict the officers for murder. In October 1924, policeman Charles Hazel killed James Emery as he emerged from a stolen car. According to witnesses, Emery was unarmed and made no attempt to resist arrest but had merely stepped from the car when Hazel started firing. Patrolman W. E. Pemberton shot two blacks on the evening of October 15, 1925; he killed a youth fleeing from a dice game, and later that evening he shot a man for leaving a store with stolen merchandise. Both victims were unarmed. On one occasion a black "Good Samaritan," attempting to catch a white burglar, was shot and killed by an off-duty policeman. The *Courier-Journal* denounced this tragedy and called for tighter restrictions on police behavior toward blacks.

19. Kentucky *Irish-American*, August 30, 1924; *Leader*, August 30, September 13, 1924.
20. *Courier-Journal*, September 12, October 5, 23, 29, 1927.

It is the same old story, perhaps a little worse than usual. A Louisville police-man shoots in the back and kills an innocent Negro, mistaken for a burglar and supposed to be trying to escape arrest. The policeman, of course, [was] oblivious of the fact that even if the Negro had been a burglar and had been trying to escape arrest, no officer had a right to shoot him to death. And it is a story whose repe-tition will be continued until the penitentiary is resorted to in order to impress upon those entrusted with firearms, whose duty is to enforce the law, that they cannot with impunity break the law.[21]

The unceasing black protest against police brutality did result in at least one instance where local officials were compelled to act. In October 1928, a white officer was killed when attempting to arrest a black. After an ex-tensive search of the black community, the police arrested Lawrence Day, whose description matched that of the suspect. After being interrogated for several hours at police headquarters, Day "confessed" and was im-mediately taken to a hospital suffering from a broken cheekbone, three broken ribs, and numerous cuts and bruises all over his body. But since he had confessed no complaints were raised about his condition.[22] Several days later, however, another man admitted killing the officer. Now an uproar occurred throughout black Louisville over Day's beating. In November a grand jury investigated the incident and charged five officers with assault. The police board, realizing that the grand jury would act, reprimanded the officers and suspended them for five days. Day sued the police department for $15,150 in damages. The department acknowledged its guilt and set-tled out of court. Sadly, however, the Day case was the exception. He was well known, his case received extensive publicity from the black press, and a number of prominent whites were outraged over his brutal beating. But most important of all, the actual murderer came forward thereby vindi-cating Day and proving that his confession had been coerced. Most blacks who were victimized by the police were not as fortunate as Day. Indeed, if the Louisville black press is to be believed, police brutality continued un-abated into the 1930s.[23]

Black leaders were surprised that instances of police brutality contin-ued in Louisville during the 1920s. However, two reasons for this contin-

21. Ibid., November 19, 1918; Kentucky Irish-American, September 6, 1924; Leader, September 5, October 25, 1924, March 7, August 15, 1925, October 10, 1927, May 19, 1928. The Courier-Journal's editorial denouncing the senseless killings of blacks was reprinted in the Leader, October 5, 1929; see also Leader, September 21, 1929.

22. Leader, November 23, 1928.

23. Ibid., December 7, 1929. Another police officer was killed by a black in October 1930. This time not one but several blacks were taken to the police station and beaten until all of them confessed to the crime. See Leader, October 29, 1930.

ued violence can be offered. First, even though the Republican party controlled the local government, the composition of the police department—especially the rank and file—had not changed. By this time the police department had an independent board that supervised the running of department affairs, and most of the jobs on the force, except for those at the very top, had been removed from political interference. Second, the hiring of blacks on the police force, the fire department, and other city jobs probably offended some whites. Moreover, it is possible that hiring blacks in minor posts might have cost some whites their jobs. Any advancement by Afro-Americans, no matter how small, could be viewed by whites as a threat and could lead to a determined resistance to keep the "uppity" blacks in their place. Regardless of the causes of police brutality, the repeated beatings and killings most surely weakened the bonds between young black leaders and the Republican party.

A further rift between Republican officials and black leaders occurred over the continuation of illegal activities in the Afro-American community. A determined drive against vice was inaugurated in July 1927 by a group of black businessmen, educators, and ministers, calling themselves "The Colored Citizens of Louisville." In a statement to the press, the black group proclaimed that "bootlegging, gambling, and prostitution are openly carried on and fighting, stealing, blasphemy, and obscenity are matters of everyday occurrences" in the black district from Seventh to Fourteenth Streets and from Jefferson to Broadway Streets. The Colored Citizens said that three classes of "undesirable" whites frequented the black area: the "viciously immoral panderer" and the patrons of dives and disorderly houses; the white men who own dives and employ blacks; and white prostitutes. As always, whites continued to come to the black district, according to the press release, because they were safe from police surveillance in black neighborhoods.[24]

Reacting to this statement, city officials and the white press began an investigation of vice in the black district. Law enforcement officials increased the number of policemen patrolling the area and began a crackdown on all known black criminals and vice joints. *Courier-Journal* investigative reporters did a series of articles detailing crime in the black area, which revealed that prostitutes and pimps continued to accost men walking through the area even though more police officers were now in the vicinity. The paper also investigated the extent of gambling and described how the gambling joints used lookouts: "Outside many black poolrooms,

24. *Courier-Journal*, July 7, 1927.

stores, or residences would be a sentry covering the same spot fourteen hours a day. Sometimes the 'buzzman' steps on a brick with a push button underneath if a stranger comes around." According to the reporters, a large number of the city's black underworld figures carried guns and other weapons. The paper concluded that black underworld figures were largely responsible for the fact that blacks were charged with committing 75 percent of the homicides in Louisville even though Afro-Americans comprised only 17 percent of the city's population.[25]

The method used by the police to rid the black district of crime was the approach that has traditionally had a short-range effect. They immediately began arresting and removing "undesirable" blacks from the area as a deterrent to crime. By Sunday, July 17, ten days after the Colored Citizens had complained about the crime, well over 100 blacks had been arrested. Yet the "undesirable" whites were free to continue their illegal activities in the black community. The July 1927 drive on crime proved to be as unsuccessful as previous reform efforts. By January 1928, for example, the newspapers were again mentioning the high incidence of crime in the black district, especially purse snatching.[26]

Even when the police did crack down on black criminals, they left untouched well-known underworld leaders. In 1920, editor Cole of the *Leader* waged a relentless campaign to close down a speakeasy owned by Andrew Ormes. A year later, in February 1921, the police made a raid and arrested seventy-nine people, including Ormes, for violating prohibition and gambling laws. All of the charges were eventually dropped. Three months later the *Leader* reported that "the 'soft drink' stand at West and Madison is the same notorious place that it was several months ago and is owned and operated by the same Andrew Ormes. Gambling, bootlegging still go on."[27] On another occasion, raids on gambling and prostitution houses resulted in the arrest of 108 persons, including several reputed vice lords. All 108 defendants had Roscoe Searcy, the brother of Chesley Searcy, as their counsel. When their cases came to trial, Searcy moved that the charges be dropped against his clients, and the judge did so.[28]

After the July 1927 "drive on crime" failed to eliminate vice from the Negro district, several blacks called for the ousting of the Republican party. In a series of editorials in his newspaper, Warley denounced blacks for al-

25. *Ibid.*, July 9, 10, 1927.
26. *Ibid.*, September 8, 1927, January 11, 1928.
27. *Leader*, February 26, May 28, December 24, 1921.
28. *Post*, March 2, 1928.

lowing themselves to be duped by the Republicans and for allowing the continuation of crime and vice in their community. As the November election approached, a stream of anonymous letters in the *Courier-Journal* called for blacks to vote for the Democrats and clean government. All of the letters claimed that the Republicans would not suppress criminals because they needed those same men to deliver the black vote. One writer quoted a Republican boss as saying that for his party to win elections in the black community all they needed was the backing of "the nigger crap shooters and preachers." Another discussed the lack of patronage given blacks by the Republicans and said that this was a result of pressure from the LIP in 1921. The writer suggested that all blacks become independents. Finally, one of the letters highlighted all of the bad results for blacks under the Republican administrations since 1917: the killing of seventeen blacks by policemen, the shooting of two young boys who were fleeing a crap game, the beating of several black women by policemen, the continuation of vice in the black district, and the exclusion of blacks from most of the public parks in the city.[29]

The Republicans swept the November election. Despite the opposition of the young leaders, the party received the overwhelming support of the black community. The printing shop owned by Warley was destroyed by a black mob on election day in retaliation for his extremely vocal opposition to the Republican party. Black leaders had failed once again to convince the race to abandon the GOP. But after the 1927 election, more and more blacks—first a few but then in the hundreds—started deserting the Republican party. By the early 1930s both parties would be compelled to court the Negro vote without either one being totally sure which way the race would go on election day.

Louisville's militant young black leaders were instrumental in several political changes that occurred in the early 1930s. In 1931 Eubank Tucker, a lawyer and the presiding bishop in the African Methodist Episcopal Zion Church, complained to the Republican party officials about the absence of black candidates on the party's campaign slate, especially in the black district. Tucker reasoned, as had the LIP before him, that the city's black voters deserved black representation. Republican officials assured Tucker that a black would be chosen to run for office. Two years later after Tucker's repeated requests for a black Republican candidate had been denied, he decided, with the backing of Cole and Warley, to declare himself a candidate for the state legislature from the Fifty-Eighth District. And in a move

29. *Courier-Journal*, September 12, October 5, 23, 29, 1927; *Crisis*, XXXV (January, 1928), 24.

that surprised the Republican party, local Democratic officials announced their support for Tucker. The Democrats hoped this strategy would draw a few blacks from the GOP and aid the Democratic mayoral race. Moreover, they had nothing to lose by backing Tucker, since they had been out of office for over a decade and their candidates traditionally fared poorly in the Republican-dominated Fifty-Eighth District. Tucker lost to the white Republican candidate, yet, as noted by Ralph J. Bunche in his study of black political activity, Tucker's switch to the Democratic party had positive repercussions for blacks: "The agitation aroused by Tucker's fight deflected enough Negro votes to the Democratic ticket to clinch the victory for the Democrats over the city administration. The new Democratic city administration gave full credit to the Negro vote for giving it the margin of victory." [30]

To show their appreciation, Democratic officials hired blacks for many city and county government jobs, including deputy in the county clerk's office, deputy in the county tax assessor's office, deputy recorder in the magistrate's court, foreman in the department of public works, and inspectors in various city departments. Remembering how blacks responded to patronage from the Republican party in the early 1920s, the Democratic party established a black fire station in the east end. Black leaders heartily approved the patronage and the improved relationship with the Democrats. But they still desired something else—the election of blacks to public office. [31]

Two years later, in 1935, the Democratic party once again backed Tucker as its candidate for the state legislature. The Republican party, fearful of losing even more of its black supporters, responded by choosing a young black attorney, Charles W. Anderson, to oppose Tucker. Anderson won easily in the predominantly Republican district, becoming Kentucky's first black legislator. [32]

Without a doubt, the founders of the LIP started Louisville's Afro-American community on the road to changes through politics. In 1921 these militant blacks had stood alone. By denouncing vice and police brutality in 1927, they gained support. And by 1930, the black vote was being courted by both political parties. The strategy of the LIP had worked after all.

30. Ralph J. Bunche, The Political Status of the Negro in the Age of FDR (Chicago, 1973), 468–69; Yater, A History of Louisville, 198.
    31. Bunche, The Political Status of the Negro, 468–69.
    32. Collins, "The Political Behavior of the Negroes," 161–62; J. A. Thomas, "Introducing Kentucky's Negro Legislator," Opportunity, XVIII (March, 1940), 76–77.

Even with these positive political changes, much remained the same for black Louisvillians. Though blacks were appointed to new positions and a few were selected to run for office, neither political party gave blacks the patronage or the respect their support deserved. Throughout the 1930s, 70 percent of the city's blacks remained Republican, yet no black served in a policymaking position in the party. Meanwhile, white Democratic officials chose the party's black precinct leaders and refused to appoint blacks to the Democratic nominating committee. Furthermore, too many of the city's black politicians appeared to be more concerned about receiving patronage positions for themselves than improving the Negro community. "A Negro politician in Louisville has been selling jobs for years. . . . He has the ear of the mayor and the Democratic machine," Ralph Bunche noted in his survey of black political activity in Louisville. The old-style Negro ward heelers were still prevalent in Louisville after they had lost their significance in most other cities.[33]

33. Bunche, *The Political Status of the Negro*, 468–69; T. Arnold Hill, "Digest and Analysis of Questionnaires Submitted by the Urban League Secretaries," research memorandum prepared for the Carnegie-Myrdal Study of the Negro in America, 1940, p. 26; Bunche, "A Brief Analysis of Negro Leadership," 129–30; Collins, "The Political Behavior of the Negroes," 107.

## 12

The "Louisville Way"
Interracial Organizations in the 1920s

In addition to the NAACP, Louisville had two other organizations attempting to improve conditions in black neighborhoods and promote interracial goodwill. The Urban League and the Commission on Interracial Cooperation (CIC) differed from the NAACP in several crucial aspects. Unlike the Louisville NAACP, which was all black, these two organizations were interracial, with whites holding the important positions on the boards. The NAACP used court battles, public outcrys, and petitions to the mayor, governor, and congressmen. They saw politics as the logical arena for the struggle for civil rights. The methods of the Urban League and the CIC were more moderate and less controversial. Urban Leaguers called for the hiring of blacks in industry. But instead of denouncing the discriminatory hiring practices in Louisville, League officials believed that developing friendly relations with powerful businessmen was the way to persuade them to include blacks in their employment program. The NAACP called for protest and agitation; the League urged negotiation and friendly persuasion. The NAACP publicized racial insults and decried injustice in Kentucky; the CIC publicized acts that showed interracial goodwill. The CIC was better organized than the NAACP. However, the CIC's main goal was not breaking down the walls of segregation (the NAACP's goal) but keeping the lines of communication open through those walls and improving the lives of blacks living behind those walls. In the CIC's vision of the future for black Americans, the walls remained.

The white members of the CIC and the Urban League set the tone of race relations in Louisville and kept racial conflict to a minimum, just as moderate whites had done in Louisville in the decades right after the Civil War. They were the legitimate heirs of Louisville's "polite racism" for they had their "way" of handling the "Negro problem." In a letter to Robert W. Bingham, former mayor and a board member of both the Urban League and the CIC, George Colvin, state superintendent of education, expressed his complete agreement with Bingham's philosophy of educating Negroes about their role in the South. Education in the North, Colvin pointed out, "gives Negroes false ideas. . . . as a member of the Inter-Racial Commission you know the problem that this presents."[1]

At the risk of portraying the more moderate blacks as passive pawns, the argument can be made that these two interracial organizations, especially the CIC, attempted to control the black civil rights movement. In the newspapers these groups were praised for solving racial problems. Black members of the organizations were hailed as race leaders. White civic leaders willingly worked in these organizations to bring about certain changes for blacks, but none as dramatic as those endorsed by the NAACP. As in the past, Louisville whites saw the necessity of improving conditions for Afro-Americans but not the importance of recognizing them as their equals. Even if William H. Steward, Charles H. Parrish, and James Bond were not pawns, they agreed fully with the "blacks-have-their-place" philosophy advocated by whites. Moreover, these black leaders were willing to compromise, to accept any concessions from whites. Throughout their careers they lectured to blacks on improving their morals, on working hard, and on the basic fairness of whites. Like white leaders, the moderate blacks continued to shift the main responsibility for the problems blacks faced onto blacks themselves while downplaying the effects of racism in society.

I.

Like the NAACP, the National Urban League was founded by an interracial group concerned about the quality of life in black communities. In October 1911 the Committee for Improving the Industrial Conditions for Negroes in New York, the National League for the Protection of Colored Women, and the Committee on Urban Conditions Among Negroes consolidated their efforts and organized the National League on Urban Conditions Among Negroes (later changed to National Urban League). The organizers announced that they would work to improve social and economic conditions for blacks living in urban areas, attempt to cooperate with other social agencies working on behalf of blacks, train Negro social workers, and conduct studies about black life in the cities. The League's founders believed in the power of interracial cooperation and the importance of bringing blacks and whites of goodwill together in an effort to benefit Afro-Americans. Urban Leaguers said that having influential whites

1. Letter from George Colvin to Robert W. Bingham, August 23, 1923, Robert W. Bingham Papers, Manuscript Division, Library of Congress.

connected with the organization would ensure a hearing from white employers and could also facilitate admission of affiliates into local community chests.[2]

A small group of Louisvillians organized one of the first Urban League
affiliates in 1913. However, little is known about the branch. It can be
speculated that Eugene Kinckle Jones, the first full-time executive secretary of the National Urban League, helped organize the Louisville affiliate.
Jones had been a teacher at Central High School for two years before accepting the post with the Urban League and was probably aware of the
need for a chapter in Louisville. In 1916 the Louisville Urban League
merged with two other social service groups, the Booker T. Washington
Community Center and the Newsboys Improvement Club. This consolidated group started a Big Brother and Big Sister Program for delinquent
black children. They also worked with juvenile authorities to promote clubs
and athletic activities for youths. Because of a lack of sustained interest
and financial support, however, the Louisville Urban League collapsed
around 1918.[3]

Several groups, all active in the black community, reorganized the
Louisville Urban League in 1920. Between 1917 and 1920, Albert E. Meyzeek worked in housing reform, James H. Hubert and John O. Blanton, a
teacher and the son-in-law of William H. Steward, directed the Big Brother
and Big Sister Program, and Mrs. Bessie Allen and several others worked
with people on probation. Blanton organized a banquet to bring the three
groups together and to promote the reestablishment of an Urban League
branch. He invited Eugene Kinckle Jones and George Haynes to speak at
the banquet on the importance of the Urban League to Louisville. The dinner was successful: the three groups agreed to merge and those attending
the banquet pledged $2,000 to help finance the Urban League. To ensure
adequate financial support for the branch, Jones suggested that the organization seek membership in the local community chest. Shortly thereafter, Dr. John A. C. Lattimore headed an Urban League delegation that
conducted talks with officials of the Welfare League about funding for the
Urban League affiliate. The Louisville Urban League was officially launched

    2. Weiss, *The National Urban League*, 29, 45, 488–98; William R. Simms (ed.), *The
Urban League Story 1910–1960, Golden Anniversary Yearbook* (New York, 1961); *Survey*, XXVII (October 28, 1911), 1080–81; *Southern Workman*, XL (November, 1911), 599–
600.
    3. Weiss, *The National Urban League*, 4, 90–91; *Opportunity*, VI (March, 1928), 84;
Bulletin of National League of Urban Conditions, VI (November, 1916), 29.

in 1921 after its acceptance as a member organization in the Louisville Welfare League.[4]

Having prominent whites on the board proved beneficial to the Louisville Urban League. The highly respected Robert W. Bingham, a former judge and soon-to-be owner of the *Courier-Journal*, served on the organization's board. Other well-known board members were Theodore Ahrens, a successful businessman and philanthropist, and George Settle, head librarian of the Louisville Free Public Library system. These whites were instrumental in securing a yearly grant from the Welfare League. The Urban League received $2,753.50 during its first full year of operation, $3,700 in 1922, and about $3,500 a year for the remainder of the decade. Though modest, these funds enabled the League to hire an executive secretary, a typist, and two part-time workers. Also, like most racial uplift organizations, the Urban League relied heavily on volunteer workers.[5]

Finding jobs for blacks was the League's main goal during the 1920s, though practically all of the positions secured for blacks were as domestics or unskilled workers. For instance, the Louisville Urban League Report for 1929, the only complete report extant for the decade, shows that 855 men and 1,190 women registered with the League for work. The League found employment for 905 of the applicants with 242 of them hired as day laborers. It can be assumed that the others who secured employment through the Urban League were placed in menial jobs as well, for if that had not been the case the League would have been quick to publicize the hiring of blacks in skilled jobs in industry or in other areas from which they had previously been excluded.[6]

The practice of the Louisville Urban League of finding employment for blacks primarily as domestics or unskilled laborers was consistent with the performance of Urban League affiliates in other cities. Urban League workers in northern cities were unsuccessful in helping blacks make breakthroughs in industry. Though working diligently, they simply lacked the power to demand that blacks be hired in skilled or white-collar jobs.

4. *Bulletin of National League of Urban Conditions*, X (January, 1921), 5. Blanton interview; her husband, J. O. Blanton, left a written sketch of his involvement in the Urban League. The *Courier-Journal* of April 27, 1959, mentions the founding of the Louisville Urban League; *Crisis*, XXI (January, 1921), 131.

5. See the National Urban League Papers, Manuscript Division, Library of Congress, Series D, Box 27 for biographical file on the Louisville Branch; see also Kerns, *The Louisville Urban League; Annual Report Welfare League, 1922* (Louisville, 1922), 72.

6. *Post*, June 28, 1923; *Herald-Post*, December 12, 1926; "Louisville Urban League Report for 1929," National Urban League Papers.

Instead, they had to plead with employers and rely on their goodwill to hire blacks. The Louisville affiliate and affiliates elsewhere had more success in finding jobs for women than men. But these were jobs black women had traditionally held. Unfortunately, it seems that the Urban League usually served as little more than a clearinghouse for whites desiring cheap black workers and not, as the League had intended, as a place where white employers could find blacks who could be trained to perform skilled jobs or placed in clerical positions.[7]

Louisville Urban League officials informed white employers of the hardships suffered by black laborers and offered classes for blacks on how to get and keep jobs in industry. Urban Leaguers lectured, wrote newspaper articles, and pleaded with white businessmen not to restrict black workers to unskilled jobs. They stressed that blacks, when given the chance, were efficient workers. But League officials, many of whom were white businessmen, also believed that bad habits and poor work performances by blacks contributed to the low number of black industrial workers. They maintained that a lack of skills, not racial discrimination, was the biggest handicap black workers faced. These white Urban Leaguers would not admit that racism kept blacks from acquiring those skills. But blacks were not allowed to enter Manual High School or Theodore Ahrens Trade School (named for Urban League board member Ahrens) where white students received invaluable training that led to skilled jobs. Moreover, blacks were denied admission to apprenticeship programs in Louisville industries. Instead of calling for changes in racial exclusion policies or hiring blacks in their own businesses, Urban Leaguers emphasized the importance of being reliable workers and told black job seekers that cleanliness and good manners were a prerequisite for obtaining and holding a desired job.[8]

In addition to seeking employment for blacks, the Urban League also conducted several social service programs and cooperated with other social service agencies in the city. The League maintained a Traveler's Aid Station at the railroad station to give information and assistance to blacks, especially young girls, traveling north and south. Quite often, they took black girls to the YWCA or the Sunshine Center for a night's lodging to prevent their being lured away from the railroad station by procurers. Although the organization occasionally gave food and shelter to the poor, the Urban League did not want to be known as a relief agency. Instead,

7. Sterling D. Spero and Abram L. Harris, *The Black Worker: The Negro and the Labor Movement* (New York, 1931), 140; Weiss, *The National Urban League*, 90, 237, 265.
8. *Post*, June 28, 1923; "Urban League Report for 1929," 1–2.

Urban Leaguers preferred to serve as a link between blacks and social service agencies. Blacks brought all kinds of problems to the League. Some were handled directly by the League; the rest were referred to such agencies as the Family Service Organization, the Children's Protective Association, and the Public Health Nursing Association. The Urban League stressed crime prevention in the black community and aided the police department by lecturing on good citizenship. A few Urban Leaguers did probation work and helped some blacks convicted of minor offenses get suspended sentences.[9]

Also, instead of agitating for integrated housing, Urban League workers strived to improve living conditions within Negro neighborhoods. Urban Leaguers, led by Meyzeek, investigated housing conditions and complained until the Board of Sanitation declared some houses unfit for habitation. They reported on streets in need of repair and secured the cooperation of the Board of Public Works in paving neglected streets. Meyzeek organized squads of young people to help clean up the streets and vacant lots in black neighborhoods. Finally, the Louisville Urban League sponsored Negro Health Week in April every year "to call the attention of the public to the causes of diseases and to secure their eradication." During Negro Health Week, a group of doctors examined black children free of charge and advised parents on how to provide proper health care for their children. Negro Health Week was promoted by organizations all over the nation, and on three occasions (1921, 1925, and 1927), Louisville's Urban League received acclaim for its efforts to improve black health. Executive secretaries Elmer Carter and John Ragland claimed that through its various programs the Louisville Urban League served more than 10,000 blacks a year. They believed that the League's efforts in employment, health care, housing, and other activities benefited not only blacks, but also white Louisvillians. As Carter explained, the Louisville Urban League made the Negro "a part of the community, not only as a recipient of its benefits, but as a participant of its responsibilities in Child Welfare, Recreation, Neighborhood Improvement, Health Education, Civic Pride, and Industrial Efficiency."[10]

II.

Similar to the National Urban League in its evolutionary and conservative approach was the Commission on Interracial Cooperation. A group

9. *Annual Report of Welfare League, 1921* (Louisville, 1921), 52–53; *Crisis*, XXII (May, 1921), 29; *Courier-Journal*, June 13, 1928.

10. *Opportunity*, VII (April, 1929) 10; *Herald*, March 4, 1923; *Herald-Post*, Decem-

of southern whites formed the CIC after World War I to prevent postwar racial conflict. The founders intended for their organization to focus on southern communities and to draw financial sustenance and leadership from prominent citizens within the South. Being interracial was, as the historian John Dittmer explains, "an innovation in the South, where whites and blacks had seldom worked together on other than an ad hoc basis." The CIC's efforts were successful: by November 1920, thirteen states had formed state CIC affiliates and numerous local branches. All told, about 800 of the nearly 1200 counties in the South formed branches of CIC. The interracial organization in Kentucky was launched under the auspices of the state YMCA with the avowed purpose of "cultivating better relations between the races and improving the conditions of the Negro along the lines agreed upon by the Interracial Commission." [11]

A few blacks took an active role in the organization. Educators Robert Moton, Robert E. Jones, and John Hope were well-known blacks who supported the work of the CIC. State affiliates in North Carolina, South Carolina, Tennessee, Louisiana, Oklahoma, and Kentucky hired blacks as state secretaries. James Bond, Kentucky's state secretary, held his post longer than any other black state secretary (1920–1929), and only L. R. Reynolds, a white man and the state secretary for both Virginia and North Carolina, served longer (1928–1941) than Bond. [12]

The ultimate goal of the CIC was to improve race relations and to elevate the status of blacks. Yet, while black members called for better schools, higher salaries for black teachers, equal justice, and better health care, they had to avoid calling for social equality or complaining too vehemently about Jim Crow practices. White CIC members believed that conditions should be improved for blacks but that segregation maintained peace between the races. One white member, John Little, operated two Negro settlement houses and worked for more than forty years to improve black health care (see chapter five). Yet Little steadfastly opposed anything that might promote equality between the races. Louisville's black CIC

---

ber 12, 1926. For information on Negro Health Week see the *Post*, August 21, 1921; *Courier-Journal*, March 15, April 7, August 2, 1925, June 14, 1926, April 6, 1927.

11. James Bond, "The Interracial Commissions of the South," *Opportunity*, I (February, 1923), 13; see also Bond's unpublished autobiography, in the possession of his daughter-in-law, Mrs. Thomas Bond, Louisville; Edward F. Burrows, "The Commission on Interracial Cooperation, 1919–1944," (Ph.D. dissertation, University of Wisconsin, 1954), 92; James Bond, "Interracial Work in Kentucky," *Southern Workman*, LIV (June, 1925), 254; *Courier-Journal*, July 13, 1920. For a very sympathetic view of the CIC, see Wilma Dykeman and James Stokely, *Seeds of Southern Change: The Life of Will Alexander* (New York, 1962).

12. Burrows, "Commission on Interracial Cooperation," 129.

board members, E. G. Harris, William H. Steward, Charles H. Parrish, and George Clement, did not challenge such stances. It was such men that DuBois had in mind when he once told a white CIC member his "greatest objection to the Interracial Commission is the kind of Negro you pick to go on it. . . . You have favored too much the sort of Colored men that we call 'WHITE FOLKS' NIGGERS.'" DuBois's statement was probably too strong an indictment of Louisville's black CIC members. But on far too many occasions the black members remained silent about racial injustices while white members proclaimed that numerous improvements were occurring in race relations.[13]

James Bond strived to balance his role as state secretary of the CIC with being an Afro-American. With the cooperation and support of influential whites, he was able to publicize the CIC all over Kentucky. Three newspapers, the Louisville *Herald-Post*, the *Courier-Journal*, which took pride in being read statewide, and the Lexington *Leader*, carried a weekly column by Bond. In his column, Bond preached interracial goodwill and attempted to eliminate racial mistrust and friction by citing instances of interracial cooperation. He emphasized Christianity and said that all racial problems could easily be solved if everyone lived according to the teachings of Jesus Christ. Only on rare occasions did he complain about park segregation, attempts to segregate blacks on streetcars, or the abolition of the black normal school. Instead, Bond apologized for the shortcomings of blacks. "The negro," Bond informed his white readers, "is intensely human and labors under the handicaps from which his white brethren have been free for hundreds of years."[14]

Although Bond's approach to racial problems was moderate, it should be kept in mind that within the context of the 1920s it was unique to have a black discussing race relations in a white newspaper. Moreover, allowing Bond to discuss racial problems meant that some whites were acknowledging the existence of racial tension and the need for something to be done. Even if his message seemed mild and often condescending to blacks, it was probably enlightening to many Kentucky whites.

13. For Bond's view of race relations in Kentucky, see "Progress in Race Relations in Kentucky," report of the Director of the Kentucky Commission on Race Relations for 1922; "Report to the Inter-Racial Commission of Kentucky by the Director of the Commission, James Bond, from November 1921 to Dece. iber 1922." For a list of white board members, see "Meeting of the Executive Committee of the Inter-Racial Commission, January 8, 1924." A few of the minutes and other papers of the CIC can be found at the Louisville Free Public Library. DuBois was quoted in Dittmer, *Black Georgia*, 208; *Crisis*, XXI (April, 1921), 6–7.

14. *Courier-Journal*, December 6, 13, 1924, October 8, 1921; *Herald-Post*, January 20, 1929.

On several occasions Bond expressed some displeasure with his role in the CIC. "The colored people looked upon me as the white man's tool to satisfy the Negro in his unrest and discontent with promises and 'taffy.' The white people looked upon me as a mischief maker and meddler, for they said, 'but for such leaders as Bond, the Negro would be content.'" He told his son that directing the CIC was extremely difficult for him since he had been outspoken throughout his life. Though troubled by his role as "interracial salesman," Bond remained secretary of the CIC until his death in November 1929.[15]

Bond claimed that the CIC made numerous achievements in Kentucky. Through the efforts of its white members, it prevented five lynchings in small Kentucky towns during the 1920s. In late October 1919, racial unrest occurred in Corbin as a white mob forced many blacks to flee the town. Members of the CIC, in cooperation with local authorities, helped restore order and started an investigation of the incident which led to a white man being sentenced to jail for instigating the disturbance. Bond reported that his meeting with railroad officials about the abuses black passengers received resulted in blacks receiving better treatment on trains in Kentucky: "Coaches set aside for colored people are cleaner, more commodious and convenient and the railroad [employees] are more polite and accommodating." Bond also claimed that the joint effort of the CIC and the Kentucky Negro Education Association resulted in salary increases for teachers in several communities.[16]

Led by members of the CIC, black Louisvillians voted in favor of several educational improvement bonds during the 1920s. The effort that James Bond and other blacks connected with the CIC put into the passing of the bonds clearly shows that they were concerned about improving schools and equally interested in working with whites. That the white establishment worked only with the moderate blacks and not the new, more militant leaders who had opposed the University of Louisville bond in 1920 is also revealing. The whites realized that without black support their bond proposals could be defeated. But since they did not want to give in to the more militant demands of the young blacks, they yielded to a few demands of the older blacks and in turn received their support for the bonds. More than likely, the whites could have counted on the support of the more moderate blacks, as demonstrated by the bond proposal in 1920. The new strategy on the part of whites, however, gave the older blacks a small mea-

15. Bond was quoted in Williams, *The Bonds*, 69; J. Max Bond interview.
16. Bond, "Interracial Work in Kentucky," 154–56; *Post*, August 21, 1921; *Crisis*, XXI (April, 1921), 250.

sure of respect because they could tell other blacks they were working for the best interests of the race.

In 1921 city officials consulted with older black leaders before submitting a bond proposal for voter approval. The city council and the Board of Education gave the CIC written guarantees that one-fourth of the total bond issue would be used for improvement in black schools. After voters approved the bond proposal, the Board of Education kept its promise and constructed a new black elementary school and allocated funds for improvements at Central High. In 1925 city officials wanted to secure two bond proposals—a $5 million bond for public education and the $1 million bond for the university. City officials realized that trying to do something for the University of Louisville might once again arouse the resentment of the young black leaders. Therefore, before announcing the bond proposal to the public, city officers met with Bond, Clement, Steward, and Parrish and assured them that blacks would receive a fair portion of the money from the University of Louisville bond. Well aware of the assurances that city officials had given to the black leaders, the university's board of trustees passed the following resolution on September 15, 1925: "There will be provided out of the proceeds of the bond issue of $1,000,000, if voted, a laboratory building for use in giving extension courses for colored students under university control and supervision, for which full credit will be given; this building is to be erected at some convenient place so that its facilities may be combined with other facilities with the view of co-ordinating all available agencies for offering complete courses to colored young men and women of Louisville." The Board of Education, also needing black support for the passing of its bond, said that two black junior high schools would be constructed if the public education bond passed.[17]

Statements by trustees of the University of Louisville and the Board of Education satisfied the members of the Urban League and the CIC. These two organizations conducted aggressive campaigns to ensure black support of the bond proposals. John M. Ragland, executive secretary of the Urban League, organized the Colored Citizen's Committee of One Hundred to promote the bonds. Immediately after its inception, the committee issued a statement to the white public of its intentions: "We wish to assure the white people of Louisville that there exists among the colored people a very sane, experienced, and quiet leadership which can be depended upon in every crisis to do the right and proper thing for the benefit of the colored people as a whole." As he had years earlier, James Bond urged blacks to

17. Wilson, "A Century of Negro Education in Louisville," 104-105; *Post*, October 21, 1925; *Courier-Journal*, October 18, 1925.

support the bond proposals. He assured them that University of Louisville officials had spent the last five years studying the higher education needs of blacks. Always promoting interracial goodwill, Bond said, "One of the by-products of this education campaign scarcely less important than the successful issue of the campaign itself, is the united cooperation of all groups of citizens which make up our diverse population, thus minimizing the things that separate us into groups and emphasizing the things which are vital and common to us all." Bond informed blacks that a "no" vote "would be an expression of a lack of confidence in the white people of Louisville who have proved their friendship, goodwill and sense of justice beyond any question or doubt." [18]

For the most part, Louisville's young black leaders remained silent on the bond proposals. They did not organize a campaign opposing the bonds in 1925 as they had in 1920. Only on one occasion did they publicly express their displeasure over the terms of the bond proposals. However, the possibility of a strong black protest had been eliminated when city officials, in conjunction with members of the Urban League and the CIC, announced what the black community would receive before the more militant blacks even learned the bonds were being proposed. Receiving little opposition, both bonds passed by more than four to one on November 4, 1925. [19]

After the bonds were approved, city officials waited several years before honoring their promises to the Afro-American community. By 1928 three white junior high schools had opened, and additions were completed on six white elementary schools. Yet construction had just begun on one of the black junior highs. [20] Both black junior highs finally opened in January 1930. However, little progress was made toward the establishment of a black junior college. After a series of futile meetings with university officials in 1926–1927, several blacks began questioning the sincerity of the university's promises to the black community. Following more setbacks and broken promises, Louisville Municipal College for Negroes opened in February 1931, almost six years after the passage of the bond proposals. [21]

Extremely sensitive to the criticism of the more militant leaders, James

18. *Courier-Journal*, October 18, 30, 1925; *Post*, October 14, 21, 1925; Louisville *Times*, October 30, 1925.

19. *Courier-Journal*, October 28, November 5, 1925.

20. Wilson, "A Century of Negro Education in Louisville," 109–10; Chicago *Defender*, December 12, 1928; *Herald-Post*, February 29, 1930.

21. Numerous sources mentioned the founding of Louisville Municipal College: Raymond Kent, "The Municipal College of Liberal Arts," *Opportunity*, XX (February, 1942),

Bond was proud of his role in the success of the bond proposals. He said that his organization, comprised of conservative people, rightfully deserved the credit for upgrading black educational facilities in Louisville.[22] What he and the others failed to acknowledge, however, was the critical role played by the more radical black leaders in 1920. By defeating the first bond proposal, city officials were forced to take black interests into consideration.

Undoubtedly, the CIC aided blacks by working for improved educational facilities, but it accomplished very little in improving race relations or ending racial discrimination. The CIC failed to speak out against injustice. Despite evidence of continued racial oppression, the CIC continued to be publicly sanguine about local race relations. In 1926, a time of racial tension in Louisville, the delegates at the CIC conference devoted most of their time to congratulating themselves on their achievements in race relations. They failed to critically analyze the true racial situation or to discuss ways their organization could become more effective. Instead, the CIC made the following observations.

1. There is an ever-increasing desire on the part of the white people of Kentucky to deal wisely with the Negro.
2. This conference believes that more liberal attitudes are being taken by white and colored people which will result in a fuller and more complete understanding of the problems involved in civil acts of the races.
3. The Interracial Commission has noticed a gradual, constant, and favorable change of the attitude of white people toward the Negro.[23]

42–43; *A Century of Municipal Higher Education: A Collection of the Addresses Delivered During the Centennial Observance of the University of Louisville, America's Oldest Municipal University* (Chicago, 1937), 381–82; "A Municipal College for Negroes," *School and Society*, XXXII (November 22, 1930), 691; Federal Writers Project of the WPA, *A Centennial History of the University of Louisville* (Louisville, n.d.), 212–15. For the various steps taken by University of Louisville officials and black leaders leading to the establishing of the black college, see the Presidential Papers of the University of Louisville on Louisville Municipal College, especially the Minutes of April 6, June 19, December 6, 1926, July 6, and August 1, 1927, Presidential Papers, Archives Department, University of Louisville.

    In 1931 Louisville Municipal College received accreditation as a junior college by the University of Kentucky. Five years later, the college had developed a four-year curriculum and was accredited as a standard four-year college by the University of Kentucky and the Southern Association of Colleges and Secondary Schools. For detailed information on the curriculum and other activities at the school, see Louisville Municipal College Papers, Archives Department, University of Louisville.

    22. James Bond, unpublished autobiography.

    23. "Report of the Executive Committee, January 21, 1925," 2; "Findings of the Seventh State Interracial Conference, Louisville, Kentucky, November 20, 1926," 1–2.

These glowing statements of the CIC were in direct contradiction to the reality of black life in Louisville in the mid-1920s. As has been shown, blacks moving into white neighborhoods did so at great risk to life and property. Police abuse remained constant. Despite a number of positive changes in politics, little had occurred elsewhere to show, as the CIC so boldly stated, that a "favorable change of the attitude of white people toward the Negro" had taken place. In fact, the one area where blacks enjoyed limited equal access was eliminated when city officials passed a resolution segregating the public parks. The CIC remained silent when the park segregation issue was debated and the ordinance was passed. As with the enactment of other discriminatory practices in Louisville, the ordinance probably would have passed even if the CIC had staunchly voiced its opposition to the measure. But this one incident shows clearly that the community leaders in the CIC were far more concerned about order and the "proper place" for blacks than about fairness and justice.

On June 13, 1924, Margaret Taylor and Naomi Anthony, two black teachers from Coleridge-Taylor Elementary School, took twenty-two students to a picnic at Iroquois Park which was located in the predominantly white east end of town. The black children remained in the park for several hours without incurring any white resentment. But upon arriving at the bus stop to return to the downtown area, they were met by park security guards and a group of over 100 white people. One of the guards informed the teachers that since Iroquois Park was reserved for whites only, they had been in violation of laws controlling picnicking in the area. Both teachers expressed their amazement at such an ordinance and said that they would investigate the matter upon returning to town. The guards, upset that the black women dared challenge their word, placed both women under arrest. Chaos soon erupted as the park guards, with the loud urgings of the white crowd behind them, roughly handled the teachers and pupils. The guards would later say that the near riot was a result of the teachers resisting arrest and striking one of the arresting officers. Meanwhile, the bus came. Fortunately the driver was sympathetic to the teachers and assured them—as they were being placed in a police car—that he would see that the children reached their downtown destination safely.[24]

Instead of taking the teachers downtown to the police headquarters, the security guards took the women to a nearby precinct station. The of-

24. Margaret Taylor, interview with author, Louisville, November 28, 1978; Helen Johnson (sister of Naomi Anthony), interview with author, Louisville, November 28, 1978; *Leader*, June 21, 1924; *Post*, June 15, 1924; *Courier-Journal*, June 14, 1924.

ficer in charge of the precinct wanted to avoid involvement in the conflict and refused to receive the teachers. After driving around for several hours and failing to have the women locked up in any of the outlying precincts, the security guards finally took them to downtown Louisville. By the time the women arrived at police headquarters, a large black crowd had gathered. Leading the group were Steward, Parrish, Meyzeek, and Warley. Meyzeek and Warley, the most outspoken of the group, bitterly expressed their anger at the arrests. Meyzeek concluded his comments by warning Republican Mayor Huston Quin that "Negroes are not going to stand for park segregation any more than they stood for residential segregation." [25]

The Louisville NAACP was inactive when this incident occurred, but it was reactivated several days later. The organization protested the harassment of blacks in city-owned parks and began raising money to fight park segregation through the courts.[26]

The NAACP leaders were not the only ones moving quickly to resolve the park controversy. The day after the incident, Mayor Quin called in Parrish, Steward, and Bond and reminded them that they had, at least in theory, called for park segregation when they campaigned for the opening of parks in Negro neighborhoods. The mayor apparently was going to support separate parks. This surprised the black leaders since they thought Quin opposed segregation. Nevertheless, at Quin's urging, several black patronage holders visited Naomi Anthony and Margaret Taylor, advising them to stay away from the NAACP and to "keep their mouths shut about the incident." Dr. Ellis Whedbee, the spokesman for the black city hall delegation, told the teachers to accept whatever local officials did. That way, he said, "everybody will keep their jobs" in the school system and at city hall.[27]

The Louisville Board of Education felt that it was involved in the park controversy since the teachers and students were on a school outing when the incident occurred. Both women were confident that once it heard all the facts, the school board would support them. But they were wrong. Two days after the incident they each received a special delivery letter (written in red ink) telling them to appear before the board on June 24 and "show why you should not be summarily dismissed for inciting the races to riot." [28]

Within several days after the park incident, blacks, city officials, and

25. Taylor interview; *Courier-Journal*, June 14, 1924.
26. *Leader*, June 28, July 5, 1924.
27. Taylor interview; Blanton interview.
28. Taylor interview; Helen Johnson interview.

the Board of Education had become actively involved in the conflict. Of the groups directly involved, only the Department of Parks and Recreation had failed to act, but its plan of action was being formulated. On June 17 the Board of Park Commissioners made known that it had adopted the following resolution:

> Pending an investigation of the complaints made regarding the ejections of certain colored people from the white playgrounds of Iroquois Park and the adoption of a permanent policy regarding the use of the parks by the white and colored people, and in view of the feeling aroused by this incident and in order to prevent any further friction, the Superintendent is hereby instructed to exclude colored people from using the following parks and playgrounds: Boone Square, Central Park, Thurston Square, Triangle Park, Victory Park, Portland Playground, Crescent Hill Playground, Lions Club Playground, Cherokee Park, Iroquois Park and Shawnee Park and, that the Superintendent be and is hereby instructed to exclude white people from the following parks and playgrounds: Chickasaw Park, Ballard Park, Baxter Square, Sixteenth and St. Catherine Playground and Plymouth Settlement Playground; provided that nothing herein contained shall be construed as prohibiting the use of Parkways, Park Roads, and paths for vehicular and pedestrian purposes.

On July 1, the board announced that the resolution of June 17 would be permanent.[29]

Naomi Anthony and Margaret Taylor went to court on June 21 to answer charges of disorderly conduct and resisting arrest. The prosecution produced a string of white witnesses who testified that the black women had acted in an unruly fashion. But a few of the last witnesses stated that only the "big woman" (Naomi Anthony) resisted arrest and assaulted the officers while the "small one" (Margaret Taylor, who weighed barely 100 pounds) cited the "preamble of the U.S. Constitution and the Declaration of Independence" as she was being arrested. The teachers denied any wrongdoing and stated that they were unaware of any ordinance barring blacks from certain parks. However, G. W. Schardin, a member of the park board, claimed that racial segregation had been enforced in the parks for years. The court found Naomi Anthony quilty of disorderly conduct for attacking the park guards and fined her $10. Charges against Margaret Taylor were dismissed.[30]

At its June 24 meeting on the park controversy, the Louisville Board of Education severely reprimanded both teachers. The board asserted that Anthony and Taylor were in a park from which blacks were prohibited

29. *Courier-Journal*, June 18, July 2, 1924.
30. *Ibid.*, June 22, 1924.

and that even if blacks had belonged there the teachers should have taken the children home without engaging in a heated discussion with park guards. The board allowed the teachers to keep their jobs, but warned that anyone else involved in such an incident would be immediately dismissed from teaching in Louisville.[31]

A rare instance of unity was displayed when the entire spectrum of Louisville's black leadership joined in writing a letter to the *Courier-Journal* sharply denouncing the institution of *de jure* segregation in the parks. They specifically condemned the Board of Park Commissioners and the Board of Education for misleading the public by saying that blacks visiting the parks were violating the law. "There never has been a law in the city of Louisville restraining certain groups from visiting certain parks or sections of parks," the letter said. The group pointed out that the "parks" reserved for blacks lacked play equipment, water fountains, restrooms, and swimming pools, and that all of them, with one possible exception, were nothing more than open fields. "The talk of restraining white people from visiting these places is a joke and is but to cite another instance of the lack of frankness on the part of certain public officials." [32]

Regardless of their claims to the contrary, the evidence suggests that Jim Crow practices existed, at least informally, in Louisville's parks before the incident of June 1924. Blacks were barred from the city's swimming pools from 1914 until 1924 when city officials opened a swimming pool for blacks. School principal Albert Meyzeek was one of the speakers at the dedication of Ballard Park in 1919 and a black chorus furnished the music. The newspapers failed to say that Ballard Park was for blacks, but the fact that the park was located in a black neighborhood and that blacks participated in the dedication leads to that conclusion. Several events occurred in 1921 that seem to indicate a change in the Quin administration regarding segregated parks. That spring, signs appeared designating black areas within the parks. In July, Rev. Noah W. Williams was arrested for straying out of the Negro area of Cherokee Park. Park officials said that they would make special arrangements whenever blacks desired to hold a big picnic, "otherwise no colored person could walk anywhere in the park, nor sit under any tree." The signs were removed after blacks protested to the mayor. But that very same summer black baseball players were barred from the public parks. In February 1922 the *Courier-Journal* stated that Chickasaw Park would open in the spring and that it would be for blacks. Warley and Cole warned blacks to not be too overjoyed with the opening

31. *Ibid.*, June 25, July 2, 1924.
32. *Ibid.*, July 4, 1924.

of Chickasaw. Warley explained that by accepting the park, blacks were agreeing to segregation. Moreover, whites quickly identified it as a black park, often calling it "Niggersaw." [33]

By the mid-1920s, blacks in Louisville were far from unique in being excluded from white parks. In fact, in relative terms, park segregation occurred in Louisville at a much later date than elsewhere. For example, blacks in Lexington were relegated to Frederick Douglass Park in the early 1900s. In other Kentucky cities, blacks either had a park of their own or were totally excluded from the parks by the 1920s. As early as 1900 race separation seemed to be the rule in public parks throughout the South. In the few instances where there was an absence of separate parks for whites and blacks, segregation was imposed within the parks. Segregation was also common in public parks in the North, especially in public parks having swimming pools or bathing beaches. [34]

It soon became apparent that the various civil rights groups were far from united in an attempt to end park segregation. The NAACP, which started by making bold statements, devoted only a portion of the year to that issue before moving on to other concerns. Warley then launched a one-man campaign against the park system. By 1929 he was still hopeful that blacks would rally against segregation in the parks as they had against housing segregation in 1914. He filed suit for the admission of blacks to all of the city's parks. But after losing in the Jefferson County Circuit Court and the Kentucky Court of Appeals, Warley was unsuccessful in raising the needed funds to appeal to the United States Supreme Court. Warley complained bitterly that "not an officer of the NAACP has shown any interest, not a preacher or other leader, business or professional, has shown any interest in the case." [35]

The Urban League, which claimed to be concerned about recreational facilities for the Afro-American community, refused to become involved in the park controversy. Maybe a fear of reprisal from city officials con-

33. On blacks and swimming pools, see *Crisis*, VIII (October, 1914), 273; IX (November, 1914), 11; *Post*, September 14, 1922; *Leader*, March 24, April 8, 1923. On blacks and park segregation, see *Courier-Journal*, October 23, 1911, February 19, 1922; *Leader*, May 21, 1921, June 25, 1921, July 23, 1921, June 3, 10, 1922.

34. Rabinowitz, *Race Relations in the Urban South*, 182–97; Wynes, *Race Relations in Virginia*, 68–84; Myrdal, *An American Dilemma*, I, 341–46.

35. *Warley v. Board of Park Commissioners*, 233 Kentucky 688, 26 S.W. 2d 554 (1930). Warley was quoted in the Chicago *Defender*, May 11, 1929. See a letter in the NAACP Papers from Cole to Robert Abbott, editor of the *Defender*, May 13, 1929, stating that contrary to what Warley said, the Louisville NAACP did its best to fight park segregation. Cole, in fact, had urged blacks to unite early in the park struggle; see the *Leader*, July 12, 1924.

vinced the League to remain aloof. Meyzeek, a member of the Urban League board and one of its strongest workers, had, along with Warley, vehemently denounced this new attempt at segregation. The Board of Education closed the Negro Normal School that Meyzeek directed for the entire school year of 1925–1926 as a way of punishing Meyzeek. Publicly, the board said that the Normal School's activities were suspended because a surplus of black teachers existed; but the black leaders knew the real reason. And the Urban League, which depended on the city for funding, was fearful of losing its main source of revenue.[36]

Under the leadership of Bond, the CIC became the most active organization in the park segregation case. But instead of denouncing the ousting of blacks, the group called for the opening of parks in black neighborhoods and the construction of playgrounds in all of the parks. City officials responded by granting $40,000 for the opening of William H. Sheppard Park at Seventeenth and Magazine, which included a playground and a swimming pool. Bond called the opening of this park one of his greatest contributions to black Louisville. Members of the CIC also were elated at the opening of Sheppard Park and the willingness of city officials to provide playground equipment in other Negro parks. In January 1925 the CIC passed a resolution praising the mayor and the park commissioners for their concern about blacks and for the allocation of funds for Negro parks. In the resolution, the CIC, an organization that claimed to be for improvements in race relations and the status of blacks, failed to state any displeasure that the new park would be for blacks only.[37]

The "Louisville way," the opening of separate parks for blacks while denying them admission to white parks, allowed whites to say that they were not only concerned but were doing something for blacks. At the same time it allowed the moderate blacks to save face with their community by pointing out the progress they were making for the race. Indeed, these more moderate blacks repeatedly said that unlike the more militant blacks, who had come up empty-handed, they had received concessions from the white establishment. In particular, William H. Steward noted that his efforts in the park matter were consistent with the work he had been doing for blacks for fifty years. What Steward and the other members of the CIC failed to comprehend or admit is that segregated parks during the mid-1920s were not comparable to the segregated institutions of the 1870s. Those of the

36. *Leader*, July 5, September 6, 1924; William H. Steward, Charles H. Parrish, *et al.*, "A Brief for the Continuation of the Colored Normal School," (Louisville, 1925). This can be found at the Louisville Free Public Library.

37. "Report of Executive Committee, January 21, 1925," 2.

earlier period were an improvement over *no* institutions, while the segregated parks were a step backward from the integrated parks that had
previously existed in Louisville.

In 1928 park officials opened a new park for whites, Seneca, and made
much of the fact that they opened Seminole, a new park for blacks, at the
same time. Whites already had many more parks than blacks and far more
space in their parks. The two new parks merely increased the discrepancy.
Seneca had 552 acres compared to 71.78 acres at Seminole. Regardless of
what city officials and moderate blacks said about their desire to provide
parks for blacks, the fact remains that, for Louisville blacks, Jim Crow
parks meant inferior parks: by 1930 whites had twenty-four parks and
blacks had five; all five of the black parks combined had only 154.1 acres,
while four of the white parks each had more than 150 acres. The white
parks also had better facilities, including tennis courts, golf courses, football fields, and baseball diamonds. Except for Chickasaw and Sheppard
the black parks were, as several NAACP spokesmen pointed out, little more
than vacant fields, lacking even such basic facilities as water fountains and
bathrooms.[38]

Furthermore, city officials assigned few employees to supervise activities in the Negro parks. All of the white parks had at least two full-time
supervisors, with the larger ones having as many as five. None of the black
parks or playgrounds had more than a single worker. Also, the city assigned few guards to the black parks, "with the result that rowdy patrons
or unscrupulous concessioners created an atmosphere that citizens of the
better class desire to avoid. The value of the park to reputable Negroes is
therefore destroyed," an investigator concluded in the late 1920s.[39]

III.

When considering the attitudes and actions of the members of the Urban League and the CIC toward park segregation and several other critical issues, the effectiveness of these organizations in Louisville during the
1920s is debatable. In the area where Urban Leaguers devoted most of their
time, seeking jobs for blacks in industry, they experienced their greatest
failure. The League did not affect black employment patterns in any sig-

38. *Post*, January 6, 1925; Louisville *Times*, October 25, 1925; *Courier-Journal*, September 7, 1928; *The Louisville Parks 1890–1930* (Louisville, 1938); *35th Annual Report
of the Board of Park Commissioners, City of Louisville* (Louisville, 1925), 7, 13.
39. Woofter, *et al.*, *Negro Problems in Cities*, 232–36.

nificant way during the decade. They found jobs for black women as domestics and for men as unskilled workers, positions blacks already occupied before the start of the program. Urban Leaguers lacked the strength to demand that changes be made in employment; they were left with making usually vain appeals to the conscience and goodwill of white businessmen. Since the organization received its funding from the city's Welfare League, it underplayed racism in Louisville as a cause of black underrepresentation in skilled positions. But perhaps the most serious shortcoming of League officials was their own belief in black inferiority, that blacks themselves were responsible for their inability to enter industry. Significantly, such board members as Theodore Ahrens and Robert Bingham could have hired blacks in responsible positions in their own businesses. They declined to do so.

The CIC concentrated its efforts on promoting good race relations. Black and white members alike believed that the best way to maintain peace between the races was to gloss over racial discrimination and segregation and to speak in glowing terms about improvements in race relations. James Bond, as state director of the CIC, informed the public about the good deeds accomplished by the group and about how blacks were beginning to receive impartial treatment. Only occasionally did he mention the injustices blacks suffered. At their annual meetings, the members of the CIC devoted far too much time to applauding themselves instead of devising ways to combat racism, and to lauding the opening of separate facilities for blacks instead of deploring the fact that these facilities further segregated the races. As one critic of the organization noted, "It is often wondered whether the inter-racial meetings result in anything further than representation of leaders of the white and colored races getting together and paying compliments to each other, when vital questions like disfranchisement, Jim Crow cars, segregation and discrimination in various forms, are not taken up."[40]

Maybe in the face of determined white resistance to black equality, the approach of the CIC was realistic or at least the best that could be expected from whites in a border city. Their approach received favorable publicity and support and was adopted by city officials. By calling for and eagerly accepting segregated institutions and facilities for Afro-Americans, the CIC assured concerned whites that the proper steps were being taken for blacks. As was so often the case, Louisville whites could be proud of their efforts because any actions they took were an improvement.

40. *Leader*, February 20, 1932.

Opening a swimming pool for blacks was progress compared to blacks being denied admission to public pools for ten years. Not only did this philosophy satisfy whites, but it effectively divided the black leadership, making some of them content while the more militant ones were viewed as ungrateful troublemakers. Segregated facilities were better than no facilities, but segregation helped perpetuate a system of inferiority for blacks.

Louisville was indeed fortunate in having a number of civic-minded white citizens who, despite their many shortcomings, attempted to solve some of the problems that blacks faced in their city. The ultimate failure of these whites resulted from their adherence to the racist belief of their day that blacks had a "place" from which they should not be moved. These white Louisvillians were the same type of people that the Rev. Martin Luther King, Jr., often encountered in the 1950s and 1960s. People who were more devoted to order than to justice. People who were constantly telling black Americans to wait for a better season.

From the end of the Civil War to the Great Depression, black Louisvillians did not devote all of their time to denouncing racial discrimination. They set about the daily business of life and gladly accepted what joy and contentment came their way. Most blacks knew that they would continue to be confined to segregated neighborhoods and excluded from white facilities and organizations, even white churches. Therefore, they established a number of institutions to fill specific community needs. Out of necessity they created their own hospitals, nursing homes, orphanages, settlement houses, and the like. These institutions not only provided services and recreational activities but also gave Louisville blacks a reason to be proud. The churches were the leading institutions and they were always more than "just church" for blacks. What is most impressive about some of the Louisville churches is their attempt to reach out to the community and be of service. Indeed, over the years the churches gave comfort and assistance to whoever came to their door. The churches consistently allowed their facilities to be used for many social functions.

A number of organizations played a vital role in the Afro-American community. To be sure, the NAACP, the Negro Outlook Committee, and others denounced racial injustices. But the real importance of black organizations goes much deeper. After being shunned by whites, blacks turned to their own fraternities and social clubs for relief from racial oppression, for a sense of belonging, and for a sense of their own importance as human beings. This last point is significant; blacks who were looked upon by whites as nothing more than servants or laborers or "negroes" were held in high esteem in the Negro community. They served in leadership positions in scores of fraternities, sororities, and social clubs in black Louisville. It was not at all uncommon for a woman to be a servant or for a man to be a chauffeur yet be fully involved in the social life of the black community.

Indeed, from the Civil War to the 1930s, black Louisville succeeded in producing a strong black community that offered numerous services and activities. That is not to say that Afro-Americans were better off behind the walls of segregation or that they liked living in an all-black community. Even though police brutality and Jim Crow patterns continued, black Louisvillians clearly believed that life in their city was not nearly as oppressive as in the Deep South nor as cold and formal as in the North. Professor Blyden Jackson writes eloquently of growing up in Louisville, and his words express what many less articulate blacks also felt.

> My Louisville was a strong and rich community. I have never felt cheated because I grew up in it. It had one high school and I still wonder if any high school anywhere ever had a better faculty. . . . Moreover, I believe my high school was what it was because my Louisville was what it was. I do not mean that it was perfect. But I do mean that when I have compared it with other worlds I have observed or studied, such as those I read about in my trade, no matter how exemplary the other worlds have been considered, I have never been able to bring myself to feel that life in any of these other worlds would have been better for me than life as I knew it in Negro Louisville, or that in any of those other worlds would the people I encountered have been of a nobler breed than those with whom I did consort as I grew up in Louisville.[1]

It is extremely important to remember that whites, too, had a hand in the formation of the community life of black Louisville, but most often with the object of ensuring that there would continue to be two distinct Louisvilles. As all blacks well knew, there was in fact another Louisville, one that Blyden Jackson remembers as existing behind a veil. That blacks failed to end discrimination and racial oppression can be attributed in some ways to their lack of consistent effort but more to the staunch resistance they encountered. White Americans have often spoken of their country as the melting pot of the world. In Louisville, European immigrants were welcomed and afforded all of the opportunities to fail or succeed like other whites. Blacks were never given this chance. Yet blacks in Louisville and elsewhere tried to do everything that whites said were important to be acceptable. As the comedian and social critic Dick Gregory once said, "Black folk are more like white folk than white folk." Ultimately, however, blacks were judged most by the color of their skin, thereby negating most of their efforts.

In the decades after the 1920s, blacks continued struggling for changes and were successful in breaking down some barriers that many blacks thought impossible. Many people forget that the successes of the recent past are merely the latest episodes in the continuing black struggle. Had it not been for the work of the Stewards and Parrishes in the 1880s and 1890s,

1. Jackson, *The Waiting Years*, 6–7.

and the Warleys and Coles in the 1910s and 1920s, the successes of the recent era would have been far more difficult, if not impossible. Though blacks can now eat, work, and live in most places in Louisville, the city's character, with its polite racism that few will acknowledge, still keeps Afro-Americans on the periphery of society.

SELECTED BIBLIOGRAPHY
Primary Sources

Manuscript Collections

Bingham, Robert W. Papers. Library of Congress, Washington, D.C.
Bradley, William O. Scrapbooks. Special Collections, University of Kentucky, Lexington.
Broadway Temple AME Zion Church. Scrapbooks. Broadway Temple AME Zion Church, Louisville.
Burroughs, Nannie H. Papers. Manuscript Division, Library of Congress, Washington, D.C.
Commission on Interracial Cooperation. Papers. Louisville Free Public Library.
Cotter, Joseph. Papers. Western Branch Library, Louisville.
Educational Division of the Bureau of Refugees, Freedmen, and Abandoned Lands. Records, 1865–1871. National Archives, Washington, D.C.
Fifth Street Baptist Church. Minutes, 1829–1930. Fifth Street Baptist Church, Louisville.
Green Street Baptist Church. Minutes, 1844–1930. Archives Department, University of Louisville.
Letters to Mayors of Louisville. Filson Club, Louisville.
Louisville Board of Education. Papers. Durrett Education Center, Louisville.
Louisville Municipal College. Papers. Archives Department, University of Louisville.
National Association for the Advancement of Colored People. Papers. Manuscript Division, Library of Congress, Washington, D.C.
National Urban League. Papers. Manuscript Division, Library of Congress, Washington, D.C.
Parrish, Charles H. Papers. Archives Department, University of Louisville.
Parrish, Charles H., Jr. Papers. Archives Department, University of Louisville.
Plymouth Congregational Church. Papers. Plymouth Congregational Church, Louisville.
Presbyterian Colored Missions. Papers. Archives Department, University of Louisville.
Presidential Papers of the University of Louisville. Archives Department, University of Louisville.
Red Cross Hospital. Papers. Archives Department, University of Louisville.
Simmons University. Papers. Archives Department, University of Louisville.

Steward, William H. Scrapbook. Located at the home of Mrs. Carolyn Steward Blanton, Louisville.
Terrell, Mary Church. Papers. Manuscript Division, Library of Congress, Washington, D.C.
Todd, George. Papers. Filson Club, Louisville.
Washington, Booker T. Papers. Manuscript Division, Library of Congress, Washington, D.C.
Watterson, Henry W. Papers. Manuscript Division, Library of Congress, Washington, D.C.

Public Documents

Acts of the General Assembly of the Commonwealth of Kentucky, 1891–93. Frankfort, 1893.
Bureau of the Census. *Eleventh Census of the United States.* Washington, D.C., 1896.
———. *Fifteenth Census of the United States.* Washington, D.C., 1932.
———. *Fourteenth Census of the United States.* Washington, D.C., 1923.
———. *Negro Population in the United States, 1790–1915.* Washington, D.C., 1918.
———. *Negroes in the United States, 1920–32.* Washington, D.C., 1935.
———. *Ninth Census of the United States.* Washington, D.C., 1872.
———. *Tenth Census of the United States.* Washington, D.C., 1883.
———. *Thirteenth Census of the United States.* Washington, D.C., 1913.
———. *Twelfth Census of the United States.* Washington, D.C., 1901.
Eleventh Biennial Compilation of General Ordinances of the City of Louisville, 1915. Louisville, 1916.
Poore, Benjamin P., ed. *The Federal and State Constitutions.* Washington, D.C., 1877.
Strattan, O. H., and J. M. Vaughn, eds. *A Collection of the State and Municipal Law in Force and Applicable to the City of Louisville.* Louisville, 1857.
Thorpe, Francis N., ed. *The Federal and State Constitutions.* Washington, D.C., 1909.

Autobiographies, Memoirs, and Travel Accounts

Duke, Basil. *Reminiscences of General Basil W. Duke.* New York, 1911.
Flexner, Abraham. *I Remember: The Autobiography of Abraham Flexner.* New York, 1940.
Green, Elisha W. *Life of Rev. Elisha W. Green, One of the Founders of the Kentucky Normal and Theological Institute.* Maysville, Ky., 1888.
King, Edward. *The Great South: A Record of Journey.* 2 vols. New York, 1875.
Krock, Arthur. *Myself When Young.* Boston, 1973.
Langston, John M. *From the Virginia Plantation to the National Capital.* Hartford, 1894.

Marrs, Elijah P. *Life of Reverend Elijah P. Marrs.* Louisville, 1885.
Palmer, John M. *Personal Recollections of John M. Palmer.* Cincinnati, 1901.
Phillips, Charles H. *From the Farm to the Bishopric.* Nashville, 1932.
Robertson, William, and W. F. Robertson. *Our American Tour,* Edinburgh, 1871.
Sheppard, William. *Pioneers in Congo.* Richmond, n.d.
Smith, James L. *Autobiography of James L. Smith.* Norwich, Conn., 1881.
Walters, Alexander. *My Life and Work.* New York, 1917.
Warner, Charles Dudley. *Studies in the South and West.* New York, 1889.

Newspapers and Periodicals

AME Christian Recorder
American Baptist
Baltimore *Afro-American*
Chicago *Defender*
Colored American Magazine
Crisis
Indianapolis *Freeman*
Indianapolis *World*
Kentucky *Irish-American*
Kentucky *Standard*
Louisville *Commercial*
Louisville *Courier-Journal*
Louisville *Daily Journal*
Louisville *Daily Courier*
Louisville *Daily Democrat*
Louisville *Daily Union Press*
Louisville *Evening Post*
Louisville *Herald*
Louisville *Herald-Post*
Louisville *Journal*
Louisville *Leader*
Louisville and Nashville Employee's Magazine
Louisville *News*
Louisville *Post*
Louisville *Times*
NAACP *Branch Bulletin*
National Urban League *Bulletin*
Ohio Falls Express
Opportunity
New York *Freeman*
New York *Times*
Southern Workman
Souvenir Magazine

Pamphlets

Brief History of Plymouth Congregational Church. Louisville, n.d.
Campaign Book of Facts Published by Democratic Campaign Committee, 1921. Louisville, 1921.
Centennial Celebration, Broadway Temple AME Zion Church 1876–1976. Louisville, 1976.
Circular of Information for the Twenty-first Annual Session of the Eckstein Norton Institute. Cane Spring, Ky., 1911.
Colored Branches of the Louisville Free Public Library. Louisville, 1915.
Company History of Mammoth. Louisville, n.d.
Grant, Roscoe C., ed. *The 1921 Louisville Colored Business, Professional, Religious, and Educational Directory.* Louisville, 1921.
Hampton, George A. *History of Fifth Street Baptist Church.* Louisville, n.d.
Hoyer, Raymond A. *Louisville Social Service Directory.* Louisville, 1921.
Little, John. *Hope Versus Hope.* Louisville, 1939.
———. *The Presbyterian Colored Missions.* Louisville, 1909.
Louisville Parks 1890–1930. Louisville, 1938.
Miles, John, ed. *Calvary Baptist Church.* Louisville, 1969.
1915–1965, 50th Anniversary Mammoth Life. Louisville, 1965.
Report of Activities of Plymouth Settlement House 1938–39. Louisville, 1939.
State University Catalogue 1883–84. Louisville, 1883.
Zion Baptist Church, 1878–1953. Louisville, 1953.

Interviews with Author

Blanton, Carolyn Steward, March 10 and May 18, 21, 1976, Louisville.
Bond, J. Max, August 20, 1979, Washington, D.C.
Bond, Mrs. Thomas, May 27, 1976, Louisville.
Clement, George, Jr., May 24, 1976, Louisville.
Cole, Rosa, May 25, 1976, Louisville.
Jackson, Blyden, August 1, 1979, Chapel Hill.
Johnson, Helen, November 28, 1978, Louisville.
Johnson, Lyman T., January 3, 1976, Louisville.
Ledbetter, Theodore, August 21, 1979, Washington, D.C.
Nutter, Rev. Homer E., July 3, 1976, Lexington.
Parrish, Dr. Charles H., Jr., January 5 and May 19, 1976, Louisville.
Perry, William H., Jr., May 20, 1976, Louisville.
Porter, Mrs. A. D., May 26, 1976, Louisville.
Schockley, Ann Allen, August 26, 1979, Nashville.
Taylor, Margaret, November 28, 1978, Louisville.
Walls, Dr. John H., September 26, 1978, Louisville.
Wesley, Dr. Charles H., December 21, 1981, Washington, D.C.
White, Robert, July 17, 1979, Louisville.

Secondary Sources

Books

Berlin, Ira. *Slaves Without Masters: The Free Negro in the Antebellum South.* New York, 1974.

Blassingame, John W. *Black New Orleans 1860–1880.* Chicago, 1973.

Bunche, Ralph J. *The Political Status of the Negro in the Age of FDR.* Chicago, 1973.

Callcott, Margaret Law. *The Negro in Maryland Politics 1870–1912.* Baltimore, 1969.

Coulter, E. Merton. *The Civil War and Readjustment in Kentucky.* Chapel Hill, 1926.

Daniels, Douglas Henry. *Pioneer Urbanites: A Social and Cultural History of Black San Francisco.* Philadelphia, 1980.

Dittmer, John. *Black Georgia in the Progressive Era 1900–1920.* Urbana, 1977.

DuBois, W. E. B. *The Philadelphia Negro.* Philadelphia, 1899.

Foner, Philip S. *Organized Labor and the Black Worker 1619–1973.* New York, 1974.

Frazier, E. Franklin. *Negro Youths at the Crossways.* Washington, D.C., 1940.

Gerber, David A. *Black Ohio and the Color Line 1860–1915.* Urbana, 1976.

Gibson, William H. *Historical Sketch of the Progress of the Colored Race in Louisville, Ky.* Louisville, 1897.

Gutman, Herbert G. *The Black Family in Slavery and Freedom, 1750–1925.* New York, 1976.

Harlan, Louis R. *Booker T. Washington: The Making of a Black Leader, 1856–1901.* New York, 1972.

———. *Booker T. Washington: The Wizard of Tuskegee, 1901–1915.* New York, 1983.

Irvin, Helen D. *Women in Kentucky.* Lexington, 1979.

Jackson, Blyden. *The Waiting Years: Essays on American Negro Literature.* Baton Rouge, 1976.

Johnson, W. D. *Biographical Sketches of Prominent Negro Men and Women of Kentucky.* Lexington, 1897.

Katzman, David M. *Before the Ghetto: Black Detroit in the Nineteenth Century.* Urbana, 1973.

Kellogg, Charles F. *A History of the National Association for the Advancement of Colored People, 1909–1920.* Baltimore, 1967.

Kemp, Janet E. *Report of the Tenement House Commission of Louisville.* Louisville, 1909.

Kerns, J. Harvey. *A Survey of the Economic and Cultural Conditions of the Negro Population of Louisville, Kentucky, and a Review of the Program and Activities of the Louisville Urban League.* New York, 1948.

Kusmer, Kenneth L. *A Ghetto Takes Shape: Black Cleveland, 1870–1930.* Urbana, 1976.

Lamon, Lester C. *Black Tennesseans 1900–1930.* Knoxville, 1977.

Leighton, George R. *Five Cities: The Stories of Their Youth and Old Age.* New York, 1939.

Lynch, Hollis, ed. *The Black Urban Condition.* New York, 1973.

Meier, August. *Negro Thought in America 1880–1915.* Ann Arbor, 1963.

Meier, August, and Elliott Rudwick. *Along the Color Line: Explorations in the Black Experience.* Urbana, 1976.

Myrdal, Gunnar. *An American Dilemma: The Negro Problem and Modern Democracy.* 2 vols. New York, 1944.

Osofsky, Gilbert. *Harlem: The Making of a Negro Ghetto.* 2nd ed. New York, 1971.

Osthaus, Carl R. *Freedmen, Philanthropy, and Fraud: A History of the Freedman's Savings Bank.* Urbana, 1976.

Parrish, Charles H., ed. *Golden Jubilee, General Association of Colored Baptists in Kentucky.* Louisville, 1915.

Parrish, Charles H., Albert E. Meyzeek, and J. B. Colbert, eds. *The History of Louisville Segregation Case and the Decision of the Supreme Court.* Louisville, 1918.

Perdue, Robert E. *The Negro in Savannah.* New York, 1973.

Rabinowitz, Howard N. *Race Relations in the Urban South, 1865–1890.* New York, 1978.

Richardson, Clement, ed. *The National Cyclopedia of the Colored Race.* Montgomery, 1919.

Richings, George F. *Evidences of Progress Among Colored People.* Philadelphia, 1899.

Simmons, William J. *Men of Mark: Eminent, Progressive, and Rising.* Cleveland, 1887.

Smith, Lucy H., ed. *Pictorial Directory of the Kentucky Association of Colored Women.* Louisville, 1945.

Spear, Allan H. *Black Chicago: The Making of a Negro Ghetto.* Chicago, 1967.

Stephenson, Gilbert T. *Race Distinction in American Law.* New York, 1910.

Tapp, Hambleton, and James C. Klotter. *Kentucky, Decades of Discord 1865–1900.* Frankfort, 1977.

Thornbrough, Emma Lou. *The Negro in Indiana.* Indianapolis, 1957.

Weare, Walter B. *Black Business in the New South: A Social History of the North Carolina Mutual Life Insurance Company.* Urbana, 1973.

Weeden, Henry Clay. *Weeden's History of the Colored People of Louisville.* Louisville, 1897.

Weiss, Nancy J. *The National Urban League 1910–1940.* New York, 1974.

Williams, Roger M. *The Bonds: An American Family.* New York, 1972.

Woodward, C. Vann. *The Strange Career of Jim Crow.* 2nd rev. ed. New York, 1966.

Woofter, Thomas Jackson, *et al. Negro Problems in Cities.* New York, 1928.
Wynes, Charles E. *Race Relations in Virginia, 1870–1902.* Charlottesville, 1961.
Yater, Georger H. *Two Hundred Years at the Falls of the Ohio: A History of Louisville and Jefferson County.* Louisville, 1979.

Journal Articles

Blassingame, John W. "The Recruitment of Colored Troops in Kentucky, Maryland, and Missouri, 1863–65." *Historian*, XXIX (August, 1967), 533-45.
Bond, James. "Interracial Work in Kentucky." *Southern Workman*, LIV (June, 1925), 254-56.
Brandt, Lilian. "The Negroes of St. Louis." *Publications of the American Statistical Association*, VIII (March, 1903), 203-304.
Gaines, Miriam. "The John Little Missions of Louisville, Kentucky." *Southern Workman*, LXII (April, 1933), 161-70.
Harris, Rachel. "The Advantages of Colored Libraries." *Southern Workman*, XLIV (July, 1915), 385-91.
Haynes, George E. "Conditions Among Negroes in the Cities." *Annals of the American Academy of Political and Social Science*, XLIX (September, 1913), 105-120.
Horton, Ben. "Life and Achievements of Albert Ernest Meyzeek." *Kentucky Negro Journal* (1958), 25-27.
Kousser, J. Morgan. "Making Separate Equal: The Integration of Black and White School Funds in Kentucky, 1882." *Journal of Interdisciplinary History*, XX (Winter, 1980), 399-428.
Lewis, Cary B. "Louisville and Its Afro-American Citizens." *Colored American Magazine*, X (April, 1906), 259-64.
Meier, August. "Booker T. Washington and the Negro Press." *Journal of Negro History*, XXXVIII (January, 1953), 67-90.
———. "Negro Class Structure and Ideology in the Age of Booker T. Washington." *Phylon*, XXIII (January, 1962), 260-65.
———. "The Vogue of Industrial Education." *Mid-West Journal*, VII (Fall, 1955), 241-66.
Messmer, Charles. "Louisville on the Eve of the Civil War." *Filson Club History Quarterly*, L (July, 1976), 249-90.
Norris, Marjorie. "An Early Instance of Non-Violence: The Louisville Demonstrations of 1870–71." *Journal of Southern History*, XXXII (November, 1966), 487-504.
Palmer, Edward M. "Negro Secret Societies." *Social Forces*, XXIII (December, 1944), 207-12.
Rabinowitz, Howard N. "The Conflict Between Blacks and the Police in the Urban South, 1865–1900." *Historian*, XXXIX (November, 1976), 62-76.

"The Record of Albert Ernest Meyzeek." Negro History Bulletin, X (May, 1947), 186-97.

Rice, Roger L. "Residential Segregation by Law, 1910–1917." Journal of Southern History, XXXIV (May, 1968), 179-99.

Rudwick, Elliott M., and August Meier. "Negro Retaliatory Violence in the Twentieth Century." New Politics, V (Winter, 1966), 41-51.

Simmons, William J. "What the Colored People Are Doing in Kentucky." American Baptist Home Mission Society, jubilee volume (1883), 85-90.

Smith, John David. "The Recruitment of Negro Soldiers in Kentucky, 1863-65." Register of the Kentucky Historical Society, LXXII (October, 1974), 366.

Speed, Louise J. "The Evolution of a Kentucky Negro Mission." Charities and the Commons, XVII (September 21, 1907), 727-28.

Wilkins, John. "Blue's Colored Branch: A 'Second Plan' That Became a First in Librarianship." American Libraries, VII (May, 1976), 256.

Wynes, Charles. "Bishop Thomas U. Dudley and the Uplift of the Negro.," Register of the Kentucky Historical Society, LXV (July, 1967), 230-38.

Dissertations, Theses, and Memoranda

Berry, Benjamin D. "Plymouth Settlement House and the Development of Black Louisville: 1900–1930." Ph.D. dissertation, Case Western Reserve University, 1977.

Bunche, Ralph J. "A Brief and Tentative Analysis of Negro Leadership." Research memorandum prepared for the Carnegie-Myrdal Study of the Negro in America, September, 1940.

———. "The Programs, Ideologies, Tactics, and Achievements of Negro Betterment and Interracial Organizations." Research memorandum prepared for the Carnegie-Myrdal Study of the Negro in America, June, 1940.

Burrows, Edward F. "The Commission on Interracial Cooperation, 1919–1944." Ph.D. dissertation, University of Wisconsin, 1954.

Collins, Ernest M. "The Political Behavior of the Negroes in Cincinnati, Ohio, and Louisville, Kentucky." Ph.D. dissertation, University of Kentucky, 1950.

DePaola, Pier Luigi Gregory. "Management and Organized Labor Relations of the Louisville and Nashville Railroads During the Depression Year 1893." M.A. thesis, University of Louisville, 1971.

Donovan, Mary S. "Kentucky Law Regarding the Negro, 1865–77." M.A. thesis, University of Louisville, 1967.

Duncan, Nancy H. "A Study of the Plymouth Settlement House Neighborhood." M.A. thesis, University of Louisville, 1965.

Finch, Herbert. "Organized Labor in Louisville, Kentucky 1880–1914." Ph.D. dissertation, University of Kentucky, 1965.

Hill, T. Arnold. "Digest and Analysis of Questionnaires Submitted by the Urban

League Secretaries." Research memorandum prepared for the Carnegie-Myrdal Study of the Negro in America, 1940.

Jackson, Brenda F. "The Policies and Purposes of Black Public Schooling in Louisville, Kentucky, 1890–1930." Ph.D. dissertation, Indiana University, 1976.

McElhone, Patrick S. "The Civil Rights Activities of the Louisville Branch of the NAACP: 1914–1960." M.A. thesis, University of Louisville, 1976.

Messmer, Charles K. "City in Conflict: A History of Louisville, 1860-65." M.A. thesis, University of Kentucky, 1953.

Metcalf, George. "The Fusion Movement in Kentucky 1905–07." M.A. thesis, Murray State University, 1969.

Ousley, Stanley. "The Irish in Louisville." M.A. thesis, University of Louisville, 1974.

Sexton, Robert F. "Kentucky Politics and Society: 1919–1932." Ph.D. dissertation, University of Washington, 1970.

Wills, James T. "Louisville Politics 1890–97." M.A. thesis, University of Louisville, 1966.

Wilson, George D. "A Century of Negro Education in Louisville." Manuscript prepared by the project workers of the WPA, n.d.

INDEX